Charles Kingsley

Village sermons, and town and country sermons

Charles Kingsley

Village sermons, and town and country sermons

ISBN/EAN: 9783744745475

Printed in Europe, USA, Canada, Australia, Japan

Cover: Foto ©Lupo / pixelio.de

More available books at **www.hansebooks.com**

VILLAGE SERMONS,

AND

TOWN AND COUNTRY SERMONS.

VILLAGE SERMONS,

AND

TOWN AND COUNTRY SERMONS.

BY

CHARLES KINGSLEY.

London:
MACMILLAN AND CO.,
AND NEW YORK.
1890.

First Edition 1877,
Reprinted 1878, 1879, 1880, 1882, 1884, 1886, 1888.
New Edition 1890.

The two volumes of Sermons contained in this book were originally
published separately.

Dedicated to

MY MOST KIND AND FAITHFUL FRIEND,

THE HONOURABLE AND VERY REVEREND

GERALD WELLESLEY,

DEAN OF WINDSOR.

CONTENTS.

VILLAGE SERMONS.

SERMON		PAGE
I.	God's World,	1
II.	Religion not Godliness,	10
III.	Life and Death,	18
IV.	The Work of God's Spirit,	25
V.	Faith,	34
VI.	The Spirit and the Flesh,	43
VII.	Retribution,	52
VIII.	Self-Destruction,	59
IX.	Hell on Earth,	65
X.	Noah's Justice,	74
XI.	The Noachic Covenant,	82
XII.	Abraham's Faith,	89
XIII.	Abraham's Obedience,	99
XIV.	Our Father in Heaven,	106
XV.	The Transfiguration,	114
XVI.	The Crucifixion,	123
XVII.	The Resurrection,	128

CONTENTS.

SERMON		PAGE
XVIII.	IMPROVEMENT,	136
XIX.	MAN'S WORKING DAY,	142
XX.	ASSOCIATION,	149
XXI.	HEAVEN ON EARTH,	155
XXII.	NATIONAL PRIVILEGES,	161
XXIII.	LENTEN THOUGHTS,	169
XXIV.	ON BOOKS,	176
XXV.	THE COURAGE OF THE SAVIOUR,	184

TOWN AND COUNTRY SERMONS.

I.	HOW TO KEEP PASSION WEEK,	193
II.	THE DIVINE HUNGER AND THIRST,	201
III.	THE TRANSFIGURATION,	207
IV.	A SOLDIER'S TRAINING,	213
V.	CHRIST'S SHEEP,	219
VI.	THE HEARING EAR AND THE SEEING EYE,	224
VII.	THE VICTORY OF FAITH,	231
VIII.	TURNING-POINTS,	237
IX.	OBADIAH,	243
X.	RELIGIOUS DANGERS,	250
XI.	BLESSING AND CURSING.	262
XII.	WORK,	269
XIII.	FALSE PROPHETS,	276
XIV.	THE ROCK OF AGES,	282
XV.	ANTIPATHIES,	290

CONTENTS.

SERMON		PAGE
XVI.	St. Paul,	296
XVII.	The Broken and Contrite Heart,	303
XVIII.	St. Peter,	309
XIX.	Elijah,	317
XX.	The Loftiness of Humility,	323
XXI.	The Knowledge of God,	331
XXII.	The Torment of Fear,	341
XXIII.	The Flesh and the Spirit,	345
XXIV.	The Unrighteous Mammon,	350
XXV.	The Sighs of Christ,	358
XXVI.	The Woman of Samaria,	362
XXVII.	The Invasion of the Assyrians,	370
XXVIII.	The Ten Lepers,	375
XXIX.	Pardon and Peace,	380
XXX.	The Central Sun,	388
XXXI.	Christmas Peace,	394
XXXII.	The Life of the Spirit,	398
XXXIII.	The Unchangeable One,	403
XXXIV.	ΕΝ ΤΟΥΤΩ ΝΙΚΑ,	408
XXXV.	The Eternal Manhood,	414
XXXVI.	The Battle Within,	422
XXXVII.	Hypocrisy,	429
XXXVIII.	A People Prepared for the Lord,	438
XXXIX.	The Wrath of Love,	446

VILLAGE SERMONS.

SERMON I.

GOD'S WORLD.

PSALM civ. 24.

O Lord, how manifold are Thy works! in wisdom hast Thou made them all: the earth is full of Thy riches.

WHEN we read such psalms as the one from which this verse is taken, we cannot help seeing, if we consider, a great difference between them and any hymns or religious poetry which are commonly written or read in these days. The hymns which are most liked now, and the psalms which people most willingly choose out of the Bible, are those which speak, or seem to speak, about God's dealings with people's own souls, while such psalms as this are overlooked. People do not care really about psalms of this kind when they find them in the Bible, and they do not expect or wish now-a-days anyone to write poetry like them. For these psalms of which I speak praise and honour God, not for what He has done to our souls, but for what He has done and is doing in the world around us. This very 104th Psalm, for instance, speaks entirely about things which we hardly care, or even think proper, to mention in church now. It speaks of this earth entirely, and the things on it; of the light, the clouds, and wind—of hills and valleys, and the springs on the hill-sides—of wild beasts and birds—of grass and corn, and wine and oil—

of the sun and moon, night and day—the great sea, the ships, and the fishes, and all the wonderful and nameless creatures which people the waters—the very birds' nests in the high trees, and the rabbits burrowing among the rocks, nothing on the earth but this psalm thinks it worth mentioning. And all this, which one would expect to find only in a book of natural history, is in the Bible, in one of the psalms, written to be sung in the temple at Jerusalem, before the throne of the living God and His glory which used to be seen in that temple,—inspired, as we all believe, by God's Spirit,—God's own word, in short : that is worth thinking of. Surely the man who wrote this must have thought very differently about this world, with its fields and woods, and beasts and birds, from what we think. Suppose, now, that we had been old Jews in the temple, standing before the Holy House, and that we believed, as the Jews believed, that there was only one thin wall and one curtain of linen between us and the glory of the living God, that unspeakable brightness and majesty which no one could look at for fear of instant death, except the high priest in fear and trembling once a year—that inside that small Holy House, He, God Almighty, appeared visibly,—God who made heaven and earth. Suppose we had been there in the temple, and known all this, should we have liked to be singing about beasts and birds, with God Himself close to us? We should not have liked it—we should have been terrified, thinking perhaps about our own sinfulness, perhaps about that wonderful majesty which dwelt inside. We should have wished to say or sing something spiritual, as we call it; at all events, something very different from the 104th Psalm, about woods, and rivers, and dumb beasts. We do not like the thought of such a thing : it seems almost irreverent, almost impertinent to God to be talking of such things in His presence. Now, does this show us that we think about this earth, and the things in it, in a very different way from those old Jews? They thought it a fit and proper thing to talk about corn and wine and oil, and cattle and fishes, in the presence of the Almighty God, and we do not think it fit and proper. We read this psalm when it comes in the Church service as a matter of course, mainly because we do not believe that God is here among us. We should not be so ready to read it if we thought that Almighty God was so near us.

That is a great difference between us and the old Jews. Whether it shows that we are better or not than they were in the main, I cannot tell; perhaps some of them had such thoughts too, and said, 'It is not respectful to God to talk about such common-place earthly things in His presence;' perhaps some of them thought themselves spiritual and pure-minded for looking down on this psalm, and on David for writing it. Very likely, for men have had such thoughts in all ages, and will have them. But the man who wrote this psalm had no such thoughts. He said himself, in this same psalm, that his words would please God. Nay, he is not speaking and preaching *about* God in this psalm, as I am now in my sermon, but he is doing more; he is speaking *to* God—a much more solemn thing, if you will think of it. He says, 'O Lord my God, *Thou* art become exceedingly glorious. Thou deckest Thyself with light as with a garment. All the beasts wait on Thee; when Thou givest them meat they gather it. Thou renewest the face of the earth.' When he turns and speaks of God as 'He,' saying, 'He appointed the moon,' and so on, he cannot help going back to God, and pouring out his wonder, and delight, and awe, to God Himself, as we would sooner speak *to* anyone we love and honour than merely speak *about* them. He cannot take his mind off God. And just at the last, when he does turn and speak to himself, it is to say, 'Praise thou the Lord, O my soul, praise the Lord,' as if rebuking and stirring up himself for being too cold-hearted and slow, for not admiring and honouring enough the infinite wisdom, and power, and love, and glorious majesty of God, which to him shines out in every hedge-side bird and every blade of grass. Truly I said that man had a very different way of looking at God's earth from what we have!

Now, in what did that difference lie? What was it? We need not look far to see. It was this,—David looked on the earth as God's earth; we look on it as man's earth, or nobody's earth. We know that we are here, with trees and grass, and beasts and birds round us. And we know that we did not put them here; and that, after we are dead and gone, they will go on just as they went on before we were born,—each tree, and flower, and animal, after its kind: but we know nothing more. The earth is here, and we on it; but who put it there, and why it is there, and why we are on it, instead of being anywhere else, few ever think. But to David the earth looked very different; it had quite another meaning; it spoke to him of God who made it. By seeing what this earth is like, he saw what God who made it is like; and we see no such thing. The earth?—we can eat the corn and cattle on it, we can earn money by farming it, and ploughing and digging it; and that is all most men know about it. But David knew something more—something which made him feel himself very weak, and yet very safe; very ignorant and stupid, and yet honoured with glorious knowledge from God,—something which made him feel that he belonged to this world, and must not forget it or neglect it; namely, that this earth was his lesson-book— this earth was his work-field; and yet those same thoughts which showed him how he was made for the land round him, and the land round him was made for him, showed him also that he belonged to another world—a spirit-world; showed him that when this world passed away, he should live for ever; showed him that while he had a mortal body, he had an immortal soul too; showed him that though his home and business were here on earth, yet that, for that very reason, his home and business were in heaven, with God who made the earth, with that blessed One of whom he said, 'Thou, Lord, in the beginning hast laid the foundation of the earth, and the heavens are the work of Thy hands. They shall perish, but Thou shalt endure ; they all shall fade as a garment, and like a vesture shalt Thou change them, and they shall be changed ; but Thou art the same, and *Thy* years shall not fail. The children of Thy servants shall continue, and their seed shall stand fast in Thy sight.' 'As a garment shalt thou change them,'—ay, there was David's secret ! He saw that this earth and skies are God's garment—the garment by which we see God ; and that is what our forefathers saw too, and just what we have forgotten ; but David had not forgotten it. Look at this very 104th Psalm again, how he refers everything to God. We say, 'The light shines :' David says something more ; he says, 'Thou, O God, adornest Thyself with light, as with a curtain.' Light is a picture of God. 'God,' says St. John, 'is light, and in Him is no darkness at all.' We say, 'The clouds fly, and the wind blows,' as if they went of themselves ; David says, 'God makes the clouds His chariot, and walks upon the wings of the wind.' We talk of the rich airs of spring, of the flashing lightning of summer, as dead things ; and men who call themselves wise say, that lightning is only matter,—'We can grind the like of it out of glass and silk, and make lightning for ourselves in a small way ;' and so they can in a small way, and in a very small one : David does not deny that, but he puts us in mind of something in that lightning and those breezes which we cannot make. He says God makes the winds His angels, and flaming fire His ministers ; and St. Paul takes the same text, and turns it round to suit his purpose, when he is talking of the blessed angels, saying, ' That text in the 104th Psalm means something more ; it means that God makes His angels spirits (that is, winds), and His ministers a flaming fire.' So showing us that in those breezes there are living spirits, that God's angels guide those thunder-clouds ; that the roaring thunderclap is a shock in the air truly, but that it is something more—that it is the voice of God, which shakes the cedar trees of Lebanon, and tears down the thick bushes, and makes the wild deer slip her young. So we read in the psalms in church; that is David's account of the thunder. I take it for a true account; you may or not, as you like. See again. Those springs in the hill-sides, how do they come there? 'Rain-water soaking and flowing out,' we say. True, but David says something more; he says God sends the springs, and He sends them into the rivers too. You may say, 'Why, water must run down-hill, what need of God?' But suppose God had chosen that water should run *up* hill, and not down, how would it have been then?—Very different I think. No, He sends them; He sends all things. Wherever there is anything useful, His spirit has settled it. The help that is done on earth, He doeth it all Himself.—Loving and merciful, —caring for the poor dumb beasts! He sends the springs, and David says, 'All the beasts of the fields drink thereof.' The wild animals in the night, He cares for them too—He, the Almighty God. We hear the foxes bark by night, and we think the fox is hungry, and there it ends with us; but not with David: he says, 'The lions roaring after their prey do seek their meat from God'—God, who feedeth the young ravens who call upon Him. He is a God! 'He did not make the world,' says a wise man, 'and then let it spin round His finger,' as we wind up a watch, and then leave it to go of itself. No; 'His mercy is over all His works.' Loving and merciful, the God of nature is the God of grace. The same love which chose us and our forefathers for His people while we were yet dead in trespasses and sins; the same only-begotten Son, who came down on earth to die for us poor wretches on the cross,—that same love, that same power, that same Word of God, who made heaven and earth, looks after the poor gnats in the winter time, that they may have a chance of coming out of the ground when the day stirs the little life in them, and dance in the sunbeam for a short hour of gay life, before they return to the dust whence they were made, to feed creatures nobler and more precious than themselves. That is all God's doing, all the doing of Christ, the King of the earth. 'They wait on Him,' says David. The beasts, and birds, and insects, the strange fish, and shells, and the nameless corals too, in the deep, deep sea, who build and build below the water for years and thousands of years, every little, tiny creature bringing his atom of lime to add to the great heap, till their heap stands out of the water and becomes dry land; and seeds float thither over the wide waste sea, and trees grow up, and birds are driven thither by storms: and men come by accident in stray ships, and build, and sow, and multiply, and raise churches, and worship the God of heaven, and Christ, the blessed One, on that new land which the little coral-worms have built up from the deep. Consider that. Who sent them there? Who contrived that those particular men should light on that new island at that especial time? Who guided thither those seeds, those birds? Who gave those insects that strange longing and power to build and build on continually? —Christ, by whom all things are made, to whom all power is given in heaven and earth; He and His Spirit, and none else. It is when *He* opens His hands, they are filled with good. It is when *He* takes away their breath, they die, and turn again to their dust. *He* lets His breath, His spirit, go forth, and out of that dead dust grow plants and herbs afresh for man and beast, and He renews the face of the earth. 'For,' says the wise man, 'all things are God's garment'—outward and visible signs of His unseen and unapproachable glory; and when they are worn out, He changes them, says the Psalmist, as a garment, and they shall be changed.

> The old order changes, giving place to the new,
> And God fulfils Himself in many ways.

But He is the same. He is there all the time. All things are His work. In all things we may see Him, if our souls have eyes. All things, be they what they may, which live and grow on this earth, or happen on land or in the sky, will tell us a tale of God,—show forth some one feature, at least, of our blessed Saviour's countenance and character,—either His foresight, or His wisdom, or His order, or His power, or His love, or His condescension, or His long-suffering, or His slow, sure vengeance on those who break His laws. It is all written there outside in the great green book, which God has given to labouring men, and which neither man nor fiend can take from them. The man who is no scholar in letters may read of God as he follows the plough, for the earth he ploughs is his Father's: there is God's mark and seal on it—His name, which, though it is written on the dust, yet neither man nor fiend can wipe it out!

The poor, solitary, untaught boy, who keeps the sheep, or minds the birds, long lonely days, far from his mother and his playmates, may keep alive in him all purifying thoughts, if he will but open his eyes and look at the green earth around him.

Think now, my boys, when you are at your work, how all things may put you in mind of God, if you do but choose. The trees which shelter you from the wind, God planted them there for your sakes, in His love. There is a lesson about God. The birds which you drive off the corn—who gave them the sense to keep together and profit by each other's wit and keen eyesight? Who but God, who feeds the young birds when they call on Him? There is another lesson about God. The sheep whom you follow—who ordered the warm wool to grow on them, from which your clothes are made? Who but the Spirit of God above, who clothes the grass of the field, and the silly sheep, and who clothes you too, and thinks of you when you do not think of yourselves? There is another lesson about God. The feeble lambs in spring, they ought to remind you surely of your blessed Saviour, the Lamb of God, who died for you upon the cruel cross, who was led as a lamb to the slaughter; and like a sheep that lies dumb and patient under the shearer's hand, so He opened not His mouth. Are not these lambs, then, a lesson from God? And these are but one or two examples out of thousands and thousands. Oh, that I could make you, young and old, all feel these things! Oh, that I could make you see God in everything, and everything in God! Oh, that I could make you look on this earth, not as a mere dull, dreary prison and workhouse for your mortal bodies, but as a living book, to speak to you at every time of the living God, Father, Son, and Holy Ghost! Sure I am that that would be a heavenly life for you,—sure I am that it would keep you from many a sin, and stir you up to many a holy thought and deed, if you could learn to find in everything around you, however small or mean, the work of God's hand, the likeness of God's countenance, the shadow of God's glory.

SERMON II.

RELIGION NOT GODLINESS.

PSALM civ. 13—15.

He watereth the hills from his chambers: the earth is satisfied with the fruit of thy works. He causeth the grass to grow for the cattle, and herb for the service of man: that he may bring forth food out of the earth; and wine that maketh glad the heart of man, and oil to make his face to shine, and bread which strengtheneth man's heart.

DID you every remark, my friends, that the Bible says hardly anything about religion—that it never praises religious people? This is very curious. Would to God we would all remember it! The Bible speaks of a religious man only once, and of religion only twice, except where it speaks of the Jews' religion to condemn it, and shows what an empty, blind, useless thing it was.

What does this Bible talk of, then? It talks of God; not of religion, but of God. It tells us not to be religious, but to be godly. You may think there is no difference, or that it is but a difference of words. I tell you that a difference in words is a very awful, important difference. A difference in words is a difference in things. Words are very awful and wonderful things, for they come from the most awful and wonderful of all beings, Jesus Christ, the Word. He puts words into men's minds. He made all things, and He makes all words to express those things with. And woe to those who use the wrong words about things! For if a man calls anything by its wrong name, it is a sure sign that he understands that thing wrongly, or feels about it wrongly; and therefore a man's words are often honester than he thinks; for as a man's words are, so is a man's heart; out of the abundance of our hearts our mouths speak; and, therefore, by right words, by the right names which we call things, we shall be justified, and by our words, by the wrong names we call things, we shall be condemned.

Therefore a difference in words is a difference in the things which those words mean, and there is a difference between religion and godliness; and we show it by our words. Now these are religious times, but they are very ungodly times; and we show that also by our words. Because we think that people ought to be religious, we talk a great deal about religion; because we hardly think at all that a man ought to be godly, we talk very little about God, and that good old Bible word 'godliness' does not pass our lips once a month. For a man may be very religious, my friends, and yet very ungodly. The heathens were very religious at the very time that, as St. Paul tells us, they would not keep God in their knowledge. The Jews were the most religious people on the earth, they hardly talked or thought about anything but religion, at the very time that they knew so little of God that they crucified Him when He came down among them. St. Paul says that he was living after the strictest sect of the Jews' religion, at the very time that he was fighting against God, persecuting God's people and God's Son, and dead in trespasses and sins. These are ugly facts, my friends, but they are true, and well worth our laying to heart in these religious, ungodly days. I am afraid if Jesus Christ came down into England this day as a carpenter's son, He would get—a better hearing, perhaps, than the Jews gave Him, but still a very bad hearing—one dare hardly think of it.

And yet I believe we ought to think of it, and, by God's help, I will one day preach you a sermon, asking you all round this fair question :—If Jesus Christ came to you in the shape of a poor man, whom nobody knew, should *you* know Him; should you admire Him, fall at His feet, and give yourself up to Him body and soul? I am afraid that I, for one, should not—I am afraid that too many of us here would not. That comes of thinking more of religion than we do of godliness— in plain words, more of our own souls than we do of Jesus Christ. But you will want to know what is, after all, the difference between religion and godliness? Just the difference, my friends, that there is between always thinking of self and always forgetting self—between the terror of a slave and the affection of a child—between the fear of hell and the love of God. For, tell me what you mean by being religious? Do you not mean thinking a great deal about your own souls, and praying and reading about your own souls, and trying by all possible means to get your own souls saved? Is not that the meaning of religion? And yet I have never mentioned God's name in describing it! This sort of religion must have very little to do with God. You may be surprised at my words, and say in your hearts, almost angrily, 'Why, who saves our souls but God? Therefore religion must have to do with God.' But, my friends, for your souls' sake, and for God's sake, ask yourselves this question on your knees this day :—If you could get your souls saved without God's help, would it make much difference to you? Suppose an angel from heaven, as they say, was to come down and prove to you clearly that there was no God, no blessed Jesus in heaven, that the world made itself, and went on of itself, and that the Bible was all a mistake, but that you need not mind, for that your gardens and crops would grow just as well, and your souls be saved just as well when you died.

To how many of you would it make any difference? To some of you, thank God, I believe it would make a difference. There are some here, I believe, who would feel that news the worst news they ever heard—worse than if they were told that their souls were lost for ever; there are some here, I do believe, who, at that news, would cry aloud in agony, like little children who had lost their father, and say, 'No Father in heaven to love? No blessed Jesus in heaven to work for, and die for, and glory and delight in? No God to rule and manage this poor, miserable, quarrelsome world, bringing good out of evil, blessing and guiding all things and people on earth? What do I care what becomes of my soul if there is no God for my soul to glory in? What is heaven worth without God? God is heaven!'

Yes, indeed, what would heaven be worth without God? But how many people feel that the curse of this day is, that most people have forgotten *that?* They are selfishly anxious enough about their own souls, but they have forgotten God. They are religious, for fear of hell; but they are not godly, for they do not love God, or see God's hand in everything. They forget that they have a Father in heaven; that He sends rain, and sunshine, and fruitful seasons; that He gives them all things richly to enjoy in spite of all their sins. His mercies are far above, out of their sight, and therefore His judgments are far away out of their sight too; and so they talk of 'the visitation of God,' as if it was something that was very extraordinary, and happened very seldom; and when it came, only brought evil, harm, and sorrow. If a man lives on in health, they say he lives by the strength of his own constitution; if he drops down dead, they say he died by 'the visitation of God.' If the corn-crops go on all right and safe, they think *that* quite natural—the effect of the soil, and the weather, and their own skill in farming and gardening. But if there comes a hailstorm or a blight, and spoils it all, and brings on a famine, they call it at once 'a visitation of God.' My friends, do you think God 'visits' the earth or you only to harm you? I tell you that every blade of grass grows by 'the visitation of God.' I tell you that every healthy breath you ever drew, every cheerful hour you ever spent, every good crop you ever housed safely, came to you by 'the visitation of God.' I tell you that every sensible thought or plan that ever came into your heads, every loving, honest, manly, womanly feeling that ever rose in your hearts, God 'visited' you to put it there. If God's Spirit had not given it you, you would never have got it of yourselves.

But people forget this, and therefore they have so little real love to God—so little real, loyal, childlike trust in God. They do not think much about God, because they find no pleasure in thinking about Him; they look on God as a taskmaster, gathering where He has not strewed, reaping where He has not sown; a taskmaster who has put them, very miserable, sinful creatures, to struggle on in a very miserable, sinful world, and, though He tells them in His Bible that they *cannot* keep His commandments, expects them to keep them just the same, and will at the last send them all into everlasting fire, unless they take a great deal of care, and give up a great many natural and pleasant things, and beseech and entreat Him very hard to excuse them after all. This is the thought which most people have of God, even religious people; they look on God as a stern tyrant, who, when man sinned and fell, could not satisfy His own justice— His own vengeance, in plain words—without killing some one, and who would have certainly killed all mankind, if Jesus Christ had not interfered, and said, 'If Thou must slay some one, slay me, though I am innocent!'

Oh, my friends, does not this all sound horrible and irreverent? And yet, if you will but look into your own hearts, will you not find some such thoughts there? I am sure you will. I believe every man finds such thoughts in his heart now and then. I find them in my own heart: I know that they must be in the hearts of others, because I see them producing their natural fruits in people's actions,—a selfish, slavish view of religion, with little or no real love to God, or real trust in Him; but a great deal of uneasy dread of Him: for this is just the dark, false view of God, and of the good news of salvation and the kingdom of heaven, which the devil is always trying to make men take. The Evil One tries to make us forget that God is love; he tries to make us forget that God gives us all things richly to enjoy; he tries to make us forget that God gives at all, and to make us think that we take, not that He gives; to make us look at God as a taskmaster, not as a Father; in one word, to make us mistake the devil for God, and God for the devil.

And therefore it is that we ought to bless God for such Scriptures as this 104th Psalm, which He seems to have preserved in the Bible just to contradict these dark, slavish notions, —just to testify that God is a *giver*, and knows our necessities before we ask, and gives us all things, even as He gave us His blessed Son—freely, long before we wanted them,—from the foundation of all things, before ever the earth and the world was made—from all eternity, perpetual Love and perpetual Bounty.

What does this text teach us? To look at God as Him who gives to all freely, and upbraideth not. It says to us, Do not suppose that your crops grow of themselves. God waters the hills from above. He causes the grass to grow for the cattle, and the green herb for the service of man. Do not suppose that He cares nothing about seeing you comfortable and happy. It is He, He only, who sends all which strengthens man's body, and makes glad his heart, and makes him of a cheerful countenance. His will is that you should be cheerful. Ah, my friends, if we would but believe all this! We are too apt to say to ourselves, 'Our earthly comforts here have nothing to do with godliness or God; God must save our souls, but our bodies we must save ourselves. God gives us spiritual blessings, but earthly blessings, the good things of this life, for them we must scramble and drudge ourselves, and get as much of them as we can without offending God;' —as if God grudged us our comforts! as if godliness had not the promise of this life as well as the life to come! If we would but believe that God knows our necessities before we ask— that He gives us daily more than we can ever get by working for it!—if we would but seek first the kingdom of God and His righteousness, all other things would be added to us; and we should find that he who loses his life should save it. And this way of looking at God's earth would not make us idle; it would not tempt us to sit with folded hands for God's blessings to drop into our mouths. No; I believe it would make men far more industrious than ever mere self-interest can make them; they would say, 'God is our Father; He gave us His only Son, He gives us all things freely; we owe Him not slavish service, but a boundless debt of cheerful gratitude. Therefore we must do His will, and we are sure His will must be our happiness and comfort; therefore we must do His will, and His will is that we should *work*, and therefore we *must* work. He has bidden us labour on this earth—He has bidden us dress it and keep it, conquer it and fill it for Him. We are His stewards here on earth, and therefore it is a glory and an honour to be allowed to work here in God's own land—in our loving Father's own garden. We do not know why He wishes us to labour and till the ground, for He could have fed us with manna from heaven if He liked, as He fed the Jews of old, without our working at all. But His will is that we should work; and work we will, not for our own sakes merely, but for His sake, because we know He likes it, and for the sake of our brothers, our countrymen, for whom Christ died.'

Oh, my friends, why is it that so many till the ground industriously, and yet grow poorer and poorer for all their drudging and working? It is their own fault. They till the ground for their own sakes, and not for God's sake and for their countrymen's sake; and so, as the Prophet says, they sow much and bring in little; and he who earns wages earns them to put in a bag full of holes. Suppose you try the opposite plan: suppose you say to yourself, 'I will work henceforward because God wishes me to work. I will work henceforward for my country's sake, because I feel that God has given me a noble and a holy calling when He set me to grow food for His children, the people of England. As for my wages and my profit, God will take care of them if they are just; and if they are unjust, He will take care of them too. He, at all events, makes the garden and the field grow, and not I. My land is filled, not with the fruit of my work, but with the fruit of His work. He will see that I lose nothing by my labour. If I till the soil for God and for God's children, I may trust God to pay me my wages.' Oh, my friends, He who feeds the young birds when they call upon Him; and far, far more, He who gave you His only-begotten Son, will He not with Him freely give you all things? For, after all done, He must give to you, or you will not get. You may fret and stint, and scrape and puzzle; one man may sow, and another man may water; but, after all, who can give the increase but God? Can you make a load of hay, unless He has first grown it for you, and then dried it for you? If you would but think a little more about Him, if you would believe that your crops were His gifts, and in your hearts offer them up to Him as thank-offerings, see if He would not help you to sell your crops as well as to house them. He would put you in the way of an honest profit for your labour just as surely as He only put you in the way of labouring at all. 'Trust in the Lord, and be doing good; dwell in the land, and verily thou shalt be fed;' for 'without me,' says our Lord, 'you can do nothing.' No: these are His own words—nothing. To Him all power is given in heaven and earth; He knows every root and every leaf, and feeds it. Will He not much more feed you, oh ye of little faith? Do you think that He has made His world so ill that a man cannot get on in it unless he is a knave? No. Cast all your care on Him, and see if you do not find out ere long that He cares for you, and has cared for you from all eternity.

SERMON III.

LIFE AND DEATH.

PSALM civ. 24, 28—30.

O Lord, how manifold are Thy works! in wisdom hast Thou made them all: the earth is full of Thy riches. That Thou gavest them they gather: Thou openest Thine hand, they are filled with good. Thou hidest Thy face, they are troubled: Thou takest away their breath, they die, and return to their dust. Thou sendest forth Thy spirit, they are created: and Thou renewest the face of the earth.

I HAD intended to go through this psalm with you in regular order; but things have happened in this parish, awful and sad, during the last week, which I was bound not to let slip without trying to bring them home to your hearts, if by any means I could persuade the thoughtless ones among you to be wise and consider your latter end :—I mean the sad deaths of various of our acquaintances. The death-bell has been tolled in this parish three times, I believe, in one day—a thing which has seldom happened before, and which, God grant, may never happen again. Within two miles of this church there are now five lying dead. Five human beings, young as well as old, to whom the awful words of the text have been fulfilled: 'Thou takest away their breath, they die, and return to their dust.' And the very day on which three of these deaths happened was Ascension-day—the day on which Jesus, the Lord of life, the conqueror of death, ascended up on high, having led captivity captive, and became the first-fruits of the grave, to send down from the heaven of eternal life the Spirit who is the Giver of life. That was a strange mixture, death seemingly triumphant over Christ's people on the very day on which life triumphed in Jesus Christ Himself. Let us see, though, whether death has not something to do with Ascension-day. Let us see whether a sermon about death is not a fit sermon for the Sunday after Ascension-day. Let us see whether the text has not a message about life and death too— a message which may make us feel that in the midst of life we are in death, and that yet in the midst of death we are in life; that however things may *seem*, yet death has not conquered life, but life has conquered and *will* conquer death, and conquer it most completely at the very moment that we die, and our bodies return to their dust.

Do I speak riddles? I think the text will explain my riddles, for it tells us how life comes, how death comes. Life comes from God: He sends forth His Spirit, and things are made, and He renews the face of the earth. We read in the very first two verses of the book of Genesis how the Spirit of God moved upon the face of the waters at the creation, and woke all things into life. Therefore the Creed well calls the Holy Ghost, the Spirit of God—that is, the Lord and Giver of Life. And the text tells us that He gives life, not only to us who have immortal souls, but to everything on the face of the earth; for the psalm has been talking all through, not only of men, but of beasts, fishes, trees, and rivers, and rocks, sun and moon. Now all these things have a life in them. Not a life like ours; but still you speak rightly and wisely when you say, 'That tree is alive, and That tree is dead. That running water is live water—it is sweet and fresh; but if it is kept standing it begins to putrefy, its life is gone from it, and a sort of death comes over it, and makes it foul, and unwholesome, and unfit to drink.' This is a deep matter, this; how there is a sort of life in everything, even to the stones under our feet. I do not mean, of course, that stones can think as our life makes us do, or feel as the beasts' life makes them do, or even grow as the trees' life makes them do; but I mean that their life keep them as they are, without changing or decaying. You hear miners and quarrymen talk very truly of the live rock. That stone, they say, was cut out of the live rock, meaning the rock as it is under ground, sound and hard—as it would be, for aught we know, to the end of time, unless it was taken out of the ground, out of the place where God's Spirit meant it to be, and brought up to the open air and the rain, in which it is not its nature to be. And then you will see that the life of the stone begins to pass from it bit by bit, that it crumbles and peels away, and, in short, decays and is turned again to its dust. Its organization, as it is called, or life, ends, and then— what? does the stone lie for ever useless? No! And there is the great blessed mystery of how God's Spirit is always bringing life out of death. When the stone is decayed and crumbled down to dust and clay, it makes *soil*—this very soil here, which you plough, is the decayed ruins of ancient hills; the clay which you dig up in the fields was once part of some slate or granite mountains, which were worn away by weather and water, that they might become fruitful earth. Wonderful! but anyone who has studied these things can tell you they are true. Anyone who has ever lived in mountainous countries ought to have seen the thing happen, ought to know that the land in the mountain valleys is made at first, and kept rich year by year, by the washings from the hills above; and this is the reason why land left dry by rivers and by the sea is generally so rich. Then what becomes of the soil? It begins a new life. The roots of the plants take it up; the salts which they find in it—the staple, as we call them—go to make leaves and seed; the very sand has its use, it feeds the stalks of corn and grass, and makes them stiff. The corn-stalks would never stand upright if they could not get sand from the soil. So what a thousand years ago made part of a mountain, now makes part of a wheat plant; and in a year more the wheat grain will have been eaten, and the wheat straw perhaps eaten too, and they will have *died*—decayed in the bodies of the animals who have eaten them, and then they will begin a third new life— they will be turned into parts of the animal's body—of a man's body. So that what is now your bone and flesh, may have been once a rock on some hill-side a hundred miles away.

Strange, but true! all learned men know that it is true. You, if you think over my words, may see that they are at least reasonable. But still most wonderful! This world works right well surely. It obeys God's spirit. Oh, my friends, if we fulfilled our life and our duty as well as the clay which we tread on does—if we obeyed God's Spirit as surely as the flint does, we should have many a heartache spared us, and many a headache too! To be what God wants us!—to be *men*, to be *women*, and therefore to live as children of God, members of Christ, fulfilling our duty in that state to which God has called us—that would be our bliss and glory. Nothing can live in a state in which God did not intend it to live. Suppose a tree could move itself about like an animal, and chose to do so, the tree would wither and die; it would be trying to act contrary to the law which God has given it. Suppose the ox chose to eat meat like the lion, it would fall sick and die; for it would be acting contrary to the law which God's Spirit had made for it—going out of the calling to which God's word has called it, to eat grass and not flesh, and live thereby. And so with us; if we will do wickedly, when the will of God, as the Scripture tells us, is our sanctification, our holiness; if we will speak lies, when God's law for us is that we should speak truth; if we will bear hatred and ill-will, when God's law for us is, Love as brothers—you all sprang from one father, Adam—you were all redeemed by one brother, Jesus Christ; if we will try to live as if there was no God, when God's law for us is, that a man can live like a man only by faith and trust in God;—then we shall *die*, if we break God's laws according to which he intended man to live. Thus it was with Adam; God intended him to obey God, to learn everything from God. He chose to disobey God, to try and know something of himself, by getting the knowledge of good and evil; and so death passed on him. He became an unnatural man, a *bad* man, more or less, and so he became a dead man; and death came into the world, that time at least, by sin, by breaking the law by which man was meant to be a man. As the beasts will die if you give them unnatural food, or in any way prevent their following the laws which God has made for them, so man dies of necessity. All the world cannot help his dying, because he breaks the laws which God has made for him.

And how does he die? The text tells us, God takes away his breath, and turns His face from him. In His presence, it is written, is life. The moment He withdraws His Spirit, the Spirit of life, from anything, body or soul, then it dies. It was by *sin* came death—by man's becoming unfit for the Spirit of God.

Therefore the body is dead because of sin, says St. Paul, doomed to die, carrying about in it the seeds of death, from the very moment it is born. Death has truly passed upon all men!

Most sad; and yet there is hope, and more than hope, there is certain assurance, for us, that though we die, yet shall we live! I have shown you, in the beginning of my sermon, how nothing that dies perishes to nothing, but begins a new and a higher life. How the stone becomes a plant—something better and more useful than it was before; the plant passes into an animal—a step higher still. And therefore we may be sure that the same rule will hold good about us men and women, that when we die, we shall begin a new and a nobler life, that is, if we have been true *men;* if we have lived fulfilling the law of our kind. St. Paul tells us so positively. He says that nothing comes to life except it first die, then God gives it a new body. He says that even so is the resurrection of the dead,—that we gain a step by dying; that we are sown in corruption, and are raised in incorruption; we are sown in dishonour, and are raised in glory; we are sown in weakness, and are raised in power; we are sown a natural body, and are raised a spiritual body; that as we now are of the earth earthy, after death and the resurrection our new and nobler body will be of the heavens heavenly; so that 'when this corruptible shall have put on incorruption, and this mortal shall have put on immortality, then death shall be swallowed up in victory.' Therefore I say, Sorrow not for those who sleep as if you had no hope for the dead; for 'Christ is risen from the dead, and become the first-fruits of them that slept. For as in Adam all die, even so in Christ shall all be made alive.'

And I say that this has to do with the text—it has to do with Ascension-day. For if we claim our share in Christ,—if we claim our share of our heavenly Father's promise, 'to give the Holy Spirit to those who ask Him,' then we may certainly hope for our share in Christ's resurrection, our share in Christ's ascension. For, says St. Paul (Rom. viii. 10, 11), 'If Christ be in you, the body is dead because of sin, but the Spirit is life because of righteousness. But if the Spirit of Him who raised up Jesus from the dead dwell in you, He that raised up Christ from the dead shall also quicken your mortal bodies, by His Spirit that dwelleth in you!' There is a blessed promise! that in that, as in everything, we shall be made like Christ our Master, the new Adam, who is a life-giving Spirit, that as He was brought to life again by the Spirit of God, so we shall be. And so will be fulfilled in us the glorious rule which the text lays down, 'Thou, O God, sendest forth Thy Spirit, and they are created, and Thou dost renew the face of the earth.' Fulfilled?—yes, but far more gloriously than ever the old Psalmist expected. Read the Revelation of St. John, chapters xxi. and xxii., for the glory of the renewed earth; read the First Epistle of Paul to the Thessalonians, chap. iv. 16—18, for the glorious resurrection and ascension of those who have died trusting in the blessed Lord, who died for them; and then see what a glorious future lies before us—see how death is but the gate of life—see how what holds true of everything on this earth, down to the flint beneath our feet, holds true ten thousand times of men—that to die and to decay is only to pass into a nobler state of life. But remember, that just as we are better than the stone, we may be also worse than the stone. It cannot disobey God's laws, therefore it can enjoy no reward, any more than suffer any punishment. We can disobey—we can fall from our calling—we can cast God's law behind us—we can refuse to do His will, to work out our own salvation; and just because our reward in the life to come will be so glorious, if we fulfil our life and law, the life of faith and the law of love, therefore will our punishment be so horrible, if we neglect the life of faith and trample under foot the law of love. Oh, my friends, choose! Death is before you all. Shall it be the gate of everlasting life and glory, or the gate of everlasting death and misery? Will you claim your glorious inheritance, and be for ever equal to the angels, doing God's will on earth as they in heaven; or will you fall lower than the stones, who, at all events, must do their duty as stones, and not *do* God's will at all, but only *suffer* it in eternal woe? You must do one or the other. You cannot be like the stones—without feeling, without joy or sorrow—just because you are immortal spirits, every one of you. You must be either happy or miserable, blessed or disgraced, for ever. I know of no middle path;—do you? Choose before the night comes, in which no man can work. Our life is but a vapour which appears for a little time, then vanishes away. 'O Lord, how manifold are Thy works! in wisdom hast Thou made them all: the earth is full of Thy riches. That Thou givest them they gather: Thou openest Thine hand, they are filled with good. Thou hidest Thy face, they are troubled: Thou takest away their breath, they die, and return to their dust. Thou sendest forth Thy Spirit, they are created: and Thou renewest the face of the earth.'

SERMON IV.

THE WORK OF GOD'S SPIRIT.

JAMES i. 16, 17.

Do not err, my beloved brethren; every good gift and every perfect gift is from above, and cometh down from the Father of lights.

THIS text, I believe more and more every day, is one of the most important ones in the whole Bible; and just at this time it is more important for us than ever, because people have forgotten it more than ever.

And, according as you firmly believe this text, according as you firmly believe that every good gift you have in body and soul comes down from above, from God the Father of Lights—according, I say, as you believe this, and live upon that belief, just so far will you be able to do your duty to God and man, worthily of your blessed Saviour's calling and redemption, and of the high honour which He has given you of being free and christened men, redeemed by His most precious blood, and led by His most noble Spirit.

Now, just because this text is so important, the devil is particularly busy in trying to make people forget it. For what is his plan? Is it not to make us forget God, to put God *out* of all our thoughts, to make us acknowledge God in none of our ways, to make us look at ourselves and not at God, so that we may become first earthly and sensual, and then devilish, like Satan himself? Therefore he tries to make us disbelieve

this text. He puts into our hearts such thoughts as these:—
"Ay, all good gifts may come from God; but that only means all spiritual gifts. All those fine, deep doctrines and wonderful feelings that some very religious people talk of, about conversion, and regeneration, and sanctification, and assurance, and the witness of the indwelling Spirit,—all those gifts come from God, no doubt, but they are quite above us. We are straightforward, simple people, who cannot feel fine fancies; if we can be honest, and industrious, and good-natured, and sober, and strong, and healthy, that is enough for us,—and all that has nothing to do with religion. Those are not gifts which come from God. A man is strong and healthy by birth, and honest and good-natured by nature. Those are very good things; but they are not *gifts*—they are not *graces*—they are not *spiritual* blessings—they have nothing to do with the state of a man's soul. Ungodly people are honest, and good-tempered, and industrious, and healthy, as well as your saints and your methodists; so what is the use of praying for spiritual gifts to God, when we can have all we want by nature?"

Did such thoughts never come into your heads, my friends? Are they not often in your heads, more or less? Perhaps not in these very words, but something like them.

I do not say it to blame you, for I believe that every man, each according to his station, is tempted to such thoughts; I believe that such thoughts are not *yours* or any man's; I believe they are the devil's, who tempts all men, who tempted even the Son of God Himself with thoughts like these at their root. Such thoughts are not *yours* or mine, though they may come into our heads. They are part of the evil which besets us—which is *not* us—which has no right or share in us—which we pray God drive away from us when we say, "Deliver us from evil." Have you not all had such thoughts? But have you not all had very different thoughts? have you not, every one of you, at times, felt in the bottom of your hearts, after all, "This strength and industry, this courage, and honesty, and good-nature of mine, must come from God; I did not get them myself. If I was born honest, and strong, and gentle, and brave, some one must have made me so when I was born, or before. The devil certainly did not make me so, therefore *God* must. These, too, are His gifts?"

Did you ever think such thoughts as these? If you did not, not much matter, for you have all acted, more or less, in your better moments, as if you had them. There are more things in a man's heart, thank God, than ever come into his head. Many a man does a noble thing by instinct, as we say, without ever *thinking* whether it is a noble thing or not—without *thinking* about it at all. Many a man, thank God, is led at times, by God's Spirit, without ever knowing whose Spirit it is that leads him.

But he *ought* to know it, for it is *willing, reasonable* service which God wants of us. He does not care to use us like tools and puppets. And why? He is not merely our Maker, He is our Father, and He wishes us to know and feel that we are His children—to know and feel that we all have come from Him; to acknowledge Him in all our ways, to thank Him for all, to look up lovingly and confidently to Him for more, as His reasonable children, day by day, and hour by hour. Every good gift we have comes from Him; but He will have us know where they all come from.

Let us go through now a few of these good gifts, which we call natural, and see what the Bible says of them, and from whom they come.

First, now, that common gift of strength and courage. Who gives you that?—who gave it David? For He that gives it to one is most likely to be He that gives it to another. David says to God, 'Thou teachest my hands to war, and my fingers to fight; by the help of God I can leap over a wall: He makes me strong, that my arms can break even a bow of steel.' That is plain-spoken enough, I think. Who gave Samson his strength, again? What says the Bible? How Samson met a young lion which roared against him, and he had nothing in his hand, and the Spirit of the Lord came mightily upon him, and he tore the lion as he would have torn a kid. And, again, how, when traitors had bound him with two new cords, the Spirit of the Lord came mightily upon him, and the cords which were on his arms became as flax that was burnt with fire, and fell from off his hands. And, for God's sake, do not give in to that miserable fancy that because these stories are what you call miraculous, therefore they have nothing to do with you—that Samson's strength came to him miraculously by God's Spirit, and yet yours comes to you a different way. The Bible is written to tell you how all that happens really happens—what all things really are. God is working among us always, but we do not see Him; and the Bible just lifts up, once and for all, the veil which hides Him from us, and lets us see, in one instance, who it is that does all the wonderful things which go on round us to this day, that when we see anything like it happen we may know whom to thank for it.

The Great Physician healed the blind and the lame in Judea; and why?—to show us who heals the blind and the lame now—to show us that the good gift of medicine and surgery, and the physician's art, comes down from Him who cured the paralytic and cleansed the lepers in Judea—to whom all power is given in heaven and earth.

So, again, with skill in farming and agriculture. From whom does that come? The very heathens can tell us that; for it is curious, that among the heathen, in all ages and countries, those men who have found out great improvements in tilling the ground have been honoured and often worshipped as divine men—as gods; thereby showing that the heathen, among all their idolatries, had a true and just notion about man's practical skill and knowledge—that it could only come from heaven; that it was by the inspiration and guidance of God above that skill in agriculture arose. What says Isaiah of that to the very same purpose? 'Doth the plowman plow all day to sow? doth he open and break the clods of his ground? When he hath made plain. the face thereof, doth he not cast abroad the vetches, and cast in the principal wheat and the appointed barley and the rye in their place? For his God doth instruct him to discretion, and doth teach him. This also,' says Isaiah, 'cometh from the Lord of Hosts, who is wonderful in counsel, and excellent in working.' Would to God you would all believe it!

Again: wisdom and prudence, and a clear, powerful mind, —are not they parts of God's likeness? How is God's Spirit described in Scripture? It is called the Spirit of wisdom and understanding, the Spirit of prudence and might. Therefore, surely, all wisdom and understanding, all prudence and strength of mind, are, like that Spirit, part of God's image? And where did we get God's image? Can we make ourselves like God? If we are like Him, He must have formed that likeness, and He alone. The Spirit of God, says the Scripture, giveth us understanding.

Or, again: good-natured and affection, love, generosity, pity,—whose likeness are they? What is God's name but love? God is love. Has not He revealed Himself as the God of mercy, full of long-suffering, compassion, and free forgiveness; and must not, then, all love and affection, all compassion and generosity, be His gift? Yes. As the rays come from the sun, and yet are not the sun, even so our love and pity, though they are not God, but merely a poor, weak image and reflection of Him, yet from Him alone they come. If there is mercy in our hearts, it comes from the fountain of mercy. If there is the light of love in us, it is a ray from the full sun of His love.

Or honesty, again, and justice,—whose image are they but God's? Is He not THE Just One—the righteous God? Is not what is just for man just for God? Are not the laws of justice and honesty by which man deals fairly with man, *His* laws—the laws by which God deals with us? Does not every book—I had almost said every page—in the Bible show us that all our justice is but the pattern and copy of God's justice, —the working out of those six latter commandments of His, which are summed up in that one command, 'Thou shalt love Thy neighbour as thyself?'

Now, here, again, I ask: If justice and honesty be God's likeness, who made us like God in this—who put into us this sense of justice which all have, though so few obey it? Can man make himself like God? Can a worm ape his Maker? No. From God's Spirit, the Spirit of Right, came this inborn feeling of justice, this knowledge of right and wrong, to us— part of the image of God in which He created man—part of the breath or spirit of life which He breathed into Adam. Do not mistake me. I do not say that the sense, and honesty, and love in us, *are* God's Spirit—they are the spirit of *man;* but that they are *like* God's Spirit, and therefore they must be given us *by* God's Spirit, to be used as God's Spirit Himself uses them. How a man shall have his share of God's Spirit, and live in, and by God's Spirit, is another question, and a higher and more blessed one; but we must master this question first—we must believe that our spirits come *from* God, then, perhaps, we shall begin to see that our spirits never can work well unless they are joined to the Spirit of God, from whom they came. From whom else, I ask again, can they come? Can they come from our bodies? Our bodies! What are they?—Flesh and bones, made up of air and water and earth,—out of the dead bodies of the animals, the dead roots and fruits of plants which we eat. They are earth—matter. Can *matter* be courageous? Did you ever hear of a good-natured plant, or an honest stone? Then this good-nature, and honesty, and courage of ours, must belong to our souls—our spirits. Who put them there? Did we? Does a child make its own character? Does its body make its character first? Can its father and mother make its character? No. Our characters must come from some spirit above us—either from God or from the devil. And is the devil likely to make us honest, or brave, or kindly? I leave you to answer that. God—God alone, my friends, is the author of good—the help that is done on earth, He doeth it all Himself: every good gift and every perfect gift cometh from Him.

Now, some of you may think this a strange sort of sermon, because I have said little or nothing about Jesus Christ and His redemption in it; but I say—No.

You must believe this much about yourselves before you can believe more. You must fairly and really believe that *God* made you one thing before you can believe that you have made yourselves another thing. You must really believe that you are not mere machines and animals, but immortal souls, before you can really believe that you have sinned; for animals cannot sin—only reasonable souls can sin. We must really believe that God made us at bottom in His likeness, before we can begin to find out that there is another likeness in us besides God's—a selfish, brutish, too often a devilish likeness, which must be repented of, and fought against, and cast out, that God's likeness in us may get the upper hand, and we may be what God expects us to be. We must know our dignity before we can feel our shame. We must see how high we have a right to stand, that we may see how low, alas! we have fallen.

Now you—I know many such here, thank God—to whom God has given clear, powerful heads for business, and honest, kindly hearts, I do beseech you consider my words, Who has given you these but God? They are talents which He has committed to your charge; and will He not require an account of them? *He* only, and His free mercy, have made you to differ from others, if you are better than the fools and profligates round you, He, and not yourselves, has made you better. What have you that you have not received? By the grace of God alone you are what you are. If good comes easier to you than to others, *He* alone has made it easier to you; and if you have done wrong,—if you have fallen short of your duty, as *all* fall short, is not your sin greater than others'? for unto whom much is given, of them shall much be required. Consider that, for God's sake, and see if you, too, have not something to be ashamed of, between yourselves and God. See if you, too, have not need of Jesus Christ and His precious blood, and God's free forgiveness, who have had so much light and power given you, and still have fallen short of what you might have been, and what by God's grace, you still may be, and, as I hope and earnestly pray, still will be.

And you, young men and women—consider;—if God has given you manly courage and high spirits, and strength and beauty—think—*God*, your Father, has given them to you, and of them He will surely require an account; therefore, 'Rejoice, young people,' says Solomon, ' in your youth, and let your hearts cheer you in the days of your youth, and walk in the ways of your heart and in the sight of your eyes. But remember,' continues the wisest of men—' remember, that for all these things God shall bring you into judgment.' Now, do not misunderstand that. It does not mean that there is a sin in being happy. It does not mean that if God has given to a young man a bold spirit and powerful limbs, or to a young woman a handsome face, and a merry, loving heart, that He will punish them for these,—God forbid ! what He gives He means to be used; but this it means, that according as you use those blessings so will you be judged at the last day; that for them, too, you will be brought to judgment, and tried at the bar of God. As you have used them for industry, and innocent happiness, and holy married love, or for riot and quarrelling, and idleness, and vanity, and filthy lusts, so shall you be judged. And if any of you have sinned in any of these ways, —God forbid that you should have sinned in *all* these ways; but surely, surely, some of you have been idle—some of you have been riotous—some of you have been vain—some of you have been quarrelsome—some of you, alas ! have been that which I shall not name here—Think, if you have sinned in any one of these ways, how can you answer it to God? Have you no need of forgiveness? Have you no need of the blessed Saviour's blood to wash you clean? Young people! God has given you much. As a young man, I speak to you Youth is an inestimable blessing or an inestimable curse, according as you use it; and if you have abused your spring-time of youth, as all, I am afraid, have—as I have—as almost all do, alas! in this fallen world, where can you get forgiveness but from Him that died on the cross to take away the sins of the world?

SERMON V.

FAITH.

HABAKKUK ii. 4.

The just shall live by faith.

THIS is one of those texts of which there are so many in the Bible, which, though they were spoken originally to one particular man, yet are meant for every man. These words were spoken to Habakkuk, a Jewish prophet, to check him for his impatience under God's hand; but they are just as true for every man that ever was and ever will be as they were for him. They are world-wide and world-old; they are the law by which all goodness, and strength, and safety, stand either in men or angels, for it always was true, and always must be true that if reasonable beings are to live at all, it is by faith.

And why? Because everything that is, heaven and earth, men and angels, are all the work of God—of one God, infinite, almighty, all-wise, all-loving, unutterably glorious. My friends, we do not think enough of this,—not that all the thinking in the world can ever make us comprehend the majesty of our Heavenly Father; but we do not remember enough what we *do* know of God. We think of God, watching the world and all things in it, and keeping them in order as a shepherd does his sheep, and so far so good; but we forget that God does more than this,—we forget that this earth, sun and moon, and all the thousand thousand stars which cover the midnight sky,—many of them suns larger than the sun we see, and worlds larger than the world on which we stand, that all these, stretching away millions of millions of miles into boundless space,—all are lying like one little grain of dust, in the hollow of God's hand, and that if He were to shut His hand upon them, He could crush them into nothing, and God would be alone in the universe again as He was before heaven and earth were made. Think of that!—that if God was but to will it, we, and this earth on which we stand, and the heaven above us, and the sun that shines on us, should vanish away, and be nowhere and nothing.

Think of the infinite power of God, and then think how is it possible to *live*, except by faith in Him, by trusting to Him, utterly? If you accustom yourselves to think in the same way of the infinite wisdom of God, and the infinite love of God, they will both teach you the same lesson; they will show you that if you were the greatest, the wisest, the holiest man that ever lived, you would still be such a speck by the side of the Almighty and Everlasting God, that it would be madness to depend upon yourselves for anything while you lived in God's world. For, after all, what *can* we do without God? *In* Him we live, and move, and have our being. He made us, He gave us our bodies, He gave us our life; what we do *He* lets us do, what we say He lets us say; we all live on sufferance. What is it but God's infinite mercy that ever brought us here, or keeps us here an instant? We may pretend to act without God's leave or help, but it is impossible for us to do so; the strength we put forth, the wit we use, are all His gifts. We cannot draw a breath of air without His leave, and yet men fancy they can do without God in the world! My friends, these are but few words, and poor words, about the glorious majesty of God and our littleness when compared with Him; but I have said quite enough, at least, to show you all how absurd it is to depend upon ourselves for anything. If we are mere creatures of God, if God alone has every blessing both of this world and the next, and the will to give them away, whom *are* we to go to but to Him for all we want? It is so in the life of our bodies, and it is so in the life of our spirits. If we wish for God's blessings, from God we must ask them. That is our duty, even though God in His mercy and long-suffering does pour down many a blessing upon men who never trust in Him for them. To us all, indeed, God gives blessings before we are old enough to trust in Him for them, and to many He continues those blessings in after-life in spite of their blindness and want of faith. 'He maketh His sun to shine on the evil and on the good, and sendeth rain on the just and on the unjust.' He gives—gives —it is His glory to give. Yet strange! that men will go on year after year, using the limbs, and eating the food, which God gives them, without ever believing so much as that God *has* given them—without so much as looking up to heaven once, and saying, 'God, I thank Thee!' But we must remember that those blessings will not last for ever. Unless a man has lived by faith in God with regard to his earthly comforts, death will come and put an end to them at once; and then it is only those who have trusted in God for all good things, and thanked Him accordingly in this life, who shall have their part in the new heavens and the new earth, which will so immeasurably surpass all that this earth can give.

And it is the same with the life of our spirits; in it, too, we must live by faith. The life of our spirits is a gift from God, the Father of spirits, and He has chosen to declare that unless we trust to Him for life, and ask Him for life, He will not bestow it upon us. The life of our bodies He in His mercy keeps up, although we forget Him; the life of our souls He will not keep up; therefore, for the sake of our spirits, even more than of our bodies, we must live by faith. If we wish to be loving, pure, wise, manly, noble, we must ask those excellent gifts of God, who is Himself infinite love and purity, wisdom and nobleness. If we wish for everlasting life, from whom can we obtain it but from God who is the boundless, eternal life itself? If we wish for forgiveness for our faults and failings, where are we to get it but from God, who is boundless love and pity, and who has revealed to us His boundless love and pity in the form of a man, Jesus Christ, the Saviour of the world? And to go a step further; it is by faith in Christ we must live—in Christ, a man like ourselves, yet God blessed for ever. For it is a certain truth, that men cannot believe in God or trust in Him unless they can think of him as a man. This was the reason why the poor heathen made themselves idols in the form of men, that they might have something like themselves to worship; and those among them who would not worship idols almost always ended in fancying that God was either a mere notion, or else a mere part of this world, or else that He sat up in heaven neither knowing nor caring what happened upon earth. But we, to whom God has given the glorious news of His Gospel, have the very Person to worship whom all the heathen were searching after and could not find, —one who is very 'God,' infinite in love, wisdom, and strength, and yet 'very man,' made in all points like ourselves, but without sin; so that we have not a High Priest who cannot be touched with the feeling of our infirmities, but one who is able to help those who are tempted, because He was tempted Himself like us, and overcame by the strength of His own perfect will, of His own perfect faith. By trusting in Him, and acknowledging Him in every thought and action of our lives, we shall be safe; for it is written, 'The just shall live by faith.'

These things are true, and always were true. All that men ever did well, or nobly, or lovingly, in this world, *was done by faith*—by faith in God of some sort or other; even in the man who thinks least about religion, it is so. Every time a man means to do, and really does, a just or generous action, he does it because he believes, more or less clearly, that there is a just and loving God above him, and that justice and love are the right thing for a man—the law by which God intended him to walk: so that this small, dim faith still shows itself in practice:

and the more faith a man has in God and in God's laws, the more it will show itself in every action of his daily life; and the more this faith works in his life and conduct, the better man he is;—the more he is like God's image, in which man was originally made;—and the more he is like Christ, the new pattern of God's image, whom all men must copy.

So that the sum of the matter is this : without Christ we can do nothing—by trusting in Christ we can do everything. See, then, how true the verse before my text must be, that he whose soul is lifted up in him is not upright ; for if a man fancies that his body and soul are his own, to do what he pleases with them, when all the time they are God's gift ;—if a man fancies that he can take perfect care of himself, while all the time it is God that is keeping him out of a thousand sins and dangers;—if a man fancies that he can do right of himself, when all the time the little good that he does is the work of God's Spirit, which has not yet left him ;—if a man fancies, in short, that he can do without God, when all the time it is in God that he lives, and moves, and has his being, how can such a man be called upright? Upright ! he is utterly wrong; he is believing a lie, and walking accordingly; and therefore, instead of keeping upright, he is going where all lies lead, into all kinds of low and crooked ways, mistakes, absurdities, and at last to ruin of body and soul. Nothing but truth can keep a man upright and straight, can keep a man where God has put him, and where he ought to be ; and the man whose heart is puffed up by pride and self-conceit, who is looking at himself and not at God, that man has begun upon a falsehood, and will soon get out of tune with heaven and earth. For consider, my friends : suppose some rich and mighty prince went out and collected a number of children, and of sick and infirm people, and said to them, 'You cannot work now, but I will give you food, medicine, everything that you require, and then you must help me to work ; and I, though you have no right to expect it of me, will pay you for the little work you can do on the strength of my food and medicine,'—is it not plain that all those persons could only live by faith in their prince, by trusting in him for food and medicine, and by acknowledging that that food and medicine came from him, and thanking him accordingly? If they wished to be true men, if they wished him to continue his bounty, they would confess that all the health and strength they had belonged to him of right, because his generosity had given it to them. Just in this position we stand with Christ the Lord. When the whole world lay in wickedness, He came and chose us, of His free grace and mercy, to be one of his peculiar nations, to work for Him and with Him; and from the time He came, all that we and our forefathers have done well has been done by the strength and wisdom which Christ has given us. Now, suppose, again, that one of the persons of whom I spoke was seized with a fit of pride—suppose he said to himself, 'My health and strength do not come from the food and medicine which the prince gave me; they come from the goodness of my own constitution; the wages which I am paid are my just due; I am a free man, and may choose what master I like.' Suppose any one of *your* servants treated you so, would you not be inclined to answer, 'You are a faithless, ungrateful fellow; go your ways, then, and see how little you can do without my bounty?' But the blessed King in heaven, though He is provoked every day, is more long-suffering than man. All He does is to withdraw His bounty for a moment, to take this world's blessings from a man, and let him find out how impossible it is for him to keep himself out of affliction—to take away His Holy Spirit for a moment from a man, and let him see how straight he rushes astray, and every way but the right; and then, if the man is humbled by his fall or his affliction, and comes back to his Lord, confessing how weak he is, and promising to trust in Christ and thank Christ only for the future, *then* our Lord will restore His blessings to him, and there will be joy among the angels of God over one sinner that repents. This was the way in which God treated Job when, in spite of all his excellence, *his* heart was lifted up. And then, when he saw his own folly, and abhorred himself, and repented in dust and ashes, God restored to him sevenfold what He had taken from him—honour, wisdom, riches, home, and children. This is the way, too, in which God treated David. 'In my prosperity,' he tells us, 'I said, I shall never be moved; Thou, Lord, of Thy goodness hast made my hill so strong'—forgetting that he must be kept safe every moment of his life, as well as made safe once for all. 'Thou didst turn Thy face from me, and I was troubled. Then cried I unto Thee, O Lord, and gat me to my Lord right humbly. And THEN,' he adds, 'God turned my heaviness into joy, and girded me with gladness' (Psalm xxx.). And again, he says, '*Before* I was troubled I went wrong, but *now* I have kept Thy word' (Psalm cxix.). And this is the way in which Christ the Lord treated St. Peter and St. Paul, and treats, in His great mercy, every Christian man when He sees him puffed up, to bring him to his senses, and make him live by faith in God. If he takes the warning, well; if he does not, he remains in a lie, and must go where all lies lead. So perfectly does it hold throughout a man's whole life, that he whose soul is lifted up within him is not upright; but that the just must live by faith.

Now, there is one objection apt to rise in men's minds when they hear such words as these, which is, that they take such a 'low view of human nature:' it is so galling to our pride to be told that we can do nothing for ourselves; but if we think of the matter more closely, and, above all, if we try to put it into practice and live by faith, we shall find that there is no real reason for thus objecting. This is not a doctrine which ought to make us despise men; any doctrine that *does*, does not come of *God.* Men are not contemptible creatures—they are glorious creatures—they were created in the image of God; God has put such honour upon them that He has given them dominion over the whole earth, and made them partakers of

His eternal reason; and His Spirit gives them understanding to enable them to conquer this earth, and make the beasts, ay, and the very winds and seas, and fire and steam, their obedient servants; and human nature, too, when it is what God made it, and what it ought to be, is not a contemptible thing: it was noble enough for the Son of God to take it upon Himself—to become man, without sinning or defiling Himself; and what was good enough for Him is surely good enough for us. Wickedness consists in *unmanliness*, in being unlike a man, in becoming like an evil spirit or a beast. Holiness consists in becoming a *true man*, in becoming more and more like the likeness of Jesus Christ. And when the Bible tells us that we can do nothing of ourselves, but can live only by faith, the Bible puts the highest honour upon us which any created thing can have. What are the things which cannot live by faith? The trees and plants, the beasts and birds, which, though they live and grow by God's providence, yet do not know it, do not thank Him, cannot ask Him for more strength and life as we can, are mere dead tools in God's hands, instead of living, reasonable beings as we are. It is only reasonable beings, like men and angels, with immortal spirits in them, who *can* live by faith; and it is the greatest glory and honour to us, I say again, that we *can* do so—that the glorious, infinite God, Maker of heaven and earth, should condescend to ask us to be loyal to Him, to love Him, should encourage us to pray to Him boldly, and then should condescend to hear our prayers—*we*, who in comparison of Him are smaller than the gnats in the sunbeam in comparison of men! And then, when we remember that He has sent His only Son into the world to take our nature upon Him, and join us all together in one great and everlasting family, the body of Christ the Lord, and that He has actually given us a share in His own Almighty Holy Spirit, that we may be able to love Him, and to serve Him, and to be joined to Him, the Almighty Father, do we not see that all this is infinitely more honourable to us than if we were each to go on his own way here without God—without knowing anything of the everlasting world of spirits to which we now belong? My friends, instead of being ashamed of being able to do nothing for ourselves, we ought to rejoice at having God for our Father and our Friend, to enable us to 'do all things through Him who strengthens us'—to do whatever is noble, and loving, and worthy of true men. Instead, then, of dreaming conceitedly that God will accept us for our own sakes, let us just be content to be accepted for the sake of Jesus Christ our King. Instead of trying to walk through this world without God's help, let us ask God to help and guide us in every action of our lives, and then go manfully forward, doing with all our might whatsoever our hands or our hearts see right to do, trusting to God to put us in the right path, and to fill our heads with right thoughts and our hearts with right feeling; and so our faith will show itself in our works, and we shall be justified at the last day, as all good men have ever been, by trusting to our Heavenly Father and to the Lord Jesus Christ, and the guidance of His Holy Spirit.

SERMON VI.

THE SPIRIT AND THE FLESH.

GALATIANS v. 16.

I say then, Walk in the Spirit, and ye shall not fulfil the lusts of the flesh. For the flesh lusteth against the Spirit, and the Spirit against the flesh, and these are contrary the one to the other.

THE more we think seriously, my friends, the more we shall see what wonderful and awful things words are—how they mean much more than we fancy,—how we do not make words, but words are given to us by one higher than ourselves. Wise men say that you can tell the character of any nation by its language, by watching the words they use, the names they give to things, for out of the abundance of the heart the mouth speaks, and by our words, our Lord tells us, we shall be justified and condemned.

It is God, and Christ, the Word of God, who gives words to men, who puts it into the hearts of men to call certain things by certain names; and, according to a nation's godliness, and wisdom, and purity of heart, will be its power of using words discreetly and reverently. That miracle of the gift of tongues, of which we read in the New Testament, would have been still most precious and full of meaning if it had had no other use than this—to teach men from whom words come. When men found themselves all of a sudden inspired to talk in foreign languages which they had never learnt, to utter words of which they themselves did not know the meaning, do you not see how it must have made them feel that all language is God's making and God's giving? Do you not see how it must have made them feel what awful, mysterious things words were, like those cloven tongues of fire which fell on the apostles? The tongues of fire signified the difficult foreign languages which they suddenly began to speak as the Spirit gave them utterance. And where did the tongues of fire come from? Not out of themselves, not out of the earth beneath, but down from the heaven above, to signify that it is not from man, from man's flesh or brain, or the earthly part of him, that words are bred, but that they come down from Christ the Word of God, and are breathed into the minds of men by the Spirit of God. Why do I speak of all this? To make you feel what awful, wonderful things words are ; how, when you want to understand the meaning of a word, you must set to work with reverence and godly fear—not in self-conceit and prejudice, taking the word to mean just what suits your own notions of things, but trying humbly to find out what the word really does mean of itself, what God meant it to mean when He put it into the hearts of wise men to use that word and bring it into our English language. A man ought to read a newspaper or a story-book in that spirit; how much more, when he takes up the Bible! How reverently he ought to examine every word in the New Testament—this very text, for instance. We ought to be sure that St. Paul, just because he was an inspired apostle, used the very best possible words to express what he meant on so important a matter; and what *are* the best words? The clearest and the simplest words are the best words; else how is the Bible to be the poor man's book? How, unless the wayfaring man, though simple, shall not err therein? Therefore we may be sure the words in Scripture are certain to be used in their simplest, most natural, most every-day meaning, such as the simplest man can understand. And therefore we may be sure that these two words, 'flesh' and 'spirit,' in my text, are used in their very simplest, straightforward sense; and that St. Paul meant by them what working-men mean by them in the affairs of daily life. No doubt St. Peter says that there are many things in St. Paul's writings difficult to be understood, which those who are unlearned and unstable wrest to their own destruction; and, most true it is, so they do daily. But what does 'wresting' a thing mean? It means twisting it, bending it, turning it out of its original straightforward, natural meaning, into some new crooked meaning of their own. This is the way we are all of us too apt, I am afraid, to come to St. Paul's Epistles. We find him difficult because we won't take him at his word, because we tear a text out of its right place in the chapter—the place where St. Paul put it, and make it stand by itself, instead of letting the rest of the chapter explain its meaning. And then, again, people use the words in the text as unfairly and unreasonably as they use the text itself; they won't let the words have their common-sense English meaning—they must stick a new meaning of their own on them. 'Oh,' they say, 'that text must not be taken literally; that word has a spiritual signification here. Flesh does not mean flesh, it means men's corrupt nature;' little thinking, all the while, that perhaps they understand those words, spiritual, and corrupt, and nature, just as ill as they do the rest of the text.

How much better, my friends, to let the Bible tell its own story; not to be so exceeding wise above what is written; just to believe that St. Paul knew better how to use words than we are likely to do,—just to believe that when he says flesh he means flesh. Everybody agrees that when he says spirit he means spirit; why, in the name of common sense, when he says flesh should he not mean flesh? For my own part, I believe that when St. Paul talks of man's flesh, he means by it man's body, man's heart and brain, and all his bodily appetites and powers—what we call a man's constitution; in a word, the *animal* part of man, just what a man has in common with the beasts who perish.

To understand what I mean, consider any animal—a dog, for instance—how much every animal has in it what men have, —a body, and brain, and heart; it hungers and thirsts as we do; it can feel pleasure and pain, anger and loneliness, and fear and madness; it likes freedom, company, and exercise, praise and petting, play and ease; it uses a great deal of cunning, and thought, and courage, to get itself food and shelter, just as human beings do: in short, it has a fleshy nature, just as we have, and yet, after all, it is but an animal, and so, in one sense, we are all animals, only more delicately made than the other animals; but we are something more—we have a spirit as well as a flesh, an immortal soul. If any one asks, what is a man? the true answer is, an animal with an immortal spirit in it; and this spirit can feel more than pleasure and pain, which are mere carnal, that is, fleshly things; it can feel trust, and hope, and peace, and love, and purity, and nobleness, and independence, and, above all, it can feel right and wrong. There is the infinite difference between an animal and a man, between our flesh and our spirit; an animal has no sense of right and wrong; a dog who has done wrong is often terrified, but not because he feels it wrong and wicked, but because he knows from experience that he will be punished for doing it: just so with a man's fleshly nature;—a carnal, fleshly man, a man whose spirit is dead within him, whose spiritual sense of right and wrong, and honour and purity, is gone, when he has done a wrong thing is often enough afraid; but why? Not for any spiritual reason, not because he feels it a wicked and abominable thing, a sin, but because he is afraid of being punished for it, because he is afraid that his body, his flesh, will be punished by the laws of the land, or by public opinion, or because he has some dim belief that this same body and flesh of his will be burnt in hell-fire; and fire, he knows by experience, is a painful thing—and so he is *afraid* of it; there is nothing spiritual in all that,—that is all fleshly, carnal; the heathens in all ages have been afraid of hell-fire; but a man's spirit, on the other hand, if it be in hell, is in a very different hell from mere fire,—a spiritual hell, such as torments the evil spirits at this very moment, although they are going to and fro on this very earth. This earth is hell to them; they carry about hell in them,—they are their own hell. Everlasting shame, discontent, doubt, despair, rage, disgust at themselves, feeling that they are out of favour with God, out of tune with heaven and earth, loving nothing, believing nothing, ever hating, hating each other, hating themselves most of all—*there* is their hell! *There* is the hell in which the soul of every wicked man *is*,—ay, is now while he is in *this* life, though he will only awake to the perfect misery of it after death, when his body and fleshly nature have mouldered away in the grave, and can no longer pamper and stupify him, and make him forget his own misery. Ay, there has been many a man in this life who had every fleshly enjoyment which this world can give—riches and pleasure, banquets and palaces, every sense and every appetite pampered,— his pride and his vanity flattered; who never knew what want, or trouble, or contradiction was on the smallest point; a man, I say, who had every carnal enjoyment which this earth can give to a man's selfish flesh, and yet whose spirit was in hell all the while, and who knew it; hating and despising himself for a mean selfish villain, while all the world round was bowing down to him and envying him as the luckiest of men. I am trying to make you understand the infinite difference between a man's flesh and his spirit; how a man's flesh can take no pleasure in spiritual things, while man's spirit of itself can take no pleasure in fleshly things. Now, the spirit and the flesh, body and soul, in every man, are at war with each other,—they have quarrelled: that is part of the corruption of our nature, the fruit of Adam's fall. And as the Article says, and as every man who has ever tried to live godly well knows from experience, 'that infection of nature does remain to the last, even in those who are regenerate.' So that, as St. Paul says, the spirit lusteth against the flesh, and the flesh against the spirit; and it continually happens that a man cannot do the things which he would; he cannot do what he knows to be right; thus, as St. Paul says again, a man may delight in the law of God in his inward man, that is, in his spirit, and yet all the while he shall find another law in his members, *i.e.* in his body, in his flesh, in his brain which thinks, and his heart which feels, and his senses which are fond of pleasure; and this law of the flesh, these appetites and passions which he has, like other animals, fight against the law of his mind, and when he wishes to do good, make him do evil. Now, how is this? The flesh is not evil; a man's body can be no more wicked than a dumb beast can be wicked. St. Paul calls man's flesh sinful flesh; not because our flesh can sin of itself, but because our sinful souls make our flesh do sinful things; for, he says, Christ came in the likeness of sinful flesh, and yet in him was no sin. The pure and spotless Saviour could not have taken man's flesh upon him if there was any sinfulness in it. The body knows nothing of right and wrong; it is not subject to the law of God, neither indeed can be, says St. Paul. And why? Because God's law is spiritual; deals with right and wrong. Wickedness, like righteousness, is a spiritual thing. If a man sins, his body is not in fault; it is his spirit, his weak, perverse will, which will sooner listen to what his flesh tells him is pleasant than to what God tells him is right; for this, my friends, is the secret of the battle of life. We stand between heaven and earth. Above is God's Spirit striving with our spirits, speaking to them in the depths of our soul, showing us what is right, putting into our hearts good desires, making us long to be honest and just, pure and manful, loving and charitable; for who is there who has not at times longed after these things, and felt that it would be a blessed thing for him if he were such a man as Jesus Christ was and is?—Above us, I say, is God's Spirit speaking to our spirits; below us is this world speaking to our flesh, as it spoke to Eve's, saying to us, 'This thing is pleasant to the eyes—this thing is good for food —that thing is to be desired to make you wise, and to flatter your vanity and self-conceit.' Below us, I say, is *this* world, tempting us to ease, and pleasure, and vanity; and in the middle, betwixt the two, stands up the third part of man—his *soul* and *will*, set to choose between the voice of God's Spirit and the temptations of this world—to choose between what is right and what is pleasant—to choose whether he will obey the desires of the spirit, or obey the desires of the flesh. He must choose. If he lets his flesh conquer his spirit, he falls; if he lets his spirit conquer his flesh, he rises; if he lets his flesh conquer his spirit, he becomes what he was not meant to be—a slave to fleshly lust; and *then* he will find his flesh set up for itself, and work for itself. And where man's flesh gets the upper hand, and takes possession of him, it can do nothing but evil—not that it is evil in itself, but that it has no rule, no law to go by; it does not know right from wrong; and therefore it does simply what it likes, as a dumb beast or an idiot might; and therefore the works of the flesh are—adulteries, drunkenness, murders, fornications, envyings, backbitings, strife. When a man's body, which God intended to be the servant of his spirit, has become the tyrant of his spirit, it is like an idiot on a king's throne, doing all manner of harm and folly without knowing that it *is* harm and folly. This is not *its* fault. Whose fault is it, then? *Our* fault—the fault of our wills and our souls. Our souls were intended to be the masters of our flesh, to conquer all the weaknesses, defilements of our constitution— our tempers, our cowardice, our laziness, our hastiness, our nervousness, our vanity, our love of pleasure—to listen to our spirits, because our spirits learn from God's Spirit what is right and noble. But if we let our flesh master us, and obey its own blind lusts, we sin against God; and we sin against God doubly; for we not only sin against God's commandments, but against ourselves, who are the image and glory of God.

Believe this, my friends; believe that, because you are all fallen human creatures, there must go on in you this sore lifelong battle between your spirit and your flesh—your spirit trying to be master and guide, as it ought to be, and your flesh rebelling, and trying to conquer your spirit and make you a mere animal, like a fox in cunning, a peacock in vanity, or a hog in greedy sloth. But believe, too, that it is your sin and your shame if your spirit does not conquer your flesh—for God has promised to help your spirits. Ask Him, and His Spirit will teach them—fill them with pure, noble hopes, with calm, clear thoughts, and with deep, unselfish love to God and man. He will strengthen your wills, that they may be able to refuse the evil and choose the good. Ask Him, and He will join them to His own Spirit—to the Spirit of Christ, your Master; for he that is joined unto the Lord is one spirit with Him. Ask Him, and He will give you the mind of Christ— teach you to see and feel all matters as Christ sees and feels them. Ask Him, and He will give you wisdom to listen to His Spirit when it teaches your spirit, and then you will be able to walk after the spirit, and not obey the lusts of the flesh; and you will be able to crucify the flesh with its passions and lusts, that is, to make it, what it ought to be, a dead thing—a dead tool for your spirit to work with manfully and godly, and not a live tyrant to lead you into brutishness and folly; and then you will find that the fruit of the spirit, of your spirit led by God's Spirit, is really, as St. Paul says, 'love, joy, peace, long-suffering, gentleness, honesty'—'whatsoever things are true, whatsoever things are honourable and of good report;' and instead of being the miserable slaves of your own passions, and of the opinions of your neighbours, you will find that where the Spirit of the Lord is, there is liberty, true freedom, not only from your neighbour's sins, but, what is far better, freedom from your own.

These are large words, my friends, and promise mighty things. But I dare speak them to you, for God has spoken to you. These promises God made you at your baptism; these promises I, on the warrant of your baptism, dare make to you again. At your baptism God gave you the right to call Him your loving Father, to call His Son your Saviour, His Spirit your Sanctifier. And He is not a man, that He should lie; nor the son of man, that He should repent! Try Him, and see whether He will not fulfil His word. Claim His promise, and though you have fallen lower than the brutes, He will make men and women of you. He will be faithful and just to forgive you your sins, and to cleanse you from all unrighteousness.

SERMON VII.

RETRIBUTION.

NUMBERS xxxii. 23.

Be sure your sin will find you out.

THE full meaning of this text is, that every sin which a man commits is certain, sooner or later, to come home to him with fearful interest.

Moses gave this warning to two tribes of the Israelites,—to the Reubenites and Gadites, who had promised to go over Jordan and help their countrymen in war against the heathen, on condition of being allowed to return and settle on the east bank of Jordan, where they then were; but if they broke their promise, and returned before the end of the war, they were to be certain that their sin would find them out; that God would avenge their falsehood on them in some way in their lifetime: in their lifetime, I say, for there is no mention made in this chapter, or in any part of the story, of heaven or hell, or any world to come. And the text has been always taken as a fair warning to all generations of men, that their sin also, even in their lifetimes, will be visited upon them.

Now, it is strange, at first sight, that these texts, which warn men that their sins will be punished in this life, are just the most unpleasant texts in the whole Bible; that men shrink from them more, and shut their eyes to them more than they do to those texts which threaten them with hell-fire and everlasting death. Strange !—that men should be more afraid of being punished in this life for a few years than in the life to come for ever and ever ;—and yet not strange if we consider; for to worldly and sinful souls, that life after death and the flames of hell seem quite distant and dim—things of which they know little and believe less, while this world they *do* know, they are quite certain that its good things are pleasant and its bad things unpleasant, and they are thoroughly afraid of losing *them*. Their hearts are where their treasure is, in this world; and a punishment which deprives them of this world's good things hits them home: but their treasure is *not* in heaven, and therefore about losing heaven they are by no means so much concerned. And thus they can face the dreadful news, that 'the wicked shall be turned into hell, and all the people that forget God;' while, as for the news that the wicked shall be recompensed on the earth, that their sins will surely find them out in this life, they cannot face that,—they shut their ears to it,—they try to persuade themselves that sin will *pay* them *here*, at all events; and as for hereafter, they shall get off somehow, —they neither know nor care much how.

Yet God's truth remains, and God's truth must be heard; and those who love this world so well must be told, whether they like or not, that every sin which they commit, every mean, every selfish, every foul deed, loses them so much enjoyment in this very present world of which they are so mighty fond. That is God's truth; and I will prove it true from common sense, from Holy Scripture, and *from the witness* of men's own hearts.

Take common sense. Does not common sense tell us, that if God made this world, and governs it by righteous and Godlike laws, this must be a world in which evil doing cannot thrive? God made the world better than that, surely! He would be a bad law-giver who made such laws, that it was as well to break them as to keep them. You would call them bad laws, surely! No, God made the world, and not the devil; and the world works by God's laws, and not the devil's; and it inclines towards good, and not towards evil; and he who sins, even the least, breaks God's laws, acts contrary to the rule and constitution of the world, and will surely find that God's laws will go on in spite of him, and grind him to powder, if he by sinning gets in the way of them. God has no need to go out of His way to punish our evil deeds. Let them alone, and they will punish themselves. Is it not so in every thing? If a tradesman trades badly, or a farmer farms badly, there is no need of lawyers to punish him; he will punish himself. Every mistake he makes will take money out of his pocket; every time he offends against the established rules of trade or agriculture, which are God's laws, he injures himself; and so, be sure, it is in the world at large,—in the world in which men and the souls of men live, and move, and have their being.

Next, to speak of Scripture. I might quote texts innumerable to prove that what I say Scripture says also. Consider but this one thing—that there is a whole book in the Bible written to prove this one thing,—that our good and bad deeds are repaid us with interest in this life; I mean the Proverbs of Solomon, in which there is little or no mention of heaven or hell, or any world to come. It is all one noble, and awful, and yet cheering sermon on that one text, 'The righteous shall be recompensed in the earth, much more the wicked and the sinner.' Put in a thousand different lights, brought home to us a thousand different roads, comes the same everlasting doom— 'Vain man, who thinkest that thou canst live in God's world and yet despise His will, know that, in every smiling, comfortable sin, thou art hatching an adder to sting thee in the days of old age, to poison thy cup of sinful joy, even when it is at thy lips; to haunt thy restless thoughts, and dog thee day and night; to rise up before thee, in the silent, sleepless hours of night, like an angry ghost, an awful foretaste of the doom that is to come; and yet a merciful foretaste, if thou wilt be but taught by the disappointment, the unsatisfied craving, the gnawing shame of a guilty conscience, to see the heinousness of sin, and would turn before it be too late.'

What, my friends,—what will you make of such texts as this, 'That he who soweth to the flesh shall of the flesh reap corruption? Do you not see that comes true far too often? Can it help *always* coming true, seeing that God's apostle spoke it? What will you make of this, too, 'That the wicked is snared by the working of his own hands'—'That *evil*'—the evil which we do —'of its own self shall slay the wicked?' What says the whole noble 37th Psalm of David, but that same awful truth of God, that sin is its own punishment?

Why should I go on quoting texts? Look for yourselves, you who fancy that it is only on the other side of the grave that God will trouble Himself about you and your meanness, your profligacy, your falsehood. Look for yourselves in the Book of God, and see if there be any writer there,—lawgiver, prophet, psalmist, apostle, up to Christ the Lord Himself,— who does not warn men again and again, that here, on earth, their sins will find them out. Our Saviour indeed, when on earth, said less about this subject than any of the prophets before Him, or the apostles after Him, and for the best of reasons. The Jews had got rooted in their minds a superstitious notion, that all disease, all sorrow, was the punishment in each case of some particular sin; and thus, instead of looking with pity and loving awe upon the sick and the afflicted, they were accustomed too often to turn from them as sinners, smitten of God, bearing in their distress the token of His anger. The Blessed One,—He who came to heal the sick and save the lost,—reproved that error more than once. When the disciples fancied a certain poor man's blindness to be a judgment from God, 'Neither did he sin,' said the Lord, 'nor his parents, but that the glory of God might be made manifest in him.' And yet, on the other hand, when He healed a certain man of an old infirmity at the pool of Bethesda, what were His words to him? 'Go thy way, sin no more, lest a worse thing come unto thee;'—a clear and weighty warning that all his long misery of eight-and-thirty years had been the punishment of some sin of his, and that the sin repeated would bring on him a still severer judgment.

What again does the apostle mean, in the Epistle to the Hebrews, when he tells us how God scourges every son whom he receives, and talks of his chastisements, whereof all are partakers. Why do we need chastising if we have nothing which needs mending? And though the innocent *may* sometimes be afflicted to make them strong as well as innocent, and the holy chastened to make them humble as well as holy, yet if the good cannot avoid their share of affliction, how will the bad escape? 'If the righteous scarcely be saved, where will the ungodly and the sinner appear?' But what use in arguing when you know that my words are true? You *know* that your sins will find you out. Look boldly and honestly into your own hearts. Look through the history of your past lives, and confess to God, at least, that the far greater number of your sorrows have been your own fault; that there is hardly a day's misery which you ever endured in your life of which you might not say, 'If I had listened to the voice of God in my conscience—if I had earnestly considered what my *duty* was—if I had prayed to God to determine my judgment right, I should have been spared this sorrow now!' Am I not right? Those who know most of God and their own souls will agree most with me; those who know little about God and their own souls will agree but hardly with me, for they provoke God's chastisements, and writhe under them for the time, and then go and do the same wrong again, as the wild beast will turn and bite the stone thrown at him, without having the sense to see why it was thrown.

Think again of your past lives, and answer in God's sight, how many wrong things have you ever done which have *succeeded*—that is, how many sins which you would not be right

glad were undone if you could but put back the wheels of time?
They may have succeeded *outwardly;* meanness will succeed
so lies—oppression —theft—adultery—drunkenness—godlessness—they are all pleasant enough while they last, I suppose:
and a man may reap what he calls substantial benefits from them
in money, and such-like, and keep that safe enough; but has his
sin succeeded? Has it not *found him out?*—found him out
never to lose him again? Is he the happier for it? Does he
feel freer for it? Does he respect himself the more for it?—
No. And, even though he may prosper now, yet does there not
run through all his selfish pleasure a certain fearful looking
forward to a fiery judgment to which he would gladly shut his
eyes, but cannot?

Cunning, fair-spoken oppressor of the poor, has not thy sin
found thee out? Then be sure it will. In the shame of thine
own heart it will find thee out;—in the curses of the poor it
will find thee out;—in a friendless, restless, hopeless death-bed,
thy covetousness and thy cruelty will glare before thee in their
true colours, and thy sin will find thee out!

Profligate woman, who art now casting away thy honest
name, thy self-respect, thy womanhood, thy baptism-vows, that
thou mayest enjoy the foul pleasures of sin for a season, has not
thy sin found thee out? Then be sure it will hereafter, when
thou hast become disgusted at thyself and thine own infamy,—
and youth, and health, and friends are gone, and a shameful
and despised old age creeps over thee, and death stalks nearer
and nearer, and God vanishes further and further off, then thy
sin will find thee out!

Foolish, improvident young man, who art wasting the noble
strength of youth and manly spirits which God has given thee
on sin and folly, throwing away thine honest earnings in cards
and drunkenness, instead of laying them by against a time
of need—has not thy sin found thee out? Then be sure it will
some day, when thou hast to bring home thy bride to a cheer-
less, unfurnished house, and there to live from hand to mouth,

—without money to provide for her sickness,—without money to give her the means of keeping things neat and comfortable when she is well,—without a farthing laid by against distress, and illness, and old age:—*then* your sin will find you out: then perhaps my text and my words may come across you, as you sigh in vain in your comfortless home, in your impoverished old age, for the money which you wasted in your youth! My friends, my friends, for your own sakes consider, and mend ere that day come, as else it surely will.

And lastly, you who, without running into any especial sins, as those which the world calls sins, still live careless about religion, without loyalty to Christ the Lord, without any honest attempt, or even wish, to serve the God above you, or to rejoice in remembering that you are His children, working for Him, and under Him,—be sure your sin will find you out. When affliction, or sickness, or disappointment come, as come they will if God has not cast you off;—when the dark day dawns, and your fool's paradise of worldly prosperity is cut away from under your feet, then you will find out your folly; you will find that you have insulted the only friend who can bring you out of affliction—cast off the only comfort which can strengthen you to bear affliction—forgotten the only knowledge which will enable you to be wiser for affliction. Then, I say, the sin of your godlessness will find you out; if you do not intend to fall, soured and sickened merely by God's chastisements, either into stupid despair or peevish discontent, you will have to go back, to go back to God and cry, 'Father, I have sinned against heaven and before Thee, and am no more worthy to be called Thy son.'

Go back at once, before it be too late. Find out your sins and mend them—before they find you out, and break your hearts.

SERMON VIII.

SELF-DESTRUCTION.

1 KINGS xxii. 23.

The Lord hath put a lying spirit in the mouth of all these thy prophets.

THE chapter from which my text is taken, which is the first lesson for this evening's service, is a very awful chapter, for it gives us an insight into the meaning of that most awful and terrible word,—temptation. And yet it is a most comforting chapter, for it shows us how God is long-suffering and merciful, even to the most hardened sinner; how to the last He puts before him good and evil, to choose between them, and warns him to the last of his path, and the ruin to which it leads.

We read of Ahab in the first lesson this morning as a thoroughly wicked man,—mean and weak, cruel and ungodly, governed by his wife Jezebel, a heathen woman, in marrying whom he had broken God's law,—a woman so famous for cruelty and fierceness, vanity and wickedness, that her name is a by-word even here in England now—'as bad as Jezebel,' we say to this day. We heard of Ahab in this morning's lesson letting Jezebel murder the righteous Naboth, by perjury and slander, to get possession of his vineyard; and then, instead of shrinking with abhorrence from his wife's iniquity, going down and taking possession of the land which he had gained by her sin. We read of God's curse on him, and yet of God's long-suffering and pardon to him on his repentance. Yet neither God's curse nor God's mercy seem to have moved him. But he had been always the same. 'He did evil,' the Bible tells us, 'in the sight of the Lord above all that were before him.' He deserted the true God for his wife's idols and false gods; and in spite of Elijah's miracle at Carmel—of which you heard last Sunday—by which he proved by fire which was the true God, and in spite of the wonderful victory which God had given him, by means of one of God's prophets, over the Syrians, he still remained an idolater. He would not be taught, nor understand; neither God's threats nor mercies could move him; he went on sinning against light and knowledge; and now his cup was full—his days were numbered, and God's vengeance was ready at the door.

He consulted all his false prophets as to whether or not he should go to attack the Syrians at Ramoth-Gilead. They knew what to say—they knew that their business was to prophesy what would pay them—what would be pleasant to him. They did not care whether what they said was true or not—they lied for the sake of gain, for the Lord had put a lying spirit into their mouths. They were rogues and villains from the first. They had turned prophets, not to speak God's truth, but to make money, to flatter King Ahab, to get themselves a reputation. We do not hear that they were all heathens. Many of them may have believed in the true God. But they were cheats and liars, and so they had given place to the devil, the father of lies: and now he had taken possession of them in spite of themselves, and they lied to Ahab, and told him that he would prosper in the battle at Ramoth-Gilead. It was a dangerous thing for them to say; for if he had been defeated, and returned disappointed, his rage would have most probably fallen on them for deceiving him. And as in those Eastern countries kings do whatever they like without laws or parliaments, Ahab would have most likely put them all to a miserable death on the spot. But however dangerous it might be for them to lie, they could not help lying. A spirit of lies had seized them, and they who began by lying because it paid them, now could not help doing so whether it paid them or not.

But the good king of Judah, Jehoshaphat, had no faith in these flattering villains. He asked whether there was not another prophet of the Lord to inquire of? Ahab told him that there was one, Micaiah the son of Imlah, but that he hated him, because he only prophesied evil of him. What a thorough picture of a hardened sinner—a man who has become a slave to his own lusts, till he cares nothing for a thing being true, provided only it is pleasant! Thus the wilful sinner, like Ahab, becomes both fool and coward, afraid to look at things as they are; and when God's judgments stare him in the face, the wretched man shuts his eyes tight, and swears that the evil is not there, just because he does not chose to see it.

But the evil was there, ready for Ahab, and it found him. When he forced Micaiah to speak, Micaiah told him the whole truth. He told him a vision, or dream, which he had seen. 'Hear thou therefore the word of the Lord: I saw the Lord sitting on His throne, and all the host of heaven standing by Him. And the Lord said, Who shall persuade Ahab, that he may go up and fall at Ramoth-Gilead? And there came forth a spirit, and said, I will go forth, and be a lying spirit in the mouth of all his prophets. And the Lord said, Thou shalt persuade him, and prevail also: go forth, and do so. Now therefore, behold, the Lord hath put a lying spirit in the mouth of all these thy prophets, and the Lord hath spoken evil concerning thee.'

What warning could be more awful, and yet more plain? Ahab was told that he was listening to a lie. He had free choice to follow that lie or not, and he did follow it. After having put Micaiah into prison for speaking the truth to him, he went up to Ramoth-Gilead; and yet he felt he was not safe He had his doubts and his fears. He would not go openly into the battle, and disguised himself, hoping that by this means he should keep himself safe from evil. Fool! God's vengeance could not be stopped by his paltry cunning. In spite of all his disguise, a chance shot struck him down between the joints of his armour. His chariot-driver carried him out of the battle, and 'he was stayed up in his chariot against the Syrians, and died at even: and the blood ran out of his wound into the midst of the chariot. And one washed the chariot in the pool of Samaria; and the dogs licked up his blood there,' according to the word of the Lord, which He spoke by the mouth of His prophet Elijah, saying, 'In the place where dogs licked the blood of Naboth, whom thou slewest, shall dogs lick thy blood, even thine.'

And do not fancy, my friends, that because this is a miraculous story of ancient times, it has nothing to do with us. All these things were written for our example. This chapter tells us not merely how Ahab was tempted, but it tells us how *we* are tempted, every one of us, here in England, in these very days. As it was with Ahab, so it is with us. Every wilful sin that we commit, we give room to the devil. Every wrong step that we take knowingly, we give a handle to some evil spirit to lead us seven steps further wrong. And yet in every temptation God gives us a fair chance. He is no cruel tyrant who will deliver us over to the devil, to be led helpless and blindfold to our ruin. He did not give Ahab over to him so. He sent a lying spirit to deceive Ahab's prophets, that Ahab might go up and fall at Ramoth-Gilead; but at the very same time, see, He sends a holy and a true man, a man whom Ahab could trust, and did trust at the bottom of his heart, to tell him that the lie was a lie, to warn him of his ruin, so that he might have no excuse for listening to those false prophets—no excuse for following his own pride, his own ambition, to his destruction. So you see, 'let no man say, when he is tempted, I am tempted of God, for God tempteth no man, but every one is tempted when he is led away by his own lusts and enticed.' Ahab was led away by his own lusts; his cowardly love of hearing what was pleasant and flattering to him, rather than what was true—rather than what he knew he deserved; that was what enticed him to listen to Zedekiah and the false prophets, rather than to Micaiah the son of Imlah. *That* is what entices us to sin—the lust of believing what is pleasant to us, what suits our own self-will—what is pleasant to our bodies—pleasant to our purses—pleasant to our pride and self-conceit. Then, when the lying spirit comes and whispers to us, by bad thoughts, by bad books, by bad men, that we shall prosper in our wickedness, does God leave us alone to listen to those evil voices without warning? No! He sends His prophets to us, as He sent Micaiah to Ahab, to tell us that the wages of sin is death—to tell us that those who sow the wind shall reap the whirlwind—to set before us at every turn good or evil, that we may choose between them, and live or die according to our choice. For do not fancy that there are no prophets in our days, unless the gift of the Holy Spirit, which is promised to all who believe, be a dream and a lie. There are prophets now-a-days—yea, I say unto you, and more than prophets. Is not the Bible a prophet? Is not every page in it a prophecy to us, foretelling God's mercies and God's punishments towards men? Is not every holy and wise book, every holy and wise preacher and writer, a prophet, expounding to us God's laws, foretelling to us God's opinions of our deeds, both good and evil? Ay, is not every man a prophet to himself? That 'still small voice' in a man's heart, which warns him of what is evil—that feeling which makes him cheerful and free when he has done right, sad and ashamed when he has done wrong—is not that a prophecy in a man's own heart? Truly it is. It is the voice of God within us—it is the Spirit of God striving with our spirits, whether we will hear, or whether we will forbear—setting before us what is righteous, and noble, and pure, and what is manly and God-like—to see whether we will obey that voice, or whether we will obey our own selfish lusts, which tempt us to please ourselves—to pamper ourselves, our greediness, covetousness, ambition, or self-conceit. And again, I say, we have our prophets. Every preacher of righteousness is a prophet. Every good tract is a prophet. That Prayer-book, those Psalms, those Creeds, those Collects, which you take into your mouths every Sunday, what are they but written prophecies, crying unto us with the words of holy men of old, greater than Micaiah, or David, or Elijah, 'Hear thou the word of the Lord?' The spirits of those who wrote that Prayer-book —the spirits of just men made perfect, filled with the spirit of the Lord—they call to us to learn the wisdom which they knew, to avoid the temptations which they conquered, that we may share in the glory in which they share round the throne of Christ for evermore.

And if you ask me how to try the spirits, how to know whether your own thoughts, whether the sermons which you hear, the books which you read, are speaking to you God's truth, or some lying spirit's falsehood, I can only answer you, 'To the law and to the testimony'—to the Bible; if they speak not according to that word, there is no truth in them. But how to understand the Bible? for the fleshly man understands not the things of God. The fleshly man, he who cares only about pleasing himself, he who goes to the Bible full of self-conceit and selfishness, wanting the Bible to tell him only just what he likes to hear, will only find it a sealed book to him, and will very likely wrest the Scriptures to his own destruction. Take up your Bible humbly, praying to God to show you its meaning, whether it be pleasant to you or not, and then you will find that God will show you a blessed meaning in it; He will open your eyes, that you may understand the wondrous things of His law; He will show you how to try the spirit of all you are taught, and to find out whether it comes from God.

SERMON IX.

HELL ON EARTH.

MATTHEW viii. 29.

And, behold, the evil spirits cried out, saying, What have we to do with Thee, Jesus, Thou Son of God? Art Thou come hither to torment us before the time?

THIS account of the man possessed with devils, and of his language to our Lord, of our Lord's casting the devils out of the poor sufferer, and His allowing them to enter into a herd of swine, is one that is well worth serious thought; and I think a few words on it will follow fitly after my last Sunday's sermon on Ahab and his temptations by evil spirits. In that sermon I showed you what temper of mind it was which laid a man open to the cunning of evil spirits: I wish now to show you something of what those evil spirits are. It is very little that we can know about them. We were intended to know very little; just as much as would enable us to guard against them, and no more. The accounts of them in the Scriptures are for our use, not to satisfy our curiosity. But we may find out a great deal about them from this very chapter, from this very story, which is repeated almost word for word in three different Gospels, as if to make us more certain of so curious and important a matter, by having three distinct and independent writers to witness for its truth. I advise all those who have Bibles to look for this story in the 8th chapter of St Matthew, and follow me as I explain it.[1]

Now, first, we may learn from this account, that evil spirits are real persons. There is a notion got abroad that it is only a figure of speech to talk of evil spirits—that all the Bible means by them are certain bad habits, or bad qualities, or diseases. There are many who will say, when they read this story, This poor man was only a madman. It was the fashion of the old Jews when a man was mad to say that he was possessed by evil spirits. All they meant was that the man's own spirit was in an evil diseased state, or that his brain and mind were out of order.

When I hear such language—and it is very common—I cannot help thinking how pleased the devil must be to hear people talk in such a way. How can people help him better than by saying that there is no devil? A thief would be very glad to hear you say, 'There are no such things as thieves; it is all an old superstition, so I may leave my house open at night without danger;' and I believe, my friends, from the very bottom of my heart, that this new-fangled disbelief in evil spirits is put into men's hearts by the evil spirits themselves. As it was once said, 'The devil has tried every plan to catch men's souls, and now, as the last and most cunning trick of all, he is shamming dead.' These may seem homely words, but the homeliest words are very often the deepest. I advise you all to think seriously on them.

---

[1] 'And when He was come to the other side, into the country of the Gergesenes, there met Him two possessed with devils, coming out of the tombs, exceeding fierce, so that no man might pass by that way. And, behold, they cried out, saying, What have we to do with Thee, Jesus, Thou Son of God? Art Thou come hither to torment us before the time? And there was a good way off from them an herd of many swine feeding. So the devils besought Him, saying, If Thou cast us out, suffer us to go away into the herd of swine. And he said unto them, Go. And when they were come out, they went into the herd of swine: and, behold, the whole herd of swine ran violently down a steep place into the sea, and perished in the waters.'

But it is impossible, surely, to read this story without seeing that the Bible considers evil spirits as distinct persons just as much as each one of us is a person, and that our Lord spoke to them and treated them as persons. 'What have *we* to do with Thee, Jesus, Thou Son of God? Art Thou come hither to torment *us* before the time?' And again, 'If Thou cast *us* out, suffer us to go into the herd of swine.' What can show more plainly that there were some persons in that poor man, besides himself, his own spirit, his own person? and that *he* knew it and Jesus knew it too? and that He spoke to these spirits, these persons who possessed that man, and not to the man himself? No doubt there was a terrible confusion in the poor madman's mind about these evil spirits, who were tormenting him, making him miserable, foul, and savage, in mind and body —a terrible confusion! We find, when Jesus asked him his name, he answers '*Legion*,' that is, an army, a multitude, 'for we are many,' he says. Again, one Gospel tells us that he says, 'What have *I* to do with Thee, Jesus, Thou Son of God?' While in another Gospel we are told that he said, 'What have *we* to do with Thee?' He seems not to have been able to distinguish between his own spirit and these spirits who possessed him. They put the furious and despairing thoughts into his heart; they spoke through his mouth; they made a slave and a puppet of him. But though he could not distinguish between his own soul and the devils who were in it, Christ could and Christ did.

The man says to Him, or rather the devils make the man say to Him, 'If Thou cast us out, suffer us to go into the herd of swine, and drive us not out into the deep.' What did Christ answer him? Christ did not answer him as our so-called wise men in these days would, 'My good man, this is all a delusion and a fancy of your own, about your having evil spirits in you—more persons than one in you—for you are wrong in saying *we* of yourself. You ought to say 'I,' as every one else does; and as for spirits going out of you, or going into a herd of swine, or anything else, that is all a superstition and a fancy. There is nothing to come out of you; there is nothing in you except yourself. All the evil in you is your own, the disease of your own brain, and the violent passions of your own heart. Your brain must be cured by medicine, and your violent passions tamed down by care and kindness, and then you will get rid of this foolish notion that you have evil spirits in you, and calling yourself a multitude as if you had other persons in you besides yourself.'

Anyone who spoke in this manner now-a-days would be thought very reasonable and very kind. Why did not our Lord speak so to this man? for there was no outward difference between this man's conduct and that of many violent mad people whom we see continually in England. We read, that this man possessed with devils would wear no clothes; that he had extraordinary strength; that he would not keep company with other men, but abode day and night in the tombs, exceeding fierce, crying, and cutting himself with stones, trying in blind rage, which he could not explain to himself, to hurt himself and all who came near him. And, above all, he had this notion, that evil spirits had got possession of him. Now, every one of these habits and fancies you may see in many raging maniacs at this day.

But did our Lord treat this man as we treat such maniacs in these days? He took the man at his word, and more; the man could not distinguish clearly between himself and the evil spirits, but our Lord did. When the devils besought him saying, 'If Thou cast us out, suffer us to go into the herd of swine,' our Lord answers, 'Go,' and 'when they were cast out they went into the herd of swine; and, behold, the whole herd of swine ran violently down a steep place into the sea, and perished in the waters.'

It was as if our Lord had meant to say to the bystanders,— ay, and to us, and to all people in all times and in all countries, 'This poor possessed maniac's notion was a true one. There were other persons in him besides himself, tormenting him, body and soul; and, behold, I can drive these out of him and send them into something else, and leave the man uninjured *himself*, and only himself, again in an instant, without any need of long education to cure him of his bad habits.' It will be but reasonable, then, for us to take this story of the man possessed by devils, as written for our example, as an instance of what *might*, and perhaps *would*, happen to any one of us, were it not for God's mercy.

St. Peter tells us to be sober and watchful, because 'the devil goes about as a roaring lion, seeking whom he may devour;' and when we look at the world around, we may surely see that that stands as true now as it did in St. Peter's time. Why, again, did St. James tell us to resist the devil, if the devil be not near us to resist? Why did St. Paul take for granted, as he did, that Christian men were, of course, not ignorant of Satan's devices, if it be quite a proof of enlightenment and superior knowledge to be ignorant of his devices,— if any dread, any thought even, about evil spirits, be beneath the attention of reasonable men? My friends, I say fairly, once for all, that that common notion, that there are no men now possessed by evil spirits, and that all those stories of the devil's power over men are only old, worn-out superstitions, has come from this, that men do not like to retain God in their knowledge, and therefore, as a necessary consequence, do not like to retain the devil in their knowledge; because they would be very glad to believe in nothing but what they can see, and taste, and handle; and, therefore, the thought of unseen evil spirits, or good spirits either, is a painful thing to them. First, they really do not believe in angels— ministering spirits sent out to minister to the heirs of salvation; then they begin not to believe in evil spirits. The Bible plainly describes their vast numbers; but these people are wiser than the Bible, and only talk of *one*—of *the* devil, as if there were not, as the text tells us, legions and armies of devils. Then they get rid of that one devil in their real desire to believe in as few spirits as possible. I am afraid many of them have gone on to the next step, and got rid of the one God out of their thoughts and their belief. I said I am afraid, I ought to have said I *know*, that they have done so, and that thousands in this day who began by saying evil spirits only mean certain diseases and bad habits in men, have ended by saying, 'God only means certain good habits in man. God is no more a person than the evil spirits are persons.'

I warn you of all this, my friends, because if you go to live in large towns, as many of you will, you will hear talk enough of this sort before your hairs are grey, put cleverly and eloquently enough; for, as a wise man said, 'The devil does not send fools on his errands.' I pray God, that if you ever do hear doctrines of that kind, some of my words may rise in your mind and help to show to you the evil path down which they lead.

We may believe, then, from the plain words of Scripture, that there are vast numbers of evil spirits continually tempting men, each of them to some particular sin; to worldliness, for instance, for we read of the spirit of the evil world; to filthiness, for we read of unclean spirits; to falsehood, for we read of lying spirits, and a spirit of lies; to pride, for we read of a spirit of pride;—in short, to all sins which a man *can* commit, to all evil passions to which a man can give way. We have a right to believe, from the plain words of Scripture, that these spirits are continually wandering up and down tempting men to sin. That wonderful story of Job's temptation, which you may all read for yourselves in the first chapter of the book of Job, is, I think, proof enough for anyone.

But next, and I wish you to pay special attention to this point: We have no right to believe—we have every right *not* to believe—that these evil spirits can make us sin in the smallest matter against our own wills. The devil cannot put a single sin into us; he can only flatter the sinfulness which is already in us. For, see; this pride, lust, covetousness, falsehood, and so on, to which the Bible tells us they tempt us, have roots already in our nature. Our fallen nature of itself is inclined to pride, to worldliness, and so on. These devils tempt us by putting in our way the occasion of sin, by suggesting to us tempting thoughts and arguments which lead to sin; so the serpent tempted Eve, not by making her ambitious and self-willed, but by using arguments to her which stirred up the ambition and self-will in her: 'Ye shall be as gods, knowing good and evil,' the devil said to her.

So Satan, the prince of the evil spirits, tempted our Lord. And as the prince of the devils tempted Christ, so do *his* servants tempt *us*, Christ's servants. Our tempers, our longings, our fancies, are not evil spirits; they are, as old divines well describe them, like greedy and foolish fish, who rise at the baits which evil spirits hold out to us. If we resist those baits—if we put ourselves under God's protection—if we claim strength from Him who conquered the devil and all his temptations, then we shall be able to turn our wills away from those tempting baits, and to resign our wills into our Father's hand, and He will take care of them, and strengthen them with His will; and we shall find out that if we resist the devil, he will flee from us. But if we yield to temptations whenever they come in our way, we shall find ourselves less and less able to resist them, for we shall learn to hate the evil spirits less and less; I mean, we shall shrink less from the evil thought they hold out to us. We shall give place to the devil, as the Scripture tells us we shall; for instance, by indulging in habitual passionate tempers, or rooted spite and malice, letting the sun go down upon our wrath: and so a man may become more and more the slave of his own nature, of his own lusts and passions, and therefore of the devils who are continually pampering and maddening those lusts and passions, till a man may end in *complete possession;* not in common madness, which may be mere disease, but as a savage and a raging maniac, such as, thank God, are rare in Christian countries, though they were common among our own forefathers before they were converted to Christianity,—men like the demoniac of whom the text speaks, tormented by devils, given up to blind rage and malice against himself and all around, to lust and blasphemy, to confusion of mind and misery of body, God's image gone, and the image of the devil, the destroyer and the corrupter, arisen in its place. Few men can arrive at this pitch of wretchedness in a civilised country. It would not answer the evil spirit's purpose to let them do so. It suits *his* spirits best in such a land as this to walk about dressed up as angels of light. Few men in England would be fools enough to indulge the gross and fierce part of their nature till they became mere savages, like the demoniac whom Christ cured; so it is to respectable vices that the devil mostly tempts us— to covetousness, to party spirit, to a hard heart, and a narrow mind; to cruelty, that shall clothe itself under the name of law; to filthiness, which excuses itself by saying, 'It is a man's nature, he cannot help it;' to idleness, which excuses itself on the score of wealth; to meanness and unfairness in trade, and in political and religious disputes—these are the devils which haunt us Englishmen—sleek, prim, respectable fiends enough; and, truly, *their* name is Legion! And the man who gives himself up to them, though he may not become a raving savage, is just as truly possessed by devils, to his own misery and ruin, that he may sow the wind and reap the whirlwind; that though men may speak well of him, and posterity praise his saying, and speak good of the covetous whom God abhorreth, yet he may go for ever unto his own, to the evil spirits to whom his own wicked will gave him up for a prey. I beseech you, my friends, consider my words; they are not mine, but the Bible's. Think of them with fear;—and yet with confidence, for we are baptized into the name of Him who conquered all devils; you may claim a share in that Spirit which is opposite to all evil spirits, —whose presence makes the agony and misery of evil spirits, and drives them out as water drives out fire. If He is on your side, why should you be afraid of any spirit? Greater is He that is in you than he that is against you; and He, Christ Himself, is with every man, every child, who struggles, however blindly and weakly, against temptation. When temptation comes, when evil looks pleasant, and arguments rise up in your mind, that seem to make it look right and reasonable, as well as pleasant, *then*, out of the very depths of your hearts, cry after Him who died for you. Say to yourselves, 'How can I do this thing, and offend against Him who bought me with His blood?' Say to Him, ' I am weak, I am confused; I do not see right from wrong; I cannot find my way; I cannot answer the devil; I cannot conquer these cunning thoughts; I know in the bottom of my heart that they are wrong, mere temptations, and yet they look so reasonable. Blessed Saviour, *Thou* must show me where they are wrong. Thou didst answer the devil Thyself out of God's Word, put into *my* mind some answer out of God's Word to these temptations; or, at least, give me spirit to toss them off—strength of will to thrust the whole temptation out of my head, and say, I will parley no longer with the devil; I will put the whole matter out of my head for a time. I don't know whether it is right or wrong for me to do this particular thing, but there are twenty other things which I *do* know are right. I will go and do *them*, and let this wait awhile.'

Believe me, my friends, you *can* do this—you *can* resist these evil spirits which tempt us all; else why did our Lord bid us pray, ' Lead us not into temptation, but deliver us from evil?' Why? Because our Father in heaven, if we ask Him, will *not* lead us *into* temptation, but *through* it safe. Tempted we must be, else we should not be men; but here is our comfort and our strength—that we have a King in heaven who has fought out and conquered all temptations, and a Father in heaven who has promised that He will not suffer us to be tempted above that we are able, but will, with the temptation, make a way to escape, that we may be able to bear it. Again, I say, draw near to God, and He will draw near to you. Resist the devil, and he will flee from you.

SERMON X.

NOAH'S JUSTICE.

GENESIS vi. 9.

Noah was a just man and perfect in his generations, and Noah walked with God.

I INTEND, my friends, according as God shall help me, to preach to you, between this time and Christmas, a few sermons on some of the saints and worthies of the Old Testament: and I will begin this day with Noah. Now, you must bear in mind that the histories of these ancient men were, as St. Paul says, written for our example. If these men in old times had been different from us, they would not be examples to us; but they were like us—men of like passions, says St. James, as ourselves; they had each of them in them a corrupt *nature*, which was continually ready to drag them down, and make beasts of them, and make them slaves to their own lusts —slaves to eating and drinking, and covetousness, and cowardice, and laziness, and love for the things which they could see and handle—just such a nature, in short, as we have. And they had also a spirit in each of them which was longing to be free, and strong, and holy, and wise—such a spirit as we have. And to them, just as to us, God was revealing Himself; God was saying to their consciences, as He does to ours, 'This is right, that is wrong; do this, and be free and clear-hearted; do that, and be dark and discontented, and afraid of thy own thoughts.' And they too, like us, had to live by faith, by continual belief that they owed a *duty* to the great God whom they could not see, by continual belief that He loved them, and was guiding and leading them through everything which happened, good or ill.

This is faith in God, by which alone we, or any man, can live worthily,—by which these old heroes lived. We read, in the twelfth chapter of Hebrews, that it was by faith these elders obtained a good report: and the whole history of the Old Testament saints is the history of God speaking to the hearts of one man after another, teaching them each more and more about Himself, and the history also of these men listening to the voice of God in their hearts, and *believing* that voice, and acting faithfully upon it, into whatever strange circumstances or deeds it might lead them. 'By faith,' we read in the same chapter—'by faith Noah, being warned of God, prepared an ark to the saving of his house, and became heir of the righteousness which is by faith.'

Now, to understand this last sentence, you must remember that Noah was not under the law of Moses. St. Paul has a whole chapter (the third chapter of Galatians) to show that these old saints had nothing to do with Moses' law any more than we have; that it was given to the Jews many hundred years afterwards. So these histories of the Old Testament saints are, in fact, histories of men who conquered by faith— histories of the power which faith in God has to conquer temptation, and doubt, and false appearances, and fear and danger, and all which besets and keeps us down from being free and holy, and children of the day, walking cheerfully forward on our heavenward road in the light of our Father's loving smile.

Noah, we read, 'was a just man and perfect in his generations;' and why? Because he was a faithful man—faithful to God, as it is written, 'The just shall live by his faith;' not by trusting in what he does himself, in his own works or deservings, but trusting in God who made him; believing that God is perfectly righteous, perfectly wise, perfectly loving; and that, because He is perfectly loving, He will accept and save sinful man when He sees in sinful man the earnest wish to be His faithful, obedient servant, and to give himself up to the rule and guidance of God. This, then, was Noah's justice in God's sight, as it was Abraham's. They believed God, and so became heirs of the righteousness which is by faith; not their own righteousness, not growing out of their own character, but given them by God, who puts His righteous Spirit into those who trust in Him.

But, moreover, we read that Noah 'was perfect in his generations;' that is, he was perfect in all the relations and duties of life,—a good son, a good husband, a good father; these were the fruits of his faith. He believed that the unseen God had given him these ties, had given him his parents, his children, and that to love them was to love God, to do his duty to them was to do his duty to God. This was part of his walking with God, continually under his great Taskmaster's eye,—walking about his daily business with the belief that a great loving Father was above him, whatever he did; ready to strengthen, and guide, and bless him if he did well, ready to avenge Himself on him if he did ill. These were the fruits of Noah's faith.

But you may think this nothing very wonderful. Many a man in England does this every day, and yet no one ever hears of him; he attends to all his family ties, doing justly, loving mercy, and walking humbly with God, like one who knows he is redeemed by Christ's blood; he lives, he dies, he is buried, and out of his own parish his name is never known; while Noah has earned for himself a world-wide fame; for four thousand years his name has been spreading over the whole earth as one of the greatest men who ever lived. Mighty nations have worshipped Noah as a God; many heathen nations worship him under strange and confused names and traditions to this day; and the wisest and holiest men among Christians now reverence Noah, write of him, preach on him, thank God for him, look up to him as, next to Abraham, their greatest example in the Old Testament.

Well, my friends, to understand what made Noah so great, we must understand in what times Noah lived. 'The wickedness of men was great in the earth in those days, and every imagination of the thoughts of their heart was only evil continually, and the earth was filled with violence through them.' And we must remember that the wickedness of men before the flood was not outwardly like wickedness now; it was not petty, mean, contemptible wickedness of silly and stupid men, such as could be despised and laughed down; it was like the wickedness of fallen angels. Men were then strong and beautiful, cunning and active, to a degree of which we can form no conception. Their enormous length of life (six, seven, and eight hundred years commonly) must have given them an experience and daring far beyond any man in these days. Their bodily size and strength were in many cases enormous. We read that 'there were giants in the earth in those days; and also after that, when the sons of God came in unto the daughters of men, and they bare children to them, the same became mighty men which were of old, men of renown.' Their powers of invention seem to have been proportionably great. We read, in the fourth chapter of Genesis, how, within a few years after Adam was driven out of Paradise, they had learned to build cities, to tame the wild beasts, and live upon their milk and flesh; that they had invented all sorts of music and musical instruments; that they had discovered the art of working in metals. We read among them of Tubal Cain, an instructor of every workman in brass and iron; and the old traditions in the East, where these men dwelt, are full of strange and awful tales of their power.

Again, we must remember that there was no law in Noah's

days before the flood, no Bible to guide them, no constitutions and acts of parliament to bind men in the beaten track by the awful majesty of law, whether they will or no, as we have.

This is the picture which the Bible gives us of the old world before the flood—a world of men mighty in body and mind, fierce and busy, conquering the world round them, in continual war and turmoil; with all the wild passions of youth, and yet all the cunning and experience of enormous old age; with the strength and the courage of young men to carry out the iniquity of old ones; every one guided only by self-will, having cast off God and conscience, and doing every man that which was right in the sight of his own eyes. And amidst all this, while men as wise, as old, as strong, as great as himself, whirled away round him in this raging sea of sin, Noah was steadfast; he, at least, knew his way,—'he walked with God, a just man and perfect in his generations.'

To Noah, living in such a world as this, among temptation, and violence, and insult, no doubt there came this command from God: 'The end of all flesh is come before me, for the earth is filled with violence through them, and I will destroy them with the earth. And behold I, even I, do bring a flood of waters upon the earth, to destroy all flesh, wherein is the breath of life; but with thee will I establish my covenant, and thou shalt make thee an ark of wood after the fashion which I tell thee; and thou shalt come into the ark, thou and thy family, and of every living thing, two of every sort, male and female, shalt thou bring into the ark, and keep them alive with thee; and take thou of all food that is eaten into the ark, for thee, and for them.' What a message, my friends! If we wish to see a little of the greatness of Noah's faith, conceive such a message coming from God to one of us! Should we believe it —much less act upon it? But *Noah* believed God, says the Scripture; and 'according as God commanded him, so did he.' Now, in whatever way this command came from God to Noah, it is equally wonderful. Some of you, perhaps, will say in your hearts, 'No! when God spoke to him, how could he help obeying Him?' But, my friends, ask yourselves seriously—for, believe me, it is a most important question for the soul and inner life of you and me, and every man—how did Noah know that it was God who spoke to him? It is easy to say God appeared to him; but no man hath seen God at any time. It is easy, again, to say that an angel appeared to him, or that God appeared to him in the form of a man; but still the same question is left to be answered, how did he know that this appearance came from God, and that its words were true? Why should not Noah have said, 'This was an evil spirit which appeared to me, trying to frighten and ruin me, and stir up all my neighbours to mock me, perhaps to murder me?' Or again; suppose that you or I saw some glorious apparition this day, which told us on such and such a day such and such a town will be destroyed, what should *we* think of it? Should we not say, I have been dreaming—I must have been ill, and so my brain and eyes must have been disordered? and treat the whole thing as a mere fancy of ill-health: now, why did not Noah do the same?

Why do I say this? To show you, my friends, that it is not apparitions and visions which can make a man believe. As it is written, " If they believe not Moses and the prophets, neither will they believe though one rose from the dead.' No; a man must have faith in his heart already. A man must first be accustomed to discern right from wrong—to listen to and to obey the voice of God within him; *that* word of God of which it is said 'the word is nigh thee, in thy heart and in thy mind,' before he can hear God's word from without; else he will only explain away miracles, and call visions and apparitions sick men's dreams.

But there was something yet more wonderful and divine in Noah's faith,—I mean his patience. He knew that a flood was to come—he set to work in faith to build his ark—and that ark was in building for one hundred and twenty years. One hundred and twenty years! It seems at first past all belief. For all that time he built; and all the while the world went on just as usual; and, before he had finished, old men had died, and children grown into years; and great cities had sprung up perhaps where there was not a cottage before; and trees which were but a yard high when that ark was begun had grown into mighty forest-timber: and men had multiplied and spread, and yet Noah built and built on steadfastly, believing that what God had said would surely one day or other come to pass. For one hundred and twenty years he saw the world go on as usual, and yet he never forgot that it was a doomed world. He endured the laughter and mockery of all his neighbours; and every fresh child who was born grew up to laugh at the foolish old man who had been toiling for a hundred years past on his mad scheme, as they thought it; and yet Noah never lost faith, and he never lost *love* either—for all those years, we read, he preached righteousness to the very men who mocked him, and preached in vain. One hundred and twenty years he warned those sinners of God's wrath, of righteousness and judgment to come, and no man listened to him! That, I believe, must have been, after all, the hardest of all his trials.

And, doubtless, Noah had his inward temptation many a time; no doubt he was ready now and then to believe God's message all a dream—to laugh at himself for his fears of a flood which seemed never coming, but in his heart was the 'still small voice' of God, warning him that God was not a man that He should lie, or repent, or deceive those who walked faithfully with Him; and around him he saw men growing and growing in iniquity, filling up the cup of their own damnation: and he said to himself, 'Verily there is a God who judgeth the earth—for all this a reckoning day will surely come; and he worked steadfastly on, and the ark was finished. And then at last there came a second call from God, 'Come thou and all thy house into the ark, for thee have I seen righteous before me in this generation. Yet seven days, and I will cause it to rain upon the earth, and every living substance that I have made will I destroy from off the earth.' And Noah entered into the ark, and seven days he waited; and louder than ever laughed the scoffers round him, at the old man and his family shut into his ark safe on dry land, while day and night went on as quietly as ever, and the world ran its usual round ; for seven days more their mad game lasted—they ate, they drank, they married, they gave in marriage, they planted, they builded ; and on the seventh day it came ; the rain fell day after day, and week after week, and the windows of heaven were opened, and the fountains of the great deep were broken up, and the flood arose, and swept them all away !

SERMON XI.

THE NOACHIC COVENANT.

GEN. ix. 8, 9.

And God spake unto Noah, and to his sons with him, saying, And I, behold, I establish my covenant with you, and with your seed after you.

IN my last sermon on Noah I spoke of the flood and of Noah's faith before the flood; I now go on to speak of the covenant which God made with Noah after the flood. Now, Noah stood on that newly-dried earth as the head of mankind; he and his family, in all eight souls, saved by God's mercy from the general ruin, were the only human beings left alive, and had laid on them the wonderful and glorious duty of renewing the race of man, and replenishing the vast world around them. From that little knot of human beings were to spring all the nations of the earth.

And because this calling and destiny of theirs was a great and all-important one—because so much of the happiness or misery of the new race of mankind depended on the teaching which they would get from their forefathers, the sons of Noah, therefore God thought fit to make with Noah and his sons a solemn covenant, as soon as they came out of the ark.

Let us solemnly consider this covenant, for it stands good now as much as ever. God made it 'with Noah, and his seed after him,' for perpetual generations. And *we* are the seed of

Noah; every man, woman, and child of us here were in the loins of Noah when the great absolute God gave him that pledge and promise. We must earnestly consider that covenant, for in it lies the very ground and meaning of man's life and business on this earth.

'And God blessed Noah and his sons, and said unto them, Be fruitful, and multiply, and replenish the earth. And the fear of you and the dread of you shall be upon every living creature. Into your hand are they delivered. Every moving thing that liveth shall be meat for you; even as the green herb have I given you all things. But flesh with the life thereof, which is the blood thereof, shall ye not eat. And surely your blood of your lives will I require; at the hand of every beast will I require it, and at the hand of man; at the hand of every man's brother will I require the life of man. Whoso sheddeth man's blood, by man shall his blood be shed; for in the image of God made He man.'

Now, to understand this covenant, consider what thoughts would have been likely to grow up in the mind of Noah's children after the flood? Would they not have been something of this kind: 'God does not love men; He has drowned all but us, and we are men of like passions with the world who perished: may we not expect the like ruin at any moment? Then what use to plough and sow, and build and plant, and work for those who shall come after us? "Let us eat and drink, for to-morrow we die."'

And again, they would have been ready to say, 'This God, whom our forefather Noah said sent floods, we cannot see Him; but the floods themselves we can see. All these clouds and tempests, lightning, sun, and stars,—are we *stronger* than they? No! They may crush us, drown us, strike us dead at any moment. They seem too to go by certain wonderful rules and laws; perhaps they have a will and understanding in them. Instead of praying to a God whom we never saw, why not pray to the thunderclouds not to strike us dead, and to the seas and rivers not to sweep us away? For this great, wonderful, awful world in which we are, however beautiful may be its flowers, and its fruits, and its sunshine, there is no trusting it; we are sitting upon a painted sepulchre, a beautiful monster, a gulf of flood and fire, which may burst up any moment, and sweep us away, as it did our forefathers.'

Again, Noah's children would have begun to say, 'These beasts here round us, they are so many of them larger than us, stronger than us, able to tear us to atoms, eat us up as they would eat a lamb. They are self-sufficient, too; they want no clothes, nor houses, nor fire, like us poor, weak, naked, soft human creatures. They can run faster than we, see further than we; their scent, too, what a wonderful, mysterious power that is, like a miracle to us! And, besides all their cunning way of getting food and building nests, they never do *wrong;* they never do horrible things contrary to their nature; they all abide as God has made them, obeying the law of their kind. Are not these beasts, then, much wiser and better than we? We will honour them, and pray to them not to devour us—to make us cunning and powerful as they are themselves. And if they are no better than us, surely they are no worse than us. After all, what difference is there between a man and a beast? The flood which drowned the beasts drowned the men too. A beast is flesh and blood; what more is a man? If you kill him, he dies, just as a beast dies; and why should not a man's carcase be just as good to eat as a beast's, and better?' And so there would have been a free opening at once into all the horrors of cannibalism!

Again, Noah's descendants would have said, ' Our forefathers offered sacrifices to the unseen God, as a sign that all they had belonged to Him, and that they had forfeited their own souls by sin, and were therefore ready to give up the most precious things they had—their cattle—as a sign that they owed all to that very God whom they had offended. But are not human creatures much more precious than cattle? Will it not be a much greater sign of repentance and willingness to give up all to God, if we offer Him the best things which we have—human creatures?—if we kill and sacrifice to Him our most beautiful and innocent things—little children—noble young men—beautiful young girls?'

My friends, these are very strange and shocking thoughts, but they have been in the hearts and minds of all nations. The heathens do such things now. Our own forefathers used to do such things once; they were tempted to worship the sun and the moon, and rivers, and the thunder, and to look with superstitious terror at the bears, and the wolves, and the snakes round them, and to kill their young children and maidens, and offer them up as sacrifices to the dark powers of this world, which they thought were ready to swallow them up. And God is my witness, my friends, when one goes through some parts of England now, and sees the mine-children and factory-children, and all the sin and misery, and the people wearying themselves in the fire for very vanity, we seem not to be so very far from the same dark superstition now, though we may call it by a different name. England has been sacrificing her sons and her daughters to the devil of covetousness of late years, just as much as our forefathers offered theirs to the devil of selfish and cowardly superstition.

But see, now, how this covenant which God made with Noah was intended just to remedy every one of those temptations which I just mentioned, into which Noah's children's children would have been certain to fall, and into which so many of them did fall. They might have become reckless, I said, from fear of a flood at any moment. God promises them—and confirms it with the sign of the rainbow—never again to destroy the earth by water. They would have been likely to take to praying to the rain and the thunder, the sun and the stars; God declares in this covenant that it is He alone who sends the rain and thunder, that He brings the clouds over the earth, that He rules the great awful world; that men are to look up and believe in God as a loving and thinking *person*, who has a will of His own, and that a faithful, and true, and loving, and merciful will; that their lives and safety depend not on blind chance, or the stern necessity of certain laws of nature, but on the covenant of an almighty and all-loving person.

Again, I said that Noah's sons would have been ready to fear, and, at last, to worship the dumb beasts; God's covenant says, 'No; these beasts are not your equals—they are your slaves—you may freely kill them for your food; the fear of you shall be upon them. The huge elephant and the swift horse shall become your servants; the lion and the tiger shall tremble and flee before you. Only claim your rights as men; believe that the invisible God who made the earth is your strength and your protector, and that He to whom the earth belongs has made you lords of the earth and all that therein is. But,' said God's covenant to Noah's sons, 'you did not *make* these beasts—you did not give them life; therefore I forbid you to eat their blood wherein their life lies, that you may never forget that all the power you have over these beasts was given you by God, who made and preserves that wonderful, mysterious, holy thing called life, which you can never imitate.' Again, I said that Noah's children, having been accustomed to the violence and bloodshed on the earth before the flood, might hold man's life cheap; that having seen in the flood men perish just like the beasts around them, they might have begun to think that man's life was not more precious than the beasts'. They might have all gone on at last, as some of them did, to those horrors of cannibalism and human sacrifice of which I just now spoke. Now, here again comes in God's covenant, 'Surely the blood of your lives will I require. At the hand of every beast will I require it, and at the hand of every man's brother will I require it. Whoso sheddeth man's blood, by man shall his blood be shed; for in the image of God made He man.' This, then, is the covenant which God made with Noah for perpetual generations, and therefore with us, the children of Noah. In this covenant you see certain truths come out into light; some, of which you read nothing before in the Bible, and other truths which, though they were given to Adam, yet had been utterly lost sight of before the flood. This has been God's method, we find from the Bible, ever since the creation,—to lead man step by step up into more and more light, up to this very day, and to make each sin and each madness of men an occasion for revealing to him more and more of truth and of the living God. And so each and every chapter in the Bible is built upon all that has gone before it; and he that neglects to understand what has gone before will never come to the understanding of what follows after. Why do I say this? Because men are continually picking out those scraps of the Bible which suit their own fancy, and pinning their own faith on them, and trying to make them serve to explain everything in heaven and earth; whereas no man can understand the Epistles unless he first understands the Gospels. No man will understand the New Testament unless he first understands the pith and marrow of the Old. No man will understand the Psalms and the Prophets unless he first understands the first ten chapters of Genesis; and lastly, no one will ever understand anything about the Bible at all, who, instead of taking it simply as it is written, is always trying to twist it into proofs of his own favourite doctrines, and make Abraham a high Calvinist, or Noah a member of the Church of England. Why do I say this? To make you all think seriously that this covenant on which I have been preaching is your covenant; that as sure as the rainbow stands in heaven, as sure as you and I are sprung out of the loins of Noah, so surely this covenant which binds us is part of our Christian covenant, and woe to us if we break it!

This covenant tells us that we are made in God's likeness, and therefore that all sin is unworthy of us, and unnatural to us. It tells that God means us bravely and industriously to subdue the earth and the living things upon it; that we are to be the masters of the pleasant things about us, and not their slaves, as sots and idlers are ; that we are stewards and tenants of this world for the great God who made it, to whom we are to look up in confidence for help and protection. It tells us that our family relationships, the blessed duties of a husband and a father, are sacred things ; that God has created them, that the great God of heaven Himself respects them, that the covenant which He makes with the father He makes with the children ; that He commands marriage, and that He blesses it with fruitfulness ; that it is He who has told us, ' Be fruitful and multiply, and replenish the earth ;' that the tie of brotherhood is His making also; that *He* will require the blood of the murdered man *at his brother's hand;* that a man's brothers, his nearest relations, are bound to protect and right him if he is injured ; so that we are all to be, in the deepest sense of the word, what Cain refused to be, our *brother's keepers*, and each member of a family is more or less answerable for the welfare and safety of all his relations. Herein lies the ground of all religion and of all society—in the covenant which God made with Noah ; and just as it is in vain for a man to pretend to be a scholar when he does not even know his letters, so it is mockery for a man to pretend to be a converted Christian man who knows not even so much as was commanded to Noah and his sons. He who has not learnt to love, honour, and succour his own family—he who has not learnt to work in honest and manful industry—he who has not learnt to look beyond this earth, and its chance, and its customs, and its glittering outside, and see and trust in a great, wise, loving God, by whose will every tree grows and every shower falls, what is Christianity to him? He has to learn the first principles which were delivered to Noah, and which not even the heathen and the savage have utterly forgotten.

SERMON XII.

ABRAHAM'S FAITH.

Hebrews xi. 9, 10.

By faith Abraham sojourned in the land of promise, as in a strange country, dwelling in tabernacles with Isaac and Jacob, the heirs with him of the same promise: for he looked for a city which hath foundations, whose builder and maker is God.

IN the last sermon which I preached in this church, I said that the Bible is the history of God's ways with mankind; how He has schooled and brought them up until the coming of Christ; that if we read the Bible histories, one after another, in the same order in which God has put them in the Bible, we shall see that they are all regular steps in a line; that each fresh story depends on the story which went before it; and yet, in each fresh history we shall find God telling men something new—something which they did not know before. And that so the whole Bible, from beginning to end, is one glorious, methodic, and organic tree of life, every part growing out of the others, and depending on the others, from the root—that foundation, other than which no man can lay, which is Christ, revealing Himself, though not by name, in that wonderful first chapter of Genesis,—up to the *fruit*, which is the kingdom of Christ, and Gospel of Christ, and the salvation in which we here now stand. I told you that the lesson which God has been teaching men in all ages, is faith in God—that the saints of old were just the men who learned this lesson of faith. Now this, as we all know, was the secret of Abraham's greatness, that he had faith in God to leave his own country at God's bidding, and become a stranger and a pilgrim on the earth, wandering on in full trust that God would give him another country instead of that which he had left—a 'city which hath foundations, whose builder and maker is God.' This was what Abraham looked for. Something of what it means we shall see presently.

You remember the story of the tower of Babel? how certain of Noah's family forgot the covenant which God had made with Noah; forgot that God had commanded them to go forth in every direction and fill the earth with human beings, solemnly promising to protect and bless them, and took on themselves to do the very opposite—set up a kingdom of their own fashion, and herded together for selfish safety, instead of going forth to all the quarters of the world in a natural way, according to their families, in their tribes, after their nations, as the eleventh chapter of Genesis says they ought to have done. 'Let us build us a city and a tower, and make us a name, lest,' they said, 'we be scattered abroad over the face of the whole world.' Here was one act of disobedience to God's order. But, besides this, they had fallen into a slavish dread of the powers of nature—they were afraid of another flood. They set to, to build a tower, on which they might worship the sun and stars, and the host of heaven, and pray to them to send no more floods and tempests. They thus fell into a slavish fear of the powers of nature, as well as into a selfish and artificial civilization. In short, they utterly broke the covenant which God had made with Noah. But by miraculously confounding their language, God drove them forth over the face of the whole earth, and so forced them to do that which they ought to have done willingly at first.

Now, we must remember that all this happened in the very

country in which Abraham lived. He must have heard of it all—for aught we know, he had seen the tower of Babel. So that, for good or for evil, the whole Babel event must have produced a strong effect on the mind of a thoughtful man like Abraham, and raised many strange questionings in his heart, which God alone could answer for him, *or for us*. Now, what did God mean to teach Abraham, by calling him out of his country, and telling him, 'I will make of thee a great nation?' I think He meant to show him, for one thing, that that Babel plan of society was utterly absurd and accursed, certain to come to nought, and so to lead him on to hope for a city which had foundations, and to see that *its* builder and maker must be, not the selfishness or the ambition of men, but the will, and the wisdom, and providence of God.

Let us see how God led Abraham on to understand this—to look for a city which had foundations; in short, to understand what a state and a nation means and ought to be. First, God taught him that he was not to cling, coward-like, to the place where he was born, but to go out boldly to colonise and subdue the earth, for the great God of heaven would protect and guide him. 'Get thee out of thy country, and from thy father's house, unto a land which I will show thee. And I will bless them that bless thee, and curse them that curse thee.' Again: God taught him what a nation was: '*I* will make of thee a great nation.' As much as to say, 'Never fancy, as those fools at Babel did, that a nation only means a great crowd of people—never fancy that men can make themselves into a nation just by feeding altogether, and breeding altogether, and fighting altogether, as the herds of wild cattle and sheep do, while there is no real union between them.' For what brought those Babel men together? Just what keeps a herd of cattle together—selfishness and fear. Each man thought he would be *safer* forsooth in company. Each man thought that if he was in company, he could use his neighbour's wits, as well as his own, and have the benefit of his neighbour's strength as well as his own. And that is all true enough; but that does not make a nation. Selfishness can join nothing: it may join a set of men for a time, each for his own ends just as a joint-stock company is made up; but it will soon split them up again. Each man, in a merely selfish community, will begin, after a time, to play on his own account, as well as work on his own account—to oppress and overreach for his own ends, as well as to be honest and benevolent for his own ends, for he will find ill-doing far easier, and more natural, in one sense, and a plan that brings in quicker profits, than well-doing; and so this godless, loveless, every-man-for-himself nation, or sham nation rather, this joint-stock company, in which fools expect that universal selfishness will do the work of universal benevolence, will quarrel and break up, crumble to dust again, as Babel did. 'But,' says God to Abraham, 'I will make of thee a great nation. I make nations, and not they themselves.' So it is, my friends: this is the lesson which God taught Abraham, the lesson which we English must learn now-a-days over again, or smart for it bitterly—that God makes nations. He is King of kings; 'by Him kings reign and princes decree judgment.' He judges all nations: He nurtureth the nations. This is throughout the teaching of the Psalms. 'It is He that hath made us, and not we ourselves; we are His people, and the sheep of His pasture;'—for this I take to be the true bearing of that glorious national hymn, the 100th Psalm, and not merely the old truism that men did not create themselves, when it exhorts *all* nations to praise God because it is He that hath made them nations, and not they themselves. The Psalms set forth the Son of God as the King of all nations. In Him, my friends—in Him all the nations of the earth are truly blessed.

He the Saviour of a few individual souls only? God forbid! To Him *all power* is given in heaven and earth; by Him were all things created, whether in heaven or earth, visible and invisible, whether they be thrones or dominions, or principalities or powers; all national life, all forms of government, whether hero-despotisms, republics, or monarchies, aristocracies of birth, or of wealth, or of talent,—all were created by Him, and for Him, and He is before all things, and by Him all things *consist* and hold together. Every thing or institution on earth, which has systematic and organic life in it—by *Him* it consists—by Him, the Life and the Light who lighteneth every man that cometh into the world. From Him come law, and order, and spiritual energy, and loving fellow-feeling, and patriotism, the spirit of wisdom, and understanding, and prudence—all, in short, by which a nation consists and holds together. It is not constitutions, and acts of parliament, and social contracts, and rights of the people, and rights of kings, and so on, which make us a nation. These are but the effects, and not the consequences of the national life. *That* is the one spirit which is shed abroad upon a country whose builder and maker is God, and which comes down from above—comes down from Christ, the King of kings, who has given each nation its peculiar work on this earth, its peculiar circumstances and history to mould and educate it for its work, and its peculiar spirit and national character, wherewith to fulfil the destiny which Christ has appointed for it.

Believe me, my friends, it takes long years, too, and much training from God and from Christ, the King of kings, to make a nation. Everything which is most precious and great is also most slow in growing, and so is a nation. The Scripture compares it everywhere to a tree; and as the tree grows, a people must grow, from small beginnings, perhaps from a single family, increasing on, according to the fixed laws of God's world, for years and hundreds of years, till it becomes a mighty nation, with one Lord, one faith, one work, one Spirit.

But again; God said to Abraham, when He had led him into this far country, 'Unto thy seed will *I give this land.*' This was a great and a new lesson for Abraham, that the earth belonged to that same great invisible God who had promised to guide and protect him, and make him into a nation—that this same God gave the earth to whomsoever He would, and allotted to each people their proper portion of it. 'He (said St. Paul on the Areopagus) hath determined the times before appointed for all nations, and the bounds of their habitation, that they may seek after the Lord and find Him.' Ah! this must have been a strange and a new feeling to Abraham; but, stranger still, though God had given him this land, he was not to take possession of a single foot of it; the land was already in the hands of a different nation, the people of Canaan; and Abraham was to go wandering about a sojourner, as the text says, in this very land of promise, which God had given him, without ever taking possession of his own, simply because it belonged to others already. How this must have taught Abraham that the rights of property were sacred things—things appointed by God; that it was an awful and heinous sin to make wanton war on other people, to drive them out and take possession of their land; that it was not mere force or mere fancy which gave men a right to a country, but the providence of Almighty God! Now, Abraham needed this warning, for the men of Babel seem from the first to have gone on the plan of driving out and conquering the tribes round them. They seem to have set up their city partly from ambition. 'Let us make us a name,' they said, meaning, 'Let us make ourselves famous and terrible to all the people around us, that we may subdue them.' And we read of Nimrod, who was their first king and the founder of Babel, that he was a mighty hunter before the Lord, that is, as most learned men explain it, a mighty conqueror and tyrant in defiance of God and His laws; as the poet says of him,

> A mighty hunter, and his game was man.

The Jews, indeed, have an old tradition that Nimrod cast Abraham into a fiery furnace for refusing to worship the host of heaven with him. The story is very likely untrue, but still it is of use in showing what sort of reputation Nimrod left behind him in his own part of the world. We may thus see that Abraham would need warning against these habits of violence, tyranny, and plunder, into which the men of Babel and other tribes were falling. And this was what God meant to teach him by keeping him a stranger and a pilgrim in the very land which God had promised to him for his own. Thus Abraham learnt respect for the rights and properties of his neighbours; thus he learnt to look up in faith to God, not only as his patron and protector, but as the lord and absolute owner of the soil on which he stood.

Now, in the 14th chapter of Genesis there is an account of Abraham's being called on to put in practice what he had learnt, and, by doing so, learning a fresh lesson. We read of four kings making war against five kings, against Chedorlaomer, king of Elam or Persia, who had been following the ways of Nimrod and the men of Babel, and conquering these foreign kings and making them serve him. We read of Chedorlaomer and four other kings coming down and wantonly ravaging and destroying other countries, besides the five kings who had rebelled against them, and at last carrying off captive the people of Sodom and Gomorrah, and Lot, Abraham's nephew. We read then how Abraham armed his trained servants, born in his own house, three hundred and eighteen men, and pursued after these tyrants and plunderers, and with his small force completely overthrew that great army. Now, that was a sign and a lesson to Abraham, as much as to say, 'See the fruits of having the great God of heaven and earth for your protector and your guide,—see the fruits of having men round you, not hirelings, keeping in your company just to see what they can get by it, but born in your own house, who love and trust you, whom you can love and trust,—see how the favour of God, and reverence for those family ties and duties which He has appointed, make you and your little band of faithful men superior to those great mobs of selfish, godless, unjust robbers,

—see how hundreds of these slaves ran away before one man, who feels that he is a member of a family, and has a just cause for fighting, and that God and his brethren are with him.'

Here, you see, was another hint to Abraham of what it was and who it was that made a great nation.

And now some of you may say, 'This is a strange sermon. You have as yet said nothing of Christ, nothing of the Holy Spirit, nothing of grace, redemption, sanctification. What kind of sermon is this?'

My friends, do not be too sure that I have not been preaching Christ to you, and Christ's Spirit to you, and Christ's redemption too, most truly in this sermon, although I have mentioned none of them by name. There are times for ornamenting the house, there are times for repairing the wall, there are times too for thoroughly examining the foundation, because, if that be not sound, it is little matter what fine work is built up upon it; and there are times when, as David says, the foundations of the earth are out of course, when men have forgotten sadly the very first principles of society and religion.

And, surely, men are doing so in these days; men are forgetting that other foundation can no man lay save that which *is* laid, which is Christ; they laugh at the thought of a city, that is, a state and form of government, 'not made with hands, eternal in the heavens;' they have forgotten that St. Paul tells them in the Hebrews that we *have* 'a city which hath foundations, whose builder and maker is God,' a kingdom which cannot be moved. Yes, men who call themselves learned and worldly wise, and good men too, alas! who fancy that they are preaching God's gospel, go about and tell men, 'The men of Babel were right, after all. What have nations to do with God and religion? Nations are merely earthly, carnal things, that were only invented by sinful men themselves, to preserve their bodies and goods, and make trading easy. Religion has only to do with a man's private opinions, his single soul; the government has nothing to do with the Church: a Christian has nothing to do with politics.' And so these men most unwittingly open a door to all sorts of covetousness and meanness in the nation, and all sorts of trickery and cowardice in the government. Tell a man that his business has nothing to do with God, and you cannot wonder if he acts without thinking of God. If you tell a nation that it is selfishness which makes it prosperous, of course you must expect it to be selfish. If you tell us Englishmen that the duties of a citizen are not duties to God, but only duties to the constable and the tax-gatherer, what wonder if men believe you and become undutiful to God in their citizenship? No, my friends, once for all, as sure as God made Abraham a great nation, so if we English are a great nation, God has made us so—as sure as God gave Abraham the land of Canaan for his possession, so did *He* give us this land of England, when He brought our Saxon forefathers out of the wild barren north, and drove out before them nations greater and mightier than they, and gave them great and goodly cities which they builded not, and wells digged which they digged not, farms and gardens which they planted not, that we too might fear the Lord our God, and serve Him, and swear by His name;—as sure as He commanded Abraham to respect the property of his neighbours, so as He commanded us; as sure as God taught Abraham that the nation which was to grow from him owed a duty to God, and could be only strong by faith in God, so it is with us: we English people owe a duty to God, and are to deal among ourselves, and with foreign countries, by faith in God, and in the fear of God, 'seeking first the kingdom of God and His righteousness,' sure that then all other things—victory, health, commerce, art, and science—will be added to us, as the first lesson says. For this is your wisdom and understanding in the sight of the nations, which shall say, Surely this great nation is a wise and understanding people! For what nation is grown so great, that hath statutes and judgments so righteous as these laws, this gospel, which God sets before us day by day?—us, Englishmen!

And I say that these are proper thoughts for this place. This is not a mere preaching-house, where you may learn every man to save his own soul; this is a far nobler place; this building belongs to the National Church of England, and we worship here, not merely as men, but as men of England, citizens of a Christian country, come here to learn not merely how to save ourselves, but how to help towards the saving of our families, our parish, and our nation; and therefore we must know what a country and a nation mean, and what is the meaning of that glorious and divine word, 'a citizen;' that by learning what it is to be a citizen of England, we may go on to learn fully what it is to be a citizen of the kingdom of God.

For this is part of the whole counsel of God, which He reveals in His Holy Bible; and this also we must not, and dare not, shun declaring in these days.

SERMON XIII.

ABRAHAM'S OBEDIENCE.

HEBREWS xi. 17—19.

By faith Abraham, when he was tried, offered up Isaac: and he that had received the promises offered up his only-begotten son, of whom it was said, 'That in Isaac shall thy seed be called: accounting that God was able to raise him up, even from the dead; from whence also he received him in a figure.

IN this chapter we come to the crowning point of Abraham's history, the highest step and perfection of his faith; beyond which it seems as if man's trust in God could no further go.

You know, most of you, doubtless, that Isaac, Abraham's son, was come to him out of the common course of nature—when he and his wife Sarah were of an age which seemed to make all chance of a family utterly hopeless. You remember how God promised Abraham that this boy should be born to him at a certain time, when He appeared to him on the plains of Mamre, in that most solemn and deep-meaning vision of which I spoke to you last Sunday. You remember, too, no doubt, most of you, how God had promised Abraham again and again, that in his seed, his children, all the nations of the earth should be blessed; so that all Abraham's hopes were wrapped up in this boy Isaac; he was his only son, whom he loved; he was the child of his old age, his glory and his joy; he was the child of God's promises. Every time Abraham looked at him he felt that Isaac was a wonderful child : that God had a great work for him to do ; that from that single boy a great nation was to spring, as many in multitude as the stars in the sky, or the sand on the sea-shore, for the great Almighty God had said it. And he knew, too, that from that boy, who was growing up by him in his tent, all the nations in the earth should be blessed: so that Isaac, his son, was to Abraham a daily sacrament, as I may say, a sign and pledge that God was with him, and would be true to him; that as surely as God had wonderfully and beyond all hope given him that son, so wonderfully and beyond all hope He would fulfil all His other promises. Conceive then, if you can, what Abraham's astonishment, and doubt, and terror, and misery must have been at such a message as this from the very God who had given Isaac to him: 'And it came to pass after these things, that God did tempt Abraham, and said unto him, Abraham; and he said, Behold, here I am. And He said, Take now thy son, thine only son Isaac, whom thou lovest, and get thee into the land of Moriah; and offer him there for a burnt-offering upon one of the mountains which I will tell thee of.'

What a storm of doubt it must have raised in Abraham's mind ! How unable he must have been to say whether that message came from a good or bad spirit, or commanded him to do a good action or a bad one; that the same God who had said, 'Whoso sheddeth man's blood, by man shall his blood be shed ;' who had forbidden murder as the very highest of crimes, should command him to shed the blood of his own son ; that the same God who had promised him that in Isaac all the nations of the earth should be blessed, should command him to put him to death that very son upon whom all his hopes depended ! Fearful indeed must have been the struggle in Abraham's mind, but the good and the right thought conquered at last. His feeling was, no doubt, 'This God who has blessed me so long, who has guided me so long, whom I have obeyed so long, shall I not trust Him a little further yet? How can I believe that He will do wrong? How can I believe that He will lead me wrong? If it is really wrong that I should kill my son, He will not let me do it: if it really *is* His will that I should kill my son, *I will do it.* Whatever He says must be right; it *is* agony and misery to me, but what of that? Do I not owe Him a thousand daily and hourly blessings? Has He not led me hither, preserved me, guided me, taught me the knowledge of Himself,—chosen me to be the father of a great nation? Do I not owe Him everything? and shall I not bear this sharp sorrow for His sake? I know, too, that if Isaac dies, all my hope, all my joy, will die with him : that I shall have nothing left to look for, nothing left to work for in this world. Nothing! shall I not have God left to me? When Isaac is dead will the Lord die? will the Lord change? will He grow weak?—Never! Years ago did He declare to me that He was the Almighty God; I will believe that He will be always Almighty; I will believe that though I kill my son, my son will be still in God's hands, and I shall be still in God's hands, and that God is able to raise him again, even from the dead. God can give him back to me, and if He will *not* give him back to me, He can fulfil His promises in a thousand other ways. Ay, and He will fulfil His promises, for in Him is neither deceit, nor fickleness, nor weakness, nor unrighteousness of any kind; and, come what will, I will believe His promise and I will obey His will.'

Some such thoughts as these, I suppose, passed through Abraham's mind. He could not have had a man's heart in him indeed, if not only those thoughts, but ten thousand more, sadder, and stranger, and more pitiful than my weak brain can imagine, did not sweep like a storm through his soul at that last and terrible temptation; but the Bible tells us nothing of them : why should the Bible tell us anything of them? the Bible sets forth Abraham as the faithful man, and therefore it simply tells us of his faith, without telling us of his doubts and struggles before he settled down into faith. It tells us, as it were, not how often the wind shifted and twisted about during the tempest, but in what quarter the wind settled when the tempest was over, and it began to blow steadily, and fixedly, and gently, and all was bright, and mild, and still in Abraham's bosom again, just as a man's mind will be bright, and gentle, and calm, even at the moment he is going to certain death or fearful misery, if he does but know that his suffering is his duty, and that his trial is his heavenly Father's will: and so all we read in the Old Testament account is simply, 'And Abraham rose up early in the morning, and saddled his ass, and took two of his young men with him, and Isaac his son, and clave the wood for the burnt-offering, and rose up, and went into the place of which God had told him. Then on the third day Abraham lifted up his eyes, and saw the place afar off. And Abraham said unto his young men, Abide ye here with the ass; and I and the lad will go yonder and worship, and come again to you. And Abraham took the wood of the burnt-offering, and laid it upon Isaac his son: and he took the fire in his hand, and a knife: and they went both of them together. And Isaac spake unto Abraham his father, and said, My father: and he said, Here am I, my son. And he said, Behold the fire and the wood: but where is the lamb for the burnt-offering? And Abraham said, My son, God will provide Himself a lamb for a burnt-offering. So they went both of them together. And they came to the place which God had told him of; and Abraham built an altar there, and laid the wood in order, and bound Isaac his son, and laid him on the altar upon the wood. And Abraham stretched forth his hand, and took the knife to slay his son.'

Really, if one is to consider the whole circumstances of Abraham's trials, they seem to have been infinite, more than mortal man could bear; more than he could have borne, no doubt, if the same God who tried had not rewarded his strength of mind by strengthening him still more, and rewarded his faith by increasing his faith; when we consider the struggle he must have had to keep the dreadful secret from the young man's mother, the tremendous effort of controlling himself, the long and frightful journey, the necessity, and yet the difficulty he seems to have felt of keeping the truth from his son, and yet of telling him the truth, which he did in those wonderful words, 'God shall provide Himself a lamb for a burnt-offering' (on which I shall have occasion to speak presently); and, last and worst of all, the perfect obedience and submission of his son; for Isaac was not a child then—he was a young man of nearly thirty years of age; strong and able enough, no doubt, to have resisted his aged father, if he had chosen. But the very excellence of Isaac seems to have been, that he did not resist, that he showed the same perfect trust and obedience to Abraham that Abraham did towards God; for he was led 'as a lamb to the slaughter, and as a sheep before her shearers is dumb, so he opened not his mouth;' as we read, 'Abraham bound Isaac his son and laid him on the wood.' Surely that was the bitterest pang of all, to see the excellence of his son shine forth just when it was too late for him to enjoy him—to find out what a perfect child he had, in simple trust and utter obedience, just at the very moment when he was going to lose him: 'And Abraham stretched forth his hand, and took the knife to slay his son.'

At that point Abraham's trial finished. He had shown the completeness of his faith by the completeness of his works, that is, by the completeness of his obedience. He had utterly given up all for God. He had submitted his will completely to God's will. He had said in heart, as our Blessed Lord said, 'Father, if it be possible, let this woe pass from me; nevertheless, not as I will, but as Thou wilt;' and thus, I say, he was justified by his works, by his actions; that is, by this faithful action he proved the faithfulness of his heart, as the Angel said to him, 'Now I know that thou fearest God, seeing thou hast not withheld thy son, thine only son, from me:' for as St. James says, 'Was not Abraham our father justified by works when he had offered Isaac his son upon the altar? Seest thou,' says he, 'how his faith wrought with his works!' how his works were the tool or instrument which his faith used; and by his works his faith was brought to perfection, as a tree is brought to perfection when it bears fruit. 'And so,' St. James continues, 'the scripture was fulfilled, which says Abraham believed God, and it was imputed to him for righteousness; and he was called the friend of God. Ye see then,' he says, 'how that by works a man is justified,' or shown to be righteous and faithful, 'and not by faith only;' that is, not by the mere feeling of faith, for, as he says, 'as the body without the spirit is dead, so faith without works is dead also.' For what is the sign of a body's being dead? It is its not being able to do anything, not being able to work; because there is no living and moving spirit in it. And what is the sign of a man's faith being dead? his faith not being able to *work*, because there is no living spirit in it, but it is a mere dead, empty shell and form of words,—a mere notion and thought about believing, in a man's head, but not a living trust and loyalty to God in his heart. Therefore, says St. James, 'show me thy faith without thy works,' if thou canst, 'and I will show thee my faith by my works,' as Abraham did by offering up Isaac his son.

Oh! my friends, when people are talking about faith and works, and trying to reconcile St. Paul and St. James, as they call it, because St. Paul says Abraham was justified by faith, and St. James says Abraham was justified by works, if they would but pray for the simple, childlike heart, and the head of common sense, and look at their own children, who, every time they go on a message for them, settle, without knowing it, this mighty difference of man's making between faith and works. You tell a little child daily to do many things the meaning and use of which it cannot understand; and the child has faith in what you tell it; and therefore it does what you tell it, and so it shows its faith in you by obedience in working for you.

But to go on with the verses: 'And the angel of the Lord called unto Abraham out of heaven the second time, and said,

By myself have I sworn, said the Lord, for because thou hast done this thing, and hast not withheld thy son, thine only son: that in blessing I will bless thee, and in multiplying I will multiply thy seed as the stars of the heaven, and as the sand which is upon the seashore; and thy seed shall possess the gate of his enemies; and in thy seed shall all the nations of the earth be blessed; because thou hast obeyed my voice.'

Now, here remark two things: first, that it was Abraham's obedience in giving up all to God, which called forth from God this confirmation of God's promises to him; and next, that God here promised him nothing new; God did not say to him, 'Because thou hast obeyed me in this great matter, I will give thee some great reward over and above what I promised thee.' No; God merely promises him over again, but more solemnly than ever, what He had promised him many years before.

And so it will be with us, my friends; we must not expect to *buy* God's favour by obeying Him,—we must not expect that the more we do for God, the more God will be bound to do for us, as the Papists do. No; God has done for us all that He will do. He has promised us all that He will promise. He has provided us, as He provided Abraham, a lamb for the burnt-offering, the Lamb without blemish and without spot, which taketh away the sins of the world. We are His redeemed people —we *have* a share in His promises—He bids us believe *that*, and show that we believe it by living as redeemed men, not our own, but bought with a price, and created anew in Christ Jesus to do good works; not that we may buy forgiveness by them, but that we may show by them that we believe that God *has* forgiven us already, and that when we have done all that is commanded us, we are still unprofitable servants; for though we should give up at God's bidding our children, our wives, and our own limbs and lives, and show as utter faith in God, and complete obedience to God, as Abraham did, we should only have done just what it was already our duty to do.

SERMON XIV.

OUR FATHER IN HEAVEN.

1 JOHN ii. 13.

I write unto you, little children, because ye have known the Father.

I PREACHED some time ago a sermon on the whole of these most deep and blessed verses of St. John.

I now wish to speak to those who are of age to be confirmed three separate sermons on three separate parts of these verses. First, to those whom St. John calls little children; next, to those whom he calls grown men. To the first I will speak to-day; to the latter, by God's help, next Sunday. And may the Blessed One bring home my weak words to all your hearts!

Now for the meaning of 'little children.' There are those who will tell you that those words mean merely 'weak believers,' 'babes in grace,' and so on. They mean that, no doubt; but they mean much more. They mean, first of all, be sure, what they say. St. John would not have said 'little children,' if he had not meant little children. Surely, God's apostle did not throw about his words at random, so as to leave them open to mistakes, and to want some one to step in and tell us that they do not mean their plain, common-sense meaning, but something else. Holy Scripture is too wisely written, and too awful a matter, to be trifled with in that way, and cut and squared to suit our own fancies, and explained away till its blessed promises are made to mean anything or nothing.

No! By little children, St. John means here children in age —of course *Christian* children and young people, for he was writing only to Christians. He speaks to those who have been christened, and brought up, more or less, as christened children should be. But, no doubt, when he says little children, he means also all Christian people, whether they be young or old, whose souls are still young, and weak, and unlearned. All, however old they may be, who have not been confirmed—I do not merely mean confirmed by the bishop, but confirmed by God's grace,—all those who have not yet come to a full knowledge of their own sins,—all who have not yet been converted, and turned to God with their whole hearts and wills, who have not yet made their full choice between God and sin,—all who have not yet fought for themselves the battle which no man or angel can fight for them—I mean the battle between their selfishness and their duty—the battle between their love of pleasure and their fear of sin—the battle, in short, between the devil and his temptations to darkness and shame, and God and his promises of light, and strength, and glory,—all who have not been converted to God, to them St. John speaks as little children— people who are not yet strong enough to stand alone, and do their duty on God's side against sin, the world, and the devil. And all of you here who have not yet made up your minds, who have not yet been confirmed in soul,—whether you were confirmed by the bishop or not,—to you I speak this day.

Now, first of all, consider this,—that though St. John calls you 'little children,' because you are still weak, and your souls have not grown to manhood, yet he does not speak to you as if you were heathens and knew nothing about God: he says, 'I have written unto you, little children, because ye have known the Father.' Consider that; that was his reason for all that he had written to them before; that they had known the Father, the God who made heaven and earth—the Father of our Lord

Jesus Christ—the Father of little children—my Father and your Father, my friends, little as we may behave like what we are, sons of the Almighty God. That was St. John's reason for speaking to little children, because they had already known the Father. So he does not speak to them as if they were heathens; and I dare not speak to you, young people, as if you were heathens, however foolish and sinful some of you may be; I dare not do it, whatever many preachers may do now-a-days; not because I should be unfair and hard upon you merely, but because I should lie, and deny the great grace and mercy which God has shown you, and count the blood of the covenant, with which you were sprinkled at baptism, an unholy thing; and do despite to the spirit of grace which has been struggling in your hearts, trying to lead you out of sin into good, out of darkness into light, ever since you were born. Therefore, as St. John said, I say, I preach this day to you, young people, because you have known your Father in heaven!

But some of you may say to me, 'You put a great honour on us; but we do not see that we have any right to it. You tell us that we have a very noble and awful knowledge—that we know the Father. We are afraid we do not know Him; we do not even rightly understand of whom or what you preach.'

Well, my young friends, these are very awful words of St. John; such blessed and wonderful words, that if we did not find them in the Bible, it would be madness and insolence to God of us to say such a thing, not merely of little children, but even of the greatest, and wisest, and holiest man who ever lived; but there they are in the Bible—the blessed Lord Himself has told us all, 'When ye pray, say, Our Father in heaven;'—and I dare not keep them back because they sound strange. They may *sound* strange, but they *are not* strange. Any one who has ever watched a young child's heart, and seen how naturally and at once the little innocent takes in the thought of his Father which is in heaven, knows that it is not a strange thought—that it comes to a little child almost by instinct—that his Father in heaven seems often to be just the thought which fills his heart most completely, has most power over him,—the thought which has been lying ready in his heart all the time, only waiting for some one to awaken it, and put it into words for him; that he will do right when you put him in mind of his Father above the skies sooner than he will for a hundred punishments. For truly says the poet—

> Heaven lies about us in our infancy,
> Not in complete forgetfulness,
> Nor yet in utter nakedness,
> But trailing clouds of glory do we come,
> From God who is our home!

And yet more truly said the Blessed One Himself, that 'children's angels always behold the face of our Father which is in heaven;' and that 'of such is the kingdom of heaven.' But you may say, some of you, perhaps, 'Whatever knowledge of our Father in heaven we had, or ought to have had, when we were young, we have lost it now. We have forgotten what we learnt at school. We have been what you would call sinful; at all events we have been thinking all our time about a great many things beside religion, and they have quite put out of our head the thought that God is our Father. So how have we known our Father in heaven?'

Well, then, to answer that,—consider the case of your earthly fathers, the men who begot you and brought you up. Now, there might be one of you who had never seen his father since he was born, but all he knows of him is, that his name is so and so, and that he is such and such a sort of man, as the case might be; and that he lives in such and such a place, far away, and that now and then he hears talk of his father, or receives letters or presents from him. Suppose I asked that young man, Do you know your father? would he not answer—would he not have a right to answer, 'Yes, I know him. I never saw him, or was acquainted with him, but I *know* him well enough;

I know who he is, and where to find him, and what sort of a man he is.' That young man might not know his father's face, or love him, or care for him at all. He might have been disobedient to his father; he might have forgotten for years that he had a father at all, and might have lived on his own way, just as if he had no father. But when he was put in mind of it all, would he not say at once, 'Yes, I know my father well enough; his name is so and so, and he lives at such and such a place? I know my father.'

Well, my young friends, and if this would be true of your fathers on earth, it is just as true of your Father in heaven. You have never seen Him—you may have forgotten Him—you may have disobeyed Him—you may have lived on your own way, as if you had no Father in heaven; still you know that you have a Father in heaven. You pray, surely, sometimes. What do you say? 'Our Father which art in heaven.' So you have a Father in heaven, else what right have you to use those words,—what right have you to say to God, 'Our Father in heaven,' if you believe that you have no Father there? That would be only blasphemy and mockery. I can well understand that you have often said those words without thinking of them —without thinking what a blessed, glorious, soul-saving meaning there was in them; but I will not believe that you never once in your whole lives said, 'Our Father which art in heaven,' without believing them to be true words. What I want is, for you *always* to believe them true. Oh, young men and young women, boys and girls—believe those words, believe that when you say, 'Our Father which art in heaven,' you speak God's truth about yourselves; that the evil devil rages when he hears you speak those words, because they are the words which prove that you do not belong to him and to hell, but to God and the kingdom of heaven. Oh, believe those words—behave as if you believed those words, and you shall see what will come of them, through all eternity for ever.

Well, but you will ask, What has all this to do with confirmation. It has everything to do with confirmation. Because you are God's children, and know that you are God's children, you are to go and confirm before the bishop your right to be called God's children. You are to go and claim your share in God's kingdom. If you were heir to an estate, you would go and claim your estate from those who held it. You are heirs to an estate—you are heirs to the kingdom of heaven; go to confirmation, and claim that kingdom; say, 'I am a citizen of God's kingdom. Before the bishop and the congregation, here I proclaim the honour which God has put upon me.' If you have a father, you will surely not be ashamed to own him! How much more when the Almighty God of heaven is your Father! You will not be ashamed to own Him? Then go to confirmation; for by doing so you own God for your Father. If you have an earthly father, you will not be ashamed to say, 'I know I ought to honour him and obey him;' how much more when your father is the Almighty God of heaven, who sent His own Son into the world to die for you, who is daily heaping you with blessings body and soul! You will not be ashamed to confess that you ought to honour and obey Him? Then go to confirmation and say, 'I here take upon myself the vow and promise made for me at my baptism. I am God's child, and therefore I will honour, love, and obey Him. It is my duty; and it shall be my delight henceforward to work for God, to do all the good I can to my life's end, because my Father in heaven loves the good, and has commanded me, poor, weak countryman though I be, to work for Him in well-doing.' So I say, if God is your Father, go and own Him at confirmation. If God is your Father, go and promise to love and obey Him at confirmation; and see if He does not, like a strong and loving Father as He is, confirm you in return,—see if He does not give you strength of heart and peace of mind, and clear, quiet, pure thoughts, such as a man or woman ought to have who considers that the great God, who made the sky and stars above their heads, is their Father. But perhaps there are some of you, young people, who do not wish to be confirmed. And why? Now, look honestly into your own hearts and see the reason. Is it not, after all, because you don't like *the trouble?* Because you are afraid that being confirmed will force you to think seriously and be religious; and you had rather not take all that trouble yet? Is it not because you do not like to look your own selves in the face, and see how foolishly you have been living, and how many bad habits you will have to give up, and what a thorough conversion and change you must make, if you are to be confirmed in earnest? Is not this why you do not wish to be confirmed? And what does that all come to? That though you know that you are God's children, you do not like to tell people publicly that you are God's children, lest they should expect you to behave like God's children—that is it. Now, young men and young women, think seriously once for all; if you have any common *sense*—I do not say grace—left in you, think! Are you not playing a fearful game? You would not dare to deny your fathers on earth—to refuse to obey them; because you know well enough that they would punish you—that if you were too old for punishment, your neighbours, at least, would despise you for mean, ungrateful, and rebellious children! But because you cannot *see* God your Father, because you have not some sign or wonder hanging in the sky to frighten you into good behavour, therefore you are not afraid to turn your backs on Him. My friends, it is ill mocking the living God. Mark my words! If a man will not turn, He will whet his sword, and make us feel it. You who can be confirmed, and know in your hearts that you ought to be confirmed, and ought to be *really* converted and confirmed in soul, and make no mockery of it,—mark my words! If you will not be converted and confirmed of your own good will, God, if He has any love left for you, will convert and confirm you against your will. He will let you go your own ways till you find out your own folly. He will bring you low with affliction perhaps with sickness, with misfortune, with shame. Some way or other, He will chastise you, again and again, till you are forced to come back to Him, and take His service on you. If He loves you, He will drive you home to your Father's house. You may laugh at my words now—see if you laugh at them when your hairs are grey. Oh, young people, if you wish in after-life to save yourselves shame and sorrow, and perhaps, in the world to come, eternal death, come to confirmation, acknowledge God for your Father, promise to come and serve Him faithfully, make those blessed words of the Lord's Prayer, 'Our Father in heaven,' your glory and your honour, your guide and guard through life, your title-deeds to heaven. You who know that the Great God is your Father, will you be ashamed to own yourselves His sons?

SERMON XV.

THE TRANSFIGURATION.

MARK ix. 2.

Jesus taketh Peter, and James, and John, and leadeth them up into a high mountain apart, and was transfigured before them.

THE second lesson for this morning's service brings us to one of the most wonderful passages in our blessed Saviour's whole stay on earth, namely, His transfiguration. The story, as told by the different Evangelists, is this—That our Lord took Peter, and John, and James his brother, and led them up into a high mountain apart, which mountain may be seen to this very day. It is a high peaked hill, standing apart from all the hills around it, with a small smooth space of ground upon the top, very fit, from its height and its loneliness, for a transaction like the transfiguration, which our Lord wished no one but these three to behold. There the apostles fell asleep; while our blessed Lord, who had deeper thoughts in His heart than they had, knelt down and prayed to *His* Father and *our* Father, which is in heaven. And as He prayed, the form of his countenance was changed, and His raiment became shining, white as the light; and there appeared Moses and Elijah talking with Him. They talked of matters which the angels desire to look into, of the greatest matters that ever happened in this earth since it was made; of the redemption of the world, and of the

THE TRANSFIGURATION.

death which Christ was to undergo at Jerusalem. And as they were talking, the apostles awoke, and found into what glorious company they had fallen while they slept. What they felt no mortal man can tell—that moment was worth to them all the years they had lived before. When they had gone up with Jesus into the mount, He was but the poor carpenter's son, wonderful enough to *them*, no doubt, with His wise, searching words, and His gentle, loving looks, that drew to Him all men who had hearts left in them, and wonderful enough, too, from all the mighty miracles which they had seen Him do; but still He was merely a man like themselves, poor and young, and homeless, who felt the heat, and the cold, and the rough roads, as much as they did. They could feel that He spake as never man spake—they could see that God's spirit and power was on Him as it had never been on any man in their time. God had even enlightened their reason by His spirit, to know that He was the Christ, the Son of the living God. But still it does seem they did not fully understand who and what He was; they could not understand how the Son of God should come in the form of a despised and humble man; they did not understand that His glory was to be a spiritual glory. They expected His kingdom to be a kingdom of this world—they expected His glory to consist in palaces, and armies, and riches, and jewels, and all the magnificence with which Solomon and the old Jewish kings were adorned; they thought that He was to conquer back again from the Roman emperor all the inestimable treasures of which the Romans had robbed the Jews, and that He was to make the Jewish nation, like the Roman, the conquerers and masters of all the nations of the earth. So that it was a puzzling thing to their minds why He should be King of the Jews at the very time that He was reputed to be but a poor man's son, living on charity. It was to show them that His kingdom was the kingdom of heaven that He was transfigured before them.

They saw His glory—the glory as of the only-begotten of the

Father, full of grace and truth. The form of His countenance was changed; all the majesty, and courage, and wisdom, and love, and resignation, and pity, that lay in His noble heart, shone out through His face, while He spoke of His death which He should accomplish at Jerusalem—the Holy Ghost that was upon Him, the spirit of wisdom, and love, and beauty —the spirit which produces everything that is lovely in heaven and earth, in soul and body, blazed out through his eyes, and all His glorious countenance, and made Him look like what He was—a God. My friends, what a sight! Would it not be worth while to journey thousands of miles—to go through all difficulties, dangers, that man ever heard of, for one sight of that glorious face, that we might fall down upon our knees before it, and, if it were but for a moment, give way to the delight of finding something that we could utterly love and utterly adore? I say, the delight of finding something to worship; for if there is a noble, if there is a holy, if there is a spiritual feeling in man, it is the feeling which bows him down before those who are greater, and wiser, and holier than himself. I say, that feeling of respect for what is noble is a heavenly feeling. The man who has lost it—the man who feels no respect for those who are above him in age, above him in knowledge, above him in wisdom, above him in goodness, *that* man shall in nowise enter into the kingdom of heaven. It is only the man who is like a little child, and feels the delight of having some one to look up to, who will ever feel delight in looking up to Jesus Christ, who is the Lord of lords, and King of kings. It was the want of respect, it was the dislike of feeling any one superior to himself, which made the devil rebel against God, and fall from heaven. It will be the feeling of complete respect —the feeling of kneeling at the feet of one who is immeasurably superior to ourselves in everything, that will make up the greatest happiness of heaven. This is a hard saying, and no man can understand it, save he to whom it is given by the Spirit of God.

That the apostles *had* this feeling of immeasurable respect for Christ there is no doubt, else they would never have been apostles. But they felt more than this. There were other wonders in that glorious vision besides the countenance of our Lord. His raiment, too, was changed, and became all brilliant, white as the light itself. Was not *that* a lesson to them? Was it not as if our Lord had said to them, 'I am a king, and have put on glorious apparel, but whence does the glory of my raiment come? *I* have no need of fine linen, and purple, and embroidery, the work of men's hands; *I* have no need to send my subjects to mines and caves to dig gold and jewels to adorn my crown: the earth is mine, and the fulness thereof. All this glorious earth, with its trees and its flowers, its sunbeams and its storms, is *mine*. *I* made it—*I* can do what I will with it. All the mysterious laws by which the light and the heat flow out for ever from God's throne, to lighten the sun, and the moon, and the stars of heaven—they are mine. *I* am the light of the world—the light of men's bodies as well as of their souls; and here is my proof of it. Look at me. I am He that "decketh himself with light as it were with a garment, who layeth the beams of His chambers in the waters, and walketh upon the wings of the wind."' This was the message which Christ's glory brought the apostles—a message which they could never forget. The spiritual glory of His countenance had shown them that He was a spiritual king—that His strength lay in the spirit of power, and wisdom, and beauty, and love, which God had given Him without measure; and it showed them, too, that there was such a thing as a spiritual body, such a body as each of us some day shall have if we be found in Christ at the resurrection of the just—a body which shall not hide a man's spirit when it becomes subject to the wear and tear of life, and disease, and decay; but a spiritual body—a body which shall be filled with our spirits, which shall be perfectly obedient to our spirits—a body through which the glory of our spirits shall shine out, as the glory of Christ's spirit shone out through His body at the transfiguration. 'Brethren, we know not yet what we shall be, but this we do know, that when He shall appear, we shall be *like Him*, for we shall see Him as He is.' (1 John iii. 3.)

Thus our Lord taught them by His appearance that there is such a thing as a spiritual body, while, by the glory of His raiment, in addition to His other miracles, He taught them that He had power over the laws of nature, and could, in his own good time, 'change the bodies of their humiliation, that they might be made like unto His glorious body, according to the mighty working by which He is able to subdue all things to Himself.'

But there was yet another lesson which the apostles learnt from the transfiguration of our Lord. They beheld Moses and Elijah talking with Him :—Moses, the great lawgiver of their nation ; Elijah, the chief of all the Jewish prophets. We must consider this a little to find out the whole depth of its meaning. You remember how Christ had spoken of Himself as having come, not to destroy the Law and the Prophets, but to fulfil them. You remember, too, how He had always said that He was the person of whom the Law and the Prophets had spoken.

Here was an actual sign and witness that His words were true—here was Moses, the giver of the Law, and Elijah, the chief of the Prophets, talking with Him, bearing witness to Him in their own persons, and showing, too, that it was His death and His perfect sacrifice that they had been shadowing forth in the sacrifices of the law and in the dark speeches of prophecy. For they talked with Him of His death, which He was to accomplish at Jerusalem. What more perfect testimony could the apostles have had to show them that Jesus of Nazareth, their Master, was He of whom the Law and the Prophets spoke —that He was indeed the Christ for whom Moses and Elijah, and all the saints of old, had looked ; and that He was come not to destroy the Law and the Prophets, but to fulfil them? We can hardly understand the awe and the delight with which the disciples must have beheld those blessed Three—Moses, and Elias, and Jesus Christ, their Lord—talking together before their very eyes. For of all men in the world, Moses and Elias were to them the greatest. All true-hearted Israelites, who knew the history of their nation, and understood the promises of God, must have felt that Moses and Elias were the two greatest heroes and saviours of their nation, whom God had ever yet raised up. And the joy and the honour of thus seeing them face to face, the very men whom they had loved and reverenced in their thoughts, whom they had heard and read of from their childhood, as the greatest ornaments and glories of their nation—the joy and the honour, I say, of that unexpected sight, added to the wonderful majesty which was suddenly revealed to their transfigured Lord, seemed to have been too much for them—they knew not what to say. Such company seemed to them for a moment heaven enough; and St. Peter, first finding words, exclaimed, 'Lord, it is good for us to be here. If Thou wilt, let us build three tabernacles, one for Thee, and one for Moses, and one for Elias.' Not, I fancy, that they intended to worship Moses and Elias, but that they felt that Moses and Elias, as well as Christ, had each a divine message, which must be listened to; and therefore they wished that each of them might have his own tabernacle, and dwell among men, and each teach his own particular doctrine and wisdom in his own school. It may seem strange that they should put Moses and Elias so on an equality with Christ; but the truth was, that as yet they understood Moses and Elias better than they did Christ. They had heard and read of Moses and Elijah all their lives—they were acquainted with all their actions and words—they knew thoroughly what great and noble men the Spirit of God had made them, but they did *not* understand Christ in like manner. They did not yet *feel* that God had given Him the Spirit without measure—they did not understand that He was not only to be a lawgiver and a prophet, but a sacrifice for sin, the conqueror of death and hell, who was to lead captivity captive, and receive inestimable gifts for men. Much less did they think that Moses and Elijah were but His servants—that all *their* spirit and *their* power had been given by Him. But this also they were taught a moment afterwards; for a bright cloud overshadowed them, hiding from them the glory of God the Father, whom no man hath seen or can see, who dwells in the light which no man can approach unto; and out of that cloud, a voice saying, 'This is my beloved Son; hear ye Him;' and then, hiding their faces in fear and wonder, they fell to the ground; and when they looked up, the vision and the voice had alike passed away, and they saw no man but Christ alone. Was not that enough for them? Must not the meaning of the vision have been plain to them? They surely understood from it that Moses and Elijah were, as they had ever believed them to·be, great and good, true messengers of the living God; but that their message and their work was done—that Christ, whom they had looked for, was come—that all the types of the law were realized, and all the prophecies fulfilled, and that henceforward Christ, and Christ alone, was to be their Prophet and their Lawgiver. Was not this plainly the meaning of the Divine voice? For when they wished to build three tabernacles, and to honour Moses and Elijah, the Law and the Prophets, as separate from Christ— that moment the heavenly voice warned them: ' *This—this* is my beloved Son—hear ye *Him*, and Him only, henceforward.' And Moses and Elijah, their work being done, forthwith vanished away, leaving Christ alone to fulfil the Law and the Prophets, and all other wisdom and righteousness that ever was or shall be. This is another lesson which Christ's transfiguration was meant to teach them and us, that Christ alone is to be henceforward our guide; that no philosophies or doctrines of any sort which are not founded on a true faith in Jesus Christ, and His life and death, are worth listening to; that God has manifested forth His beloved Son, and that Him, and Him only, we are to hear. I do not mean to say that Christ came into the world to put down human learning. I do not mean that we are to despise human learning, as so many are apt to do now-a-days; for Christ came into the world not to destroy human learning, but to fulfil it—to sanctify it—to make human learning true, and strong, and useful, by giving it a sure foundation to stand upon, which is the belief and knowledge of His blessed self. Just as Christ came not to destroy the Law and the Prophets, but to fulfil them—to give them a spirit and a depth in men's eyes which they never had before—just so He came to fulfil all true philosophies, all the deep thoughts which men had ever thought about this wonderful world and their own souls, by giving *them* a spirit and a depth which *they* never had before. Therefore, let no man tempt you to despise learning, for it is holy to the Lord.

There is one more lesson which we may learn from our Lord's transfiguration. When St. Peter said, 'Lord, it is good for us to be here,' he spoke a truth. It *was* good for him to be there; nevertheless, Christ did not listen to his prayers. He and his two companions were not allowed to *stay* in that glorious company. And why? Because they had a work to do. They had glad tidings of great joy to proclaim to every creature, and it was, after all, but a selfish prayer, to wish to be allowed to stay in ease and glory on the mount while the whole world was struggling in sin and wickedness below them: for there is no meaning in a man's calling himself a Christian, or saying that he loves God, unless he is ready to hate what God hates and to fight against that which Christ fought against, that is sin. No one has any right to call himself a servant of God, who is not trying to do away with some of the evil in the world around him. And therefore Christ was merciful, when, instead of listening to St. Peter's prayer, He led the apostles down again from the mount, and sent them forth, as he did afterwards, to preach the Gospel of the kingdom to all nations. For Christ put a higher honour on St. Peter by that than if He had let him stay on the mount all his life, to behold His glory, and worship and adore. And He made St. Peter more like Himself by doing so. For what was Christ's life? Not one of deep speculations, quiet thoughts, and bright visions, such as St. Peter wished to lead; but a life of fighting against evil; earnest, awful prayers and struggles within, continual labour of body and mind without, insult, and danger, and confusion, and violent exertion, and bitter sorrow. This was Christ's life—this is the life of almost every good man I ever heard of;—this was St. Peter, and St. James, and St. John's life afterwards. This was Christ's cup, which they were to drink of as well as He;—this was the baptism of fire with which they were to be baptized of as well as He;—this was to be their fight of faith;—this was the tribulation through which they, like all other great saints, were to enter into the kingdom of heaven; for it is certain that the harder a man fights against evil, the harder evil will fight against him in return; but it is certain too that the harder a man fights against evil, the more he is like his Saviour Christ, and the more glorious will be his reward in heaven. It is certain too that what was good for St. Peter is good for us. It is good for man to have holy and quiet thoughts, and at moments to see into the very deepest meaning of God's word and God's earth, and to have, as it were, heaven opened before his eyes; and it is good for a man sometimes actually to *feel* his heart overpowered with the glorious majesty of God, and to *feel* it gushing out with love to his blessed Saviour: but it is not good for him to stop there, any more than it was for the apostles: they had to leave that glorious vision and come down from the mount, and do Christ's work; and *so have we*; for, believe me, one word of warning spoken to keep a little child out of sin,—one crust of bread given to a beggarman, because he is your brother, for whom Christ died,—one angry word checked, when it is on your lips, for the sake of Him who was meek and lowly of heart; in short, any, the smallest endeavour of this kind to lessen the quantity of evil which is in yourselves, and in those around you, is worth all the speculations, and raptures, and visions, and frames, and feelings in the world; for those are the good *fruits* of faith, whereby alone the tree shall be known whether it be good or evil.

SERMON XVI.

THE CRUCIFIXION.

ISAIAH liii. 7.

He is brought as a lamb to the slaughter.

ON this day, my friends, was offered up upon the cross, the Lamb of God,—slain in eternity and heaven before the foundation of the world, but slain in time and space upon this day. All the old sacrifices, the lambs which were daily offered up to God in the Jewish Temple, the lambs which Abel, and after him the patriarchs offered up, the Paschal Lamb slain at the Passover, our Eastertide, all these were but figures of Christ—tokens of the awful and yet loving law of God, that without shedding of blood there is no remission of sin. But the blood of dumb animals could not take away sin. All mankind had sinned, and it was therefore necessary that all mankind should suffer. Therefore He suffered, the new Adam, the Man of all men, in whom all mankind were, as it were, collected into one and put on a new footing with God; that henceforward to be a man might mean to be a holy being, a forgiven being, a being joined to God, wearing the likeness of the Son of God—the human soul and body in which He offered up all human souls and bodies on the cross. For man was originally made in Christ's likeness; He was the Word of God who walked in the garden of Eden, who spoke to Adam with a human voice; He was the Lord who appeared to the patriarchs in a man's figure, and ate and drank in Abraham's tent, and spoke to him with a human voice; He was the God of Israel, whom the Jewish elders saw with their bodily eyes upon Mount Sinai, and under His feet a pavement as of a sapphire stone. From Him all man's powers came—man's speech, man's understanding. All that is truly noble in man was a dim pattern of Him in whose likeness man was originally made. And when man had fallen and sinned, and Christ's image was fading more and more out of him, and the likeness of the brutes growing more and more in him year by year, then came Christ, the head and original pattern of all men, to claim them for His own again, to do in their name what they could never do for themselves, to offer Himself up a sacrifice for the sins of the whole world : so that He is the real sacrifice, the real lamb; as St. John said when he pointed Him out to his disciples, 'Behold the Lamb of God, which taketh away the sin of the world!'

Oh, think of that strong and patient Lamb, who on this day showed Himself perfect in fortitude and nobleness, perfect in meekness and resignation. Think of Him who, in His utter love to us, endured the cross, despising the shame. And what a cross! Truly said the prophet, 'His visage was marred more than any man, and His form more than the sons of men:' in hunger and thirst, in tears and sighs, bruised and bleeding, His forehead crowned with thorns, His sides torn with scourges, His hands and feet gored with nails, His limbs stretched from their sockets, naked upon the shameful cross, the Son of God hung, lingering slowly towards the last gasp, in the death of the felon and the slave! The most shameful sight that this earth ever saw, and yet the most glorious sight. The most shameful sight, at which the sun in heaven veiled his face, as if ashamed, and the skies grew black, as if to hide those bleeding limbs from the foul eyes of men; and yet the noblest sight, for in that death upon the cross shone out the utter fulness of all holiness, the utter fulness of all fortitude, the utter fulness of that self-sacrificing love which had said, 'The Son of Man came to seek and to save that which was lost;' the utter fulness of obedient patience, which could say, 'Father, not My will, but Thine be done;' the utter fulness of generous forgiveness, which could pray, 'Father, forgive them, for they know not what they do;' the utter fulness of noble fortitude and endurance, which could say at the very moment when a fearful death stared Him in the face, 'Thinkest thou that I cannot now pray to the Father, and He will send me at once more than twelve armies of angels? But how then would the Scriptures be fulfilled that thus it must be?'

Oh, my friends, look to Him, the author and perfecter of all faith, all trust, all loyal daring for the sake of duty and of God! Look at His patience. See how He endured the cross, despising the shame. See how He endured—how patience had her perfect work in Him—how in all things He was more than conqueror. What gentleness, what calmness, what silence, what infinite depths of Divine love within Him! A heart which neither shame, nor torture, nor insult, could stir from its God-like resolution. When looking down from that cross He beheld none almost but enemies, heard no word but mockery; when those who passed by reviled Him, wagging their heads and saying, 'He saved others, Himself He cannot save;' His only answer was a prayer for forgiveness for that besottec mob who were yelling beneath Him like hounds about theii game. Consider Him, and then consider ourselves, ruffled and put out of temper by the slightest cross accident, the slightest harsh word, too often by the slightest pain—not to mention insults, for we pride ourselves in not bearing them. Try, my friends, if you can, even in the dimmest way, fancy yourselves for one instant in His place this day 1815 years. Fancy yourselves hanging on that cross—fancy that mocking mob below—fancy—but I dare not go on with the picture. Only think—think what would have been *your* temper there, and then you may get some slight notion of the boundless love and the boundless endurance of the Saviour whom *we* love so little, for whose sake most of us will not endure the trouble of giving up a single sin.

And then consider that it was all of His own free will; that at any moment, even while He was hanging upon the cross, He might have called to earth and sun, to heaven and hell, 'Stop! thus far, but no further,' and they would have obeyed Him; and all that cross, and agony, and the fierce faces of those furious Jews, would have vanished away like a hideous dream when one awakes. For they lied in their mockery. Any moment He might have been free, triumphant again in His eternal bliss, but He would not. He Himself kept Himself on that cross till His Father's will was fulfilled, and the sacrifice was finished, and we were saved. And then at last, when there was no more human nobleness, no more agony left for Him to fulfil, no gem in the crown of holiness which He had not won as His own; no drop in the cup of misery which He had not drained as His own; when at last He was made perfect through suffering, and His strength had been made perfect in weakness, then He bowed that bleeding, thorn-crowned head, and said, 'It is finished. Father, into Thy hands I commend my spirit.' And so He died.

How can our poor words, our poor deeds, thank Him? How mean and paltry our deepest gratitude, our highest loyalty, when compared with Him to whom it is due—that adorable victim, that perfect sin-offering, who this day offered up Himself upon the altar of the cross, in the fire of His own boundless zeal for the kingdom of God, His Father, and of His boundless love for us, His sinful brothers! 'Oh, thou blessed Jesus! Saviour agonizing for us! God Almighty, who didst make Thyself weak for the love of us! oh, write that love upon our hearts so deeply that neither pleasure nor sorrow, life nor death, may wipe it away! Thou hast sacrificed Thyself for us; oh, give us the hearts to sacrifice ourselves for Thee! Thou art the Vine, we are the branches. Let Thy priceless blood shed for us on this day flow like life-giving sap through all our hearts and minds, and fill us with Thy righteousness, that we may be sacrifices fit for Thee. Stir us up to offer to Thee, O Lord, our bodies, our souls, our spirits, in all we love and all we learn, in all we plan and all we do, to offer our labours, our pleasures, our sorrows, to Thee; to work for Thy kingdom through them, to live as those who are not their own, but bought with Thy blood, fed with Thy body; and enable us now, in Thy most holy Sacrament, to offer to Thee our repentance, our faith, our prayers, our praises, living, reasonable, and spiritual sacrifices,—Thine from our birth-hour, Thine now, and Thine for ever!'

SERMON XVII.

THE RESURRECTION.

LUKE XXIV. 6.

He is not here—He is risen.

WE are assembled here to-day, my friends, to celebrate the joyful memory of our blessed Saviour's Resurrection. All Friday night, Saturday, and Saturday night, His body lay in the grave; His soul was—where we cannot tell. St. Peter tells that He went and preached to the spirits in prison—the sinners of the old world, who are kept in the place of departed souls —most likely in the depths of the earth, in the great fire-kingdom, which boils and flames miles below our feet, and breaks out here and there through the earth's solid crust in burning mountains and streams of fire. There some say—and the Bible seems to say—sinful souls are kept in chains until the judgment-day; and hither they say Christ went to preach—no doubt to save some of those sinful souls who had never heard of Him. However this may be, for those two nights and day there was no sign, no stir in the grave where Christ was laid. His body seemed dead—the stone lay still over the mouth of the tomb where Joseph and Nicodemus laid him; the seal which Pilate had put on it was unbroken; the soldiers watched and watched, but no one stirred; the priests and Pharisees were keeping their sham Passover, thinking, no doubt, that they were well rid of Christ and of His rebukes for ever.

THE RESURRECTION.

But early on the Sunday morn—this day, as it might be—in the grey dawn of morning there came a change—a wondrous change. There was a great earthquake; the solid ground and rocks were stirred—the angel of the Lord came down from heaven, and rolled back the stone from the door, and sat upon it, waiting for the King of glory to arise from His slumber, and go forth the conqueror of Death.

His countenance was like lightning, and His raiment white as snow; and for fear of Him those fierce, hard soldiers, who feared neither God nor man, shook, and became as dead men. And Christ arose and went forth. *How* He rose—how He looked when He arose, no man can tell, for no man saw. Only before the sun was risen came Mary Magdalene, and the other Mary, and found the stone rolled away, and saw the angel sitting clothed in white, who said, 'Fear not, for I know that ye seek Jesus, who was crucified. He is not here, for He is risen. Come, see the place where the Lord lay.'

What must they have thought, poor, faithful souls, who came, lonely and broken-hearted, to see the place where *He*, their only hope, was, as they thought, shut up and lost for ever, to hear that He was risen and gone? Half terrified, half delighted, they went back with other women who had come on the same errand, with spices to anoint the blessed body, and told the apostles. Peter and John ran to the sepulchre, and saw the linen clothes lie, and the napkin that was about His blessed head, wrapped together by itself. They then believed. Then first broke on them the meaning of His old saying, that He must rise from the dead; and so, wondering and doubting what to do, they went back home.

But Mary—faithful, humble Mary—stood without, by the sepulchre, weeping. The angel called to her, 'Woman, why weepest thou?' 'They have taken away my Lord,' said she; 'and I know not where they have laid Him.'

Then, in a moment, out of the air, He appeared behind her. His body had been changed; it was now a glorified, spiritual body, which could appear and disappear when and how He liked. She turned back, and saw Him standing, but she knew Him not. A wondrous change had come over Him since last she saw Him hanging, bleeding, pale, and dying, on the cross of shame. 'Woman,' said He, 'why weepest thou?' She, fancying it was the gardener, said to Him, 'Sir, if thou hast borne Him hence, tell me where thou hast laid Him, and I will take Him away.' Jesus said to her, 'Mary.' At the sound of that beloved voice—His own voice—calling her by her name, her recollection came back to her. She knew Him—knew Him for her risen Lord; and, falling at His feet, cried out, 'My Master!'

So Jesus Christ, the Son of God, rose from the dead!

Now come the questions, *Why* did Christ rise from the dead?—and *how* did He rise? And, first, I will say a few words about *how* He rose from the dead. And this the Bible will answer for us, as it will everything else about the spirit-world. Christ, says the Bible, was put to death in the flesh; but quickened, that is, brought to life, by the Spirit. Now, what is the Spirit but the Lord and Giver of Life,—life of all sorts—life to the soul—life to the body—life to the trees and plants around us? With that Spirit Christ is filled infinitely without measure; it is *His* spirit. He is the Prince of Life; and the Spirit which gives life is His Spirit, proceeding from the Father and the Son. *Therefore* the gates of hell could not prevail against Him—*therefore* the heavy gravestone could not hold Him down—*therefore* His flesh could not see corruption and decay as other bodies do; not because His *body* was different from other bodies in its substance, but because *He* was filled, body and soul, with the great Spirit of Life. For this is the great business of the Spirit of God, in all nature, to bring life out of death—new generations out of old. What says David? 'When Thou, O God, turnest away Thy face, things die and return again to the dust; when Thou lettest Thy breath (which is the same as Thy Spirit) go forth, they are made, and Thou renewest the face of the earth.' This is the way that seeds, instead of rotting and perishing, spring up and become new plants—God breathes His spirit on them. The seeds must have heat, and damp, and darkness, and electricity, before they can sprout; but the heat, and damp, and darkness do not make them sprout; they want something more to do that. A philosopher can find out exactly what a seed is made of, and he might make a seed of the proper materials, and put it in the ground, and electrify it— but would it grow? Not it. To grow it must have life—life from the fountain of life—from God's Spirit. All the philosophers in the world have never yet been able, among all the things which they have made, to make a single living thing— and say they never shall; because, put together all they will, still one thing is wanting—*life*, which God alone can give. Why do I say this? To show you what God's Spirit is; to put you in mind that it is near you, above you, and beneath you, about your path in your daily walk. And also to explain to you how Christ rose by that Spirit,—how your bodies, if you claim your share in Christ's Spirit, may rise by it too.

You can see now, how Christ, being filled with God's Spirit rose of Himself. People had risen from the dead before Christ's time, but they had been either raised in answer to the prayers of holy men who had God's Spirit, or at some peculiar time when heaven was opened, and God chose to alter His laws (as we call it) for a moment.

But here was a Man who rose of Himself. He was raised by God, and therefore He raised Himself, for He was God.

You all know what life and power a man's own spirit will often give him. You may have heard of 'spirited' men in great danger, or 'spirited' soldiers in battle; when faint, wounded, having suffered enough, apparently, to kill them twice over, still struggling or fighting on, and doing the most desperate deeds to the last, from the strength and courage of their spirits conquering pain and weakness, and keeping off, for a time, death itself. We all know how madmen, diseased in their spirits, will, when the fit is on them, have for a few minutes ten men's strength. Well, just think, if a man's own spirit, when it is powerful, can give his body such life and force, what must it have been with Christ, who was filled full of *the* Spirit—God's Spirit, the Lord and Giver of life. The Lord could not *help* rising. All the disease, and poison, and rottenness in the world, could not have made His body decay: mountains on mountains could not have kept it down. His body—the Prince of Life!—He that was the life itself! It was impossible that death could hold Him.

And does not this show us *why* He rose, that we might rise with Him? What did He say about His own death? 'Except a corn of wheat fall into the ground and die, it abideth alone, but if it die it bringeth forth much fruit.' He was the grain which fell into the ground and died, and from His dead body sprung up another body—His glorified body; and we, His church, His people, fed with that body—His members, however strange it may sound—St. Paul said it, and therefore I dare to say it, little as I know what it means—members of His flesh and of His bones. But think! Remember what St. Paul tells you about this very matter in that glorious chapter which is read in the burial service, 'how when thou sowest seed, thou sowest not that body which it will have, but bare grain; but God gives it a body as it hath pleased Him, and to every seed its own body.' For the wheat-plant is in reality the same thing as the wheat-seed, and its life the same life, different as the outside of it may look. Dig it up just at this time of year, and you will find the seed-corn all gone, sucked dry; the life of the wheat-seed has formed it into a wheat plant—yet it is the same individual thing. The substance of the seed has gone into the root and the young blade; but it is the same individual substance. You know it is, and though you cannot tell why, yet you say, 'What a fine plant that seed has grown into,' because you feel it is so, that the seed is the very same thing as the plant which springs up from it, though its shape is changed, and its size, and its colour, and the very stuff of which it was made is changed, since it was a mere seed. And yet it is at bottom the same individual thing as the seed was, with a new body and shape.

So with Christ's body. It was changed after He rose. It had gone through pain, and weakness, and death, gone down to the lowest depth of them, and conquered them, and passed triumphant through them and far beyond their power. His body was now a nobler, a more beautiful, a glorified body, a spiritual body, one which could do whatever His Spirit chose to make it do, one which could never die again, one which could come through closed doors, appear and vanish as He liked, instead of being bound to walk the earth, and stand cold and heat, sickness and weariness.

Yet it was the very same body, just as the wheat-plant is the same as the wheat-seed—the very same body. Everyone knew His face again after His resurrection. There was the very print of the nails to be seen in His hands and feet, the spear wound in His blessed side. So shall it be with us, my friends. We shall rise again, and we shall be the same as we are now, and yet not the same ; our bodies shall be the same bodies, and yet nobler, purer, spiritual bodies, which can know neither death, nor pain, nor weariness. Then, never care, my friends, if we drop like ripe grain into the bosom of mother earth,—if we are to spring up again as seedling plants, after death's long winter, on the resurrection morn. Truly says the poet,* how

> Mother earth, she gathers all
> Into her bosom, great and small:
> Oh, could we look into her face,
> We should not shrink from her embrace.

No, indeed! for if we look steadily with the wise, searching eye of faith into the face of mother earth, we shall see how death is but the gate of life, and this narrow churchyard, with

* Von Stolberg.

its corpses close-packed underneath the sod, would not seem to us a frightful charnel-house of corruption. No! it would seem like what it is—a blessed, quiet, seed-filled God's garden, in which our forefathers, after their long life-labour, lay sown by God's friendly hand, waiting peaceful, one and all, to spring up into leaf, and flower, and everlasting paradise-fruit, beneath the breath of God's Spirit at the last great day, when the Sun of Righteousness arises in glory, and the summer begins which shall never end.

One and all, did I say? Alas! would God it were so! We cannot hope as for all; but they are dead and gone, and we are not here to judge the dead. They have another Judge, and all shall be as He wills.

But we—we in whose limbs the breath of life still stirs—we who can still work, let us never forget all grain ripens not. There is some falls out of the ear unripe, and perishes; some is picked out by birds; some withers and decays in the ear, and yet gets into the barn with the ripe wheat, and is sown too with it, of which I never heard that any sprang up again—ploughed up again it may be—a withered, dead husk of chaff as it died, ploughed up to the resurrection of damnation to burn as chaff in unquenchable fire; but the good seed alone, ripe, and safe with the wheat-plant till it is ripe, that only will *spring up* to the resurrection of eternal life.

Now, consider again that parable of the wheat-plant. After it has sprung up, what does it next, but *tiller?*—and every new shoot that tillers out bears its own ear, ripens its own grain, twenty, thirty, or forty stems, and yet they are all the same plant, living with the life of that one original seed. So with Christ's Church—His body the Church. As soon as He rose, that new plant began to tiller. He did not keep His Spirit to Himself, but poured it out on the apostles, and from them it spread and spread—each generation of Christians ripening, and bearing fruit, and dying, a fresh generation of fruit springing up from them, and so on, as we are now at this day. And yet all these plants, these millions and millions of Christian men and women, who have lived since Christ's blessed resurrection, all are parts of that one original seed, the body of Christ, whose members they are, and all owe their life to that one spirit of Christ, which is in them all and through them all, as the life of the original grain is in the whole crop which springs from it.

And what can you learn from this? Learn this, that in Christ you are safe, out of Christ you are lost. But *really* in Christ, I mean—not like the dead and dying grains, mildewed and worm-eaten, which you find here and there on the finest wheat-plant. Their end is to be burned, and so will ours be, for all our springing out of Christ's root, if the angel reapers find us not good wheat, but chaff and mildew. Every branch in Christ which beareth not fruit, His heavenly Father taketh away. Therefore, never pride yourself on having been baptized into Christ, never pride yourself on showing some signs of God's Spirit, on being really good, right in this and right in that,—the question is, not so much, Are you *in Christ* at all, are you part of His tree, a member of His body? but, Are you *ripening* there? If you are not ripening, you are decaying, and your end will be as God has said. And do you wish to know whether you are in Christ, safe, ripening? see whether you are like Him. If the young grain does not show like the seed grain, you may be sure it is making no progress; and as surely as a wheat-plant never brought forth rye, or a grape-tree thistles, so surely, if you are not like Christ in your character, in patience, in meekness, in courage, truth, purity, piety, and love, you may be of His planting, but you are none of His ripening, and you will not be raised with Him at the last day, to flower anew in the gardens of Paradise, world without end.

SERMON XVIII.

IMPROVEMENT.

PSALM xcii. 12.

The righteous shall flourish like the palm-tree: he shall grow like the cedar in Lebanon. Those that be planted in the house of the Lord shall flourish in the courts of our God. They shall still bring forth fruit in old age: they shall be fat and flourishing.

THE Bible is always telling Christian people to *go forwards* —to grow—to become wiser and stronger, better and better day by day; that they ought to become better and better, because they can, if they choose, improve. This text tells us so; it says that we shall bring forth more fruit in our old age. Another text tells us, that 'those who wait on the Lord shall renew their strength;' another tells us, that we 'shall go from strength to strength.' Not one of St. Paul's Epistles but talks of growing in grace, and in the knowledge of God, of being *filled* with God's Spirit, of having our eyes more and more open to understand God's truth. Not one of St. Paul's Epistles but contains prayers of St. Paul that the men to whom he writes may become holier and wiser. And St. Paul says that he himself needed to go forward—that he wanted fresh strength—that he had to forget what was past, and consider all he had done and felt as nothing, and press forward to the prize of his high calling; that he needed to be daily conquering himself more and more, keeping down his bad feelings, hunting out one bad habit after another, lest, by any means when he had preached to others, he himself should become a castaway. Therefore, I said rightly, that the Bible is always bidding us to go forwards. You cannot read your Bibles without seeing this. What else was the use of St. Paul's Epistles? They were written to Christian men, redeemed men, converted men, most of them better, I fear, than ever we shall be; and for what? to tell them not to be content to remain as they were, but to go forwards, to improve, to remember that they were only just inside the gate of God's kingdom, and that if they would go on to perfection, they would find strength, and holiness, and blessing, and honour, and happiness, which they as yet did not dream of. 'Be ye perfect, even as your Father which is in heaven is perfect,' said our blessed Lord to all men. 'Be ye perfect,' says St. Paul to the Corinthians and the Ephesians, and all to whom he wrote; and so say I to you now in God's name, for Christ's sake, as citizens of God's kingdom, as heirs of everlasting glory, 'Be you perfect, even as your Father in heaven is perfect.'

Now, I ask you, my friends, is not this reasonable? It is reasonable, for the Bible always speaks of our souls as living things. It compares them to limbs of a body, to branches of a tree, often to separate plants—as in our Lord's parable of the tares and the wheat. Again, St. Paul tells us that we have been planted in baptism in the likeness of Christ's death; and again, in the 1st Psalm, which says that the good man shall be like a tree planted by the waterside; and again in the text of my sermon, which says, that 'those who are planted in the house of the Lord shall flourish in the courts of our God. They shall still bring forth fruit in old age: they shall be fat 'and flourishing.'

Now, what does all this mean? It means that the life of our souls is in some respects like the life of a plant; and therefore, that as plants grow, so our souls are to grow. Why do you plant anything, but in order that it may *grow*, and become larger, stronger, bear flower and fruit? Be sure God has planted us in His garden, Christ's Church, for no other reason. Consider again—What is life but a continual growing, or a continual decaying? If a tree does not get larger and stronger year by year, is not that a sure sign that it is unhealthy, and that decay has begun in it, that it is unsound at heart? And what happens then? It begins to become weaker and smaller, and cankered and choked with scurf and moss till it dies. If a tree is not growing, it is sure in the long run to be dying; and so are our souls. If they are not growing, they are dying; if they are not getting better, they are getting worse. This is why the Bible compares our souls to trees—not out of a mere pretty fancy of poetry, but for a great, awful, deep, world-wide lesson, that every tree in the fields may be a pattern, a warning, to us thoughtless men, that as that tree is meant to grow, so our souls are meant to grow. As that tree dies unless it grows, so our souls must die unless they grow. Consider that!

But how does a tree grow? How are our souls to grow? Now, here again, we shall understand heavenly things best by taking and considering the pattern from among earthly things which the Bible gives us—the tree, I mean. A tree grows in two ways. Its roots take up food from the ground, its leaves take up food from the air. Its roots are its mouth, we may say, and its leaves are its lungs. Thus the tree draws nourishment from the earth beneath, and from the heaven above; and so must our souls, my friends: if they are to live and grow, they must have food both from earth and from heaven. And this is what I mean—

Why has God given us senses, eyes, and ears, and understanding? That by them we may feed our souls with things which we see and hear—things which are going on in the world round us. We must read, and we must listen, and we must watch people and their sayings and doings, and what becomes of them, and we must try and act, and practise what is right for ourselves: and so we shall, by using our eyes and ears and our bodies, get practice, and experience, and knowledge, from the world around us—such as Solomon gives us in his Proverbs—and so our eyes, and ears, and understandings are to be to us like roots, by which we may feed our souls with earthly learning and experience. But is this enough? No, surely. Consider, again, God's example which He has given us—a tree. If you keep stripping all the leaves off a tree as fast as they grow, what becomes of it? It dies, because without leaves it cannot get nourishment from the air, and the rain, and the sunlight. Again, if you shut up a tree, where it can get neither rain, air, nor light, what happens? The tree certainly dies, though it may be planted in the very richest soil, and have the very strongest roots: and why?—because it can get no food from the sky above. So with our souls, my friends. If we get no food from above, our souls will die, though we have all the wit, and learning, and experience in the world. We must be fed, and strengthened, and satisfied, with the grace of God from above—with the Spirit of God. Consider how the Bible speaks of God's Spirit as the breath of God; for the very word *spirit* means, originally, breath, or air, or gas, or a breeze of wind, showing us that as without the airs of heaven the tree would become stunted and cankered, so our souls will without the fresh purifying breath of God's Spirit. Again, God's Spirit is often spoken of in Scripture as dew and rain. His grace, or favour, we read, is as dew on the grass; and again, that God shall come unto us as the rain, as the former and latter rain upon the earth; and again, speaking of the outpourings of God's Spirit on His Church, the Psalmist says, that ' He shall come down as the rain upon the mown grass, as showers that water the earth:' and to show us that as the tree puts forth buds and leaves, and tender wood, when it drinks in the dew and rains, so our hearts will become tender, and bud out into good thoughts and wise resolves, when God's Spirit fills them with His grace.

Moreover, the Scripture tells us again and again that our souls want light from above; and we all know by experience that the trees and plants which grow on the earth want the light of the sun to make them grow. So, doubtless, in this case also, the Scripture example of a tree will hold good. Now, what does the sunlight do for the tree? It does everything, for without light, the soil, and air, and rain, are all useless. It stirs up the sap, it hardens the wood, it brings out the blossom, it colours the leaves and the flowers, it ripens the fruit. The light is the life of the tree; and is there not one, my friends, of whom these words are written—that He is the Life, and that He is the Light—that He is the Sun of Righteousness and the bright and morning star—that He is the Light which lighteth every man that cometh into the world—that in Him was life, and the life was the light of men? Do you not know of whom I speak? Even of Him that was born at Bethelem and died on the cross, who now sits at God's right hand, praying for us, offering to us His body and His blood;—Jesus the Son of God. He is the Light and the Life. From Him alone our light must come, from Him alone our life must come, now and for ever, Oh, think seriously of this—and think too how a short time before He died on earth He spoke of Himself as the Bread of life—the living Bread which comes down from heaven; how He declared to men, that unless they eat His flesh and drink His blood, they have no life in them. And lastly, consider this, how the same night that He was betrayed, He took bread, and when He had given thanks, He brake it, and said, 'Take, eat; this is my body, which is given for you; this do in remembrance of me.' And how, likewise, He took the cup, and when He had blessed it, He gave it to them, saying, 'Drink ye all of this, for this is the new covenant in my blood, which is shed for you and for many, for the forgiveness of sins; this do, as oft as ye drink it, in remembrance of me.' Oh, consider these words, my friends—to you all and every one they were spoken. 'Drink ye *all* of this,' said the Blessed One; and will you refuse to drink it? He offers you the bread of life, the sign and the pledge of His body, which shall feed your souls with everlasting strength and life; and will you refuse what the Son of God offers you, what He bought for you with His death? God forbid, my friends! This is your blessed right and privilege—the right and the privilege of every one of you—to come freely and boldly to that holy table, and there to remember your Saviour. At that table to confess your Saviour before men —at that table to show that you really believe that Jesus Christ died for you—at that table to claim your share in the strength of His body, in the pardon of His blood, which cleanses from all sin—and at that table to receive what you claim, to receive at that table the wine, as a sign from Christ Himself, that His blood has washed away your sins; and the bread, as a sign that His body and His spirit are really feeding your spirits, that your souls are strengthened and refreshed by the body and blood of Christ, as your bodies are with the bread and wine. I have shown you that your souls must be fed from heaven,—that the Lord's Supper is a sign to you that they *are* fed from heaven. You pray to God, I hope, many of you, that He would give you His Holy Spirit, that He would change, and renew, and strengthen your souls—you pray God to do this, I hope. Well, then, there is the answer to your prayers. There your souls *will* be renewed and strengthened—there you will claim your share in Christ, who alone can renew and strengthen them The bread which is there broken is the communion, the sharing of the body of Christ; the cup which is there blessed is the communion of the blood of Christ: to that heavenly treat, to that spiritual food of your souls, Jesus Himself invites you, He who is the life of men. Do not let it be said at the last day of any one of you, that when the Son of God Himself invites you, you would not come to Him that you might have life.

SERMON XIX.

MAN'S WORKING DAY.

JOHN xi. 9, 10.

Jesus answered, Are there not twelve hours in the day? If any man walk in the day, he stumbleth not, because he seeth the light of this world. But if a man walk in the night, he stumbleth, because there is no light in him.

THIS was our blessed Lord's answer to His disciples when they said to Him, 'Master, the Jews of late tried to stone Thee, and goest Thou among them again?' And 'Jesus answered, Are there not twelve hours in the day? If any man walk in the day, he stumbleth not, because he seeth the light of this world. But if a man walk in the night, he stumbleth, because there is no light in him.'

Now, at first sight, one does not see what this has to do with the disciples' question—it seems no answer at all to it. But we must remember who it was who gave that answer. The Son of God, from whom all words come, who came to do good, and only good, every minute of his life. And, therefore, we may be sure that He never threw away a single word. And we must remember, too, to whom He spoke—to His disciples, whom He was training to be apostles to the whole world, teaching them in everything some deep lesson, to fit them for their glorious calling, as preachers of the good news of His coming. So we may be sure that He would never put off any question of theirs; we may be certain that whatever they asked Him, He would give them the best possible answer; not perhaps just the answer for which they wished, but the answer which would teach them most. Therefore I say, we must believe that there is some deep, wonderful lesson in this text—that it is the very best and fullest answer which our Lord could have made to His disciples when they asked Him why He was going again to Judea, where He stood in danger of His life.

Let us think a little about this text in faith, that is, sure that there is a deep, blessed meaning in it, if we can but find it out. Let us take it piece by piece; we shall never get to the bottom of it, of course, but we may get deep enough into it to set us thinking a little between now and next Sunday.

'Are there not twelve hours in the day?' said our Lord. We know there are, and we know, too, that if any man walks in the day, and keeps his eyes open, he does not stumble, because he has the light of this world to guide him. Twelve hours for business, and twelve for food, and sleep, and rest, is our rule for working men, or, indeed, not our rule, but God's. He has set the sun for the light of this world, to rule the day, to settle for us how long we are to work. In this country days vary. In summer they are more than twelve hours, and then men work early and late; but that is made up to us by winter, when the days are less than twelve hours, and men work short time. In the very cold countries, again, far away in the frozen north, the sun never sets all the summer, and never rises all the winter, and there is six months day and six months night. Wonderful! But even there God has fitted the land and men's lives to that strange climate, and they can gather in enough meat in the summer to keep them all the winter, that they may be able to spend the long six months' night of winter warm in their houses, sleeping and resting, with plenty of food. So that even to them there are twelve hours in the day, though their hours are each a fortnight long,—I mean a certain fixed time in which to work, and do the business which they have to do before the long frozen night comes wherein no man can work, because the sun, the light of this world, is hid from them below the ice for six whole months. So that our Lord's words hold true of all men, even of those people in the icy north. But in by far the most parts of the world, and especially in the hot countries, where our Lord lived, there are twelve common hours in every day, wherein men may and ought to work.

Now, what did our Lord mean by reminding His disciples of this, which they all knew already? He meant this,—that God His Father had appointed Him a certain work to do, and a certain time to do it in; that though His day was short, only thirty-three years in all, while we have, many of us, seventy years given us, yet that there were twelve hours in His day in which He must work—that God would take care that He lived out His appointed time, provided He was ready and earnest in doing God's work in it—and that He *must* work in that time which God had given Him, whatever came of it, and do His appointed work before the night of death came, in which no man can work.

There was a heathen king once, named Philip of Macedon, and a very wise king he was, though he was a heathen, and one of the wisest of his plans was this :—he had a slave, whom he ordered to come in to him every morning of his life, whatever he was doing, and say to him in a loud voice, 'Philip, remember that thou must die!'

He was a heathen, but a great many who call themselves Christians are not half so wise as he, for they take all possible care not to remember that they must die, but to *forget* that they must die; and yet every living man has a servant who, like King Philip's, puts him in mind, whether he likes it or not, that his day will run out at last, and his twelve hours of life be over, and then die he must. And who is that servant? A man's own body. Happy for him though if his body is his servant—not his *master* and his tyrant. But still, be that as it may, every finger-ache that one's body has, every cough and cold one's body catches, ought to be to us a warning like King Philip's servant, 'Remember that thou must die.' Every little pain and illness is a warning, a kindly hint from our Father in heaven, that we are doomed to death; that we have but twelve hours in this short day of life, and that the twelve must end; and that we must get our work done and our accounts settled, and be ready for our long journey, to meet our Father and our King, before the night comes wherein no man can work, but only take his wages; for them who have done good the wages of life eternal, and for them who have done evil—God help them! we know what is written—'the wages of sin is death!'

Now, observe next, that those who walk in the day do not stumble, because they see the light of this world, and those who walk in the night stumble—they have no light in them. If they are to see, it must be by the help of some light outside themselves, which is not part of themselves, or belonging to themselves at all. We only see by the light which God has made; when that is gone, our eyes are useless.

So it is with our souls. Our wits, however clever they may be, only understand things by the light which God throws on those things. He must explain and enlighten all things to us. Without His light—His Spirit, all the wit of the world is as useless as a pair of eyes in a dark night.

Now, this earthly world which we do see is an exact picture and pattern of the spiritual, heavenly world which we do not see; as Solomon says in the Proverbs, 'The things which are seen are the doubles of the things which are not seen.' And as there is a light for us in this earth, which is *not ourselves*, namely, the sun, so there is a light to us in the spirit-world, which is *not ourselves*. And who is that? The blessed Lord shall answer for Himself. He says, 'I am the light of the world;' and St. John bears witness to Him, 'In Him was life, and the life was the light of men.' And does not St. Paul say the same thing, when he blessed God so often for having called him and his congregations out of darkness into that marvellous light? If you read his Epistles, you will find what he meant by the darkness, what he meant by the light. The darkness was heathendom, knowing nothing of Christ. The light was Christianity, knowing Christ the light; and more being *in* the light, belonging to Christ—being joined to Him, as the leaves are to the tree,--living by trust in Christ, being taught and made true men and true women of, by the Noble and Holy Spirit of Christ—seeing their way through this world by trust in Christ and His promises,—That was light.

And there is no other light. If a man does not work trusting in Christ, whom God has set for the light of the world, he works in the night, where God never set or meant him to work; and stumble he will, and make a fool of himself sooner or later, because he is walking in the night, and sees nothing plainly or in a right view. For, as our Lord says truly, 'There is no light in him.' No light in him? In one sense there is no light in any one, be he the wisest or holiest man who ever lived. But this is just what three people out of four will not believe. They will not believe that the Spirit of God gives man understanding. They fancy that they have light in themselves. They try, conceitedly and godlessly, to walk by the light of their own eyes—to make their own way plain before their face for themselves. They will not believe David, a man who worked, and fought, and thought, and saw far more than any one of us will ever do, when he tells them again and again in his Psalms, that the Lord is his light, that the Lord must guide a man, and inform him with His eye, and teach him in the way in which he should go. And therefore they will not pray to God for light—therefore they will not look for light in God's Word, and in the writings of godly men; and they are like a man in the broad sunshine, who should choose to shut his eyes close, and say, 'I have light enough in my own head to do without the sun;' and therefore they walk on still in darkness, and all the foundations of the earth are out of course, because men forget the first universal ground rules of common sense, and reason, and love, which God's Spirit teaches. I tell you, all the mistakes that you ever made—that ever were made since Adam fell, came from this, that men will not ask God for light and wisdom; they love darkness rather than light, and therefore, though God's light is ready for every man, shining in the darkness to show every man his way, yet the darkness will not comprehend it—will not take it in, and let God change its blindness into day.

Now, then, to gather all together, what better answer could our Lord have given to His disciples' question than this, 'Are there not twelve hours in the day? If a man walk in the day he does not stumble, because he seeth the light of this world; but if a man walk in the night, he stumbleth, because there is no light in him.'

It was as if He had said, 'However short my day of life may be, there are twelve hours in it, of my Father's numbering and measuring, not of mine. My times are in His hand; as long as He pleases I shall live. He has given me a work to do, and He will see that I live long enough to do it. Into his hands I commend my spirit, for, living or dying, He is with me. Though I walk through the valley of the shadow of death, He will be with me. He will keep me secretly in His tabernacle from the strife of tongues, and will turn the furiousness of my enemies to His glory; and as my day my strength will be. And I have no fear of running into danger needlessly. I have prayed to Him daily and nightly for light, for His Spirit—the spirit of wisdom and understanding, of prudence and courage; and His word is pledged to keep me in all my ways, so that I dash not my foot against a stone. Know ye not that I must be about my Father's business? While I am about that, I am safe. It is only if I go about my own business—my own pleasure; if I forget to ask Him for His light and guidance, that I shall put myself into the night, and stumble and fall.

Well, my friends, what is there in this which we may not say as well as our Lord? In this, as in all things, Christ set Himself up as our pattern. Oh, believe it—believe that your time —your measure of life, is in God's hand. Believe that He is your light, that He will teach and guide you into all truth, and that all your mistakes come from not asking counsel of Him in prayer, and thought, and reading of His Holy Bible. Believe His blessed promise, that He will give His Holy Spirit to those who ask Him. Believe, too, that He has given you a work to do—prepared good works already for you to walk in. Be you labourer or gentleman, maid, wife, or widow, God has given you a work to do; there is good to be done lying all round you, ready for you. And the blessed Jesus who bought you, body and soul, with His own blood, commands you to work for Him: 'Whatsoever your hand finds to do, do it with all your might.'

> Work ye manful while ye may,
> Work for God in this your day;
> Night must stop you, rich or poor—
> Godly deeds alone endure.

And then, whether you live or die, your Father's smile will be on you, and His everlasting arms beneath you, and at your last hour you shall find that 'Blessed are the dead that die in the Lord, for they rest from their labour, and their works do follow them.'

SERMON XX.

ASSOCIATION.

GALATIANS vi. 2.

Bear ye one another's burdens, and so fulfil the law of Christ.

IF I were to ask you, my friends, why you were met together here to-day, you would tell me, I suppose, that you were come to church as members of a benefit club ; and quite right you are in coming here as such, and God grant that we may meet together here on this same errand many more Whit-Mondays. But this would be no answer to my question ; I wish to know *why* you come to *church* to-day sooner than to any other place? What has the church to do with the benefit club? Now this is a question which I do not think all of you could answer very readily, and therefore I wish to make you, especially the younger members of the club, think a little seriously about the meaning of your coming here to-day. You will be none the less cheerful this evening for having had some deep and godly thoughts in your heads this morning.

Now, these benefit clubs are also called provident societies, and a very good name for them. You become members of them, because you are prudent, or provident—that is, because you are careful, and look forward to a rainy day. But why does not each of you lay up his savings for himself, instead of putting them into a common purse, and so forming a club?

Because you have found out, what everyone else in the world, but madmen, ought to have found out, that two are better than one; that if a great many men join together in any matter, they are a great deal stronger when working together than if they each worked just as hard, but each by himself; that the way to be safe is not to stand each of you alone, but to help each other; in short, that there is no getting on without bearing one another's burdens.

Now, this plan of bearing one another's burdens is not only good in benefit clubs—it is good in families, in parishes, in nations, in the Church of God, which is the elect of all mankind. Unless men hold together, and help each other, there is no safety for them.

Let us consider what there is bearing on this matter of prudence, that makes one of the greatest differences between a man and a brute beast. It is not that the man is prudent, and the beast is not. Many beasts have forethought enough; the very sleepmouse hoards up acorns against the winter; a fox will hide the game he cannot eat. No; the great difference between man and beast is, that the beast has forethought only for himself, but the man has forethought for others also; beasts have not reason enough to bear each other's burdens, as men have. And what is it that makes us call the ant and the bee the wisest of animals, except that they do, in some degree, behave like men, in helping one another, and having some sort of family feeling, and society, and government among them, by which they can help bear each other's burdens? So that we all confess, by calling them wise, how wise it is to help each other. Consider a family, again. In order that a family may be happy and prosperous, all the members of it must bear each other's burdens. If the father only thought of himself, and the mother of herself, and each of the children did nothing but take care of themselves, would not that family come to misery and ruin? But if they all helped each other— all thought of each other more than of themselves—all were ready to give up their own comfort to make each other comfortable, that family would be peaceful and prosperous, and would be doing a great deal towards fulfilling the law of Christ.

It is just the same in a parish. If the rich help and defend the poor, and the poor respect and love the rich, and are ready to serve them as far as they can—in short, if all ranks bear each other's burdens, that parish is a happy one; and if they do not, it is a miserable one.

Just the same with a nation. If the king only cares about making himself strong, and the noblemen and gentlemen about their rank and riches, and the poor people, again, only care for themselves, and are trying to pull down the rich, and so get what they can for themselves,—if a country is in this state, what can be more wretched? Neither a house nor a country divided against itself can ever stand. But if the king and the nobles give their whole minds to making good laws, and seeing justice done to all, and workmen fairly paid; and if the poor, in their turns, are loyal and ready to fight and work for their king and their nobles, then will not that country be a happy and a great country? Surely it will, because its people, instead of caring every man for himself only, help each other and bear one another's burdens.

And just in the same way with Christ's Church, with the company of true Christian men. If the clergymen thought only of themselves, and neglected the people, and forgot to labour among them, and pray for them, and preach to them; and if each of the people cared for himself, and never prayed to God to give him a spirit of love and charity, and never helped his neighbours, or did unto others as he wished to be done by; and, above all, if Christ, our Head, left His Church, and cared no more about us, what would become of Christ's Church? What would happen to the whole race of sinful man, but misery in this world, and ruin in the next? But if the people love and help each other, and obey their ministers, and pray for them;

and if the ministers labour earnestly after the souls and bodies of their people ; and Christ in heaven helps both minister and people with His Spirit, and His providence and protection ; in short, if all in the whole Church bear each other's burdens, then Christ's Church will stand, and the gates of hell will not prevail against it.

Thus you see that this text of bearing one another's burdens is no new or strange commandment, but the very state in which every man is meant to live, both in his family, his parish, his country, and his Church—all his life helping others, and being helped by them in turn. And because families and nations, and the Church of Christ above all, are good, and holy, and beautiful, therefore any society which is formed upon the same plan—I mean of helping each other—must be good also. And therefore benefit societies are right and reasonable things ; and among all the good which they do, they do this one great good, that they teach men to remember that there is no use trying to stand alone, but that the way to be safe and happy is to bear each other's burdens.

Thus benefit societies are patterns of Christ's Church. But now, my friends, there is another point for each of you to consider, which is this—the benefit club is a good thing, but are you a good member of the club ? Do you do your duty, each of you, in the club as Christian men should ?

I do not ask whether you pay your subscriptions regularly or not—that is quite right and necessary, but there is something more than that wanted to make a club go on rightly. Mere paying and receiving money will never keep men together any more than any other outward business. A man may pay his club-money regularly, and yet not be a really good member. And how is this ? You remember that I tried to show you that a family, and a nation, and a church, all were kept together by the same principle of bearing one another's burdens, just as a benefit club is. Now, what makes a man a good member of Christ's Church,—a good Christian, in short ? A man may pay his tithes to the rector, and his church-rates to repair God's house, and his poor-rates to maintain God's poor, all very regularly, and yet be a very bad member of Christ's Church. These payments are all right and good; but they are but the outside, the letter of what God requires of him. What is wanted is, to serve God in the *spirit*, to have the spirit—*the will*, of a Christian in him; that is, to do all these things for *God's* sake—not of constraint, but willingly—'not grudgingly, for God loveth a cheerful giver." No! If a man is really a good member of Christ's Church, he lives a life of faith in Jesus Christ, and of thankfulness to Him for His infinite love and mercy in coming down to die for us, and thus the love of God and man is shed abroad in his heart by God's Spirit, which is given to him. Therefore, that man thinks it an honour to pay church-rates, and so help towards keeping God's house in repair and neatness. He pays his tithes cheerfully, because he loves God's ministers, and feels their use and worth to him. He pays his poor-rates with a willing mind, for the sake of that God who has said, that 'he who gives to the poor lends to the Lord.' And so he obeys not only the letter but the spirit of the law.

But the man does more than this. Besides obeying not only the letter but the spirit of the law, he helps his brethren in a thousand other ways. He shows, in short, by every action, that he believes in God and loves his neighbour.

And why should it not be just the same in a benefit club? There the good member is *not* the man who pays his money merely to have a claim for relief when he himself is sick, and yet grudges every farthing that goes to help other members. That man is not a good member. He has come into the club merely to take care of himself, and not to bear others' burdens. He may obey the letter of the club rules by paying in his subscriptions and by granting relief to sick members, but he does not obey the spirit of them. If he did, he would be glad to bear his sick neighbour's burden with so little trouble to himself. He would therefore grant club relief willingly and cheerfully when it was wanted,—ay, he would thank God that he had an opportunity of helping his neighbours. He would feel that all the members of the society were his brothers in a double sense : first, because they had joined with him to help and support each other in the society; and next, that they were his brothers in Christ, who had been baptized into the same Church of God with himself. And he would therefore delight in supporting them in their sickness, and honouring them when they died, and in helping their widows and orphans in their affliction; in short, in bearing his neighbour's burdens, and so fulfilling the law of Christ. And do you not see, that if any of you subscribe to this benefit society in such a spirit as this, that they are the men to give an answer to the question I asked at first, 'Why are you all here at church to-day?' They come here for the same reason that you all ought to come, to thank God for having kept them well, and out of the want of relief for the past year, and to thank Him, too, for having enabled them to bear their sick neighbours' burdens. And they come also to pray to God to keep them well and strong for the year to come, and to raise up those members who are in sickness and distress, that they may all worship God here together another year, as a company of faithful friends, helping each other on through this life, and all on the way to the same heavenly home, where there will be no more poverty, nor sorrow, nor sickness, nor death, and God shall wipe away tears from all widows' and orphans' eyes.

And now, my friends, I have tried to put some new and true thoughts into your head about your club and your business in this church to-day. And I pray, God grant that you may remember them, and think of this whole matter as a much more solemn and holy one than you ever did before.

SERMON XXI.

HEAVEN ON EARTH.

1 COR. x. 31.

Whether ye eat, or drink, or whatsoever ye do, do all to the glory of God.

THIS is a command from God, my friends, which is well worth a few minutes' consideration this day;—well worth considering, because though it was spoken eighteen hundred years ago, yet God has not changed since that time; He is just as glorious as ever: and Christian men's relation to God has not changed since that time; they still live, and move, and have their being in God; they are still His children—His beloved; Christ who died for us is still our King; God's spirit is still with us, God's mercy still saves us: we owe God as much as any people ever did. If it was ever any one's duty to show forth God's glory, surely it is our duty too.

Worth considering, indeed, is this command; for though it is in the Bible, and has been there for eighteen hundred years, it is seldom read, seldomer understood, and still more seldom put into practice. Men eat, and drink, and do all manner of things, with all their might and main; but how many of them do they do to the glory of God? No; this is the fault—the especial curse of our day, that religion does not mean any longer, as it used, the service of God—the being like God, and showing forth God's glory. No; religion means, now-a-days, the art of getting to heaven when we die, and saving our own miserable souls from hell, and getting God's wages without doing God's work—as if that was godliness,—as if that was anything but selfishness; as if selfishness was any the better for being everlasting selfishness! If selfishness is evil, my friends, the sooner we get rid of it the better, instead of mixing it up as we do with all our thoughts of heaven, and making our own enjoyment and our own safety the vile root of our hopes for all eternity. And therefore it is that people have forgotten what God's glory is. They seem to think that God's highest glory is saving them from hell-fire. And they talk not of God and the wondrous majesty of God, but only of the wonder of God's having saved them—looking at themselves all the time, and not at God. We must get rid of this sort of religion, my friends, at all risks, in order to get rid of all sorts of irreligion, for one is the father of the other.

It is a wonder, indeed, that we are saved from hell, much more raised to heaven, such peevish, cowardly, pitiful creatures as the best of us are; and yet the more we think of it, the less wonder we shall find it. The more we think of the wonder of all wonders,—God Himself, His majesty, His power, His wisdom, His love, His pity, His infinite condescension, the less reason we shall have to be surprised that he has stooped to save us. Yes, do not be startled—for it is true, that God has done for sinful men nothing contrary to Himself, but just what was to be expected from such unutterable condescension, and pity, and generosity, as God's is. And so recollecting this, we shall begin to forget ourselves, and look at God; and in thinking of Him we shall get beyond mere wondering at Him, to something higher—to worshipping Him.

Yes, my friends, this is what we must try at if we would be really godly—to find out what God is—to find out His likeness, His character, as He is: and has He not shown us what He is? He who has earnestly read Christ's story—he who has understood, and admired, and loved Christ's character, and its nobleness and beauty—he who can believe that Jesus Christ is now, at this minute, raising up his heart to good, guiding his thoughts to good, he has seen God; for he has seen the Son, who is the exact likeness of the Father's glory, in whom dwells all the fulness of the Godhead in a bodily shape. Remember, he who knows Christ knows God; and that knowledge will help us up a noble step further—it will help us to show forth God's glory. For when we once know what God's glory is, we shall see how to make others know it too. We shall know how to *do God justice*, to set men right as to their notions of God, to give them, at all events, in our own lives and characters, a pattern of Christ, who is the pattern of God ; and whatsoever we do, we shall be able to do all to God's glory.

For what is doing everything to the glory of God? It is this :—we have seen what God's glory is : He is His own glory. As you say of any very excellent man, you have but to know him to honour him ; or of any very beautiful woman, you have but to see her to love her; so I say of God, men have but to see and know Him to love and honour Him.

Well, then, my friends, if we call ourselves Christian men, if we believe that God is our Father, and delight, as on the grounds of common feeling we ought, to honour our Father, we should try to make every one honour Him. In short, whatever we do we should make it tend to His glory—make it a lesson to our neighbours, our friends, and our families. We should preach God's glory day by day, not by *words* only, often not by words at all, but by our conduct. Ay, there is the secret.— If you wish other men to believe a thing, just behave as if you believed it yourself. Nothing is so infectious as example. If you wish your neighbours to see what Jesus Christ is like, let them see what He can make *you* like. If you wish them to know how God's love is ready to save them from their sins, let them see His love save *you* from *your* sins. If you wish them to see God's tender care in every blessing and every sorrow they have, why, let them see you thanking God for every sorrow and every blessing you have. I tell you, friends, example is everything. One good man,—one man who does not put his religion on once a week with his Sunday coat, but wears it for his working dress, and lets the thought of God grow into him, and through and through him, till everything he says and does becomes religious, that man is worth a thousand sermons—he is a living Gospel—he comes in the spirit and power of Elias—he is the image of God. And men see his good works, and admire them in spite of themselves, and see that they are Godlike, and that God's grace is no dream, but that the Holy Spirit is still among men, and that all nobleness and manliness is His gift, His stamp, His picture; and so they get a glimpse of God again in His saints and heroes, and glorify their Father who is in heaven.

Would not such a life be a heavenly life? Ay, it would be more, it would be heaven—heaven on earth: not in mere fine words, but really. We should then be sitting, as St. Paul tells us, in heavenly places with Jesus Christ, and having our conversation in heaven. All the while we were doing our daily work, following our business, or serving our country, or sitting at our own firesides with wife and child, we should be all that time in heaven. Why not? we are in heaven now—if we had but faith to see it. Oh, get rid of those carnal, heathen notions about heaven, which tempt men to fancy that, after having misused this place—God's earth—for a whole life, they are to fly away when they die, like swallows in autumn, to another place—they know not where—where they are to be very happy—they know not why or how, nor do I know either. Heaven is not a mere *place*, my friends. All places are heaven if you will be heavenly in them. Heaven is where God is and Christ is; and hell is where God is not and Christ is not. The Bible says, no doubt, there is a place now—somewhere beyond the skies—where Christ especially shows forth His glory—a heaven of heavens: and for reasons which I cannot explain, there must be such a place. But, at all events, here is heaven; for Christ is here and God is here, if we will open our eyes and see them. And how?—How? Did not Christ Himself say, 'If a man will love Me, My Father will love him; and we, My Father and I, will come to him, and make our abode with him, and we will show ourselves to him?' Do those words mean nothing or something? If they have any meaning, do they not mean this, that in this life we can see God—in this life we can have God and Christ abiding with us? And is not that heaven? Yes, heaven is where God is. You are in heaven if God is with you, you are in hell if God is not with you; for where God is not, darkness and a devil are sure to be.

There was a great poet once—Dante by name—who described most truly and wonderfully, in his own way, heaven and hell, for indeed he had been in both. He had known sin and shame, and doubt and darkness and despair, which is hell. And after long years of misery, he had got to know love and hope, and holiness and nobleness, and the love of Christ and the peace of God, which is heaven. And so well did he speak of them, that the ignorant people used to point after him with awe in the streets, and whisper, There is the man who has been in hell. Whereon some one made these lines on him:—

> Thou hast seen hell and heaven? Why not? since heaven and hell
> Within the struggling soul of every mortal dwell.

Think of that!—thou—and thou—and thou!—for in thee, at this moment, is either heaven or hell. And which of them? Ask thyself, ask thyself, friend. If thou art not in heaven in this life, thou wilt never be in heaven in the life to come. At death, says the wise man, each thing returns into its own element, into the ground of its life; the light into the light, and the darkness into the darkness. As the tree falls, so it lies. My friends, you who call yourselves enlightened Christian folk, do you suppose that you can lead a mean, worldly, covetous, spiteful life here, and then, the moment your soul leaves the body, that you are to be changed into the very opposite character, into angel and saints, as fairy tales tell of beasts changed into men? If a beast can be changed into a man, then death can change the sinner into a saint—but not else. If a beast would enjoy being a man, then a sinner would enjoy being in heaven—but not else. A sinful, worldly man enjoy being in heaven? Does a fish enjoy being on dry land? The sinner would long to be back in this world again. Why, what is the employment of spirits in heaven, according to the Bible (for that is the point to which I have been trying to lead you round again? What but glorifying God? Not *trying* only to do .everything to God's glory, but actually succeeding in *doing* it—basking in the sunshine of His smile, delighting to feel themselves as nothing before His glorious majesty, meditating on the beauty of His love, filling themselves with the sight of His power, searching out the treasures of His wisdom, and finding God in all and all in God—their whole eternity one act of worship, one hymn of praise. Are there not some among us who will have had but little practice at that work? Those who have done nothing for God's glory here, how do they expect to be able to do everything for God's glory hereafter? Those who will not take the trouble of merely standing up at the Psalms, like the rest of their neighbours, even if they cannot sing with their voices God's praises in this church, how will they like singing God's praises through eternity? No; be sure that the only people who will be fit for heaven, who will like heaven even, are those who have been in heaven in this life—the only people who will be able to do everything to God's glory in the new heavens and new earth, are those who have been trying honestly to do all to His glory in this heaven and this earth.

Think over, in the meantime, what I have said this day; consider it, and you will have enough to think of, and pray over too, till we meet here again.

SERMON XXII.

NATIONAL PRIVILEGES.

LUKE x. 23.

Blessed are the eyes which see the things which ye see : for I tell you, that many prophets and kings have desired to see those things which ye see, and have not seen them; and to hear those things which ye hear, and have not heard them.

THIS is a noble text, my friends—and yet an awful one, for if it does not increase our godliness, it will certainly increase our condemnation. It tells us that we, even the meanest among us, are more favoured by God than the kings, and judges, and conquerors of the old world, of whom we read this afternoon in the first lesson ; that we have more light, and knowledge of God, than even the prophets David, Isaiah, Jeremiah, and Ezekiel, to whom God's glory appeared in visible shape. It tells us that we see things which they longed to see, and could not ; that words are spoken to us for which their ears longed in vain ; that they, though they died in hope, yet received not the promises, God having provided some better things for us, that they without us should not be made perfect.

Now, what was this which they longed for, and had not, and yet we have? It is this—a Saviour and a Saviour's kingdom. All wise and holy hearts for ages—as well heathens as Jews— had had this longing. They wanted a Saviour—one who should free them from sin and conquer evil—one who should explain to them all the doubt and contradiction and misery of the world, and give them some means of being freed from it—one who should set them the perfect pattern of what a man should be, and join earth and heaven, and make godliness part of man's daily life. They longed for a Saviour, and for a heavenly kingdom also. They saw that all the laws in the world could never make men good; that one half of men broke them, and the other half only obeyed them unwillingly, through slavish fear, loving the sin they dared not do. That men got worse and worse as time rolled on. That kings, instead of being shepherds of their people, were only wolves and tyrants to keep them in ignorance and misery. That priests only taught the people lies, and fattened themselves at their expense. That, in short, as David said, men would not learn or understand, and all the foundations of the earth, the grounds and principles of society, politics, and religion, were out of course, and the devil very truly the king of this lower world; so they longed for a heavenly kingdom—a kingdom of God—one in which men should obey God for love and not for fear, and man for God's sake; a spiritual kingdom—a kingdom whose laws should be written in men's hearts and spirits, and be their delight and glory, not their dread. They longed for a King of kings, who should teach all kings and magistrates to rule in love and wisdom. They longed for a High-priest, who should teach all priests to explain the wonder and the glory that there is in every living man, and in heaven and earth, and all that therein lies, and lead men's hearts into love and purity, and noble thoughts and deeds. They longed, in short, for a kingdom of God, a golden age, a regeneration of the world, as they called it, and rightly. Of course the Jewish prophets saw most clearly how this would be brought about, and how utterly necessary a Saviour and his kingdom was to save mankind from utter ruin. They, I say, saw this best. But still all the wise and pious heathens, each according to his measure of light, saw the same necessity, or else were restless and miserable because they could not see it. So that in all ages of the world, in a thousand different shapes, there was rising up to heaven a mournful, earnest prayer,—' Thy kingdom come!'

And now this kingdom is come, and the King of it, the Saviour of men, is Jesus Christ, the Son of God. Long men prayed, and long men waited, and at last, in the fulness of God's good time, just when the night seemed darkest, and, under the abominations of the Roman Empire, religion, honesty, and common decency seemed to have died out, the Sun of Righteousness rose on the dead and rotten world, to bring life and immortality to light. God sent forth His Son made of a woman, not to condemn the world, but that the world through Him might be saved. He sent Him to be our Saviour, to die on the cross for our sins and our children's, that all our guilt might be washed away, and that we might come boldly to the throne of grace, with our hearts sprinkled from an evil conscience, and our bodies washed in the waters of baptism. He sent Him to be our Teacher in the perfect law of love, our pattern in everything which a man should be and is not. He sent Him to conquer death by rising from the dead, that He might have power to raise us also to life and immortality. He sent Him to fill men with His Spirit, the Spirit of reason and truth, the Spirit of love and courage, that they might know the will of God, and do it as our Saviour did before us. He sent Him to found a Church, to join all men into one brotherhood, one kingdom of God, whose rulers are kings and parliaments, whose ministers are the clergy, whose prophets are all poets and philosophers, authors and preachers, who are true to their own calling : whose signs and tokens are the sacraments : a kingdom which should never be moved, but should go on for ever, drawing it into all honest and true hearts, and preserving them ever for Christ their Lord.

And that we might not doubt that we too belonged to this kingdom, He has placed in this land His ministers and teachers, Christ's sacraments, Christ's churches in every parish in the land, Christ's Bible, or the means of attaining the Bible, in every house and every cottage; that from our cradle to our grave we might see that we belonged, as sworn servants and faithful children, to the great Father in heaven and Jesus Christ, the King of the earth.

Thus, my friends, all that all men have longed for we possess; we want no more, and we shall have no more. If, under the present state of things, we cannot be holy, we shall never be holy. If we cannot use our right in this kingdom of Christ, how can we become citizens of God's everlasting kingdom, when Christ shall have delivered up the dominion to His father, and God shall be all in all? God has done all for us, as far as we know, that God will do. He has given us His Son for a Saviour, and a Church in which and by which to worship that Saviour; and what more would we have? Alas! my friends, have we yet used fairly what God has given us? and if not, how terrible will be our guilt! 'How shall we escape if we neglect so great salvation?' And yet how many do neglect!—how few live as if they were citizens of Christ's kingdom! It seems as if God had been too good to us, and heaped us so heavily with blessings, that we were tired of them, and despised them as common things. Common things? They are the very things, as I said, which the great and the wise in all ages have longed for and prayed for, and yet never found! Surely, surely, God may well say to us, 'What could have been done unto my vineyard which has not been done to it?' What, indeed! I wish I could take some of you into a heathen country for a single week, that you might see what it is not to know of a Saviour—not to be members of His Church, as we are. Why, we here in England are in the very garden of the Lord. We have but to stretch out our hand to the tree of life, and eat, and live for ever. From our cradle to our grave, Christ the King is ready to guide, to teach, to comfort, to deliver us. When we are born, we are christened in His name, made members of Christ, children of God, and inheritors by hope of the kingdom of heaven. Is that nothing? It is, alas! nothing in the eyes of most parents. As we grow older, are we not taught who we are — taught to call God our Father — taught about Jesus Christ, who He is, and what He is? Is that, too, nothing? Alas! that knowledge is generally a mere meaningless school-lesson, cared for neither by child nor by man. At confirmation, again, we solemnly declare that we belong to Christ's kingdom, and that we will live as His subjects, and His alone. And we are brought to His bishops, to be received as free, reasonable, Christian people, to claim our citizenship in the kingdom of God. Is that nothing? Yet that, too, is nothing with three-fourths of us. Nothing? Hear me, young people—as I have often told you—you are ready enough to excuse yourselves from your confirmation vows by saying you were not taught to understand them—were not taught how to put them into practice. That may be true, or it may not; your sin is just the same. No one with any common honesty or common sense could answer as you have to the bishop's questions at confirmation, without knowing that you did make a promise, and knowing well enough what you promised— and you who carried to confirmation a careless heart and a lying tongue, have only yourselves to blame for it!—But to proceed. Is not Christ present, or ready to be present, with us? Sunday after Sunday, for years, have not the churches been opened all around us, inviting us to enter and worship Christ, knowing that where two or three are gathered together, there is Christ in the midst of them? Is that nothing? This Creed — these lessons — these prayers, which Sunday after Sunday you have used; are they nothing? Are they not all proofs that the kingdom of God is come to you, and means whereby you can behave like children of the kingdom? And not on Sundays alone. Have we not been taught daily, in our own houses, in our own hearts, in all danger and trouble, and temptation, to pray to Jesus Christ, our King, knowing that He will hear and save all them that put their trust in Him? Is that nothing? On our happy marriage morn, too, was it not in God's house, before Christ's minister, in Christ's name, that we were married? Surely the kingdom of God is come to us, when our wedlock, as well as our souls and bodies, is holy to the Lord. Is that nothing? How few think of their marriage joys as holy things—an ordinance of Christ's kingdom, which He delights in and blesses with His presence and His special smile, seeing that it is the noblest and the purest of all things on earth—the picture of the great mystery which shall be the bridal of all bridals, the marriage of Christ and His Church! People do not now-a-days believe in marriage as a part of their religion; and so, according to their want of faith, it happens to them, their marriage is not holy, and the love and joy of their youth wither into a peevish, careless, lonely old age;—and yet over their heads these words were said, 'They are man and wife together, in the name of the Father, and of the Son, and of the Holy Ghost!' This comes of not believing in Christ's presence and Christ's favour; of not believing, in short, in what the Creed truly calls the Holy Catholic Church. Neither after that does Christ leave us. Every time a woman is churched, is not that meant to be a sign of thankfulness to Christ, the Great Physician, to whom she owes her life and health once more? Then season after season is the sacrament of Christ's body and blood offered you. Is that no sign that Christ is here among us? Ah! blessed are the eyes which see that—blessed are the ears which hear those words, 'Take, eat; this is My body which is given for you.' Truly, that honour—that blessing— is so vast, the love and the condescension of Christ, the Lamb of God, are so unutterable, that prophets and kings, whatever they believed, never could have desired, never could have imagined, that the Son of God should offer to the sons of men, year after year, in their little parish churches, His most precious body, His most precious blood. And another thing, too, those prophets and kings would never have imagined—that when Christ, in those churches, offers His body and His blood, nine-tenths of the congregation, calling themselves Christians, should quietly walk out, and go home, and leave the sacraments of Christ's body and Christ's blood behind as a useless and unnecessary matter! That indeed the old prophets and kings never saw, and never expected to see—but so it is. Christ is among us, and our eyes are holden, and we know Him not.

And then, at last, after all these blessed privileges, these tokens of God's kingdom, have been neglected through a long life, does Christ neglect us in the hour of death? Ah, no! He is at the grave, as He was at the font, at the marriage-bed, at His own holy table in God's house; and the body is laid in the ground by Christ's minister, in the certain hope of a joyful resurrection. But what—a sure and certain hope for each and all? The resurrection is a joyful hope—but is it so for all? Only, too often, a faint, dim longing that clings to the last chance, and dares not confess to itself how hopeless must be the death of that man or woman whose life was spent in the kingdom of God, in the midst of blessings which kings and prophets desired in vain to see, and yet who neglected them all—never entered into the spirit of them—never loved them— never lived according to them, but despised and trampled under foot the kingdom of God from their childhood to their grave, as three-fourths of us do. Christ came to judge no man, and therefore Christ's ministers judge no man, and read the Christian funeral service over all, and pray Christ to be there, and to remember His blessed promise of raising up the body and soul to everlasting life. But how can they help fearing that Christ will not hear them—that after all His offers and gifts in this life have been despised, He will give nothing after death but death; and that it were better for the sinful worldly, sham Christian, when lying in his coffin, if he had never been born? How can those escape who neglect such great salvation?

Ah, my friends—my friends, take this to heart! Blessed indeed are the eyes which see what you see, and hear what you hear; prophets and kings have desired to see and hear them, and have not seen or heard! But if you, cradled among all these despised honours and means of grace, bring forth no fruit in your lives—shut out from yourselves the thought of your high calling in Jesus Christ, what shall be your end but ruin? He that despises Christ, Christ will despise him. And say not to yourselves, as many do, We are church-goers—we are all safe. I say to you, God is able, from among the Negro and the Savage—ay, God is able of these stones to raise up children to the Church of England, while those of you, the children of the kingdom, who lived in the Church of your fathers, and never used or loved her or Christ her King, shall be cast into outer darkness, where there shall be weeping and gnashing of teeth.

SERMON XXIII.

LENTEN THOUGHTS.

HAGGAI i. 5.

Now therefore thus saith the Lord of Hosts, Consider your ways.

NEXT Wednesday is Ash-Wednesday, the first day of Lent, the season which our forefathers have appointed for us to consider and mend our ways, and to return, year by year, heart and soul to that Lord and Heavenly Father from whom we are daily wandering. Now, we all know that we ought to have repented long ago; we all know that, sinning in many things daily, as we do, we ought all to repent daily. But that is not enough; we do want, unless we are wonderfully better than the holy men of old,—we do want, I say, a particular time in which we may sit down deliberately and look our own souls steadily in the face, and cast up our accounts with God, and be thoroughly ashamed and terrified at those accounts when we find, as we shall, that we cannot answer God one thing in a thousand. It is all very well to say, 'I confess and repent of my sins daily; why should I do it especially in Lent?' Very true. Let us see, then, by your altered life and conduct, that you have repented during this Lent, and then it will be time to talk of repenting every day after Lent. But, in fact, a man might just as well argue, 'I say my prayers every day, and God hears them; why should I say them more on Sundays than any other day?' Why? not only because your forefathers, and the Church of your forefathers, have advised you, which, though not an imperative reason, is still a strong one, surely, but because the thing is good, and reasonable, and right in itself. Because, as they found, in their own case, and as you may find in yours, if you will but think, the hurry and bustle of business is daily putting repentance and self-examination out of our heads. A man may think much, and pray much, thank God, in the very midst of his busiest work, but he is apt to be hurried; he has not set his thoughts especially on the matters of his soul, and so the soul's work is not thoroughly done. Much for which he ought to pray he forgets to pray for. Many sins and failings of which he ought to repent, slip past him out of sight in the hurry of life. Much good that might be done is put off and laid by, often till it is too late. But now here is a regular season in which we may look back and say to ourselves, 'How have I been getting on for this twelvemonth, not in pocket, but in character? not in the appearance of character in my neighbour's eyes, but in real character—in the eyes of God? Am I more manly, or more womanly—more godly, more true, more humble, above all, more loving, than I was this time last year? What bad habits have I conquered? What good habits have grown upon me? What chances of doing good have I let slip? What foolish, unkind things have I done? My duty to God and my neighbours is so and so; how have I done it? Above all, this Saviour and King in heaven, in whom I profess to believe, to whom I have sworn to be loyal and true, and to help His good cause, the cause of godliness, manliness, and happiness among my neighbours, in my family, in my own heart,—how have I felt towards Him? Have I thought about Him more this year than I did last? Do I feel any more loyalty, respect, love, gratitude to Him than I did? Ay, more, do I think about Him at all as a living man, much less as my King and Saviour; or, is all I really know about Him the sound of the words, "Jesus Christ," and the story about Him in the Apostles' Creed? Do I really *believe* and trust in "Jesus Christ," or do I not?' These are sharp, searching questions, my friends,—good Lenten food for any man's soul,—questions which it is much more easy to ask soberly and answer fairly now when you look quietly back on the past year, than it is, alas ! to answer them day by day amid all the bustle of your business and your families. But you will answer, ' This bustle will go on just as much in Lent as ever. Our time and thoughts will be just as much occupied. We have our livings to get. We are not fine gentlemen and ladies who can lie by for forty days and do nothing but read and pray, while their tradesmen and servants are working for them from morning to night. How, then, can we give up more time to religion now than at other times?'

This is all true enough ; but there is a sound and true answer to it. It is not so much more *time* which you are asked to give up to your souls in Lent, as it is more *heart*. What do I talk of? *Giving up* more time to your souls? And yet this is the way we all talk, as if our time belonged to our bodies, and so we had to rob them of it, to give it up to our souls— as if our bodies were ourselves, and our souls were troublesome burdens, or peevish children hanging at our backs, which would keep prating and fretting about heaven and hell, and had to be quieted, and their mouths stopped as quickly and easily as possible, that we might be rid of them, and get about our true business, our real duty,—this mighty work of eating and drinking, and amusing ourselves, and making money. I am afraid— afraid there are too many who, if they spoke out their whole hearts, would be quite as content to have no souls, and no necessity to waste their precious time (as they think) upon religion. But, my friends, my friends, the day will come when you will see yourselves in a true light ; when your soul will not seem a mere hanger-on to your body, but you will find out *that you are your soul*. Then there will be no more forgetting that you have souls, and thrusting them into the background, be to fed at odd minutes or left to starve,—no more talk of *giving up* time to the care of your souls; your souls will take the time for themselves then—and the eternity, too; they will be all in all to you then, perhaps when it is too late!

Well, I want you, just for forty days, to let your souls be all in all to you now; to make them your first object—your first thought in the morning, the last thing at night, your thought at every odd moment in the day. You need not neglect your business; only for one short forty days do not make your business your God. We are all to apt to try the heathen plan, of seeking first everything else in the world, and letting the kingdom of God and His righteousness be added to us over and above—or *not* added, as it may happen. Try for once the plan the Lord of heaven and earth advises, and seek first the kingdom of God and His righteousness, and see whether everything else will not be added to you. Again, you need not be idle a moment more in Lent than at any other time. But I daresay that none of you are so full of business that you have not a free ten minutes in the morning, and ten minutes at night of which the best of uses may be made. What do I say? Why, of all men in the world, farmers and labourers have most time, I think, to themselves; working, as they do, the greater part of their day in silence and alone; what opportunities for them to have their souls busy in heaven, while they are pacing over the fields, ploughing and hoeing! I have read of many, many labouring men who had found out their opportunities in this way, and used them so well as to become holy, great, and learned men. One of the most learned scholars in England at this day was once a village carpenter, who used, when young, to keep a book open before him on his bench while he worked, and thus contrived to teach himself, one after the other, Latin, Greek, and Hebrew. So much time may a man find who *looks* for time.

But after all, and above all, believe this—that if your business or your work does actually give you no time to think about God and your own souls,—if in the midst of it all you cannot find leisure enough night and morning to pray earnestly, to read your Bible carefully,—if it so swallows up your whole thoughts during the day, that you have no opportunity to recollect yourself, to remember that you are an immortal being, and that you have a Saviour in heaven, whom you are serving faithfully, or unfaithfully,—if this work or business of yours will not give you time enough for that, then it is not God's business, and ought not to be yours either.

But you have time,—you have all time. When there is a will there is a way. Make up your minds that there shall be a will, and pray earnestly to God to give it you, if it is but for forty days: and in them think seriously, slowly, solemnly over your past lives. Examine yourselves and your doings. Ask yourselves fairly—'Am I going forward or back?' Am I living like a child of God, or like a mere machine for making food and wages? Is my conduct such as the Holy Scripture tells me that it should be? You will not need to go far for a set of questions, my friends, or rules by which to examine yourselves. You can hardly open a page of God's book without finding something which stares you in the face with the question, ' Do I do thus? or, Do I not do thus?' Take, for example, the Epistle of this very day. What better test can we have for trying and weighing our own souls?

What says it? That though we were wise, charitable, eloquent—all that the greatest of men can be, and yet had not charity—*love*, we are nothing!—nothing! And how does it describe this necessary, indispensable, heavenly love? Let us spend the last few minutes of this sermon in seeing how. And if that description does not prick all our hearts on more points than one, they are harder than I take them for—far harder, certainly, than they should be.

This charity, or love, we hear, which each of us ought to have and must have, ' suffers long, and is kind.' What shall we say to that? How many hasty, revengeful thoughts and feelings have arisen in the hearts of most of us in the last year?—Here is one thought for Lent. 'Charity envies not.' Have we envied any their riches, their happiness, their good name, health, and youth?—Another thought for Lent. 'Charity boasts not herself.' Alas! alas! my friends, are not the best of us apt to make much of the little good we do—to pride ourselves on the petty kindnesses we show—to be puffed up with easy self-satisfaction, just as charity is *not* puffed up?—Another Lenten thought. 'Charity does not behave herself unseemly;' is never proud, noisy, conceited; gives every man's opinion a fair kindly hearing; making allowances for all mistakes. Have we done so?—Then there is another thought for Lent. 'Charity seeks not her own;' does not stand fiercely and stifly on her own rights, on the gratitude due to her; while we—are we not too apt, when we have done a kindness, to fret and fume, and feel ourselves deeply injured, if we do not get repaid at once with all the humble gratitude we expected? Of this also we must think. 'Charity thinks no evil;' sets down no bad motives for any one's conduct, but takes for granted that he means well, whatever appearances may be; while we (I speak of myself just as much as of any one), are we not continually apt to be suspicious, jealous, to take for granted that people mean harm; and even when we find ourselves mistaken, and that we have cried out before we are hurt, not to consider it as any sin against our neighbour, whom in reality we have been silently slandering to ourselves? 'Charity rejoices not in iniquity,' but in the truth, whatever it may be; is never glad to see a high professor prove a hypocrite, and fall into sin, and show himself in his true foul colours; which we, alas! are too apt to think a very pleasant sight. Are not these wholesome meditations for Lent? 'Charity hopes all things' of every one; 'believes all things,' all good that is told of every one; 'endures all things,' instead of flying off and giving up a person at the first fault. Are not all these points which our own hearts, consciences, common sense, or whatever you like to call it (I shall call it God's Spirit), tell us are right, true, necessary? And is there one of us that can say that he has not offended in many, if not in all these points? And is not that unrighteousness—going out of the right, straightforward, child-like, loving way of looking at all people? And is not all unrighteousness sin? And must not all sin be repented of, and that *as soon as we find it out?* And can we not all find time this Lent to throw over these sins of ours—to confess them with shame and sorrow—to try like men to shake them off? Oh, my friends! you who are too busy for forty short days to make your immortal souls your first business, take care—take care lest the day shall come when sickness, and pain, and the terror of death shall keep you too busy to prepare those unrepenting, unforgiven, sin-besotted souls of yours for the kingdom of God.

SERMON XXIV.

ON BOOKS.

JOHN i. 1.

In the beginning was the Word, and the Word was with God, and the Word was God.

I DO not pretend to be able to explain this text to you, for no man can comprehend it but He of whom it speaks, Jesus Christ, the Word of God. But I can, by God's grace, put before you some of the awful and glorious truths of which it gives us a sight, and may Christ, who is *the* Word, direct you, and grant me words to bring the matter home to you, so as to make some of you, at least, ask yourselves the golden question, 'If this is true, what must we *do* to be saved?'

The text says, that the Word was from the beginning with God, ay, God Himself. Who the Word is, there is no doubt, from the rest of the chapter, which you heard read this morning. But why is Christ called the Word of all words—the Word of God? Let us look at this. Is not Christ *the man*, the head and pattern of all men who are what men ought to be? And did He not tell me that He is *the* Life? That all life is given by Him and out of Him? And does not St. John tell us that Christ the Life is the light of men—the true light which lighteth every man who cometh into the world?

Remember this, and then think again, what is it which makes

men different from all other living things we know of. Is it not speech—the power of words? The beasts may make each other understand many things, but they have no speech. These glorious things—words—are man's right alone, part of the image of the Son of God—the Word of God, in which man was created. If men would but think what a noble thing it is merely to be able to speak in words, to think in words, to write in words! Without words we should know no more of each other's hearts and thoughts than the dog knows of his fellow-dog;—without words to think in; for if you will consider, you always think to yourself in *words*, though you do not speak them aloud; and without them all our thoughts would be mere blind longings, feelings which we could not understand our ownselves. Without words to write in we could not know what our forefathers did—we could not let our children after us know what to do. But now books—the written word of man—are precious heirlooms from one generation to another, training us, encouraging us, teaching us, by the words and thoughts of men, whose bodies are crumbled into dust ages ago, but whose words —the power of uttering themselves, which they got from the Son of God—still live and bear fruit in our hearts, and in the hearts of our children after us, till the last day!

But where did these words—this power of uttering our thoughts, come from? Do you fancy that men first began like brute beasts or babies, with strange cries and mutterings, and so gradually found out words for themselves? Not they; the beasts have been on the earth as long as man, and yet they can no more speak than they could when God created Adam; but Adam, we find, could speak at once. God spoke to Adam the moment he was made, and Adam understood Him; so he knew the power and the meaning of words. Who gave him that power? Who but Jehovah—Jesus—the Word of God, who imparted to him the word of speech and the light of reason? Without words what use would there have been in saying to him, 'Thou shalt not eat of the tree of knowledge?'

Without words what would there have been in God's bringing to him all the animals to see what he would call them, unless He had first given Adam the power of understanding words, and thinking of words, and speaking words? This was the glorious gift of Christ—the Voice or Word of the Lord God, as we read in the second chapter of Genesis, whom Adam heard another time with fear and terror—'The voice of the Lord walking in the garden in the cool of the day.'—A text and a story strange enough, till we find in the first chapter of St. John the explanation of it, telling us that the Word was in the beginning with God—very God, and that He was the light which lighteth every man who cometh into the world. Therefore Christ is the light which lighteth every man who cometh into the world. How are we to understand that, when there are so many who live and die heathens or reprobates—some who never hear of Christ—some, alas! in Christian lands, who are dead to every doctrine or motive of Christianity? Yet the Bible says that Christs lights *every man* who comes into the world. Difficult to understand at first sight, yet most true, and simple too, at bottom.

For how is every one, whether heathen or Christian child or man, enlightened or taught, to live and behave? Is it not by the words of those around him, by the words he reads in books, by the thoughts which he thinks out and puts into shape for himself? All this is the light which every human being has his share of. And has not every man, too, the light of reason and good feeling, more or less, to tell him whether each thing is right or wrong, noble or mean, ugly or beautiful? This is another way by which the light which lighteth every man works. And St. John tells us in the text, that He who works in this way—He who gives us the power of understanding, and thinking, and judging, and speaking, is the very same Word of God who was made flesh, and dwelt among men, and died on the cross for us: 'the Lamb of God, who taketh away the sins of the world!'

He is the Word of God—by Him God has spoken to man in all ages. He taught Adam. He spoke to Abraham as a man speaketh with his friend. It was He, Jehovah, whom we call Jesus, whom Moses and the seventy elders saw—saw with their bodily eyes on Mount Sinai, who spoke to them with human voice from amid the lightning and the rainbow. It must have been only He, the Word, by whom God the Father utters Himself to man, for no man hath seen God at any time ; only the Word, the only-begotten Son, who is in the bosom of the Father, He hath declared Him. And who put into the mouth of David those glorious Psalms—the songs in which all true men for three thousand years have found the very things they longed to speak themselves, and could not? Who but Christ, the Word of God, the Lord, as David calls Him, put a new song into the mouth of His holy poet, the sweet singer of Israel? Who spake by the prophets, again ? What do they say themselves?—'The Word of the Lord came to me, saying.' And then, when the Spirit of God stirred them up, the Word of God gave them speech, and they spake the sayings which shall never pass away till all be fulfilled. And who was it who, when He was upon earth, spake as never man spake—whose words were the simplest, and yet the deepest—the tenderest, and yet the most awful, which ever broke the blessed silence upon this earth—whose words, now to this day, come home to men's hearts, stirring them up to the very roots, piercing through the marrow of men's souls? Whose but Christ's, the Word, who was made flesh and dwelt among us, full of grace and truth ? And who since then, do you think, has it been who has given to all wise and holy poets, philosophers, and preachers, the power to speak and write the wonderful truths which, by God's grace, they thought out for themselves and for all mankind—who gave them utterance? Who but Christ, the Lord of men's spirits, the Word of God, who promised to give to all His true disciples a mouth and wisdom, which their enemies should not be able to gainsay or resist?

Well, my friends, ought not the knowledge of this to make us better and wiser? Ought it not to make us esteem, and reverence, and use many things of which we are apt to think too lightly? How it should make us reverence the Bible, the written word of God's saints and prophets, of God's apostles, of Christ, the Word Himself! Oh, that men would use that treasure of the Bible as it deserves;—oh, that they would believe from their hearts, that whatever is said there is truly said, that whatever is said there is said to them, that whatever names things are called there are called by their right names. Then men would no longer call the vile person beautiful, or call pride and vanity honour, or covetousness respectability, or call sin worldly wisdom; but they would call things as Christ calls them—they would try to copy Christ's thoughts and Christ's teaching; and instead of looking for instruction and comfort to lying opinions and false worldly cunning, they would find their only advice in the blessed teaching, and their only comfort in the gracious promises, of the word of the Book of Life.

Again, how these thoughts ought to make us reverence all books. Consider! except a living man, there is nothing more wonderful than a book! a message to us from the dead—from human souls whom we never saw, who lived perhaps thousands of miles away; and yet these, in those little sheets of paper, speak to us, amuse us, terrify us, teach us, comfort us, open their hearts to us as brothers.

Why is it that neither angels, nor saints, nor evil spirits, appear to men now to speak to them as they did of old? Why, but because we have *books*, by which Christ's messengers and the devil's messengers too, can tell what they will to thousands of human beings at the same moment, year after year, all the world over! I say, we ought to reverence books, to look at them as awful and mighty things. If they are good and true, whether they are about religion or politics, farming, trade, or medicine, they are the message of Christ, the Maker of all things, the Teacher of all Truth, which He has put into the heart of some man to speak, that he may tell us what is good for our spirits, for our bodies, and for our country. And at the last day, be sure of it, we shall have to render an account —a strict account—of the good books which we have read, and of the way in which we have obeyed what we read, just as if we had had so many prophets or angels sent to us.

If, on the other hand, books are false and wicked, we ought to fear them as evil spirits loose among us, as messages from the father of lies, who deceives the hearts of evil men, that they may spread abroad the poison of his false and foul messages, putting good for evil, and evil for good, sweet for bitter, and bitter for sweet—saying to all men, 'I too have a tree of knowledge, and you may eat of the fruit thereof, and not die.' But believe him not. When you see a wicked book, when you find in a book anything which contradicts God's book, cast it away, trample it under foot; believe that it is the devil tempting you by his cunning, alluring words, as he tempted Eve, your mother. Would to God all here would make that rule, —never to look into an evil book, or a filthy ballad! Can a man take a snake into his bosom and not be bitten?—can we play with fire and not be burnt?—can we open our ears and eyes to the devil's message, whether of covetousness, or filth, or folly, and not be haunted afterwards by its wicked words, rising up in our thoughts like evil spirits, between us and our pure and noble duty—our baptismal vows?

I might say much more about these things, and, by God's help, in another sermon I will go on and speak to you of the awful importance of spoken words, of the sermons and the conversation to which you listen, the awful importance of every word which comes out of your own mouth. But I have spoken only of books this morning; for this is the age of books—the time, one would think, of which Daniel prophesied that many should run to and fro, and knowledge should be increased. A flood of books, newspapers, writings of all sorts, good and bad, is spreading over the whole land, and young and old will read them. We cannot stop that; we ought not; it is God's ordinance. It is more; it is God's grace and mercy that we have a free press in England—liberty for every man, that if he have any of God's truth to tell, he may tell it out boldly, in books or otherwise. A blessing from God! one which we should reverence, for God knows it was dearly bought. Before our forefathers could buy it for us, many an honoured man left house and home to die in the battle-field or on the scaffold, fighting and witnessing for the right of every man to whom God's Word comes, to speak God's Word openly to his countrymen. A blessing, and an awful one! for the same gate which lets in good, lets in evil. The law dare not silence bad books. It dare not root up the tares, lest it root up the wheat also. The men who died to buy us liberty, knew that it was better to let in a thousand bad books than shut out one good one; for a grain of God's truth will ever outweigh a ton of the devil's lies. We cannot, then, silence evil books, but we can turn away our eyes from them; we can take care that what we read, and what we let others read, shall be good and wholesome. Now, if ever, are we bound to remember that books are words, and that words come either from Christ or the devil; now, if ever, we are bound to try all books by the Word of God; now, if ever, are we bound to put holy and wise books, both religious and worldly, into the hands of all around us, that if, poor souls! they must needs eat of the fruit of the tree of knowledge, they may also eat of the tree of life; and now, if ever, are we bound to pray to Christ, the Word of God, that He will raise up among us wise and holy writers, and give them words and utterance to speak to the hearts of all Englishmen the message of God's covenant, and that He may confound the devil and his lies, and all that swarm of writers who are filling England with trash, filth, blasphemy, and covetousness, with books which teach men that our wise forefathers, who built our churches, and founded our constitution, and made England the queen of nations, were but ignorant knaves and fanatics, and that selfish money-making and godless licentiousness are the only true wisdom; and so turn the divine power of words, and the inestimable blessing of a free press, into the devil's engine, and not Christ's, the Word of God. But their words shall be brought to nought.

May God preserve us and all our friends from that defilement! and may He give you all grace, in these strange times, to take care what you read and how you read, and to hold fast by the Book of all books, and Christ the Word of God! Try by them all books and men; for if they speak not according to God's law and testimony, it is because there is no truth in them.

SERMON XXV.

THE COURAGE OF THE SAVIOUR.

JOHN xi. 7, 8.

Then after that saith He to His disciples, Let us go into Judea again. His disciples say to Him, Master, the Jews of late sought to stone Thee, and goest Thou thither again?

WE all admire a brave man. And we are right. To be brave is God's gift. To be brave is to be like Jesus Christ. Cowardice is only the devil's likeness. But we must take care what we mean by being brave. Now, there are two sorts of bravery—courage and fortitude. And they are very different: courage is of the flesh, fortitude is of the spirit. Courage is good, but dumb animals have it just as much as we. A dog, a tiger, and a horse, have courage, but they have no fortitude; because fortitude is a spiritual thing, and beasts have no spirits like ours.

What is fortitude? It is the courage which will make us not only fight in a good cause, but suffer in a good cause. Courage will help us only to give others pain; fortitude will help us to bear pain ourselves. And more, fortitude will make a fearful person brave, and very often the more brave the more fearful they are. And thus it is that women are so often braver than men. We men are made of coarser stuff; we do not feel pain as keenly as women; and if we do feel, we are rightly ashamed to show it. But a tender woman, who feels pain and sorrow infinitely more than we do, who need not be ashamed of being frightened, who perhaps is terrified at every mouse and spider,—to see her bearing patiently pain, and sorrow, and shame, in spite of all her fearfulness, because she knows it is her duty—that is Christ's likeness—that is true fortitude—that is a sight nobler than all the 'bull-dog courage' in the world. For what is the courage of the bull-dog after all, or of the strong quarrelsome man? He is confident in his own strength; he is rough and hard, and does not care for pain; and when he thrusts his head into a fight, like a surly dog, he does it not because it is his duty, but because he likes it, because he is angry; and then every blow and every wound makes him more angry, and he fights on, forgetting his pain from blind rage.

That is not altogether bad; men ought to be courageous. But, oh! my friends, is there not a more excellent way to be brave? and which is nobler, to suffer bravely for God's sake, or to beat men made in God's image bravely for one's own sake? Think of any fight you ever saw, and then compare with that the stories of those old martyrs who died rather than speak a word against their Saviour. If you want to see true fortitude, think of what has happened thousands of times when the heathen used to persecute the Christians. How delicate women, who would not venture to set the sole of their foot to the ground·for tenderness, would submit, rather than give up their religion and deny the Lord who died for them, to be torn from husband and family, and endure nakedness, and insult, and tortures, to read of which makes one's blood run cold, till they were torn slowly piecemeal, or roasted in burning flames, without a murmur or an angry word—knowing that Christ, who had borne all things for them, would give them strength to bear all things for Him; trusting that if they were faithful unto death, He would give them a crown of life. There was true fortitude—there was true faith—there was God's strength made perfect in woman's weakness! Do you not see, my friends, that such a death was truly brave? How does bull-dog courage show beside that courage—the courage which conquers grief and pain for duty's sake, instead of merely forgetting them in rage and obstinacy?

And do you not see how this bears on my text? how it bears on our Lord's whole life? Was He not indeed the perfectly brave man—the man who endured more than all living men put together, at the very time that He had the most intense fear of what He was going to suffer? And, stranger still, endured it all of His own will, while He had it in His power to shake it all off at any instant, and free Himself utterly from pain and suffering.

Now, this speech of our Lord's in the text is just a case of true fortitude. He was beyond Jordan. He had been forced to escape thither to save His life from the mad, blinded Jews. He had no foolhardiness; He knew that He had no more right than we have to put His life in danger when there was no good to be done by it. But now there *was* good to be done by it. Lazarus was dead, and He wanted to raise Him to life. Therefore He said to His disciples, 'Let us go into Judea again.' They knew the danger; they said, 'Master, the Jews of late sought to stone Thee, and goest Thou thither again?' But He would go; He had a work to do, and He dared bear anything to do his work. Aye, here is the secret, this is the feeling which gives a man true courage—the feeling that he has a work to do at all costs—the sense of duty. Oh! my friends, let men, women, or children once feel that they have a duty to perform; let them once say to themselves, 'I am bound to do this thing —it is right for me to do this thing; I owe it as a duty to my family; I owe it as a duty to my country; I owe it as a duty to God, who called me into this station in life; I owe it as a duty to Jesus Christ, who bought me with His blood, that I might do His will and not my own pleasure. When a man has once said that *honestly* to himself, when that glorious heavenly thought, '*It is my duty*,' has risen upon his soul, like the sun upon the earth, warming his heart and enlightening it and making it bring forth all good and noble fruits, then that man will feel a strength come to him, and a courage from God above, which will conquer all his fears and his selfish love of ease and pleasure, and enable him to bear insults, and pain, and poverty, and death itself, provided he can but do what is right, and be found by God, whatever happens to him, working God's will where God has put him. This is fortitude—this is true courage —this is Christ's likeness—this is the courage which weak women on sick beds may have as well as strong men on the battle-field. Even when they shrink most from suffering, God's Spirit will whisper to them, 'It is *thy* duty, it is thy Father's will,' and then they will find His strength made perfect in their weakness; and when their human weakness fails most, God will give them heavenly fortitude, and they will be able, like St Paul, to say, 'When I am weak, then I am strong, for I can do all things through Christ, who strengtheneth me.'

And now, remember, that there was no pride, no want of feeling, to keep up our Lord's courage. He has tasted sorrow for every man, woman, and child, and therefore He has tasted fear also; tempted in all things like as we are, that in all things He might be touched with the feeling of our infirmities,—that there might be no poor souls terrified at the thought of pain or sorrow, but could comfort themselves with the thought, Well, the Son of God knows what fear is. He who said that His soul was troubled—He who at the thought of death was in such agony of terror that His sweat ran down to the ground like great drops of blood—He who cried in His agony, ' Father, if it be possible, let this cup pass from me '—He understands my pain,—He tells me not to be ashamed of crying in my pain, like him, 'Father, if it be possible, let this cup pass from me;' for He will give me the strength to finish that prayer of His, and in the midst of my trouble say, 'Nevertheless, Father, not as I will, but as Thou wilt.' Remember, again, that our Lord was not like the martyrs of old, forced to undergo His sufferings whether He liked them or not. We are too apt to forget that, and therefore we misunderstand our Lord's example; and therefore we misunderstand what true fortitude is. Jesus Christ was the Son of God; He had made the very men who were tormenting him; He had made the very wood of the cross on which He hung, the iron which pierced His blessed hands; and, for aught we know, one wish of His, and they would all have crumbled into dust, and He have been safe in a moment. But He would not; He *endured* the Cross. He was the only man who ever really endured anything at all, because He alone of all men had perfect power to save Himself, even when He was nailed to the tree, fainting, bleeding, dying. It was never too late for Him to stop. As He said to Peter when he wanted to fight for Christ, 'Thinkest thou that I cannot pray to my Father, and He will send me instantly more that twelve legions of angels?' But *He would not.* He had to save the world, and He was determined to do it, whatever agony or fear it cost Him. St. Peter was a *brave* man. He drew his sword in the garden, and attacked, single-handed, that great body of armed soldiers; cutting down a servant of the high-priest's. But he was only brave; our Lord was more. The blessed Jesus had true fortitude; He could *bear* patiently, while Peter could only rage and fight uselessly. And see how Christ's fortitude lasted Him, while Peter's mere courage failed him. While our Lord was witnessing that glorious confession of His before Pilate, bearing on through without shrinking, even to the cross itself, where was Peter? He had denied his Master, and ran shamefully away. He had a long lesson to learn before he was perfect, had Peter. He had to learn, not how to fight, but how to suffer—and he learnt it; and in his old age that strong, fierce St. Peter had true fortitude to give himself up to be crucified, like his Lord, without a murmur, and preach Christ's Gospel as he hung for twelve whole days upon the torturing cross. There was fortitude; that violence of his in the garden was only courage as of a brute animal— courage of the flesh, not the true courage of the spirit. Oh, my friends, that we could all learn this lesson, that it is better to suffer than revenge, better to be killed than to kill! There are times when a man must fight—for his country, for just laws, for his family, but for himself it is very seldom that he must fight. He who returns good for evil, —he who, when he is cursed, blesses those who curse him,—he who takes joyfully the spoiling of his goods, who submits to be cheated in little matters, and sometimes in great ones, sooner than ruin the poor sinful wretch who has ill-used him,—that man has really put on Christ's likeness, that man is really going on to perfection, and fulfilling the law of love; and for everything which he gives up for the sake of peace and mercy, that is, for God's sake, God will reward him sevenfold into his bosom. There are times when a man is bound to go to law, bound to expose and punish evil-doers, lest they should, being unpunished, become confident and go on from bad to worse, and so hurt others as well as him. A man sometimes is bound by his duty to his neighbours and to society to defend himself, to go to law with those who injure him—sometimes; but never bound to revenge himself, never bound to say, 'He has hurt me, and I will pay him off for it at law;' that is abusing law, which is God's ordinance, for mere selfish revenge. You may say, it is difficult to know which is which, when to defend oneself, and when not. It is difficult; without the light of God's Spirit, I think no man will know. But let a man live by God's Spirit, let him pray for kindliness, mercifulness, manliness, and patience, for true fortitude to bear and to forbear, and God will surely open his eyes to see when he is called on to avenge an injury, and when he is called on to suffer patiently. God will show him. If a man wishes to be like Christ, and to work like Christ, at doing good, God will teach him and guide him in all puzzling matters like this. And do not be afraid of being called cowards and milksops for bearing injuries patiently; those who call you so will be likely to be the greatest cowards themselves. Patience is the truest sign of courage. Ask old soldiers, who have seen real war, and they will tell you that the bravest men, the men who endured best, not in mere fighting, but in standing still for hours to be mowed down by cannon-shot; who were most cheerful and patient in shipwreck, and starvation, and defeat—all things ten times worse than fighting,—ask old soldiers, I say, and they will tell you that the men who showed best in such miseries, were generally the stillest and meekest men in the whole regiment: that is true fortitude; that is Christ's image —the meekest of men, and the bravest too. And so books say, and seem to prove it by many strange stories, that the lion, while he is the strongest and bravest of beasts of prey, is also the most patient and merciful. He knows his own strength and courage, and therefore he does not care to be showing it off. He can afford to endure an affront. It is only the cowardly cur who flies out and barks at every passer-by. And so it is with our blessed Lord. The Bible calls Him the Lion of Judah; but it also calls Him the Lamb dumb before the shearers. Ah! my friends, we must come back to Him; for all the little that is great or noble in man or woman, or dumb beast even, is perfected in Him: He only is perfectly great, perfectly noble, brave, meek. He who, to save us sinful men, endured the cross, despising the shame, till He sat down at the right hand of the Majesty on high, perfectly brave He is, and perfectly gentle, and will be so for ever; for even at his second coming, when He shall appear the Conqueror of hell, with tens of thousands of angels, to take vengeance on those who know not God, and destroy the wicked with the breath of His mouth, even then, in His fiercest anger, the Scripture tells us His anger shall be 'the anger of the Lamb.' Almighty vengeance and just anger, and yet perfect gentleness and love all the while.— Mystery of mysteries!—The wrath of the Lamb. May God give us all to feel in that day, not the wrath, but the love, of the Lamb who was slain for us!

TOWN AND COUNTRY SERMONS.

SERMON I.

HOW TO KEEP PASSION WEEK.

(*Preached before the Queen.*)

PHILIPPIANS ii. 5-11.

Let this mind be in you, which was also in Christ Jesus: who, being in the form of God, thought it not robbery to be equal with God: but made himself of no reputation, and took upon him the form of a servant, and was made in the likeness of men: and being found in fashion as a man, he humbled himself, and became obedient unto death, even the death of the cross. Wherefore God also hath highly exalted him, and given him a name which is above every name: that at the name of Jesus every knee should bow, of things in heaven, and things in earth, and things under the earth; and that every tongue should confess that Jesus Christ is Lord, to the glory of God the Father.

THIS is the first day of Passion Week; and this text is the key-note of Passion Week. It tells us of the obedience of Christ; of the unselfishness of Christ; and, therefore, of the true glory of Christ.

It tells us of One who was in the form of God; the Co-equal and Co-eternal Son; the brightness of his Father's glory, the express image of his Father's person: but who showed forth his Father's glory, and proved that he was the express likeness of his Father's character, by the very opposite means to those which man takes, when he wishes to show forth his own glory.

He was in the form of God. But he did not (so the text seems to mean) think that the bliss of God was a thing to be seized on greedily for himself. He did not think fit merely to glorify himself; to enjoy himself. He was not like the false gods of whom the heathen dreamed, who sat aloft in heaven and enjoyed themselves, careless of mankind.

No. He obeyed his Father utterly, and at all costs. He emptied himself (says St. Paul). He took on him the form of a slave. He humbled himself. He became obedient; obedient to death; and that death the shameful and dreadful death of the cross.

Therefore God has highly exalted him; has declared him to be perfectly good, worthy of all praise, honour, glory, power, and dominion; and has given him a name above all names, the name of Jesus—Saviour. One who saved others, and cared not to save himself.

And therefore, too, God has given him that dominion of which he is worthy, and has proclaimed him Lord and Creator of all beings and all worlds, past, present, and to come.

It is of him; of his obedience; of his unselfishness, that Passion Week speaks to us. It tell us of the mind of Christ, and says, 'Let this mind be in you, which was also in Christ Jesus.'

How, then, shall we keep his Passion Week? There are several ways of keeping it, and all more or less good. Wisdom is justified of all her children.

But no way will be safe for us, unless we keep in mind the mind of Christ—obedience and self-sacrifice.

Some, for instance, are careful this week to attend church as often as possible; and who will blame them?

But unless they keep in mind the mind of Christ, they are apt to fall into the mistake of using vain repetitions, as the heathen do; and of fancying, like them, that they shall be heard for their much speaking, forgetting their Father in heaven knows what they have need of, before they ask him. And that is not like the mind of Christ. It is not like the mind of Christ to fancy that God dwells in temples made with hands; or that he can be worshipped with men's hands, as though he needed anything; seeing he giveth to all life, and breath, and all things. For in him we live, and move, and have our being; and (as even the heathen poet knew), are the offspring, the children, of God.

It is *not* according to the mind of Christ, to worship God as the heathen do, in order to win him to do our will. It *is* according to the mind of Christ to worship God, in order that we may do his will; to believe that God's will is a good will, good in itself, and good for us, and for all things and beings; and, therefore, to ask for strength to do God's will, whatever it may cost us. That is the mind of Christ, who came not to do his own will, but the will of him who sent him; who taught us to pray, as the greatest blessing for which we can ask, 'Father, thy will be done on earth, as it is in heaven;' who himself, in his utter agony, cried, 'Father, not my will, but thine, be done.'

Therefore, it is good to go to church; and good, for some at least, to go as often as possible: but only if we remember why we go, and whom we go to worship—a Father, who asks of us to worship him in spirit and in truth. A Father who has told us what that worship is like.

'Is this (God asked the Jews of old) the fast which I have chosen? Is it a day for a man to afflict his soul, and bow down his head like a bulrush, and to spread sackcloth and ashes under him (playing at being sad, while God has not made him sad)? Wilt thou call this a fast, and an acceptable day to the Lord?'

'Is not this the fast which I have chosen? to loose the bands of wickedness, to undo the heavy burdens, and to let the oppressed go free, and that ye break every yoke? Is it not to deal thy bread to the hungry, and to bring the poor that are cast out to thine house; when thou seest the naked, that thou cover him, and that thou hide not thyself from thine own flesh.'

This is that pure worship and undefiled before God and the Father, of which St. James tells us; and says that it consists in this—'to visit the fatherless and widows in their affliction; and to keep ourselves unspotted from the world.'

In a word, this worship in the spirit, and in truth, is nought else but the mind of Christ. To believe in, to adore the Father's perfect goodness; to long and try to copy that goodness here on earth. That is what Christ did utterly and perfectly, that is what we have to do, each according to our powers; and without it, without the spirit of obedience, all our church-going is of little worth in the eyes of our heavenly Father.

Others, again, go into retirement for this week, and spend it in examining themselves, and thinking over the sufferings of Christ. And who, again, will blame them, provided they do not neglect their daily duty meanwhile?

But they, too, need to keep in mind the mind of Christ, if they mean to keep Passion Week aright.

They need it, indeed. And such a man, before he shuts himself up, and begins to examine himself, would do well *to examine himself as to why he is going to examine himself*, and to ask, Why am I going to do this? Because it is my interest? Because I think I shall gain more safety for my soul? Because I hope it will give me more chance of pleasure and glory in the next world? But, it so; have I the mind of Christ? For he did *not* think of his own interest, his own gain, his own pleasure, his own glory. How is this, then? I confess that the root of all my faults is selfishness. Shall I examine into my own selfishness for a selfish end—to get safety and pleasure by it hereafter? I confess that the very glory of Christ is, that there is no selfishness in him. Shall I think over the sufferings of the unselfish Christ for a selfish end—to get something by it after I die? I am too apt already to make myself the centre, round which all the world must turn : to care for everything only as far as it does *me* good or harm. Shall I make myself the centre round which heaven is to turn? Shall I think of God and of Christ only as far as it will profit *me?* And this week, too, of all weeks in the year? God forgive me! Into what a contradiction I am running unawares !

No If I do shut myself up from my fellowmen, it shall be only to think how I may do my duty better to my fellowmen. If I do think over Christ's sufferings, it shall be only that I may learn from him how to suffer, if need be, at the call of duty ; at least, to stir up in me obedience, usefulness, generosity, that I may go back to my work cheerfully, willingly, careless what reward I get, provided only I can do good in my station.

But, after all, will not the text tell us best how to keep Passion Week? Will not our Lord's own example tell us? Can we go wrong, if we keep our Passion Week as Christ kept his?

And how did he keep it? Certainly not by shutting himself up apart. Certainly not by mere thinking over the glory of self-sacrifice He taught daily, we read, in the temple. Instead of giving up his work for a while, he seems to have worked more earnestly than ever. As the terrible end drew near ; and his soul was troubled; and he was straitened as he looked forward to his baptism of fire; and the struggle in him grew fiercer (for the Bible tells us that there was a struggle) between the Man's natural desire to save his life, and the God's heavenly desire to lay down his life, he threw himself more and more into the work which he had to do. We hear more, perhaps, of our Lord's saying and doings during this week, up to the very moment before he was betrayed to death, than we do of the whole three years of his public life. His teaching was never, it seems, so continual ; his appeals to the nation which he was trying to save were never so pathetic as at the very last ; his warnings to the bigots who were destroying his nation never so terrible; his contempt for personal danger never so clear. The Bible seems to picture him to us as gathering up all his strength for one last effort, if by any means he might save that doomed city of Jerusalem, and in his divine spirit, courting death the more, the more his human flesh shrank from it.

This—the pattern of perfect obedience, perfect unselfishness, perfect generosity, perfect self-sacrificing love—is what we are to look at in Passion Week. This, I believe, is what we are meant to copy in Passion Week; that we may learn the habit of copying it all our lives long.

Why should not we, then, keep Passion Week somewhat as our Lord kept it before us? Not by merely hiding in our closets to meditate, even about *him:* but by going about our work, each in his place, dutifully, bravely, as he went? By doing the duty which lies nearest us, and trying to draw our lesson out of it.

Thus we may keep Passion Week in spirit and in truth; though some of us may hardly have time to enter a church, hardly have time for an hour's private thought about religion.

Amid the bustle of daily duties; amid the buzz of petty cares; amid the anxieties of great labours; amid the roar of the busy world, which cannot stop (and which ought not to stop), for our convenience; we may keep Passion Week in spirit and in truth, if we will do the duty which lies nearest us, and try to draw our lesson out of it.

For practice—and, I believe, practice alone—will teach us to restrain ourselves, and conquer ourselves. Experience—and, I believe, experience alone—will show us our own faults and weaknesses.

Every man—every human spirit on God's earth has spiritual enemies—habits and principles within him—if not other spirits without him, which hinder him, more or less, from being all that God meant him to be. And we must find out those enemies, and measure their strength, not merely by reading of them in books; not merely by fancying them in our own minds; but by the hard blows, and sudden falls, which they too often give us in the actual battle of daily life.

And how can we find them out?

This at least we can do.

We can ask ourselves at every turn,—For what end am I doing this, and this? For what end am I living at all? For myself, or for others?

Am I living for ambition? for fame? for show? for money? for pleasure? If so, I have not the mind of Christ. I have not found out the golden secret. I have not seen what true glory is; what the glory of Christ is—to live for the sake of doing my duty—for the sake of doing good.

And am I—I surely shall be if I am living for myself—struggling, envying, casting an evil eye on those more fortunate than I; perhaps letting loose against them a cruel tongue? If I am doing thus, God forgive me. What have I of the mind of Christ? What likeness between me and him who emptied himself of self, who humbled himself, gave himself up utterly, even to death? Is this the mind of Christ? Is this the spirit whose name is Love?

And yet there should be a likeness. A likeness between Christ and us. A likeness between God and us. For Chris' is the likeness of his Father; and not only of his Father, but of our Father, The Father in heaven. And what should a child be, but like his father? What should man be, but like God?

But how shall we get that likeness? How shall we get the mind of Christ which is the Spirit of God?

This at least we know. That the father will surely hear the child, when the child cries to him. Perhaps will hear him all the more tenderly, the more utterly the child has strayed away.

Our highest reason, the instincts of our own hearts, tell us so. Christ himself has told us so; and said to the Jews of old : 'If ye, being evil, know how to give good gifts to your children, how much more shall your heavenly Father give the Holy Spirit to those who ask *him?*'

Shall give? Yes; and has given already. From that Spirit of God have come, and will always come, all our purest, highest, best thoughts and feelings.

From him comes all which raises us above the animals, and makes us really and truly men and women. All sense of duty, obedience, order, justice, law; all tenderness, pity, generosity, honour, modesty; all this, if you will receive it, is that Christ in us of whom St. Paul tells us, and tells us that he is our hope of glory.

Yes, these feelings in us, which, just as far as we obey them, make us respect ourselves, and make us blessings to our fellow-men; what are they but the Spirit of Christ, the likeness of Christ, the mind of Christ in us; the hope of our glory; because, if we obey them, we shall attain to something of the true glory, the glory with which Christ himself is glorious.

Then let us pray to God, now in this Passion Week, to stir up in us that generous spirit; to deepen in us that fair likeness; to fill us with that noble mind. Let us ask God to quench in us all which is selfish, idle, mean; to quicken to life in us all which is godlike, and from God; that so we may attain, at last, to the true glory, the glory which comes not from selfish ambition; not from selfish pride; not from selfish ease; but from getting rid of selfishness, in all its shapes. The glory which Christ alone has in perfection. The glory before which every knee will one day bow, whether in earth or heaven. Even the glory of doing our duty, regardless of what it costs us in the station to which each of us has been called by his Father in heaven. Amen.

SERMON II.

THE DIVINE HUNGER AND THIRST.

(*Preached before the Queen.*)

PSALM xxxvi. 7, 8, 9.

How excellent is thy loving-kindness, O God! therefore the children of men put their trust under the shadow of thy wings. They shall be abundantly satisfied with the fatness of thy house; and thou shalt make them drink of the river of thy pleasures. For with thee is the fountain of life: in thy light shall we see light.

THIS is a great saying. So great that we shall never know, certainly never in this life, how much it means.

It speaks of being satisfied; of what alone can satisfy a man. It speaks of man as a creature who is, or rather ought to be, always hungering and thirsting after something better than he has, as it is written: 'Blessed are they which hunger and thirst after righteousness; for they shall be filled.' So says David, also, in this Psalm.

I say man ought to be always hungering and thirsting for something better. I do not mean by that that he ought to be discontented. Nothing less. For just in as far as a man hungers and thirsts after righteousness and truth, he will hunger and thirst after nothing else. As long as a man does not care for righteousness, does not care to be a better man himself, and to see the world better round him, so long will he go longing after this fine thing and that, tormenting himself with lusts and passions, greediness and covetousness of divers sorts; and little satisfaction will he get from them. But, when he begins to hunger and thirst after righteousness, that heavenly and spiritual hunger destroys the old carnal hunger in him. He cares less and less to ask, What shall I eat and drink, wherewithal shall I be clothed?—Or how shall I win for myself admiration, station, and all the fine things of this world?—What he thinks of more and more is,—How can I become better and more righteous? How can I make my neighbours better likewise? How the world? As for the good things of this life, if they will make me a better man, let them come. If not, why should I care so much about them? What I want is, to be righteous like God, beneficent and good-doing like God.

That is the man of whom it is written, that he shall be satisfied with the plenteousness of God's house, God's kingdom; for with God is the fountain of life.

Again, as long as a man has no hunger and thirst after truth, he is easily enough interested, though he is not satisfied. He reads, perhaps, and amuses his fancy, but he does no more. He reads again, really to instruct his mind, and learns about this and that: but he does not learn the causes of things; the reasons of the chances and changes of this world; and so he is not satisfied; he takes up doctrines, true ones, perhaps, at secondhand out of books and out of sermons, without having had any personal experience of them; and so, when sickness or sorrow, doubt or dread, come, they do not satisfy him. Then he longs—he ought at least to long—for truth. He thirsts for truth. O that I could know the truth about myself; about my fellow-creatures; about this world. What am I really? What are they? Where am I? What can I know? What ought I to do? I do not want secondhand names and notions. I want to be sure.

That is the divine thirst after truth, which will surely be satisfied. He will drink of the pleasure of true knowledge, as out of an overflowing river; and the more he knows, the more he will be glad to know, and the more he will find he can know, if only he loves truth for truth's own sake; for, as it is written, in God's light shall that man see light.

With God is the well of life; and in his light we shall see light. The first is the answer to man's hunger after righteousness, the second answers to his thirst after truth.

With God is the well of life. There is the answer. Thou wishest to be a good man; to live a good life; to live as a good son, good husband, good father, good in all the relations of humanity; as it is written, 'And Noah was a just man, and perfect in his generations; and Noah walked with God.' Then do thou walk with God. For in him is the life thou wishest for. He alone can quicken thee, and give thee spirit and power to fulfil thy duty in thy generation. Is not his Spirit the Lord and Giver of life—the only fount and eternal spring of life? From him life flows out unto the smallest blade of grass beneath thy feet, the smallest gnat which dances in the sun, that it may live the life which God intends for it. How much more to thee, who hast an altogether boundless power of life; whom God has made in his own likeness, that thou mayest be called his son, and live his life, and do, as Christ did, what thou seest thy heavenly Father do.

Thou feelest, perhaps, how poor and paltry thine own life is, compared with what it might have been. Thou feelest that thou hast never done thy best. When the world is praising thee most, thou art most ashamed of thyself. Thou art ready to cry all day long, 'I have left undone that which I ought to have done;' till, at times, thou longest that all was over, and thou wert beginning again in some freer, fuller, nobler, holier life, to do and to be what thou hast never done nor been here; and criest with the poet—

> 'Tis life, whereof my nerves are scant;
> 'Tis life, not death, for which I pant;
> More life, and fuller, that I want.

Then have patience. With God is the fount of life. He will refresh and strengthen thee; and raise thee up day by day to that new life for which thou longest. Is not Holy communion his own pledge that he will do so? Is not that God's own sign to thee, that though thou canst not feed and strengthen thine own soul, he can and will feed and strengthen it; and feed it—mystery of mysteries—with himself; that God may dwell in thee, and thou in God. And if God and Christ live in thee, and work in thee to will and to do of their own good pleasure, that shall be enough for thee, and thou shalt be satisfied.

And just so, again, with that same thirst after truth. That, too, can only be satisfied by God, and in God. Not by the reading of books, however true; not by listening to sermons, however clever; can we see light: but only in the light of God. Know God. Know that he is justice itself, order itself, love itself, patience itself, pity itself. In the light of that, all things will become light and bright to thee. Matters which seemed to have nothing to do with God, the thought of God will explain to thee, if thou thinkest aright concerning God; and the true knowledge of him will be the key to all other true knowledge in heaven and earth. For the fear of the Lord is the beginning of wisdom, and a good understanding have all they that do thereafter. Must it not be so? How can it be otherwise? For in God all live and move and have their being; and all things which he has made are rays from off his glory, and patterns of his perfect mind. As the Maker is, so is his work; if, therefore, thou wouldest judge rightly of the work, acquaint thyself with the Maker of it, and know first, and know for ever, that his name is Love.

Thus, sooner or later, in God the Father's good time, will thy thirst for truth be satisfied, and thou shalt see the light of God. He may keep thee long waiting for full truth. He may send thee by strange and crooked paths. He may exercise and strain thy reason by doubts, mistakes, and failures; but sooner or later, if thou dost not faint and grow weary, he will show to thee the thing which thou knewest not; for he is thy Father, and wills that all his children, each according to their powers, should share not only in his goodness, but in his wisdom also.

Do any of you say, 'These are words too deep for us; they are for learned people, clever, great saints?' I think not.

I have seen poor people, ignorant people, sick people, poor old souls on parish pay, satisfied with the plenteousness of God's house, and drinking so freely of God's pleasure, that they knew no thirst, fretted not, never were discontented. All vain longings after this and that were gone from their hearts. They had very little; but it seemed to be enough. They had nothing indeed, which we could call pleasure in this world; but somehow what they had satisfied them, because it came from God. They had a hidden pleasure, joy, content, and peace.

They had found out that with God was the well of life; that in God they lived and moved, and had their being. And as long as their souls lived in God, full of the eternal life and goodness, obeying his laws, loving the thing which he commanded, and desiring what he promised, they could trust him for their poor worn-out dying bodies, that he would not let them perish, but raise them up again at the last day. They knew very little; but what they did know was full of light. Cheerful and hopeful they were always; for they saw all things in the light of God. They knew that God was light, and God was love; that his love was shining down on them and on all around them, warming, cheering, quickening into life all things which he had made; so that when the world should have looked most dark to them, it looked most bright, because they saw it lightened up by the smile of their Father in heaven.

O may God bring us all to such an old age, that, as our mortal bodies decay, our souls may be renewed day by day;

that as the life of our bodies grows cold and feeble, the life of our souls may grow richer, warmer, stronger, more useful to all around us, for ever and ever; that as the light of this life fades, the light of our souls may grow brighter, fuller, deeper; till all is clear to us in the everlasting light of God, in that perfect day for which St. Paul thirsted through so many weary years; when he should no more see through a glass darkly, or prophesy in part, and talk as a child, but see face to face, and know even as he was known.

SERMON III.

THE TRANSFIGURATION.

(*Preached before the Queen.*)

MATTHEW xvii. 2 and 9.

And he was transfigured before them. . . . . And he charged them, saying, Tell the vision to no man, until the Son of Man be risen again from the dead.

ANY one who will consider the gospels, will see that there is a peculiar calm, a soberness and modesty about them, very different from what we should have expected to find in them. Speaking, as they do, of the grandest person who ever trod this earth, of the grandest events which ever happened upon this earth—of the events, indeed, which settled the future of this earth for ever,—one would not be surprised at their using grand words—the grandest they could find. If they had gone off into beautiful poetry; if they had filled pages with words of astonishment, admiration, delight; if they had told us their own thoughts and feelings at the sight of our Lord; if they had given us long and full descriptions of our Lord's face and figure, even (as forged documents have pretended to do) to the very colour of his hair, we should have thought it but natural.

But there is nothing of the kind in either of the four gospels, even when speaking of the most awful matters. Their words are as quiet and simple and modest as if they were written of things which might be seen every day. When they tell of our Lord's crucifixion, for instance, how easy, natural, harmless, right, as far as we can see, it would have been to have poured out their own feelings about the most pitiable and shameful crime ever committed upon earth; to have spoken out all their own pity, terror, grief, indignation; and to have stirred up ours thereby. And yet all they say is,—'And they crucified him.' They feel that is enough. The deed is too dark to talk about. Let it tell its own story to all human hearts.

So with this account of the Lord's transfiguration. 'And he took Peter, and James, and John, his brother, up into a high mountain, apart, and was transfigured before them; and his face did shine as the sun; and his raiment was white as the light; . . . and while he yet spake a bright cloud overshadowed them; and, behold, a voice out of the cloud, which said: This is my beloved Son, in whom I am well pleased. Hear ye him.'

How soberly, simply, modestly, they tell this strange story. How differently they might have told it. A man might write whole poems, whole books of philosophy, about that transfiguration, and yet never reach the full depth of its beauty and of its meaning. But the evangelists do not even try to do that. As with the crucifixion, as with all the most wonderful passages of our Lord's life, they simply say what happened, and let the story bring its own message home to our hearts.

What may we suppose is the reason of this great stillness and soberness of the gospels? I believe that it may be explained thus. The men who wrote them were too much *awed* by our Lord, to make more words about him than they absolutely needed.

Our Lord was too utterly *beyond* them. They felt that they could not understand him; could not give a worthy picture of him. He was too noble, too awful, in spite of all his tenderness, for any words of theirs, however fine. We all know that the holiest things, the deepest feelings, the most beautiful sights, are those about which we talk least, and least like to hear others talk. Putting them into words seems impertinent, profane. No one needs to gild gold, or paint the lily. When we see a glorious sunset; when we hear the rolling of the thunder-storm; we do not *talk* about them; we do not begin to cry, How awful, how magnificent; we admire them in silence, and let them tell their own story. Who that ever truly loved his wife talked about his love to her? Who that ever came to Holy Communion in spirit and in truth, tried to put into words what he felt as he knelt before Christ's altar? When God speaks, man had best keep silence.

So it was, I suppose, with the writers of the gospels. They had been in too grand company for them to speak freely of what they felt there. They had seen such sights, and heard such words, that they were inclined to be silent, and think over it all, and only wrote because they must write. They felt that our Lord, as I say, was utterly beyond them, too unlike any one whom they had ever met before; too perfect, too noble, for them to talk about him. So they simply set down his words as he spoke them, and his works as he did them, as far as they could recollect, and left them to tell their own story. Even St. John, who was our Lord's beloved friend, who seems to have caught and copied exactly his way of speaking, seems to feel that there was infinitely more in our Lord than he could put into words, and ends with confessing,—'And there are also many more things which Jesus did, the which if they should be written every one, I suppose that even the world itself could not contain the books that should be written.'

The first reason then, I suppose, for the evangelists' modesty, was their awe and astonishment at our Lord. The next, I think, may have been that they wished to copy him, and so to please him. It surely must have been so, if, as all good Christians believe, they were inspired to write our Lord's life. The Lord would inspire them to write as he would like his life to be written, as he would have written it (if it be reverent to speak of such a thing) himself. They were inspired by Christ's Spirit; and, therefore, they wrote according to the Spirit of Christ, soberly, humbly, modestly, copying the character of Christ.

Think upon that word *modestly*. I am not sure that it is the best; I only know that it is the best which I can find, to express one excellence which we see in our Lord, which is like what we call modesty in common human beings.

We all know how beautiful and noble modesty is; how we all admire it; how it raises a man in our eyes to see him afraid of boasting; never showing off; never requiring people to admire him; never pushing himself forward; or, if his business forces him to go into public, not going for the sake of display, but simply because the thing has to be done; and then quietly withdrawing himself when the thing is done, content that none should be staring at him or thinking of him. This is modesty; and we admire it not only in young people, or those who have little cause to be proud: we admire it much more in the greatest, the wisest, and the best; in those who have, humanly speaking, most cause to be proud. Whenever, on the other hand, we see in wise and good men any vanity, boasting, pompousness of any kind, we call it a weakness in them, and are sorry to see them lowering themselves by the least want of divine modesty.

Now, this great grace and noble virtue should surely be in our Lord, from whom all graces and virtues come; and I think we need not look far through the gospels to find it.

See how he refused to cast himself down from the temple, and make himself a sign and a wonder to the Jews. How he refused to show the Pharisees a sign. How in this very text, when it seemed good to him to show his glory, he takes only three favourite apostles, and commands them to tell no man till he be risen again. See, again, how when the Jews wanted to take him by force, and make him a king, he escaped out of their hands. How when He had been preaching to, or healing the multitude, so that they crowded on him, and became excited about him, he more than once immediately left them, and retired into a desert place to pray.

See, again, how when he did tell the Jews who he was, in words most awfully unmistakeable, the confession was, as it were, drawn from him, at the end of a long argument, when he was forced to speak out for truth's sake. And, even then, how simple, how modest (if I dare so speak), are his words. 'Before Abraham was, I am.' The most awful words ever spoken on earth; and yet most divine in their very simplicity. The Maker of the world telling his creatures that he is their God! What might he *not* have said at such a moment? What might we not fancy his saying? What words, grand enough, awful enough, might not the evangelists have put into his mouth, if they had not been men full of the spirit of truth? And yet what does the Lord say? 'Before Abraham was, I am.' Could he say more? If you think of the matter, No. But could he say less? If you think of the manner, No, likewise.

Truly, 'never man spake as he spake:' because never man was like him. Perfect strength, wisdom, determination, endurance; and yet perfect meekness, simplicity, sobriety. Zeal and modesty. They are the last two virtues which go together most seldom. In him they went together utterly; and were one, as he was one in spirit.

Him some of the evangelists saw, and by him all were inspired; and, therefore, they toned their account of him to his likeness, and, as it were, took their key-note from him, and made the very manner and language of their gospels a pattern of his manners and his life.

And, if we wanted a fresh proof (as, thank God, needs not) that the gospels are true, I think we might find it in this. For when a man is inventing a wonderful story out of his own head, he is certain to dress it up in fine words, fancies, shrewd reflections of his own, in order to make people see, as he goes on, how wonderful it all is. Whereas, no books on earth which describe wonderful events, true or false, are so sober and simple as the gospels, which describe the most wonderful of all events. And this is to me a plain proof (as I hope it will be to you) that Matthew, Mark, Luke, and John were not inventing but telling a plain and true story, and dared not alter it in the least; and, again, a story so strange and beautiful, that they dared not try to make it more strange, or more beautiful, by any words of their own.

They had seen a person, to describe whom passed all their powers of thought and memory, much more their power of words. A person of whom even St. Paul could only say, 'that he was the brightness of his Father's glory, and the express image of his person.'

Words in which to write of him failed them; for no words could suffice. But the temper of mind in which to write of him did not fail them; for, by gazing on the face of the Lord, they had been changed, more or less, into the likeness of his glory; into that temper, simplicity, sobriety, gentleness, modesty, which shone forth in him, and shines forth still in their immortal words about him. God grant that it may shine forth in us. God grant it truly. May we read their words till their spirit passes into us. May we (as St. Paul expresses it) looking on the face of the Lord, as into a glass, be changed into his likeness, from glory to glory. May he who inspired them to write, inspire us to think and work, like our Lord, soberly, quietly, simply. May God take out of us all pride and vanity, boasting and forwardness; and give us the true courage which shows itself by gentleness; the true wisdom which show itself by simplicity; and the true power which show itself by modesty. Amen.

SERMON IV.

A SOLDIER'S TRAINING.

LUKE vii. 2-9.

And a certain centurion's servant, who was dear unto him, was sick, and ready to die. And when he heard of Jesus, he sent unto him the elders of the Jews, beseeching him that he would come and heal his servant. And when they came to Jesus, they besought him instantly, saying, That he was worthy for whom he should do this: For he loveth our nation, and he hath built us a synagogue. Then Jesus went with them. And when he was now not far from the house, the centurion sent friends to him, saying unto him, Lord, trouble not thyself; for I am not worthy that thou shouldest enter under my roof: Wherefore neither thought I myself worthy to come unto thee: but say in a word, and my servant shall be healed. For I also am a man set under authority, having under me soldiers, and I say unto one, Go, and he goeth; and to another, Come, and he cometh; and to my servant, Do this, and he doeth it. When Jesus heard these things he marvelled at him, and turned him about, and said unto the people that followed him, I say unto you, I have not found so great faith, no, not in Israel.

THERE is something puzzling in this speech of the centurion's. One must think twice, and more than twice, to understand clearly what he had in his mind. *I*, indeed, am not quite sure that I altogether understand it. But I may, perhaps, help you to understand it, by telling you what this centurion was.

He was not a Jew. He was a Roman, and a heathen; a man of our race, very likely. And he was a centurion, a captain in the army; and one, mind, who had risen from the ranks, by good conduct, and good service. Before he got his vine-stock, which was the mark of his authority over a hundred men, he had, no doubt, marched many a weary mile under a heavy load, and fought, probably, many a bloody battle in foreign parts. That had been his education, his training, namely, discipline, and hard work. And because he had learned to obey, he was fit to rule. He was helping now to keep in order those treacherous, unruly Jews, and their worthless puppet-kings, like Herod; much as our soldiers in India are keeping in order the Hindoos, and their worthless puppet-kings.

Whether the Romans had any *right* to conquer and keep down the Jews as they did, is no concern of ours just now. But we have proof that what this centurion did, he did wisely and kindly. The elders of the Jews said of him, that he loved the Jews, and had built them a synagogue, a church. I suppose that what he had heard from them about a one living God, who had made all things in heaven and earth, and given them a law, which cannot be broken, so that all things obey him to this day—I suppose, I say, that this pleased him better than the Roman stories of many gods, who were capricious, and fretful, and quarrelled with each other in a fashion which ought to have been shocking to the conscience and reason of a disciplined soldier.

There was a great deal, besides, in the Old Testament, which would, surely, come home to a soldier's heart, when it told him of a God of law, and order, and justice, and might, who defended the right in battle, and inspired the old Jews to conquer the heathen, and to fight for their own liberty. For what was it, which had enabled the Romans to conquer so many great nations? What was it which enabled them to keep them in order, and, on the whole, make them happier, more peaceable, more prosperous, than they had ever been? What was it which had made him, the poor common soldier, an officer, and a wealthy man, governing, by his little garrison of a hundred soldiers, this town of Capernaum, and the country round?

It was this. Discipline; drill; obedience to authority. That Roman army was the most admirably disciplined which the world till then had ever seen. So, indeed, was the whole Roman Government. Every man knew his place, and knew his work. Every man had been trained to obey orders; if he was told to go, to go; if he was told to do, to do, or to die in trying to do, what he was bidden.

This was the great and true thought which had filled this good man's mind—duty, order, and obedience. And by thinking of order, and seeing how strength, and safety, and success lie in order, and by giving himself up to obey orders, body and soul, like a good soldier, had that plain man (who had certainly no scholarship, perhaps could barely read or write) caught sight of a higher, wider, deeper order than even that of a Roman army. He had caught sight of that divine and wonderful order, by which God has constituted the services of men, and angels, and all created things; that divine and wonderful order by which sun and stars, fire and hail, wind and vapour, cattle and creeping things fulfil his word.

Fulfil God's word. That was the thought, surely, which was in the good soldier's mind, and which he was trying to speak out; clumsily, perhaps, but truly enough. I suppose, then, that he thought in his own mind somewhat in this way. 'There is a word of command among us soldiers. Has God, then, no word of command likewise? And that word of command is enough. Is not God's word of command enough likewise? I merely speak, and I am obeyed. I am merely spoken to, and I obey. Shall not God merely speak, and be obeyed likewise? There is discipline and order among men, because it is necessary. An Army cannot be manœuvred, a Government cannot be carried on, without it. Is there not a discipline and order in all heaven and earth? And that discipline is carried out by simple word of command. A word from me will make a man rush upon certain death. A word from certain other men will make me rush on certain death. For I am a man under authority. I have my tribune (colonel, as we should say) over me; and he, again, the perfect (general of brigade) over him. Their word is enough for me. If they want me to do a thing, they do not need to come under my roof, to argue with me, to persuade me, much less to thrust me about, and make me obey them by force. They say to me, 'Go,' and I go; and I say to those under me, 'Go,' and they go likewise.

And if I can work by a word, cannot this Jesus work by a word likewise? He is a messenger of God, with commission and authority from God, to work his will on his creatures. Are not God's creatures as well ordered, disciplined, obedient, as we soldiers are? Are they not a hundred times better ordered? A messenger from God? Is he not a God himself; a God in goodness and mercy; a God in miraculous power? Cannot he do his work by a word, far more certainly than I can do mine? If my word can send a man to death, cannot his word bring a man back to life? Surely it can. 'Lord, thou needest not to come under my roof; speak the word only, and my servant shall be healed.'

By some such thoughts as these, I suppose, had this good soldier gained his great faith; his faith that all God's creatures were in a divine, and wonderful order, obedient to the will of God who made them; and that Jesus Christ was God's viceroy and lieutenant (I speak so, because I suppose that is what he, as a soldier, would have thought), to carry out God's commands on earth.

Now remember that he was the first heathen man of whom we read, that he acknowledged Christ. Remember, too, that the next heathen of whom we read, that he acknowledged

Christ, was also a Roman centurion, he whom the old legends call Longinus, who, when he saw our Lord upon the cross, said, ' Truly this *was* the Son of God.' Remember, again, that the next heathen of whom we read as having acknowledged Christ, he to whom St. Peter was sent, at Joppa, who is often called the first fruits of the heathen, was a Roman centurion likewise.

Surely, there must have been a reason for this. There must be a lesson in this; and this, I think, is the lesson. That the soldierlike habit of mind is one which makes a man ready to receive the truth of Christ. And why? Because the good soldier's first and last thought is Duty. To do his duty by those who are set over him, and to learn to do his duty to those who are set under him. To turn his whole mind and soul to doing, not just what he fancies, but to what must be done, because it is his duty. This is the character which makes a good soldier, and a good Christian likewise. If we be undisciplined and undutiful, and unruly; if we be fanciful, self-willed, disobedient; then we shall not understand Christ, or Christ's rule on earth and in heaven. If there be no order within us, we shall not see his divine and wonderful order all around us. If there be no discipline and obedience within us, we shall never believe really that Christ disciplines all things, and that all things obey him. If there be no sense of duty in us, governing our whole lives and actions, we shall never perceive the true beauty and glory of Christ's character, who sacrificed himself for his duty, which was to do his Father's will.

I tell you, my friends, that nothing prevents a man from gaining either right doctrines or right practice, so much as the undutiful, unruly, self-conceited heart. We may be full of religious knowledge, of devout sentiments, of heavenly aspirations: but in spite of them all, we shall never get beyond false doctrine, and loose practice, unless we have learned to obey; to rule our own minds, and hearts, and tempers, soberly and patiently; to conform to the laws, and to all reasonable rules of society, to believe that God has called us to our station in life, whatever it may be; and to do our duty therein, as faithful soldiers and servants of Christ. For, if you will receive it, the beginning and the middle, and the end of all true religion is simply this. To do the will of God on earth, as it is done in heaven.

SERMON V.

CHRIST'S SHEEP.

MARK vi. 34.

And Jesus, when he came out, saw much people, and was moved with compassion toward them, because they were as sheep not having a shepherd: and he began to teach them many things.

THIS is a text full of comfort, if we will but remember one thing: that Jesus Christ is the same yesterday, to-day, and for ever; and, therefore, what he did when he was upon earth, he is doing now, and will do till the end of the world. If we will believe this, and look at our Lord's doings upon earth as patterns and specimens, as it were, of his eternal life and character, then every verse in the gospels will teach us something, and be precious to us.

The people came to hear Jesus in a desert place; a wild forest country, among the hills on the east side of the Lake of Gennesaret. 'And Jesus, when he came out, saw much people, and was moved with compassion toward them, because they were as sheep having no shepherd: and he taught them many things.'

And, what kind of people were these, who so moved our Lord's pity? The text tells us, that they were like sheep. Now, in what way were they like sheep?

A sheep is simple, and harmless, and tractable, and so, I suppose, were these people. They may not have been very clever and shrewd; not good scholars. No doubt they were a poor, wild, ignorant, set of people; but they were tractable; they were willing to come and learn; they felt their own ignorance, and wanted to be taught. They were not proud and self-sufficient, not fierce or blood-thirsty. The text does not say that they were like wild beasts having no keeper: but like sheep having no shepherd. And therefore Christ pitied them, because they were teachable, willing to be taught, and worth teaching; and yet had no one to teach them.

The Scribes and Pharisees, it seems, taught them nothing. They may have taught the people in Jerusalem, and in the great towns, something: but they seem, from all the gospels, to have cared little or nothing for the poor folk out in the wild mountain country. They liked to live in pride and comfort in the towns, with their comfortable congregations round them, admiring them; but they had no fancy to go out into the deserts, to seek and to save those who were lost. They were bad shepherds, greedy shepherds, who were glad enough to shear God's flock, and keep the wool themselves: but they did not care to feed the flock of God. It was too much trouble; and they could get no honour and no money by it. And most likely they did not understand these poor people; could not speak, hardly understand, their country language; for these Galileans spoke a rough dialect, different from that of the upper classes.

So the Scribes and Pharisees looked down on them as a bad, wild, low set of people, with whom nothing could be done; and said, 'This people who knoweth not the law, is accursed.'

But what they would not do, God himself would. God in Christ had come to feed his own flock, and to seek the lost sheep, and bring them gently home to God's fold. He could feel for these poor wild foresters and mountain shepherds; he could understand what was in their hearts; for he knew the heart of man; and, therefore, he could make them understand him. And it was for this very reason, one might suppose, that our Lord was willing to be brought up at Nazareth, that he might learn the country speech, and country ways, and that the people might grow to look on him as one of themselves. Those Scribes and Pharisees, one may suppose, were just the people whom they could not understand; fine, rich scholars, proud people talking very learnedly about deep doctrines. The country folk must have looked at them as if they belonged to some other world, and said,—Those Pharisees cannot understand us, any more than we can them, with their hard rules about this and that. Easy enough for rich men like them to make rules for poor ones. Indeed our Lord said the very same of them— 'Binding heavy burdens, and grievous to be borne, and laying them on men's shoulders; while they themselves would not touch them with one of their fingers.'

Then the Lord himself came and preached to these poor wild folk, and they heard him gladly. And why? Because his speech was too deep for them? Because he scolded and threatened them? No.

We never find that our Lord spoke harshly to them. They had plenty of sins, and he knew it: but it is most remarkable that the Evangelists never tell us what he said about those sins. What they do tell us is, that he spoke to them of the common things around them, of the flowers of the field, the birds of the air, of sowing and reaping, and feeding sheep; and taught them by parables, taken from the common country life which they lived, and the common country things which they saw; and shewed them how the kingdom of God was like unto this and that which they had seen from their childhood, and how earth was a pattern of heaven. And they could understand that. Not all of it perhaps: but still they heard him gladly. His preaching made them understand themselves, and their own souls, and what God felt for them, and what was right and wrong, and what would become of them, as they never felt before. It is plain and certain that the country people could understand Christ's parables, when the Scribes and Pharisees could not. The Scribes and Pharisees, in spite of all their learning, were those who were without (as our Lord said); who had eyes and could not see, and ears and could not hear, for their hearts were grown fat and gross. With all their learning, they were not wise enough to understand the message which God sends in every flower and every sunbeam; the message which Christ preached to the poor, and the poor heard him gladly; the message which he confirmed to them by his miracles. For what were his miracles like? Did he call down lightning to strike sinners dead, or call up earthquakes, to swallow them? No; he went about healing the sick, cleansing the leper, feeding the hungry in the wilderness; that therefore they might see by his example, the glory of their Father in heaven, and understand that God is a God of Love, of mercy, a deliverer, a Saviour, and not, as the Scribes and Pharisees made him out, a hard task-master, keeping his anger for ever, and extreme to mark what was done amiss.

Ah that, be sure, was what made the Scribes and Pharisees more mad than anything else against Christ, that he spoke to the poor ignorant people of their Father in heaven. It made them envious enough to see the poor people listening to Christ, when they would not listen to them; but when he told these poor folk, whom they called 'accursed and lost sinners,' that God in heaven was their Father, then no name was too bad for our Lord; and they called him the worst name which they could think of,—a friend of publicans and sinners. That was the worst name, in their eyes: and yet, in reality, it was the highest honour. But they never forgave him. How could they? They felt that if he was doing God's work, they were doing the devil's; that either he or they must be utterly wrong: and they never rested till they crucified him, and stopped him for ever, as they fancied, from telling poor ignorant people laden with sins to consider the flowers of the field how they grow, and learn from them that they have a Father in heaven who knoweth what they have need of before they ask him.

But they did not stop Christ: and, what is more, they will never stop him. He has said it, and it remains true for ever; for he is saying it over and over again, in a thousand ways, to his sheep, when they are wandering without a shepherd.

Only let them be Christ's sheep, and he will have compassion on them, and teach them many things. Many may neglect them: but Christ will not. Whoever you may be, however simple you are, however ignorant, however lonely, still, if you are one of Christ's sheep, if you are harmless and teachable, willing and wishing to learn what is right, then Christ will surely teach you in his good time. There never was a soul on earth, I believe, who really wished for God's light, but what God's light came to it at last, as it will to you, if you be Christ's sheep. If you are proud and conceited, you will learn nothing. If you are fierce and headstrong, you will learn nothing. If you are patient and gentle, you will learn all that you need to know; for Christ will teach you. He has many ways of teaching you. By his ministers; by the Bible; by books; by good friends; by sorrows and troubles; by blessings and comforts; by stirring up your mind to think over the common things which lie all around you in your daily work. But what need for me to go on counting by how many ways Christ will lead you, when he has more ways than man ever dreamed of? Who hath known the mind of the Lord; or who shall be his counsellor? Only be sure that he will teach you, if you wish to learn; and be sure that this is what he will teach you—to know the glory of his Father and your Father, whose name is Love.

SERMON VI.

THE HEARING EAR AND THE SEEING EYE.

PROVERBS xx. 12.

The hearing ear, and the seeing eye, the Lord hath made even both of them.

THIS saying may seem at first a very simple one; and some may ask, What need to tell us that? We know it already. God, who made all things, made the ear and the eye likewise.

True, my friends: but the simplest texts are often the deepest; and that, just because they speak to us of the most common things. For the most common things are often the most wonderful, and deep, and difficult to understand.

The hearing of the ear, and the seeing of the eye.—Every one hears and sees all day long, so perpetually that we never think about our hearing or sight, unless we find them fail us. And yet, how wonderful are hearing and sight. How we hear, how we see, no man knows, and perhaps ever will know.

When the ear is dissected and examined, it is found to be a piece of machinery infinitely beyond the skill of mortal man to make. The tiny drum of the ear, which quivers with every sound which strikes it, puts to shame with its divine workmanship all the clumsy workmanship of man. But recollect that *it* is not all the wonder, but only the beginning of it. The ear is wonderful: but still more wonderful is it how the ear *hears*. It is wonderful, I mean, how the ear should be so made, that each different sound sets it in motion in a different way : but still more wonderful, how that sound should pass up from the ear to the nerves and brain, so that we *hear*. Therein is a mystery which no mortal man can explain.

So of the eye. All the telescopes and microscopes which man makes, curiously and cunningly as they are made, are clumsy things compared with the divine workmanship of the eye. I cannot describe it to you; nor, if I could, is this altogether a fit place to do so. But if any one wishes to see the greatness and the glory of God, and be overwhelmed with the sense of his own ignorance, and of God's wisdom, let him read any book which describes to him the eye of man, or even of beast, and then say with the psalmist, ' I am fearfully and wonderfully made. Marvellous are thy works, O Lord, and that my soul knoweth right well.'

And remember, that as with the ear, so with the eye, the mere workmanship of it is only the beginning of the wonder. It is very wonderful that the eye should be able to take a picture of each thing in front of it; that on the tiny black curtain at the back of the eye, each thing outside should be printed, as it were, instantly, exact in shape and colour. But that is not sight. Sight is a greater wonder, over and above that. Seeing is this, that the picture which is printed on the back of the eye, is also printed on our brain, so that we *see* it. There is the wonder of wonders.

Do some of you not understand me? Then look at it thus. If you took out the eye of an animal, and held it up to anything, a man or a tree, a perfect picture of that man or that tree would be printed on the back of the dead eye : but the eye would not *see* it. And why ? Because it is cut off from the live brain of the animal to which it belonged; and therefore, though the picture is still in the eye, it sends no message about itself up to the brain, and is not seen.

And how does the picture on the eye send its message about

itself to the brain, so that the brain sees it? And how, again—for here is a third wonder, greater still—do *we* ourselves see what our brain sees?

That no man knows, and, perhaps, never will know in this world. For science, as it is called, that is, the understanding of this world, and what goes on therein, can only tell us as yet what happens, what God does: but of how God does it, it can tell us little or nothing; and of why God does it, nothing at all; and all we can say is, at every turn, " God is great."

Mind, again, that these are not all the wonders which are in the ear and in the eye. It is wonderful enough, that our brains should hear through our ears, and see through our eyes: but it is more wonderful still, that they should be able to recollect what they have heard and seen. That you and I should be able to call up in our minds a sound which we heard yesterday, or even a minute ago, is to me one of the most utterly astonishing things I know of. And so of ordinary recollection. What is it that we call remembering a place, remembering a person's face? That place, or that face, was actually printed, as it were, through our eye upon our brain. We have a picture of it somewhere; we know not where, inside us. But that we should be able to call that picture up again, and look at it with what we rightly call our mind's eye, whenever we choose; and not merely that one picture only, but thousands of such;—that is a wonder, indeed, which passes understanding. Consider the hundreds of human faces, the hundreds of different things and places, which you can recollect; and then consider that all those different pictures are lying, as it were, over each other in hundreds in that small place, your brain, for the most part without interfering with, or rubbing out each other, each ready to be called up, recollected, and used in its turn.

If this is not wonderful, what is? So wonderful, that no man knows, or, I think, ever will know, how it comes to pass. How the eye tells the brain of the picture which is drawn upon the back of the eye—how the brain calls up that picture when it likes—these are two mysteries beyond all man's wisdom to explain. These are two proofs of the wisdom and the power of God, which ought to sink deeper into our hearts than all signs and wonders;—greater proofs of God's power and wisdom, than if yon fir-trees burst into flame of themselves, or yon ground opened, and a fountain of water sprung out. Most people think much of signs and wonders. Just in proportion as they have no real faith in God, just in proportion as they forget God, and will not see that he is about their path, and about their bed, and spying out all their ways, they are like those godless Scribes and Pharisees of old, who must have signs and wonders before they would believe. So it is: the commonest things are as wonderful, more wonderful, than the uncommon; and yet, people will hanker after the uncommon, as if they belonged to God more immediately than the commonest matters.

If yon trees burst out in flame; if yon hill opened, and a fountain sprang up, how many would cry, 'How awful! How wonderful! Here is a sign that God is near us! It is time to think about our souls now! Perhaps the end of the world is at hand!' And all the while they would be blind to that far more awful proof of God's presence, that all around them, all day long, all over the world, millions of human ears are hearing, millions of human eyes are seeing, God alone knows how; millions of human brains are recollecting, God alone knows how. That is not faith, my friends, to see God only in what is strange and rare: but this is faith, to see God in what is most common and simple; to know God's greatness not so much from disorder, as from order; not so much from those strange sights in which God seems (but only seems) to break his laws, as from those common ones in which he fulfils his laws.

I know it is very difficult to believe that. It has been always difficult; and for this reason. Our souls and minds are disorderly; and therefore order does not look to us what it is, the likeness and glory of God. I will explain. If God, at any moment, should create a full-grown plant with stalk, leaves, and flowers, all perfect, all would say, There is the hand of God! How great is God! There is, indeed, a miracle!—Just because it would seem not to be according to order. But the tiny seed sown in the ground, springing up into root-leaf, stalk, rough leaf, flower, seed, which will again be sown and spring up into leaf, flower, and seed;—in that perpetual miracle, people see no miracle: just because it is according to order: because it comes to pass by regular and natural laws. And why? Because, such as we are, such we fancy God to be. And we are all of us more or less disorderly: fanciful; changeable; fond of doing not what we ought, but what we like; fond of showing our power, not by keeping rules, but by breaking rules; and we fancy too often that God is like ourselves, and make him in our image, after our own likeness, which is disorder, and self-will, and changeableness; instead of trying to be conformed to his image and his likeness, which is order and law eternal: and, therefore, whenever God seems (for he only *seems* to our ignorance) to be making things suddenly, as we make, or working arbitrarily as we work, then we acknowledge his greatness and wisdom. Whereas his greatness, his wisdom, are rather shown in not making as we make, not working as we work: but in this is the greatness of God manifest, in that he has ordained laws which must work of themselves, and with which he need never interfere: laws by which the tiny seed, made up only (as far as we can see) of a little water, and air, and earth, must grow up into plant, leaf, and flower, utterly unlike itself, and must produce seeds which have the truly miraculous power of growing up in their turn, into plants exactly like that from which they sprung, and no other. Ah, my friends, herein is the glory of God: and he who will consider the lilies of the field, how they grow, that man will see at last that the highest, and therefore the truest, notion of God is, not that the universe is continually going wrong, so that he has to interfere and right it: but that the universe is continually going right, because he hath given it a law which cannot be broken.

And when a man sees that, there will arise within his soul a clear light, and an awful joy, and an abiding peace, and a sure hope ; and a faith as of a little child.

Then will that man crave no more for signs and wonders, with the superstitious and the unbelieving, who have eyes, and see not ; ears, and cannot hear ; whose hearts are waxen gross, so that they cannot consider the lilies of the field, how they grow : but all his cry will be to the Lord of Order, to make him orderly ; to the Lord of Law, to make him loyal ; to the Lord in whom is nothing arbitrary, to take out of him all that is unreasonable and self-willed ; and make him content, like his Master Christ before him, to do the will of his Father in heaven, who has sent him into this noble world. He will no longer fancy that God is an absent God, who only comes down now and then to visit the earth in signs and wonders : but he will know that God is everywhere, and over all things, from the greatest to the least ; for in God, he, and all things created, live and move and have their being. And therefore, knowing that he is always in the presence of God, he will pray to be taught how to use all his powers aright, because all of them are the powers of God ; pray to be taught how to see, and how to hear ; pray that when he is called to account for the use of this wonderful body which God has bestowed on him, he may not be brought to shame by the thought that he has used it merely for his own profit or his own pleasure, much less by the thought that he has weakened and diseased it by misuse and neglect : but comforted by the thought that he has done with it what the Lord Jesus did with his body—made it the useful servant, and not the brutal master, of his immortal soul.

And he will do that, I believe, just as far as he keeps in mind what a wonderful and useful thing his body is ; what a perpetual token and witness to him of the unspeakable greatness and wisdom of God ; just in proportion as he says day by day, with the Psalmist, 'Thou hast fashioned me behind and before, and laid thine hand upon me. Such knowledge is too wonderful and excellent for me; I cannot attain unto it. Whither shall I go, then, from thy Spirit; or whither shall I go from thy presence? If I climb up into heaven, thou art there. If I go down to hell, thou art there also. If I take the wings of the morning, and remain in the uttermost parts of the sea, even there also shall thy hand lead me, thy right hand shall hold me.'—

Just in proportion as he recollects that, will he utter from his heart the prayer which follows, 'Try me, O God, and seek the ground of my heart; prove me, and examine my thoughts. Look well if there be any way of wickedness in me, and lead me in the way everlasting.'

SERMON VII.

THE VICTORY OF FAITH.

(*First Sunday after Easter.*)

---

1 JOHN v. 4, 5.

Whatsoever is born of God overcometh the world: and this is the victory which overcometh the world, even our faith. Who is he that overcometh the world, but he that believeth that Jesus is the Son of God?

WHAT is the meaning of 'overcoming the world?' What is there about the world which we have to overcome? lest it should overcome us, and make worse men of us than we ought to be. Let us think awhile.

1. In the world all seems full of chance and change. One man rises, and another falls, one hardly knows why: they hardly know themselves. A very slight accident may turn the future of a man's whole life, perhaps of a whole nation. Chance and change—there seems to us, at times, to be little else than chance and change. Is not the world full of chance? Are not people daily crushed in railways, burnt to death, shot with their own guns, poisoned by mistake, without any reason that we can see, why one should be taken, and another left? Why should not an accident happen to us, as well as to others? Why should not we have the thing we love best snatched from us this day? Why not, indeed? What, then, will help us to overcome the fear of chances and accidents? How shall we

keep from being fearful, fretful, full of melancholy forebodings! Where shall we find something abiding and eternal, a refuge sure and steadfast, in which we may trust, amid all the chances and changes of this mortal life? St. John tells us—In that within you which is born of God.

2. In the world so much seems to go by fixed law and rule. That is even more terrible to our minds and hearts—to find that all around us, in the pettiest matters of life, there are laws and rules ready made for us, which we cannot break; laws of trade; laws of prosperity and adversity; laws of health and sickness; laws of weather and storms; laws by which not merely we, but whole nations, grow, and decay, and die.—All around us, laws, iron laws, which we do not make, and which we dare not try to break, lest they go on their way, and grind us to powder.

Then comes the awful question, Are we at the mercy of these laws? Is the world a great machine, which goes grinding on its own way without any mercy to us or to anything; and are we each of us parts of the machine, and forced of necessity to do all we do? Is it true, that our fate is fixed for us from the cradle to the grave, and perhaps beyond the grave? How shall we prevent the world from overcoming us in this? How shall we escape the temptation to sit down and fold our hands in sloth and despair, crying, What we are, we must be; and what will come, must come; whether it be for our happiness or misery, our life or death? Where shall we find something to trust in, something to give us confidence and hope that we can mend ourselves, that self-improvement is of use, that working is of use, that prudence is of use, for God will reward every man according to his work? St. John tells us—In that within you which is born of God.

3. Then, again, in the world how much seems to go by selfishness. Let every man take care of himself, help himself, fight for himself against all around him, seems to be the way of the world, and the only way to get on in the world. But is it really to be so? Are we to thrive only by thinking of our-

selves? Something in our hearts tells us, No. Something in our hearts tells us that this would be a very miserable world if every man shifted for himself; and that even if we got this world's good things by selfishness, they would not be worth having after all, if we had no one but ourselves to enjoy them with. What is that? St. John answers—That in you which is born of God. It will enable you to overcome the world's deceits, and to see that selfishness is *not* the way to prosper.

4. Once, again; in the world how much seems to go by mere custom and fashion. Because one person does a thing right or wrong, everybody round fancies himself bound to do likewise. Because one man thinks a thing, hundreds and thousands begin to think the same from mere hearsay, without examining and judging for themselves. There is no silliness, no cruelty, no crime into which people have not fallen, and may still fall, for mere fashion's sake, from blindly following the example of those round him. 'Everybody does so; and I must. Why should I be singular?' Or, 'Everybody does so; what harm can there be in my doing so?'

But there is something in each of us which tells us that that is not right; that each man should act according to his own conscience, and not blindly follow his neighbour, not knowing whither, like sheep over a hedge; that a man is directly responsible at first for his own conduct to God, and that 'my neighbours did so' will be no excuse in God's sight. What is it which tells us this? St. John answers, That in you which is born of God; and it, if you will listen to it, will enable you to overcome the world's deceit, and its vain fashions, and foolish hearsays, and blind party-cries; and not to follow after a multitude to do evil.

What, then, is this thing? St. John tells us that it is born of God; and that it is our faith. *Faith* will enable us to overcome the world. We shall overcome by believing and trusting in something which we do not see. But in what? Are we to believe and trust that we are going to heaven? St. John does not say so; he was far too wise, my friends, to say so: for a man's trusting that he is going to heaven, if that is all the faith he has, is more likely to make the world overcome him, than him overcome the world. For it will make him but too ready to say, 'If I am sure to be saved after I die, it matters not so very much what I do before I die. I may follow the way of the world here, in money-making and meanness, and selfishness; and then die in peace, and go to heaven after all.'

This is no fancy. There are hundreds, nay thousands, I fear, in England now, who let the world and its wicked ways utterly overcome them, just because their faith is a faith in their own salvation, and not the faith of which St. John speaks—Believing that Jesus is the Son of God.

But some may ask, 'How will believing that Jesus is the Son of God help us more than believing the other? For, after all, we do believe it. We all believe that Jesus is the Son of God: but as for overcoming the world, we dare not say too much of that. We fear we are letting the world overcome us; we are living too much in continual fear of the chances and changes of this mortal life. We are letting things go too much their own way. We are trying too much each to get what he can by his own selfish wits, without considering his neighbours. We are following too much the ways and fashions of the day, and doing and saying and thinking anything that comes uppermost, just because others do so round us.'

Is it so, my friends? But do you really believe that Jesus is the Son of God? For sure I am, that if you did, and I did, really and fully believe that, we could all lead much better lives than we are leading, manful and godly, useful and honourable, truly independent and yet truly humble; fearing God and fearing nothing else. But do you believe it? Have you ever thought of all that those great words mean, 'Jesus is the Son of God'?—That he who died on the cross, and rose again for us, now sits at God's right hand, having all power given to him in heaven and earth? For, think, if we really believed that, what power it would give us to overcome the world, and all its chances and changes; all its seemingly iron laws; all its selfish struggling; all its hearsays and fashions.

1. Those chances and changes of mortal life of which I spoke first. We should not be afraid of them, then, even if they came. For we should believe that they were not chances and changes at all, but the loving providence of our Lord and Saviour, a man of the substance of his mother, born in the world, who therefore can be touched with a feeling of our infirmities, and knows our necessities before we ask, and our ignorance in asking, and orders all things for good to those who love him, and desire to copy his likeness.

2. Those stern laws and rules by which the world moves, and will move as long as it lasts—we should not be afraid of them either, as if we were mere parts of a machine forced by fate to do this thing and that, without a will of our own. For we should believe that these laws were the laws of the Lord Jesus Christ; that he had ordained them for the good of man, of man whom he so loved that he poured out his most precious blood upon the cross for us; and therefore we should not fear them; we should only wish to learn them, that we might obey them, sure that they are the laws of life; of health and wealth, peace and safety, honour and glory in this world and in the world to come; and we should thank God whenever men of science, philosophers, clergymen, or any persons whatsoever, found out more of the laws of that good God, in whom we and all created things live and move and have our being.

3. If we believe really that Jesus was the Son of God, we should never believe that selfishness was to be the rule of our lives. One sight of Christ upon his cross would tell us that not selfishness, but love, was the likeness of God, that not selfishness, but love, which gives up all that it may do good, was the path to honour and glory, happiness and peace.

4. If we really believe this, we should never believe that custom and fashion ought to rule us. For we should live by

the example of some one else: but by the example of only one —of Jesus himself. We should set him before us as the rule of all our actions, and try to keep our conscience pure, not merely in the sight of men who may mistake, and do mistake, but in the sight of Jesus, the Word of God, who pierces the very thoughts and intents of the heart; and we should say daily with St. Paul, 'It is a small thing for me to be judged by you, or any man's judgment, for he that judges me is the Lord.'

And so we should overcome the world. Our hearts and spirits would rise above the false shows of things, to God who has made all things; above fear and melancholy; above laziness and despair; above selfishness and covetousness; above custom and fashion; up to the everlasting truth and order, which is the mind of God; that so we might live joyfully and freely in the faith and trust that Christ is our king, Christ is our Saviour, Christ is our example, Christ is our judge; and that as long as we are loyal to him, all will be well with us in this world, and in all worlds to come.—Amen.

SERMON VIII.

TURNING-POINTS.

LUKE xix. 41, 42.

And when Jesus was come near, he beheld the city, and wept over it, saying, If thou hadst known, even thou, at least in this thy day, the things which belong unto thy peace! but now they are hid from thine eyes.

MY dear friends, here is a solemn lesson to be learnt from this text. What is true of whole nations, and of whole churches, is very often true of single persons—of each of us.

To most men—to all baptized Christian men, perhaps—there comes a day of visitation, a crisis, or turning-point in our lives. A day when Christ sets before us, as he did to those Jews, good and evil, light and darkness, right and wrong, and says, Choose! Choose at once, and choose for ever; for by what you choose this day, by that you must abide till death. If you make a mistake now, you will rue it to the last. If you take the downward road now, you will fall lower and lower upon it henceforth. If you shut your eyes now to the things which belong to your peace, they will be hid from your eyes for ever; and nothing but darkness, ignorance, and confusion will be before you henceforth.

What will become of the man's soul after he dies, I cannot say. Christ is his judge, and not I. He may be saved, yet so as by fire, as St. Paul says. Repentance is open to all men, and forgiveness for those who repent. But from that day, if he chooses wrongly, true repentance will grow harder and harder to him—perhaps impossible at last. He has made his bed, and he must lie on it. He has chosen the evil, and refused the good; and now the evil must go on getting more and more power over him. He has sold his soul, and now he must pay the price. Again, I say, he may be saved at last. Who am I, to say that God's mercy is not boundless, when the Bible says it is? But one may well say of that man, 'God help him,' for he will not be able to help himself henceforth.

It is an awful thing, my friends, to think that we may fix our own fate in this world, perhaps in the world to come, by one act of wilful folly or sin: but so it is. Just as a man may do one tricky thing about money, which will force him to do another to hide it, and another after that, till he becomes a confirmed rogue in spite of himself. Just as a man may run into debt once, so that he never gets out of debt again; just as a man may take to drink once, and the bad habit grow on him till he is a confirmed drunkard to his dying day. Just as a man may mix in bad company once, and so become entangled as in a net, till he cannot escape his evil companions, and lowers himself to their level day by day, till he becomes as bad as they. Just as a man may be unfaithful to his wife once, and so blunt his conscience till he becomes a thorough profligate, breaking her heart, and ruining his own soul. Just as—but why should I go on, mentioning ugly examples, which we all know too well, if we will open our own eyes and see the world and mankind as they are? I will say no more, lest I should set you on judging other people, and saying, 'There is no hope for them. They are lost.' No; let us rather judge ourselves, as any man can, and will, who dares face fact, and look steadily at what he is, and what he might become. Do we not know that we could, any one of us, sell our own souls, once and for all, if we choose? I know that I could. I know that there are things which I might do, which if I did from that moment forth, I should have no hope, but only a fearful looking forward to judgment and fiery indignation. And have you never felt, when you were tempted to do wrong: 'I dare not do it for my own sake; for if I did this one wickedness, I feel sure that I never should be an honest man again?' If you have felt that, thank God, indeed; for then you have seen the things which belong to your peace; you have known the day of your visitation; and you will be a better man as long as you live, for having fought against that one temptation, and chosen the good, and refused the evil, when God put them unmistakeably before you.

No; the real danger is, lest a man should be as those Jews, and not know the day of his visitation. Ah, that is ruinous indeed, when a man's eyes are blinded as those Jews' eyes were; when a great temptation comes on him, and he thinks it no temptation at all; when hell is opening beneath him, with the devils trying to pluck him down, and heaven opening above him, with God's saints and martyrs beckoning him up, looking with eyes of unutterable pity and anxiety and love on a poor soul; and that poor soul sees neither heaven nor hell, nor anything but his own selfish interest, selfish pleasure, or selfish pride, and snaps at the devil's bait as easily as a silly fish; while the devil, instead of striking to frighten him, lets him play with the bait, and gorge it in peace, fancying that he is well off, when really he is fast hooked for ever, led captive thenceforth from bad to worse by the snare of the devil. Oh miserable blindness, which comes over men sometimes, and keeps them asleep at the very moment that they ought to be most wide awake!

And what throws men into that sleep? What makes them do in one minute something which curses all their lives afterwards? Love of pleasure? Yes: that is a common curse enough, as we all know. But a worse snare than even that is pride and self-conceit. That was what ruined those old Jews. That was what blinded their eyes. They had made up their minds that they saw; therefore they were blind : that they could not go wrong; therefore they went utterly and horribly wrong thenceforth : that they alone of all people knew and kept God's law; therefore they crucified the Son of God himself for fulfilling their law. They were taken unawares, because they were asleep in vain security.

And so with us. By conceit and carelessness, we may ruin ourselves in a moment, once and for all. When a man has made up his mind that he is quite worldly-wise; that no one can take him in; that he thoroughly understands his own interest; then is that man ripe and ready to commit some enormous folly, which may bring him to ruin.

When a man has made up his mind that he knows all doctrines, and is fully instructed in religion, and can afford to look down on all who differ from him; then is that man ripe and ready for doing something plainly wrong and wicked, which will blunt his conscience from that day forth, and teach him to call evil good, and good evil more and more; till, in the midst of all his fine religious professions, he knows not plain right from plain wrong—full of the form of godliness, but denying the power of it in scandal of his every-day life.

Yes, my friends, our only safeguard is humility. Be not high-minded, but fear. Avoid every appearance of evil. Believe that in every temptation heaven and hell may be at stake: and that the only way to be safe is to do nothing wilfully wrong at all, for you never know how far downward one wilful sin may lead you. The devil is not simple enough to let you see the bottom of his pitfall: but it is so deep, nevertheless, that he who falls in, may never get out again.

And do not say in your hearts about this thing and that, 'Well, it is wrong : but it is such a little matter.' A little draught may give a great cold; and a great cold grow to a deadly decline. A little sin may grow to a great bad habit; and a great bad habit may kill both body and soul in hell. A little bait may take a great fish; and the devil fishes with a very fine line, and is not going to let you see his hook. The only way to be safe is to avoid all appearance of evil, lest when you fancy yourself most completely your own master, you find yourself the slave of sin.

Oh, may God give us all the spirit of watchfulness and godly fear! Of watchfulness, lest sin overtake us unawares; and of godly fear, that we may have strength to say with Joseph, 'How can I do this great wickedness, and sin against God?' Of watchfulness, too, not only against sin, but for God; of godly fear, not only fear of God's anger, but fear of God's love.

Do you ask what I mean? This, my friends; that as we cannot tell at any moment what danger may be coming on us, so we cannot tell at any moment what blessing from God may be coming on us. Those Jews, in the day of their visitation, were blind, and they rejected Christ: but recollect, that it was *Christ* whom they rejected; that Christ was there, not in anger, but in love; not to judge, but to save; that the power of the Lord was present, not to destroy, but to heal them. They would have none of him. True; but they might have had him if they had chosen. They denied him; but he could not deny himself. He was there to teach and to save, as he comes to teach and to save every man.

Therefore, I say, be watchful. Believe that Christ is looking for you always, and expect to meet him at any moment. I do not mean in visible form, in vision or apparition. No. He comes, not by observation, that a man may say, 'Lo, here; and lo, there;' but he comes within you, to your hearts, with the still, small voice, which softens a man and sobers him for a moment, and makes him yearn after good, and say in his heart, 'Ah, that I were as when I was a child upon my mother's knee.' Oh! listen to that softening, sobering voice. Through very small things it may speak to you: but it is Christ himself who speaks. Whenever your heart is softened to affection toward parent, or child, or your fellowman, then Christ is speaking to you, and showing you the things which belong to your peace. Whenever the feeling of justice, and righteous horror of all meanness rises strong in you, then Christ is speaking to you. Whenever your heart burns within you with admiration of some noble action, then Christ is speaking to you. Whenever a chance word in sermons or in books touches your conscience, and reproves you, then Christ is speaking to you. Oh turn not a deaf ear to those instincts. They may be the very turning-points of your lives. One such godly motion, one such pure inspiration of the Spirit of God listened to humbly, and obeyed heartily, may be the means of putting you into the right path thenceforward, that you may go on and grow in strength and wisdom, and favour with God and man; till you become again, in the world to come, what you were when you were carried home from the baptismal font, a little child, pure from all spot of sin.

SERMON IX.

OBADIAH.

1 KINGS, xviii. 3, 4.

And Ahab called Obadiah, which was the governor of his house. (Now Obadiah feared the Lord greatly : for it was so, when Jezebel cut off the prophets of the Lord, that Obadiah took an hundred prophets, and hid them by fifty in a cave, and fed them with bread and water.)

THIS is the first and last time throughout the Bible, that we find this Obadiah mentioned. We find the same name elsewhere, but not the same person. It is a common Jewish name, Obadiah, and means, I believe, the servant of the Lord.

All we know of the man is contained in this chapter. We do not read what became of him afterwards. He vanishes out of the story as quickly as he came into it, and, as we go on through the chapter and read of that grand judgment at Carmel between Elijah and the priests of Baal, and the fire of God which came down from heaven, to shew that the Lord was God, we forget Obadiah, and care to hear of him no more.

And yet Obadiah was a great man in his day. He was, it seems, King Ahab's vizier, or prime minister; the second man in the country after the king; and a prime minister in those eastern kingdoms had, and has now, far greater power than he has in a free country like this. Yes, Obadiah was a great man in his day, I doubt not; and people bowed before him when he went out, and looked up to him, in that lawless country, for life or death, for ruin or prosperity. Their money, and their land, their very lives might depend on his taking a liking toward them, or a spite against them. And he had wealth, no doubt, and his fair and great house there among the beautiful hills of Samaria, ceiled with cedar and painted with vermilion, with its olive groves and vineyards, and rich gardens full of gay flowers and sweet spices, figs and peaches, and pomegranates, and all the lovely vegetation which makes those Eastern gardens like Paradise itself. And he had his great household of slaves, menservants and maidservants, guards and footmen, singing men and singing women—perhaps a hundred souls and more eating and drinking in his house day by day for many a year. A great man; full of wealth, and pomp, and power. We know that it must have been so, because we know well in what luxury those great men in the East lived. But where is it now?

Where is it now? Vanished and forgotten. Be not thou afraid, though one be made rich, or if the glory of his house be increased. For he shall carry nothing away with him when he dieth; neither shall his pomp follow him.

See—of all Obadiah's wealth and glory, the Bible does not say one word. It is actually not worth mentioning. People admired Obadiah, I doubt not, while he was alive; envied him too, tried to thrust him out of his place, slander him to King Ahab, drive him out of favour, and step into his place, that they might enjoy his wealth and his power instead of him. The fine outside of Obadiah was what they saw, and coveted, and envied —as we are tempted now to say in our hearts, 'Ah, if I was rich like that man. Ah, if I could buy what I liked, go where I liked, do what I liked, like that great Lord!'—and yet, that is but the outside, the shell, the gay clothing, not the persons themselves. The day must come, when they must put off all that; when nothing shall remain but themselves; and they themselves, naked as they were born, shall appear before the judgment-seat of God.

And did Obadiah, then, carry away nothing with him when he died? Yes; and yet again, No. His wealth and his power he left behind him: but one thing he took with him into the grave, better than all wealth and power; and he keeps it now, and will keep it for ever; and that is, a good, and just, and merciful action—concerning which it is written, 'Blessed are the dead which die in the Lord; for they rest from their labours, and their works do follow them.' Yes, though a man's wealth will not follow him beyond the grave, his works will; and so Obadiah's one good deed has followed him. 'He feared the Lord greatly, and when Jezebel cut off the prophets of the Lord, Obadiah took a hundred prophets, and hid them by fifty in a cave, and fed them with bread and water.'

That has followed Obadiah; for by it we know him, now two thousand years and more after his death, here in a distant land of the name of which he never heard. By that good deed he lives. He lives in the pages of the Holy Bible; he lives in our minds and memories; and more than all, by that good deed he lives for ever in God's sight; he is rewarded for it, and the happier for it, doubt it not, at this very moment, and will be the happier for it for ever.

Oh blessed thought! that there is something of which death cannot rob us! That when we have to leave this pleasant world, wife and child, home and business, and all that has grown up round us here on earth, till it has become like a part of ourselves, yet still we are not destitute. We can turn round on death and say—'Though I die, yet canst thou not take my righteousness from me!' Blessed thought! that we cannot do a good deed, not even give a cup of cold water in Christ's name, but what it shall rise again, like a guardian angel, to smooth our death-bed pillow, and make our bed for us in our sickness, and follow us into the next world, to bless us for ever and ever!

And blessed thought, too, that what you do well and lovingly, for God's sake, will bless you here in this world before you die!

Yes, my friends, in the dark day of sorrow and loneliness, and fear and perplexity, you will find old good deeds, which you perhaps have forgotten, coming to look after you, as it were, and help you in the hour of need. Those whom you have helped, will help you in return : and if they will not, God will ; for he is not unrighteous, to forget any work and labour of love, which you have showed for his name's sake, in ministering to his saints. So found Obadiah in that sad day, when he met Elijah.

For he was in evil case that day, as were all souls, rich and poor, throughout that hapless land. For three weary years, there had been no drop of rain : the earth beneath their feet had been like iron, and the heavens above them brass ; and Obadiah had found poverty, want, and misery, come on him in the midst of all his riches: he had seen his fair gardens wither, and his olives and his vines burnt up with drought ;—his cattle had perished on the hills, and his servants, too, perhaps, in his house. Perhaps his children at home were even then crying for food and water, and crying in vain, in spite of all their father's greatness.

What was the use of wealth ? He could not eat gold, nor drink jewels. What was the use of his power? He could not command the smallest cloud to rise up off the sea, and pour down one drop of water to quench their thirst. Yes, Obadiah was in bitter misery that day, no doubt; and all the more, because he felt that all was God's judgment on the people's sins. They had served Baalim and Ashtaroth, the sun and moon and stars, and prayed to them for rain and fruitful seasons, as if they were the rulers of the weather and the soil, instead of serving the true God who made heaven and earth, and all therein : and now God had *judged* them : he had given his sentence and verdict about that matter, and told them, by a sign which could not be mistaken, that he, and not the sun and moon, was master of the sky and the sea, and the rain and the soil. They had prayed to the sun and moon ; and this was the fruit of their prayers—that their prayers had not been heard: but instead of rain and plenty, was drought and barrenness;— carcasses of cattle scattered over the pastures—every village full of living skeletons, too weak to work (though what use in working, when the ground would yield no crop?)—crawling about, their tongues cleaving to the roof of their mouths, in vain searching after a drop of water. Fearful and sickening sights must Obadiah have seen that day, as he rode wearily on upon his pitiful errand. And the thought of what a pitiful errand he was going on, and what a pitiful king he served, must have made him all the more miserable; for, instead of turning and repenting, and going back to the true God, which was the plain and the only way of escaping out of that misery, that wretched King Ahab seems to have cared for nothing but his horses.

We do not read that he tried to save one of his wretched people alive. All his cry was, 'Go into the land, to all fountains of water and all brooks; perhaps we shall find grass enough to save the horses and mules alive: that we lose not all the beasts.' The horses were what he cared for more than the human beings, as many of those bad kings of Israel did. Moses had expressly commanded them not to multiply horses to themselves; but they persisted always in doing so, nevertheless. And why? Because they wanted horses to mount their guards; to keep up a strong force of cavalry and chariots, in order to oppress the poor country people, whom they had brought down to slavery, from having been free yeomen, as they were in the days of Moses and Joshua. And what hope could he have for his wretched country? The people shewed no signs of coming to their senses; the king still less. His wicked Queen Jezebel was as devoted as ever to her idols; the false prophets of Baal were four hundred and fifty men, and the prophets of the groves (where the stars were worshipped) four hundred; and these cheats contrived (as such false teachers generally do) to take good care of themselves, and to eat at Jezebel's table, while all the rest of the people were perishing. What could be before the country, and him, too, but utter starvation, and hopeless ruin? And all this while his life was in the hands of a weak and capricious tyrant, who might murder him any moment, and of a wicked and spiteful queen, who certainly would murder him, if she found out that he had helped and saved the prophets of the Lord. Who so miserable as he? But on that day, Obadiah found that his alms and prayers had gone up before God, and were safe with God, and not to be forgotten for ever. When he fell on his face before Elijah, in fear for his life, he found that he was safe in God's hands; that God would not betray him or forsake him. Elijah promised him, with a solemn oath, that he would keep his word with him; he kept it, and before many days were past, Obadiah had an answer to all his prayers, and a relief from all his fears; and the Lord sent a gracious rain on his inheritance, and refreshed it when it was weary.

Yes, my friends, though well-doing seems for a while not to profit you, persevere: in due time you shall reap, if you faint not. Though the Lord sometimes waits to be gracious, he only waits, he does not forget; and it is to be *gracious* that he waits, not ungracious. Cast, therefore, thy bread upon the waters, and thou shalt find it after many days. Give a portion to seven, and also to eight, for thou knowest not what evil shall be upon the earth. Do thy diligence to give of what thou hast; for so gatherest thou thyself in the day of necessity, in which, with what measure you have measured to others, God will measure to you again.

This is true, for the Scripture says so; this *must* be true, for reason and conscience—the voice of God within us—tell us that God is just; that God must be true, though every man be a liar. 'Hear,' says our Lord, 'what the *unjust* judge says: And shall not God (the just judge), avenge his own elect, who cry day and night to him, though he bear long with them?' Yes, my friends, God's promise stands sure, now and for ever. 'Trust in the Lord, and do good; so shalt thou dwell in the land, and verily thou shalt be fed.'

But now comes in a doubt—and it ought to come in—What are our works at best? What have we which is fit to offer to God? Full of selfishness, vanity, self-conceit, the best of them; and not half done either. What have we ever done right, but what we might have done more rightly, and done more of it, also? Bad in quality our good works are, and bad in quantity, too. How shall we have courage to carry them in our hand to that God who charges his very angels with folly; and the very heavens are not clean in his sight?

Too true, if we had to offer our own works to God. But, thanks be to his holy name, we have not to offer them ourselves; for there is one who offers them for us—Jesus Christ the Lord. He it is who takes these imperfect, clumsy works of ours, all soiled and stained with our sin and selfishness, and washes them clean in his most precious blood, which was shed to take away the sin of the world: he it is who, in some wonderful and unspeakable way, cleanses our works from sin, by the merit of his death and sufferings, so that nothing may be left in them but what is the fruit of God's own spirit; and that God may see in them only the good which he himself put into them, and not the stains and soils which they get from our foolish and sinful hearts.

Oh, my friends, bear this in mind. Whensoever you do a thing which you know to be right and good, instead of priding yourself on it, as if the good in it came from you, offer it up to the Lord Jesus Christ, and to your Heavenly Father, from whom all good things come, and say, 'Oh Lord, the good in this is thine, and not mine; the bad in it is mine, and not thine. I thank thee for having made me do right, for without thy help I should have done nothing but wrong; for mine is the laziness, and the weakness, and the selfishness, and the self-conceit; and thine is the kingdom, for thou rulest all things; and the power, for thou doest all things; and the glory, for thou doest all things well, for ever and ever. Amen.'

SERMON X.

RELIGIOUS DANGERS.

(*Preached at the Chapel Royal, Whitehall,* 1861, *for the London Diocesan Board of Education.*)

ST. MARK viii. 4, 5, 8.

And the disciples answered him, From whence can a man satisfy these men with bread here in the wilderness? . . . How many loaves have ye? And they said, Seven. . . . so they did eat and were filled; and they took up of the broken meat that was left seven baskets.

I THINK that I can take no better text for the subject on which I am about to preach, than that which the Gospel for this day gives me.

For is not such a great city as this London, at least in its present amorphous, unorganised state, having grown up, and growing still, any how and any whither, by the accidental necessities of private commerce, private speculation, private luxury —is it not, I say, literally a wilderness?

I do not mean a wilderness in the sense of a place of want and misery; on the contrary, it is a place of plenty and of comfort. I think that we clergymen, and those good people who help our labours, are too apt exclusively to forget London labour, in our first and necessary attention to the London poor; to fix our eyes and minds on London want and misery, till we almost ignore the fact of London wealth and comfort. We must remember, if we are to be just to God, and just to our great nation, that there is not only more wealth in London, but that that wealth is more equitably and generally diffused through all classes, from the highest to the lowest, than ever has been the case in any city in the world. We must remember that there is collected together here a greater number of free human beings than were ever settled on the same space of earth, earning an honest, independent, and sufficient livelihood, and enjoying the fruits of their labour in health and cheapness, freedom and security, such as the world never saw before. There is want and misery. I know it too well. There are great confusions to be organised, great anomalies to be suppressed. But remember, that if want and misery, confusion and anomaly were *the rule* of London, and not (as they are) the exception, then London, instead of increasing at its present extraordinary pace, would decay; London work, instead of being better and better done, would be worse and worse done, till it stopped short in some such fearful convulsion as that of Paris in 1793. No, my friends; compare London with any city on the Continent; compare her with the old Greek and Roman cities; with Alexandria, Antioch, Constantinople, with that Imperial Rome itself, which was like London in nothing but its size, and then thank God for England, for freedom, and for the Church of Christ.

And yet I have called London a wilderness. I have. There is a wilderness of want; but there is a wilderness of wealth likewise. And the latter is far more dangerous to human nature than the former one. It is not in the waste and howling wilderness of rock, and sand and shingle, with its scanty acacia copses, and groups of date trees round the lonely well, that nature shews herself too strong for man, and crushes him down to the likeness of the ape. There the wild Arab, struggling to exist, and yet not finding the struggle altogether too hard for him, can gain and keep, if not spiritual life, virtue and godliness, yet still something of manhood; something of—

> The reason firm, the temperate will,
> Endurance, foresight, thought, and skill.

No; if you would see how low man can fall, you must go to the tropic jungle, where geniality of climate, plenty and variety of food, are in themselves a cause of degradation to the soul, as long as the Spirit of Christ is absent from it. Not in the barren desert, but in the rich forest, wanders the true savage, eating and eating all day long, like the ape in the trees above his head; and (I had almost said), like the ape, too, with no thoughts save what his pampered senses can suggest. I had almost said it. Thank God, I dare not say it altogether; for, after all, the savage is a man, and not an ape. Yes, to the lowest savage in the forests of the Amazon, comes a hunger of the soul, and whispers from the unseen world, to remind him of what he might have been, and still may be. In the dreams of the night they come; in vague terrors of the unseen, vague feelings of guilt and shame, vague dread of the powers of nature; driving him to unmeaning ceremonies, to superstitious panics, to horrible and bloody rites—as they might drive, to-morrow, my friends, an outwardly civilized population, debauched by mere peace and plenty, entangled and imprisoned in the wilderness of a great city.

I can imagine—imagine?—Have we not seen again and again human souls so entangled and opprest by this vast labyrinth of brick and mortar, as never to care to stir outside it and expand their souls with the sight of God's works as long as their brute wants are supplied, just as the savage never cares to leave his accustomed forest haunt, and hew himself a path into the open air through the tangled underwood. I can imagine—nay, have we not seen that, too?—and can we not see it any day in the street?—human souls so dazzled and stupefied, instead of being quickened, by the numberless objects of skill and beauty, which they see in their walks through the streets, that they care no more for the wonders of man's making, than the savage does for the wonders of God's making, which he sees around him in every insect, bird, and flower. The man who walks the streets every day, is the very man who will see least in the streets. The man who works in a factory, repeating a thousand times a day some one dull mechanical operation, or even casting up day after day the accounts of it, is the man who will think least of the real wonderfulness of that factory; of the amount of prudence, skill, and science, which it expresses; of its real value to himself and to his class; of its usefulness to far nations beyond the seas. He is like a savage who looks up at some glorious tree, capable, in the hands of civilized man, of a hundred uses, and teeming to him with a hundred scientific facts; and thinks all the while of nothing but his chance of finding a few grubs beneath its bark.

Think over, I beseech you, this fact of the stupefying effect of mere material civilization; and remember that plenty and comfort do not diminish but increase that stupefaction; that Hebrew prophets knew it, and have told us, again and again, that, by fulness of bread the heart waxeth gross; that Greek sages knew it, and have told us, again and again, that need, and not satiety, was the quickener of the human intellect. Believe that man requires another bread than the bread of the body; that sometimes the want of the bodily bread will awaken the hunger for that bread of the soul. Bear in mind that the period during which the middle and lower classes of England were most brutalized, was that of their greatest material prosperity, the latter half of the eighteenth century. Remember that with the distress which came upon them, at the end of the French war, their spiritual hunger awakened— often in forms diseased enough: but growing healthier, as well as keener, year by year; and that if they are not brutalized once more by their present unexampled prosperity, it will be mainly owing to the spiritual life which was awakened in those sad and terrible years. Remember that the present carelessness of the masses about either religious or political agitation.

though it may be a very comfortable sign to those who believe that a man's life consists in the abundance of the things which he possesses, is a very ominous sign to some who study history, and to some also who study their Bibles: and ask yourselves earnestly the question, 'From where shall a man find food for these men in this wilderness, not of want, but of wealth?' For, believe me, that spiritual hunger, though stopped awhile by physical comfort, will surely reawaken. Any severe and sudden depression in trade—the stoppage of the cotton crop, for instance, will awaken in the minds of hundreds of thousands deep questions—for which we, if we are wise, shall have an explicit answer ready.

For it is a very serious moment, my friends, when large masses have had enough to eat and drink, and have been saying, 'Let us eat and drink, for to-morrow we die;' and then, suddenly, by *not* having enough to eat and drink, and yet finding themselves still alive, are awakened to the sense that there is more in them than the mere capacity for eating and drinking. Then begin once more the world-old questions, Why are we thus? Who put us here? Who made us? God? Is there a God? and if there be, what is he like? What is his will toward us, good or evil? Is it hate or love?

My friends, those are questions which have been asked often enough in the world's history, by vast masses at once. And they may be answered in more ways than one.

They may be answered as the weavers of a certain country (thank God, not England) answered them in the potato famine with their mad song, "We looked to the earth, and the earth deceived us. We looked to the kings, and the kings deceived us. We looked to God, and God deceived us. Let us lie down and die.'

Or they may answer them—they will be more likely to answer them in England just now, because there are those who will teach them so to answer—in another, but a scarcely less terrible tone. 'Yes, there is a God; and he is angry with us.

And why? Because there is something, or some one, in the nation which he abhors—heretics, papists'—what not—any man, or class of men, on whom cowardly and terrified ignorance may happen to fix as a scapegoat, and cry, 'These are the guilty! We have allowed these men, indulged them; the accursed thing is among us, therefore the face of the Lord is turned from us. We will serve him truly henceforth—and hate those whom he hates. We will be orthodox henceforth—and prove our orthodoxy by persecuting the heretic.'

Does this seem to you extravagant, impossible? Remember, my friends, that within the last century Lord George Gordon's riots convulsed London. Can you give me any reason why Lord George Gordon's riots cannot occur again? Believe me, the more you study history, the more you study human nature, the more possible it will seem to you. It is not, I believe, infidelity, but fanaticism, which England has to fear just now. The infidelity of England is one of mere doubt and denial, a scepticism; which is in itself weak and self-destructive. The infidelity of France in 1793 was strong enough, but just because it was no scepticism, but a faith; a positive creed concerning human reason, and the rights of man, which men could formulize, and believe in, and fight for, and persecute for, and, if need was, die for. But no such exists in England now. And what we have most to fear in England under the pressure of some sudden distress, is a superstitious panic, and the wickedness which is certain to accompany that panic; mean and unjust, cruel and abominable things, done in the name of orthodoxy: though meanwhile, whether what the masses and their spiritual demagogues will mean by orthodoxy, will be the same that we and the Church of England mean thereby, is a question which I leave for your most solemn consideration. That, however, rather than any proclamation of the abstract rights of man, or installations of a goddess of Reason, is the form which spiritual hunger is most likely to take in England now. Alas! are there not tokens enough around us now, whereby we may discern the signs of this time?

I say, the spiritual hunger will reawaken; and woe to us who really understand and love the Church of England; woe to us who are really true to her principles, honestly subscribe her formulas, if we cannot appease it in that day.

But wherewith? We may look, my friends, appalled at the danger and the need. We may cry to our Lord, 'From whence can a man satisfy these men with bread in the wilderness?' But his answer will be, as far as I dare to predict it, the same as to his apostles of old on another and a similar occasion, 'Give ye them to eat. They need not depart'

I am not going to draw any far-fetched analogy between the miracle recorded in the gospel, and the subject on which I am speaking. I am not going to put any mystical and mediæval interpretation on the seven loaves, or the two small fishes. I only ask you to accept the plain moral practical lesson which the words convey.——

Use the means which you have already, however few and weak they seem. If Christ be among you, as he is indeed, he will bless them, and multiply them you know not how.

Use the means which you have; though they may seem to you inadequate, though they may seem to the world antiquated, and decrepit, try them. They need not depart from us, these masses, to seek spiritual food, they know not where, if we have but faith. Let us give them what we have; the organization of the Church of England, and the teaching of the Church of England.

The organization of the Church. Not merely its Parochial system, but its Diocesan system. In London, more than in any part of England, the Diocesan system is valuable. A London parish is not like a country one, a self-dependent, corporate body, made up of residents of every rank, capable of providing for the physical and spiritual wants of its own stationary population. In London, population fluctuates rapidly, sometimes rolling away from one quarter, always developing itself in fresh quarters; in London all ranks do not dwell side by side within sight and sound of each other: but the rich and the poor, the employed and the unemployed, dwell apart, work apart, and are but too often out of sight, out of mind. These, and many other reasons, make it impossible for the mere parochial system to bring out the zeal and the liberality of London Churchmen. If they are to realize their unity and their strength, they must do so not as members of a Parish, but of a Diocese; their Bishop must be to them the sign that they are one body; their good works must be organized more and more under him, and round him. This is no new theory of mine; it is a historic law. The Priest for the village, the Bishop for the city, has been the natural and necessary organization of the Church in every age; and it was in strict accordance with this historic law, that the London Diocesan Board of Education was founded in 1846, not to override the parochial system, but to do for it what it cannot, in a great city, do for itself; to establish elementary schools (and now I am happy to say, evening schools also) in parishes which were too poor to furnish them for themselves. I, as the son of a London Rector, can bear my testimony to the excellent working of that Board; and it is with grief I hear that, in spite of the vast work which it has done since 1846, and which it is still doing, on an income which is now not £300 a year—proving thereby how cheaply and easily your work may be done when it is done in the right way—it is with grief, I say, that I hear that it is more and more neglected by the religious public.

With grief: but not with surprise. For the religious public, even the Church portion of it, has of late been more and more inclined to undervalue the organization and the teaching of the Church of England, and to supply its place with nostrums, borrowed from those denominations who disagree with the Church, alike in their doctrines of what man should be, and of what God is. How have their energies, their zeal, their money (for zealous they are, and generous too) been frittered away! But I will not particularize, lest I hurt the feelings of better people than myself, by holding up their good works to the ridicule of those who do us no good works at all. But I entreat them to look at their own work; to look at the vastness of its expense, compared with the smallness of its results; and then to ask themselves, whether the one cause of their failure—for failures I must call too many of the religious movements of this day, in spite of their own loud self-laudations —whether, I say, one cause of these failures may not be, that the religious world is throwing itself into anything and everything novel and exciting, rather than into the simple and unobstrusive work of teaching little children their Catechism, that they may go home as angels of God and missionaries of Christ, teaching their parents in turn as they have been taught themselves, and so awakening that sacred family life, without which there can be no sound Christianity. I know well that there has been much work done in the right direction; but when I look at the ugly fact, that the population of London is increasing far faster than its schools; that in 25 of the poorest parishes thereof there are now nearly 60,000 children who go to no school at all; and that the proportion of scholars to the population is lower in Middlesex than in almost any county in England, while the proportion of crime is highest; I cannot but sigh over the thousands which I see squandered yearly on rash novelties by really pious and generous souls, and cry, Ah, that one-fourth, one-tenth of it all had been spent in the plain work of helping elementary schools; I cannot but call on all London churchmen of the plain old school, to stand by the organization and the doctrines of the Church to which they belong; to rally in this matter round their bishop; and work for him, and with him.

And now, there may be some here who will ask, scornfully enough, And do you talk of nostrums? and then, after confessing that the masses are hungering for the bread of life, offer them nothing but your own nostrum, the Catechism?

Yes, my friends, I do. I know that the Church Catechism is not the bread of life. Neither, I beg you to remember, is any other Catechism, or doctrine, or tract, or sermon, or book or anything else whatsoever. Christ is the Bread of Life. But how shall they know Christ, unless they be taught what Christ is; and how can they be taught what Christ is, unless the conception of him which is offered them be true?

And, I say, that the Catechism does give a true conception of Christ; and more, a far truer one—I had almost said, an infinitely truer—than any which I have yet seen in these realms: that from the Catechism a child may learn who God is, who Christ is, who he himself is, what are his relation and duty to God, what are his relation and duty to his neighbours, to his country, and to the whole human race, far better than from any document of the kind of which I am aware.

I know well the substitutes for the Catechism which are becoming more and more fashionable; the limitations, the explainings away, the non-natural and dishonest interpretations, which are more and more applied to it when it is used; and I warn you, that those substitutes for, and those defacements of, the Catechism, will be no barrier against an outburst of fanaticism, did one arise; nay, that many of them would directly excite it; and prove, when too late, that instead of feeding the masses with the bread of life, which should preserve them, soul and body, some persons had been feeding them with poison, which had maddened them, soul and body. But I see no such danger in the Catechism. I see in the Catechism; in its freedom alike from sentimental horror and sentimental raptures; its freedom alike from slavish terror, and from Pharisaic assurance; a guarantee that those who learn it will learn something of that sound religion, sober, trusty, cheerful, manful, which may be seen still, thank God, in country Church folk of the good old school ; and which will, in the day of trial, be proof against the phantoms of a diseased conscience, and the ravings of spiritual demagogues.

And therefore I preach gladly for this institution; therefore I urge strongly its claims on you, whom I am bound to suppose honest Churchmen, because the fact of its being a Diocesan Board of Education is, at least in this diocese, a guarantee that the schools which it supports will teach their children, honestly and literally, the Catechism of the Church of England, which may God preserve!

Not that I expect it to teach only that. I take for granted, that that will be its primary object, the guarantee that all the rest is well done: but I know that much more than that must be done; that much more will be done, even unintentionally.

For, shall I—-I trust that I shall not—make a too fanciful application of the last fact recorded of this great miracle, if I bid you find in it a fresh source of hope in your work?

'And they took up of the fragments which were left seven baskets full.'

The plain historic fact is, that not only do the seven loaves feed 4,000, but that what they leave, and are about to throw away, far exceeds the original supply.

I believe the fact: I ask you to consider why it was recorded? Surely, like all facts in the gospels, to teach us more of the character of Christ, which (a fact too often forgotten in these days) is the character of God. To teach us that he is an utterly bountiful God. That as in him there is no weakness, nor difficulty, so in him is no grudging, no parsimony. That he is not only able, but willing, to give exceeding abundantly, beyond all that we can ask or think. That there is a magnificence in God and in God's workings, which ought to fill us with boundless hope, if we are but fellow-workers with God.

You see that magnificence in the seeming prodigality of nature; in the prodigality which creates a thousand beautiful species of butterfly, where a single plain one would have sufficed; in the prodigality which creates a thousand acorns, only one of which is destined to grow into an oak. Everywhere in the kingdom of nature it shows itself; believe that it exists as richly in the higher kingdom of grace. Yes. Believe, that whenever you begin to work according to God's law and God's will, let your means seem as inadequate as they may, not only will your work multiply, as by miracle, under your hands; but the very fragments of it, which you are inclined to neglect and overlook, will form in time a heap of unexpected treasure. Plans which you have thrown aside, because they seemed to fail, details which seemed to encumber you, accessory work which formed no part of your original plan, all will be of use to some one, somehow, somewhere.

You began, for instance, by wishing to educate the masses of London; you are educating over and above, indirectly, thousands who never saw London. You began by wishing to teach them spiritual truth; you have been drawn on to give them an excellent secular education besides. You intended to make them live as good Christians here at home. But since you began, the inter-penetration of town and country by railroads, and the rush of emigrants to our colonies, have widened infinitely the sphere of your influence; and you are now teaching them also to live as useful men in the farthest corners of these isles, and in far lands beyond the seas, to become educated emigrants, loyal colonists; to raise, by their example, rude settlers, and ruder savages; and so, the very fragments of your good work, without your will or intent, will bless thousands of whom you never heard, and help to sow the seeds of civilization and Christianity, wherever the English flag commands Justice, and the English Church preaches Love.

SERMON XI.

BLESSING AND CURSING.

(Preached at the Chapel Royal, Whitehall, Ash Wednesday, 1860.)

DEUTERONOMY xxviii. 15.

It shall come to pass, if thou wilt not hearken unto the voice of the Lord thy God, to observe to do all his commandments and his statutes which I command thee this day; that all these curses shall come upon thee, and overtake thee.

MANY good people are pained by the Commination Service which we have just heard read. They dislike to listen to it. They cannot say 'Amen' to its awful words. It seems to them to curse men; and their conscience forbids them to join in curses. To imprecate evil on any living being seems to them unchristian, barbarous, a relic of dark ages and dark superstitions.

But does the Commination Service curse men? Are these good people (who are certainly right in their horror of cursing) right in the accusations which they bring against it? Or have they fallen into a mistake as to the meaning of the service, owing, it may be supposed, to that carelessness about the exact use of words, that want of accurate and critical habits of mind, which is but too common among religous people at the present day?

I cannot but think that they mistake, when they say that the

Commination Service curses men. For to curse a man, is to pray and wish that God may become angry with him, and may vent his anger on the man by punishing him. But I find no such prayer and wish in any word of the Commination Service. Its form is not, 'Cursed *be* he that doeth such and such things,' but ' Cursed *is* he that doeth them.'

Does this seem to you a small difference? A fine-drawn question of words? Is it, then, a small difference whether I say to my fellow-man, I hope and pray that you may be stricken with disease, or whether I say, You are stricken with disease, whether you know it or not. I warn you of it, and I warn you to go to the physician? For so great, and no less, is the difference.

And if any one shall say, that it is very probable that the authors of the Liturgy were not conscious of this distinction; but that they meant by cursing what priests in most ages have meant by it; I must answer, that it is dealing them most hard and unfair measure, to take for granted that they were as careless about words as we are ; that they were (like some of us) so ignorant of grammar as not to know the difference between the indicative and the imperative mood ; and to assume this, in order to make them say exactly what they do *not* say, and to impute to them a ferocity of which no hint is given in their Commination Service.

But some will say, Granted that the authors of the Commination Service did not wish evil to sinners—granted that they did not long to pray, with bell, book, and candle, that they might be tormented for ever in Gehenna—granted that they did not desire to burn their bodies on earth ; those words are still dark and unchristian. They could only be written by men who believed that God hates sinners, that his will is to destroy them on earth, and torture them for ever after death.

We may impute, alas ! what motives and thoughts we choose, in the face of our Lord's own words, Judge not, and ye shall not be judged. But we shall not be fair and honest in imputing, unless we first settle what these men meant, in the words which they have actually written. What did they mean by 'cursed' is the question. And that we can only answer by the context of the Commination Service. And that again we can only answer by seeing what it means in the Bible, which the Reformers profess to follow in all their writings.

Now, what does the Bible mean by a curse, and cursing?— For we are bound to believe, in all fairness, that the Reformers meant the same, and neither more nor less.

The text, I think, tells us plainly enough.

We know that its words came true. We know that the Jews *did* perish out of their native land, as the Author of this book foretold, in consequence of doing that against which Moses warned them. We know also that they did not perish by any miraculous intervention of Providence : but simply as any other nation would have perished; by profligacy, internal weakness, civil war, and, at last, by foreign conquest.

We know that their destruction was the natural consequence of their own folly. Why are we to suppose that the prophet meant anything but that? He foretells the result. Why are we to suppose that he did not foresee the means by which that result would happen? Why are we, in the name of all justice, to impute to him an expectation of miraculous interferences, about which he says no word? The curse which he foretold was the natural consequence of the sins of the nation. Why are we not to believe that he considered it as such? Why are we not to believe that the Bible meaning of a curse, is simply the natural ill-consequence of men's own ill-actions? I believe that if you will apply the same rule to other places of Scripture, you will have reason to reverence the letter and the Spirit of Scripture more and more, and will free your minds from many a superstitious and magical fancy, which will prevent you alike from understanding the Bible and the Commination Service.

The Book of Deuteronomy, like the rest of Moses' laws, says nothing whatever about the life to come. It says, that sin is to be punished, and virtue rewarded, in this life; and the Commination Service, when it quotes the Book of Deuteronomy, means so, so I presume, likewise. Indeed, if we look at the very remarkable, and most invaluable address which the Commination Service contains, we shall find its author saying the same thing, in the very passages which are to some minds most offensive.

For even in this life the door of mercy may be shut, and we may cry in vain for mercy, when it is the time for justice. This is not merely a doctrine: it is a fact; a common, patent fact. Men do wrong, and escape, again and again, the just punishment of their deeds; but how often there are cases in which a man does not escape; when he is filled with the fruit of his own devices, and left to the misery which he has earned; when the covetous and dishonest man ruins himself past all recovery; when the profligate is left in a shameful old age, with worn-out body and defiled mind, to rot into an unhonoured grave; when the hypocrite who has tampered with his conscience is left without any conscience at all.

They have chosen the curse, and the curse is come upon them to the uttermost. So it is. Is the commination service uncharitable, is the preacher uncharitable, when they tell men so? No more so, than the physician is uncharitable, when he says,—'If you go on misusing thus your lungs, or your digestion, you will ruin them past all cure.' Is God to be blamed because this is a fact? Why then because the other is a fact likewise?

Now if this be, as I believe, the doctrine of the commination service; if this be, as I believe, the message of Ash-Wednesday, it is one which is quite free from superstition or cruelty: but it is a message more disagreeable, and more terrible too, than any magical imprecations of harm to the sinner could bring. More disagreeable. For which is more galling to human pride, to be told,—Sin is certainly a clever, and politic, and successful trade, as far as this world is concerned. It is only in the next world, or in the case of rare and peculiar visitations and judgments in this world, that it will harm you? Or to be told,—Sin is no more clever, politic, or successful here, than hereafter. The wrong-doing which looks to you so prudent is folly. You, man of the world as you may think yourself, are simply, as often as you do wrong, blind, ignorant, suicidal. You are your own curse; your acts are their own curse. The injury to your own character and spirit, the injury to your fellow-creatures, which will again re-act on you,—these are the curses of God, which you will feel some day too heavy to be borne. And which is more terrible? To tell a man, that God will judge and curse him by unexpected afflictions, or at least by casting him into Gehenna in the world to come: or to tell him, 'You are judged already. The curse is on you already?'

The first threat he may get rid of, by denying the fact; by saying that God does not generally interfere to punish bad men in this life; that he does not strike them dead, swallow them up; and he may even quote Scripture on his side, and call on Solomon to bear witness how as dieth the fool, so dieth the wise man; and that there is one event to the righteous and to the wicked.

As for the fear of Gehenna, again, after he dies: that is too dim and distant; too unlike anything which he has seen in this life (now that the tortures and *Autos da fé* of the middle age have disappeared) to frighten him very severely, except in rare moments, when his imagination is highly excited. And even then, he can—in practice he does—look forward to 'making his peace with God' as it is called, at last, and fulfilling Baalam's wish of dying the death of the righteous, after living the life of the wicked. He knows well, too, that when that day comes, he can find—alas! that it should be so—priests and preachers in plenty, of some communion or other, who will give him his viaticum, and bid him depart in peace to that God, who has said that there is no peace to the wicked.

But terrible, truly terrible and heart searching for the wrong-doer is the message—God does not curse thee: thou hast cursed thyself. God will not go out of his way to punish thee : thou hast gone out of his way, and thereby thou art punishing thyself. Just as, by abusing thy body, thou bringest a curse upon it; so by abusing thy soul. God does not break his laws to punish drunkenness or gluttony. The laws themselves, the laws of nature, the beneficent laws of life, nutrition, growth, and health, they punish thee; and kill by the very same means by which they make alive. And so with thy soul, thy character, thy humanity. God does not break his laws to punish its sins. The laws themselves punish; every fresh wrong deed, and wrong thought, and wrong desire of thine sets thee more and more out of tune with those immutable and eternal laws of the Moral Universe, which have their root in the absolute and necessary character of God himself. All things that he has ordained; the laws of the human body, the laws of the human soul, the laws of society, the laws of all heaven and earth are arrayed against thee; for thou hast arrayed thyself against them. They have not excommunicated thee : thou hast, single-handed, excommunicated thyself. In thine own self-will, thou hast set thyself to try thy strength against God and his whole universe. Dost thou fancy that he needs to interfere with the working of that universe, to punish such a worm as thee? No more than the great mill engine need stop, and the overseer of it interfere with the machinery, if the drunken or careless workman should entangle himself among the wheels. The wheels move on, doing their duty, spinning cloth for the use of man: but the workman who should have worked with them, is entangled among them. He is out of his place; and slowly, but irresistibly, they are grinding him to powder, as the whole universe is grinding thee.

Heart-searching, indeed, is such a message; for it will come home, not merely to that very rare character, the absolutely wicked man, the ideal sinner, at whom the preacher too often aims ideal arrows, which vanish in the air : not to him merely will it come home, but to ourselves, to us average human beings, inconsistent, half-formed, struggling lamely and confusedly between good and evil. Oh let us take home with us to-day this belief, the only belief in this matter possible in an age of science, which is daily revealing more and more that God is a God, not of disorder, but of order. Let us take home, I say, the awful belief, that every wrong act of ours does of itself sow the seeds of its own punishment; and that those seeds will assuredly bear fruit, now, here in this life. Let us believe that God's judgments, though they will culminate, no doubt, hereafter in one great day, and "one divine far-off event, to which the whole creation moves," are yet about our path and about our bed, now, here, in this life. Let us believe, that if we are to prepare to meet our God, we must do it now, here in this life, yea and all day long; for he is not far off from any one of us, seeing that in him we live, and move, and have our being; and can never go from his presence, never flee from his spirit. Let us believe that God's good laws, and God's good order, are in themselves and of themselves, the curse and punishment of every sin of ours; and that Ash-Wednesday, returning year after year, whether we be glad or sorry, good or evil, bears witness to that most awful and yet most blessed fact.

My friends, this is the preacher's Ash-Wednesday's message: but, thanks be to God, it is not all. It is written—'If thou, Lord, wilt be extreme to mark what is done amiss: Oh Lord, who may abide it? For there is mercy with thee; therefore shalt thou be feared.'

It is written—'On whomsoever this stone shall fall, it shall grind him to powder:' but it is written too—'Whosoever shall fall on this stone shall be broken;' and again, 'The broken and the contrite heart, O God, thou shall not despise.' There is such a thing as pardon; pardon full and free, for the sake of the precious blood of Christ. Lent may be a time of awe and of shame: but it is not a time of despair. Meanwhile remember this; that God has set before you blessing and cursing, and that you may turn your life and God's whole universe, as you will, either into that blessing or into that curse.

SERMON XII.

WORK.

(*Twenty-fourth Sunday after Trinity.*)

PROVERBS xiv. 23.
In all labour there is profit.

I FEAR there are more lessons in the Book of Proverbs than most of us care to learn. There is a lesson in every verse of it, and a shrewd one. Certain I am, that for a practical, business man, who has to do his duty and to make his way in this world, there is no guide so safe as these same Proverbs of Solomon. In *this* world, I say; for they say little about the world to come. Their doctrine is, that what is good for the next world, is good for this; that he who wishes to go out of this world happily, must first go through this world wisely; and more, that he who wishes to go through this world happily, must likewise go through it wisely.

The righteous, says Solomon, shall be recompensed in the earth, and not merely at the end of judgment hereafter: much more the wicked and the sinner.

That is the doctrine of the Proverbs; that men do, to a very great extent, earn for themselves their good or their evil fortunes, and are filled with the fruit of their own devices; and it is that doctrine which makes them the best of text-books for the practical man.

For the Proverbs do not look on religion as a thing to be kept out of our daily dealings, and thought of only on Sundays: they look on true religion, which is to obey God, as a thing which mixes itself up with all the cares and business of this mortal life, this work-day world; and, therefore, they are written in work-day language; in homely words taken from the common doings of this mortal life, as our Lord's parables are. And, like the most simple of those parables, the most simple of the proverbs have often the very deepest meaning.

'In all labour there is profit.' Whatsoever is worth doing, is worth doing well. It is always worth while to take pains. In another proverb, homely enough—but if it be in the Bible, it is not too homely for us—'Where no oxen are, the crib is clean,' Solomon says the same thing as in the text. He says, 'Where no oxen are, the farmer is saved trouble; the clearing away of dirt and refuse; and all the labour required to keep his cattle in condition: but all that trouble,' Solomon says, if a man will but undergo it, will repay itself; for much increase is in the strength of the ox.' For the ox, in that country, as in most parts of the world now, is the beast used for ploughing, and for all the work of the farm.

Now, herein, I think, Solomon gives us a lesson which holds good through all matters of life. That it is a short-sighted mistake to avoid taking trouble; for God has so well ordered this world, that industry will always repay itself. No doubt it is much easier and pleasanter for the savage to scratch the seed into the ground with some rude wooden tool, and sit idle till the grain ripens: much easier and pleasanter, than to breed and break in beasts, and to labour all the year round at the different duties of a well-ordered farm: but here is the mighty difference; that the savage, growing only enough for himself, is in continual danger of famine, he and all his tribe; while the civilized farmer, producing many times more than he needs for himself, gains food, comfort, and safety, not only for himself, but for many other human beings. The savage has an easy life enough, if that be any gain : but it is a life of poverty, uncertainty, danger of starvation. The civilized man works hard and heavily, using body and mind more in one month than the savage does in the whole year: but he gains in return a life of safety, comfort, and continually increasing prosperity.

This is Solomon's lesson: and be sure it holds good, not only of tilling the ground, but of all other labours, all other duties, to which God may call us. 'Whatsoever thy hand findeth to do,' says Solomon, 'do it with all thy might.' God has set thee thy work; then fulfil it. Fill it full. Throw thy whole heart and soul into it. Do it carefully, accurately, completely. It will be better for thee, and for thy children after thee. All neglect, carelessness, slurring over work, is a sin; a sin against God, who has called us to our work; a sin against our country and our neighbours, who ought to profit by our work; and a sin against ourselves also, for we (as I shall shew you soon) ought to be made wiser and better men by our work.

Oh, if there is one rule above another which I should like to bring home to young men and women setting out in life, it is this—*Take pains*. Take trouble. Whatever you do, do thoroughly. Whatever you begin, finish. It may not seem to be worth your while at the moment, to be so very painstaking, so very exact. In after years, you will find that it was worth your while; that it has *paid* you, by training your character and soul; paid you, by giving you success in life; paid you, by giving you the respect and trust of your fellowmen; paid you, by helping you towards a good conscience, and enabling you in old age to look back, and say, I have been of use upon the earth; I leave this world, according to my small powers, somewhat better than I found it : instead of having to look back, as too many have, upon opportunities thrown away, plans never carried out, talents wasted, a whole life a failure, for want of taking pains.

Why do I say these things to you? To persuade you to work? Thank God, there is no need of that, for you are Englishmen; and it has pleased God to put into the hearts of Englishmen a love of work, and a power of work, which has helped to make this little island one of the greatest nations upon earth. No, thanks be to God, I say, there is no need to bid you work. What I ask you to do, is to look upon your work as an honourable calling, and as a blessing to yourselves, not merely as a hard necessity, a burden which must be borne merely to keep you from starvation. It is not that, my friends, but far more than that. For what is more honourable than to be of use? And in all labour, as Solomon says, there is profit; it is all of use. And all trade, manufacture, tillage, even of the smallest, all management and ordering, whether of an estate, a parish, or even of the pettiest office in it, all is honourable, because all is of use; all helping forward, more or less, the well-being of God's human creatures, and of the whole world.

And therefore all is worth taking trouble over, worth doing as diligently and honestly as possible, in sure trust that it will bring its reward with it. Why not? Almsgiving is blessed in God's sight, and charity to the poor; and God will repay it: but is not useful labour blessed in his sight also? and shall he not repay it? Will he not say of it, as well as of almsgiving, 'Inasmuch as ye have done it unto one of the least of these little ones, ye have done it unto me?' We may trust so, my friends; indeed, I may say more than, 'We may trust.' We can see; see that industry has its reward. By increasing the well-being of others, and the safety of others, you increase your own. So it is, and so it should be; for God has knit us all together as brethren, members of one family of God; and the well-being of each makes up the well-being of all, so that sooner or later, if one member rejoice, all the others rejoice with it.

But more. And here I speak to young people; for their elders, I doubt not, have found it out long since for themselves. Work, hard work, is a blessing to the soul and character of the man who works. Young men may not think so. They may say, What more pleasant than to have one's fortune made for one, and have nothing before one than to enjoy life? What more pleasant than to be idle: or, at least, to do only what one likes, and no more than one likes? But they would find themselves mistaken. They would find that idleness makes a man restless, discontented, greedy, the slave of his own lusts and passions, and see too late, that no man is more to be pitied than the man who has nothing to do. Yes; thank God every morning, when you get up, that you have something to do that day which must be done, whether you like or not. Being forced to work, and forced to do your best, will breed in you temperance and self-control, diligence and strength of will, cheerfulness and content and a hundred virtues which the idle man will never know. The monks in old time found it so. When they shut themselves up from the world to worship God in prayers and hymns, they found that, without working, without hard work either of head or hands, they could not even be good men. The devil came and tempted them, they said, as often as they were idle. An idle monk's soul was lost, they used to say; and they spoke truly. Though they gave up a large portion of every day, and of every night also, to prayer and worship, yet they found they could not pray aright without work. And 'working is praying,' said one of the holiest of them that ever lived; and he spoke truth, if a man will but do his work for the sake of duty, which is for the sake of God. And so they worked, and worked hard, not only at teaching the children of the poor, but at tilling the ground, clearing the forests, building noble churches, which stand unto this day; none among them were idle at first; and as long as they worked, they were good men, and blessings to all around them, and to this land of England, which they brought out of heathendom to the knowledge of Christ and of God; and it was not till they became rich and idle, and made other people work for them and till their great estates, that they sank into sin and shame, and became despised and hated, and at last swept off the face of the land. Lastly, my friends, if you wish to see how noble a calling Work is, consider God himself; who, although he is perfect, and does not need, as we do, the training which comes by work, yet works for ever with and through his Son, Jesus Christ, who said, 'My Father worketh hitherto, and I work.' Yes; think of God, who, though he needs nothing, and therefore need not work to benefit himself, yet does work, simply because, though he needs nothing, all things need him. Think of God as a king working for ever for the good of his subjects, a Father working for ever for the good of his children, for ever sending forth light and life and happiness to all created things, and ordering all things in heaven and earth by a providence so perfect, that not a sparrow falls to the ground without his knowledge, and the very hairs of your head are all numbered.

And then think of yourselves, called to copy God, each in his station, and to be fellow-workers with God for the good of each other and of yourselves. Called to work, because you are made in God's image, and redeemed to be the children of God. Not like the brutes, who cannot work, and can therefore never improve themselves, or the earth around them; but like children of God, whom he has called to the high honour of subduing and replenishing this earth which he has given you, and of handing down by your labour blessings without number to generations yet unborn. And when you go back, one to his farm, another to his shop, another to his daily labour, say to yourselves, 'This, too, as well as my prayers in church, is my heavenly Father's command; in doing this my daily duty honestly and well, I can do Christ's will, copy Christ, approve myself to Christ; single-eyed and single-handed, doing my work as unto God, and not unto men; and so hear, I may hope at last, Christ's voice saying to me. 'Well done, thou good and faithful servant. I set thee not to govern kingdoms, to lead senates, to command armies, to preach the gospel, to build churches, to give large charities, to write learned books, to do any great work in the eyes of men. I set thee simply to buy and sell, to plough and reap like a Christian man, and to bring up thy family thereby, in the fear of God and in the faith of Christ. And thou hast done thy duty more or less; and, in doing thy duty, has taught thyself deeper and sounder lessons about thy life, character, and immortal soul, than all books could teach thee. And now thou hast thy reward. Thou hast been faithful over a few things: I will make thee ruler over many things. Enter thou into the joy of thy Lord.'

SERMON XIII.

FALSE PROPHETS.

(*Eighth Sunday after Trinity.*)

MATTHEW vii. 16.

Ye shall know them by their fruits.

PEOPLE are apt to overlook, I think, the real meaning of these words. They do so, because they part them from the words which go just before them, about false prophets

They consider that 'fruit' means only a man's conduct,—that a man is known by his conduct. That professions are worth nothing, and practice worth everything. That the good man, after all, is the man who does right; and the bad man, the man who does wrong. Excellent doctrine; and always needed. God grant that we may never forget it.

But the text surely does not quite mean that. 'Fruit' here does not mean a man's own conduct, but the conduct of those whom he teaches. For see,—our Lord is talking of prophets; that is preachers, who set up to preach the Word of God, in the name of God. 'Beware,' he says, 'of false prophets. By their fruits ye shall know them. By what you gather from them,' he says. 'For do men gather grapes off thorns, or figs off thistles?'

Now what is a preacher's fruit? Surely the fruit of his

preaching; and that is, not what he does himself, but what he makes you do. His fruit is what you gather from him; and what you gather from him is, not merely the notions and doctrines which he puts into your head, but the way of life in which he makes you live. What he makes you do, is the fruit which you get from him. Does he make you a better man, or does he not? that is the question. That is the test whether he is a false prophet, or a true one; whether he is preaching to you the eternal truth of God, or man's inventions and devil's lies.

Does he make you a better man? Not—Does he make you feel better? but—Does he make you behave better? There is too much preaching in the world which makes men *feel* better —so much better, indeed, that they go about like the Pharisee, thanking God that they are not as other men, before they have any sound reason to believe that they are *not* as other men; because they live just such lives as other men do, as far as respectability, and the fear of hurting their custom or their character, allow them to do. They have their prophets, their preachers who teach them; and by their fruits in these men, the preachers may be known, by those who have eyes to see, and hearts to understand.

Therefore beware of false prophets. There are too many of them in the world now, as there were in our Lord's time; men who go about with the name of God on their lips, and the Bible in their hands, in sheep's clothing outwardly; but inwardly ravening wolves. In sheep's clothing, truly, smooth and sanctimonious, meek, and sleek. But wolves at heart; wolves in cunning and slyness, as you will find, if you have to deal with them; wolves in fierceness and cruelty, as you will find if you have to differ from them; wolves in greediness and covetousness, and care of their own interest and their own pockets. And wolves, too, in hardness of heart; in the hard, dark, horrible, unjust doctrines, which they preach with a smile upon their lips, not merely in sermons, but in books and tracts innumerable, making out the Heavenly Father, the God whose name is Love and Justice, to be even such a one as themselves. Wolves, too, in their habit of hunting in packs, each keeping up his courage by listening to the howl of his fellows. They may come in the name of God. They may tell you that they preach the Gospel; that no one but they preach the Gospel. But by their fruits ye shall know them.

Will they make you better men? Is it not written, 'The disciple is not above his master?' What will you learn from them, but to be like them? And the more you take in their doctrines, the more like them you will be; for is it not written, 'He that is perfect shall be as his master.' Can they lead you to eternal life? Is it not written, 'If the blind lead the blind, both shall fall into the ditch?'

But by their fruits ye shall know them. By their fruits in the world at large, if you have eyes to see it. By their fruits in your own lives, if you give yourselves up to listen to their false doctrines, for you will surely find, that, in the first place, they will not make you honest men. They will not teach you to be just and true in all your dealings. They will not teach you common morality. No, my friends, it is most sad to see, how much preaching and tract-writing there is in England now, which talks loud about Protestant doctrine, and Gospel truths, while all the fruit of it seems to be, to teach men to abuse the Pope, and to fancy that every one is going to hell, who does not agree with their opinions; while their own lives, their own conduct, their own morality, seems not improved one whit by all this preaching. And yet men like such preaching, and run to hear it. Of course they do; for it leaves them to behave all the week as if there was no Law of God, if only they will go on Sundays, and listen to what is called, I fear most untruly, the Gospel of God; leaves them, on condition of belonging to some particular party, and listening to some favourite preacher, free to give way to their passions, their spite, their meanness; to grind their servants, cheat their masters, trick their customers, adulterate their goods, and behave in money-matters as if all was fair in business, and the Gospel of Jesus Christ had nothing to do with common honesty; and all the while,

> Compound for sins they are inclined to,
> By damning those they have no mind to.

My friends, these things ought not so to be. There is a Gospel of God, which preaches full forgiveness for the sake of Jesus Christ, to all who turn from their sins. But there is a Law of God, likewise, which executes sure vengeance against all who do *not* turn from their sins; be their professions as high, or their doctrines as correct as they may. A law which is in the Gospel itself, and says, by the mouth of the Apostle St. John, 'Little children, let no man deceive you: he that *doeth* righteousness is righteous, even as God is righteous'—he—and not he who expects to be saved by listening to some false preacher who teaches his congregation how to go to heaven without having thought one heavenly thought, or done one heavenly deed.

Yes. There is an eternal law of God, which people are forgetting, I often fear, more and more, in England just now. I sometimes dread, lest we should be sinking into that hideous state of which the old Hebrew prophet speaks—'The prophets prophesy falsely, and the priests bear rule by their means; and my people love to have it so: and what will ye do in the end thereof?' What, indeed; if people are to be taught more and more, that religion is a matter merely of doctrines and fancies and feelings, and has nothing to do with common morality, and common honesty, and common self-control and improvement of character and conduct?

My friends, in these dangerous days, for dangerous they truly are—like those of the Scribes and Pharisees of old; days in which bigotry and hardness of heart, hypocrisy and lip-profession stalk triumphant; days, in which men, like the Scribes and Pharisees of old, boast of the Bible, worship the Bible, think they have eternal life in the Bible, spend vast sums every year in spreading the Bible; and yet will neither read the Bible honestly, nor obey its plain commands—In such days as these, what prophet shall we fall back upon? What preacher shall we trust?

We can at least trust our Bible. We can read it honestly, if only there be in us the honest and good heart; we can obey its plain commands, if only we hunger and thirst after righteousness, and desire really to become good men. Read your Bibles for yourselves with a single eye, and with a pure heart which longs to know God's will because it longs to *do* God's will; and you will need no false prophets, under pretence of explaining it to you, to draw you away from the Holy Catholic faith into which you were baptized.

But if you must have a commentary on the Bible; if you must have some book to give you a general notion of what the Bible teaches you, and what it expects of you; go to the prayer-book. Go to the good old Catechism which you learnt at school. There, though not from the popular preachers, you will learn that God is just and true, loving and merciful, and no respecter of persons. There you will learn, that Christ died not for a few elect, but for the sins of the whole world. There you will learn that in baptism, by God's free grace, and not by any experiences or feelings of your own, you were made children of God, members of Christ, and inheritors of the kingdom of heaven. There you will learn, that the elect whom the Holy Spirit sanctifies, are not merely a favoured few, but *you*—every baptized man, woman, and child. That the Holy Spirit is with you, every one of you, to sanctify you, if you will open your hearts to his gracious inspirations. And there you will learn what sanctification really means. Not a few fancies and feelings about which any man can deceive himself, and any man, also, deceive his neighbours. No, that sanctification means being made holy, righteous, virtuous, good. That sanctification means 'To love your neighbour as yourself, and to do to all men as they should do unto you—to love, honour, and succour your father and mother'—Shall I go on? Or do you all know the plain old duty to your neighbours, which stands in the Church Catechism. If you do, thank God that you were taught it in your youth. Read it over and over again. Think over it. Pray to God to give you grace to act upon it, and to shew the fruit of it in your lives. And then, 'By its fruits you shall know it.' By its fruits you shall know the virtue of the Catechism, and of the great and good men, true prophets of God, who wrote that Catechism. Yes. Cling to that Catechism, even if it convinces you of many sins, and makes you sadly ashamed of yourselves again and again; for, believe me, it will prove your best safeguard in doctrine, your best teacher in practice, in these dangerous days—days in which every man who believes that right is right, and wrong is wrong, has need to pray with all his heart—' From all false doctrine, heresy, and schism; from hardness of heart, and contempt of thy word and commandments : good Lord, deliver us!'

SERMON XIV.

THE ROCK OF AGES.

(*Ninth Sunday after Trinity.*)

---

1 CORINTHIANS x. 4.

They drank of that Spiritual Rock which followed them; and that Rock was Christ.

ST. PAUL has been speaking to the Corinthians about the Holy Communion.

In this text, St. Paul is warning the Corinthians about it. He says, 'You may be Christian men; you may have the means of grace; you may come to the Communion and use the means of grace; and yet you may become castaways.' St. Paul himself says, in the very verse before, 'I keep under my body, and bring it into subjection: lest . . . . I myself should be a castaway.' Look, he says then, 'at the old Jews in the wilderness. They all partook of God's grace: but they were not all saved. They were all baptized to Moses in the cloud and in the sea. They all ate the same spiritual meat, the manna from heaven. They all drank the same spiritual drink, the water out of the rock in Horeb. And yet with many of them God was not well pleased;' for they were overthrown—their corpses were scattered far and wide—in the wilderness. The spiritual meat and the spiritual drink could not keep them alive, if they sinned, and deserved death. 'So,' says St. Paul, 'with you. You are members of Christ's body. The cup of blessing which we bless, is the communion of the blood of Christ; the bread which we break, is the communion of the body of Christ:' but beware, they will not save you, if you sin. Nothing will save you, if you sin. If you lust after evil things, as those old Jews did; if you are idolaters, as they were; if you are profligates, as they were; if you tempt Christ, as they did; if you murmur against God, as they murmured, you will be destroyed like them.

Note here two things. First, that St. Paul says that we really receive Christ in the Holy Communion. He does *not* say, as some do, that the Communion is merely a remembrance of Christ's death. He says that the faithful verily and indeed receive Christ's body and blood in the Sacrament. He says so, distinctly, plainly, literally; and if that be not true, his whole argument goes for nothing, and will not stand. The Jews, he says, drank of the spiritual Rock which followed them, and that Rock was Christ; and so he says to you. But that did not save them from the punishment of their sins, when they went and sinned afresh: neither will it save you.

But now—What are these strange words which St. Paul uses? These old Jews drank of the spiritual Rock which followed them, and that Rock was Christ? Where in the Old Testament do we read of the Rock following them? We read of Moses striking the rock in Horeb, at the beginning of their wanderings in the wilderness; but not of its following them afterwards.

St. Paul is here using a beautiful old tradition of the Rabbis, that the rock which Moses struck in Horeb followed the Jews through all their forty years' wanderings, and that on every Sabbath day when they stoped, it stopped also, and the elders called to it, 'Flow out, O fountain,' and the water flowed. A beautiful old story, which St. Paul turns into an allegory, to teach, as by a picture, the deepest and the highest truth. Whether that rock followed them or not, he says, there was One who did follow them, from whom flowed living water; and that Rock is Christ. Christ followed them. Christ the creator, the preserver, the inspirer, the light, the life, the guide of men, and of all the universe. It was to Christ they owed their deliverance from Egypt; to Christ they owed their knowledge of God, and of the law of God, to Christ they owed whatever reason, justice, righteousness, good government, there was among them. And to Christ we owe the same.

The rock was a type of him from whom flows living water. As he himself said on earth, 'Whosoever drinketh of the water which I shall give him, shall never thirst; but the water which I shall give him shall be in him a well of water, springing up to everlasting life.' Just as the manna also was a type of him, as he himself declared, when the Jews talked to him of the manna; 'Our fathers did eat manna in the desert, as it is written, He gave them bread from heaven to eat.' Then Jesus said to them, 'Verily, verily, I say unto you, Moses gave you not that bread from heaven.' No: but only a type and picture of it. 'My Father giveth you the true bread from heaven. For the bread of God is he which cometh down from heaven, and giveth life unto the world. . . . I am that bread of life.'

My friends, herein is a great mystery. Something of what it means, however, we may learn from that wise and good Jew, Philo, who was St. Paul's teacher according to the flesh, before he became a Christian; and who himself was so near to the kingdom of God, that St. Paul often in his epistles uses Philo's very words, putting into them a Christian meaning. And what says he concerning the Rock of living waters?

The soul, he says, falls in with a scorpion in the wilderness; and then thirst, which is the thirst of the passions—of the lusts which war in our members—seizes on it; till God sends forth on it the stream of his own perfect wisdom, and causes the changed soul to drink of unchangeable health. For the steep rock is the wisdom of God (by whom he means the Word of God, whom Philo knew not in the flesh, but whom we know, as the Lord Jesus Christ), which, being both sublime and the first of all things; he quarried out of his own powers; and of it he gives drink to the souls which love God; and they, when they have drunk, are filled with the most universal manna.

So says Philo, the good Jew, who knew not Christ; and therefore he says only a part of the truth. If you wish to learn the whole truth, you must read St. John's Gospel, and St. Paul's Epistles, especially this very text; and again, the opening of the Epistle to the Ephesians; and again, that most royal passage in the opening of the Colossians, where he speaks of the Everlasting Being of Christ, who is before all things, and by whom all things consist—in whom dwells all the fulness of the Godhead bodily, and in whom are hid all the treasures of wisdom and knowledge.

Therefore he is rightly called the Rock, the Rock of Ages, the Eternal Rock; because on him all things rest, and have rested since the foundation of the world, being made, and kept together, and ruled, and inspired by him alone. Therefore he is rightly called the Rock of living waters; for in him are hid all the treasures of wisdom and knowledge, and from him they flow forth freely to all who cry to him in their thirst after truth and holiness. Yes, my friends, by Christ all things live; and therefore, most of all, by Christ our souls live. To be parted from Christ is death. To be joined to Christ and the body of Christ is life.

But what life? The life of the soul. And what is the life of the soul? Holiness, righteousness, sanctification, virtue,—call it what pleases you best. I shall call it goodness. That is the only life of the soul. And why? Because it is the life of Christ. That is the only wisdom of the soul. And why? Because it is the mind of Christ. That is the living water. And why? Because it flows eternally from Christ.

For who is Christ, but the likeness of God, and the glory of

God? And what is the likeness of God, but goodness; and what is the glory of God, but goodness? Therefore Christ is goodness itself, as it is written, 'Now the Lord is that Spirit.' Yes, if you will believe it, Christ, the only-begotten Son, co-equal and co eternal, is the very and essential goodness of the Father, coming out everlastingly in action and in life, in himself, and in his people, who are his mystical body, filled with the Spirit of him and his Father; who is the Holy Spirit, the spirit of goodness. From Christ, and not from any created being, comes all goodness in man or angel. Comes from Christ? It were more right, and more according to St. Paul's own words, to say, that all goodness *is* Christ; Christ dwelling in a man, Christ forming himself in a man, little by little, step by step, as he grows in grace, in purity, in self-control, in experience, in knowledge, in wisdom, in strength, in patience, in love, in charity; till he comes to the stature of a perfect man, to the measure of the fulness of Christ.

Meanwhile, let the good which a man does be much, or be it little, he must say, 'The good which I do, *I* do not, but Christ who dwelleth in me.'

For in every age of man, it is Christ who is awakening in him the hunger and thirst after righteousness, and then satisfying it with the only thing which can satisfy them, namely, his most blessed self.

Yes, believe it. It is Christ in the child which makes it speak the truth; Christ in the child which makes it shrink from whatever it has been told is wrong. It is Christ in the young man, which fills him with lofty aspirations, hopes of bettering the world around him, hopes of training his soul to be all that it can be, and of putting forth all his powers in the service of Christ. It is Christ in the middle-aged man, which makes him strong in good works, labouring patiently, wisely, and sturdily; so that having drunk of the living waters himself, they may flow out of him again to others in good deeds; a fountain springing up in him to an eternal life of goodness. It is Christ in the old man, which makes him look on with calm content while his own body and mind decay, knowing that the kingdom of God cannot decay; for Christ is ruling it in righteousness; and all will be well with him, and with his children after him, and with all mankind, and all heaven and earth, if they themselves only will it, long after he has been gathered to his fathers.

Yes, such a man knows in whom he has believed. He knows that the spiritual Rock has been following him through all his wanderings in this weary world; and that that Rock is Christ. He can recollect how, again and again, at his Sabbath haltings in his life's journey, it was to him in the Holy Communion as to the Israelites of old in their haltings in the wilderness, when the priests of Jehovah cried to the mystic rock, 'Flow forth, O fountain,' and the waters flowed. So can he recollect how, in Holy Communion, there flowed into his soul streams of living water, the water of life, quenching that thirst of his soul, which no created thing could slake; the water of life; of Christ's life, which is the light of men, shewing them what they ought to be and do; the life which is the light; the life which is according to the eternal and divine reason; the life of wisdom; which is the life of love; which is the life of justice; which is the life of Christ; which is the life of God.

But if these things are so—and so they are, for Christ has said it, St. Paul has said it, St. John has said it—but if these things are so, will they not teach us much about Holy Communion, how we may receive it worthily, and how unworthily?

If what we receive in the Communion be Christ himself, the good Christ who is to make us good; then how can we receive it worthily, if we do not hunger and thirst after goodness? If we do not come thither, longing to be made good, and sanctified, then we come for the wrong thing, to the wrong place. We are like those Corinthians who came to the Lord's supper not to be made good men, but to exalt their own spiritual self-conceit; and so only ate and drank their own damnation, not discerning the Lord's body, that it was a holy body, a body of righteousness and goodness.

But if we come hungering and thirsting to be made good men, then we come for the right thing, to the right place. Then we need not stay away, because we feel ourselves intolerably burdened with many sins; that will be our very reason for coming, that we may be cleansed from our sins—cleansed not only from their guilt, but from their power; and cry, in spirit and in truth, as we kneel at that holy table—

> Rock of ages, cleft for me,
> Let me hide myself in thee;
> By the water and the blood,
> From thy riven side which flowed,
> Be of sin the double cure,
> Cleanse me from its guilt and power.

Yes, from its guilt and from its power also. Let us all pray, each in his own fashion :—

Oh Lamb eternal, beyond all place and time! Oh Lamb slain eternally, before the foundation of the world! Oh Lamb, which liest slain eternally, in the midst of the throne of God! Let the blood of life, which flows from thee, procure me pardon for the past; let the water of life, which flows from thee, give me strength for the future. I come to cast away my own life, my life of self and selfishness, which is corrupt according to the deceitful lusts, that I may live it no more; and to receive thy life, which is created after the likeness of God, in righteousness and true holiness, that I may live it for ever and ever, and find it a well of life springing up in me to everlasting life. Eternal Goodness, make me good like thee. Eternal Wisdom, make me wise like thee. Eternal Justice, make me just like thee. Eternal Love, make me loving like thee. Then I shall hunger no more, and thirst no more; for

> Thou, O Christ, art all I want;
>   More than all in thee I find;
> Raise me, fallen; cheer me, faint;
>   Heal me, sick; and lead me, blind.
> Thou of life the fountain art;
>   Freely let me take of thee;
> Spring thou up within my heart;
>   Rise to all eternity.

Oh come to Holy Communion with the words of that glorious hymn not merely on your lips, but in your hearts; and you will never come amiss.

SERMON XV.

ANTIPATHIES.

(*Tenth Sunday after Trinity.*)

---

1 Cor. xii. 3, 4, 5, 6.

Wherefore, I give you to understand, that no man speaking by the Spirit of God calleth Jesus accursed: and that no man can say that Jesus is the Lord, but by the Holy Ghost. Now there are diversities of gifts, but the same Spirit. And there are differences of administrations, but the same Lord. And there are diversities of operations, but it is the same God which worketh all in all.

WE are to come to the Communion this day in love and charity with all men. But are we in love and charity with all men?

I do not mean, are there any persons whom we hate; against whom we bear a spite; whom we should be glad to see in trouble or shame? God forbid, my friends, God forbid. There are, indeed, devil's tempers. And yet more easy for us to keep in the bottom of our hearts, and more difficult to root them out, than we fancy.

It is easy enough for us to forgive (in words at least) a man who has injured us. Easy enough to make up our minds that we will not revenge ourselves. Easy enough to determine, even, that we will return good for evil to him, and do him a kindness when we have a chance. Yes, we would not hurt him for the world: but what if God hurt him? What if he hurt himself? What if he lost his money? What if his children turned out ill? What if he made a fool of himself, and came to shame? What if he were found out and exposed, as we fancy that he deserves? Should we be so very sorry? We should not punish him ourselves. No. But do we never catch ourselves thinking whether God may not punish him; thinking of that with a base secret satisfaction; almost hoping for it, at last? Oh if we ever do, God forgive us! If we ever find those devil's thoughts rising in us, let us flee from them as from an adder; flee to the foot of Christ's Cross, to the cross of him who prayed for his murderers, Father, forgive them, for they know not what they do; and there cry aloud for the blood of life, which shall cleanse us from the guilt of those wicked thoughts, and for the water of life, which shall cleanse us from the power of them: lest they get the dominion over us, and spring up in us, and spread over our whole hearts; not a well of life, but a well of poison, springing up in us to everlasting damnation. Oh let us pray to him to give us truth in our inward parts; that we may forgive and love, not in word only, but in deed and in truth.

I could not help saying this in passing. But it is not what the text is speaking of; not what I want to speak of myself to-day. I want to speak of a matter which is smaller, and not by any means so sinful: and which yet in practice is often more tormenting to a truly tender conscience, because it is more common and more continual.

How often, when one examines oneself, whether one be in love and charity with all men, one must recollect that there are many people whom one does not like. I do not mean that one hates them. Not in the least: but they do not suit one. There is something in them which we cannot get on with, as the saying is. Something in their opinions, manners, ways of talking; even—God forgive us—merely in their voice, or their looks, or their dress, which frets us, and gives us what is called an antipathy to them. And one dislikes them; though they never have harmed us, or we them; and we know them, perhaps, to be better people than ourselves. Now, are we in love and charity with these people? I am afraid not.

I know one is tempted to answer; but I am afraid the answer is worth very little—Why not? We cannot help it. You cannot expect us to like people who do not suit us; any more than you can expect us to like a beetle or a spider. We know the beetle or the spider will not harm us. We know that they are good in their places, and do good, as all God's creatures are and do; and there is room enough in the world for them and us: but we have a natural dislike to them, and cannot help it; and so with these people. We mean no harm in disliking them. It is natural to us; and why blame us for it.

Now what is the mistake here? Saying that it is *natural* to us. We are not meant to live according to nature, but according to grace; and grace must conquer nature, my friends, if we wish to save our souls alive. It is nature, brute nature, which makes some dogs fly at every strange dog they meet. It is nature, brute nature, which makes a savage consider every strange savage as his enemy, and try to kill him. But unless nature be conquered in that savage, it will end, where following brute nature always ends, in death; and the savages will (as all savages are apt to do) destroy each other off the face of the earth, by continual war and murder. It is brute nature which makes low and ignorant persons hate foreign people, because their dress and language seem strange. But unless that natural feeling had been in most of us conquered by the grace of God, which is the spirit of justice and of love, then England would have remained alone in conceit and ignorance, hated by all the nations; instead of being what, thank God! she is—the Sanctuary of the world; to which all the oppressed of the earth may flee; and find a welcome, and safety, and freedom, and justice, and peace.

And so with us, my friends. It is natural, and according to the brute nature of the old Adam, to dislike this person and that, just because they do not suit us. But it is according to grace, and the new Adam, who is the Lord from heaven, to honour all men; to love the brotherhood; to throw away our own private fancies and personal antipathies; and, like the Lord Jesus Christ, copy the all-embracing charity of God. And no one has a right to answer, 'But I must draw the line somewhere.' Thou must not. I am afraid that thou *wilt*, and that I shall, too, God forgive us both ! because we are sinful human beings. We may, but we *must* not, draw a line as to whom we shall endure in charity. For Christ draws no line. Is it not written, 'No man can say that Jesus is the Lord, but by the Holy Ghost.' Is not the Spirit of Christ in a Christian man, unless he be a reprobate? and who is reprobate, we know not, and dare not try to know; for it is written, 'Judge not, and ye shall not be judged: condemn not, and ye shall not be condemned.'

But what has the text to do with all this?

My friends, is not this just what the text is telling us? I said this moment, that the Spirit of Christ was in a Christian man, unless he be a reprobate. And the text says further, that there are diversities of gifts in Christian men: but the same spirit in all of them.

Yes: people *will* be different one from another. There are diversities of gifts. Differences in talents, in powers, in character, in kinds of virtue and piety; so that you shall find no two good men, no two useful men, like each other. But there is the same Spirit. The same Spirit of God is in each, though bearing different fruit in each. And there are differences of administrations, of offices, in God's kingdom. God sets one man to do one work, and another to do another: but it is the same Lord who puts each man in his place, and shows him his work, and gives him power to do it. And there are diversities of operations, that is, of ways of working; so that if you put any two men to do the same thing, they will most probably do it each in a different way, and yet both do it well. But it is the same God, who is working in them both; the God who works all in all, and has his work done by a thousand different hands, by a thousand different ways.

And it is right and good that people should be so different from each other. 'For the manifestation of the Spirit is given to every man to profit withal.' To profit, to be of use. If all men were alike, no one could learn from his neighbour. If all mankind were as like each other as a flock of sheep, there would be no more work, no more progress, no more improvement in mankind, than there is in a flock of sheep. Now each man can bring his own little share of knowledge or usefulness into the common stock. Each man has, or ought to have, something to teach his neighbour. Each man can learn something from his neighbour: at least he can learn this—to have patience with his neighbour. To live and let live. To bear with what in him seems odd and disagreeable, trusting that God may have put it there; that God has need of it; that God will make use of it. God makes use of many things which look to us ugly and disagreeable. He makes use of the spider and of the beetle. How much more of our brethren, members of Christ, children of God, inheritors of the kingdom of heaven. Shall they be to us, even if they be odd or disagreeable in some things—shall they be to us as the beetle or the spider, or any other merely natural things? They are men and women, in whom is the Spirit of the living God. And my friends, if they are good enough for God, they are good enough for us. Think but one moment. God the Father adopts a man as his child, God the Son dies for that man, God the Holy Ghost inspires that man; and shall we be more dainty than God? If, in spite of the man's little weaknesses and oddities, God shall condescend to come down and dwell in that man, making him more or less a good man, doing good work; shall we pretend that we cannot endure what God endures? Shall we be more dainty, I ask again, than the holy and perfect God? Oh my friends, let us pray to him to take out of our hearts all selfishness, fancifulness, fastidiousness, and hasty respect of persons, of all which there is none in God. Let us ask for his Spirit, the Spirit of Charity, which sees God in all, and all in God, and therefore sees good in all, and sees all in love.

Then we shall see how much more there is in our neighbours to like, than to dislike. Then all these little differences will seem to us trifles not to be thought of, before the broad fact of a man's being, after all, a man, an Englishman, a Christian, and a good Christian, doing good work where God has put him. Then we shall be ashamed of our old narrowness of heart; ashamed of having looked so much at the little evil in our neighbours, and not at the great good in them. Then we shall go about the world cheerfully; and our neighbour's faces will seem to us full of light: instead of seeming full of darkness, because our own eyes and minds are dark for want of charity. Then we shall come to the Communion, not with hearts narrowed and shut up, perhaps, from the very person who kneels next to us: but truly open-hearted; with hearts as wide—ah God, that it were possible!—as the sacred heart of Christ, in which is room for all mankind. And so receiving his body, which is the blessed company of all faithful people, we shall receive Christ, who dwelleth in them, and they in him.

SERMON XVI.

ST. PAUL.

(Eleventh Sunday after Trinity.)

---

1 COR. xv. 8.

Last of all he was seen of me, also, as of one born out of due time. For I am the least of the Apostles, that am not meet to be called an apostle, because I persecuted the church of God.

YOU heard in this text (part of the epistle for this day) St. Paul's opinion of himself. You heard, also, in the Second Lesson for this day, the ninth chapter of Acts, the extraordinary story of his conversion.

And what may we learn from that story? We may learn many lessons; lessons without number.

We may learn, first; not to be astonished, if we have to change our opinions as we grow older. When we are young, we are very positive about this thing and that, as St. Paul was; violent in favour of our own opinions; ready to quarrel with any one who differs from us, as St. Paul was. But let ten years, twenty years, roll over our heads, and we may find our opinions utterly changed, as St. Paul did, and look back with astonishment on ourselves, for having been foolish enough to believe what we did, as St. Paul looked back; and with shame, as did St. Paul likewise, at having said so many violent and unjust things against people, who, we now see, were in the right after all.

Next; we may learn not to be ashamed of changing our minds: but if we find ourselves in the wrong, to confess it boldly and honestly, as St. Paul did. What a fearful wrench to his mind and his heart; what a humiliation to his self-conceit, to have to change his mind once for all on all matters in heaven and earth. What must it not have cost him to throw up at once all his friends and relations; to part himself from all whom he loved and respected on earth, to feel that henceforth they must look upon him as a madman, an infidel, an enemy. To an affectionate man, and St. Paul was an extremely affectionate man, what a bitter struggle that must have cost him. But he faced that struggle, and conquered in it, like a brave and honest man. And the consequence was, that he had, in time, and after many lonely years, many Christian friends for each Jewish friend that he had lost; and to him was fulfilled (as it will be to all men) our Lord's great saying, 'There is no man that hath left house, or brethren, or sisters, or father, or mother, or wife, or children, or lands for my sake, and the gospel's, but he shall receive an hundredfold now in this time, . . . and in the world to come eternal life.'

Next; we may take comfort, in the hope that God will not impute to us these early follies and mistakes of ours; if only there be in us, as there was in St. Paul, the honest and good heart; that is, the heart which longs to know what is true and right, and bravely acts up to what it knows. St. Paul did so. God, when he set him apart, as he says, from his very birth, gave him a great grace, even the honest and good heart; and he was true to it, and used it. He tried to learn his best, and do his best. He profited in the Jews' religion, beyond all his fellows. He was, touching the righteousness which was in the law, blameless. He was so zealous for what he thought right, that he persecuted the Church of Christ, as the Pharisees, his teachers, had taught him to do. In all things, whether right or wrong in each particular case, he was an honest, earnest seeker after truth and righteousness. And therefore Christ, instead of punishing him, fulfilled to him his own great saying,—'To him that hath shall be given, and he shall have abundance.' He had not yet, as he himself says, again and again, the grace of Christ, which is love to his fellow-men ; and therefore his works were not pleasing to God, and had, as the article says, the nature of sin. His empty forms and ceremonies could not please God. His persecuting the Church had plainly the nature of sin. But there was something which God had put in him, and which God would not lose sight of, or suffer to be lost ; and that was, the honest and good heart, of which our Lord speaks in the parable of the sower. In that Christ sowed the word of God, even himself, and his grace and Holy Spirit ; and, behold, it sprang up and bore fruit a hundredfold, over all Christian nations to this day.

Keep, therefore, if you have it, the honest and good heart. If you have it not, pray for it earnestly. Determine to learn what is true, whatever be the trouble ; and to do what is right, whatever be the cost ; and then, though you may make many mistakes, and have more than once, perhaps, to change your mind in shame and confusion, yet all will come right at last, for the grace of Christ, sooner or later, will lead you into all truth which you require for this world and all worlds to come.

Again, we may learn from St. Paul this lesson. That though God has forgiven a man, that is no reason that he should forgive himself. That may seem a startling saying just now. For the common teaching now is, that if a man finds, or fancies, that God has forgiven him, he may forgive himself at once ; that if he gets assurance that his sins are washed away in Christ's blood, he may go swaggering and boasting about the world (I can call it no less), as if he had never sinned at all ; that he may be (as you see in these revivals, from which God defend us !) one moment in the deepest agonies of conscience, and dread of hell-fire, and the next moment in raptures of joy, declaring himself to be in heaven. Alas, alas ! such people forget that sin leaves behind it wounds, which even the grace of

Christ takes a long time in healing, and which then remain as ugly, but wholesome scars, to remind us of the fools which we have been. They are like a man who is in great bodily agony, and gets sudden relief from a dose of laudanum. The pain stops; and he feels himself, as he says, in heaven for the time: but he is too apt to forget that the cause of the pain is still in his body, and that if he commits the least imprudence, he will bring it back again; just as happens, I hear, in too many of these hasty and noisy conversions now-a-days.

That is one extreme. The opposite extreme is that of many old Roman Catholic saints and hermits who could not forgive themselves at all, but passed their whole lives in fasting, poverty, and misery, bewailing their sins till their dying day. That was a mistake. It sprang out of mistaken doctrines, of which I shall not speak here: but it did not spring entirely from them. There was in them a seed of good, for which I shall always love and honour them, even though I differ from them; and that was, a noble hatred of sin. They felt the sinfulness of sin; and they hated themselves for having sinned. The mercy of God made them only the more ashamed of themselves for having rebelled against him. Their longing after holiness only made them loathe the more their past unholiness. They carried that feeling too far: but they were noble people, men and women of God; and we may say of them, that, 'Wisdom is justified of all her children.'

But I wish you to run into neither extreme. I only ask you to look at your past lives, if you have ever been open sinners, as St. Paul looked at his. There is no sentimental melancholy in him; no pretending to be miserable; no trying to make himself miserable. He is saved, and he knows it. He is an apostle, and he stands boldly on his dignity. He is cheerful, hopeful, joyful: but whenever he speaks of his past life (and he speaks of it often), it is with noble shame and sorrow. Then he looks to himself the chief of sinners, not worthy to be called an apostle, because he persecuted the Church of Christ. What he is, he will not deny. What he was, he will not forget, he dare not forget, lest he should forget that the good which he does, *he* does not—for in him (that is, in his flesh, his own natural character), dwelleth no good thing—but Christ, who dwells in him; lest he should grow puffed up, careless, self-indulgent; lest he should neglect to subdue his evil passions; and so, after having preached to others, himself become a castaway.

So let us do, my friends. Let us not be too hasty in forgiving ourselves. Let us thank God cheerfully for the present. Let us look on hopefully to the future; let us not look back too much at the past, or rake up old follies which have been pardoned and done away. But let us thank God whenever he thinks fit to shew us the past, and bring our sin to our remembrance. Let us thank him, when meeting an old acquaintance, passing by an old haunt, looking over an old letter, reminds us what fools we were ten, twenty, thirty years ago. Let us thank him for those nightly dreams, in which old tempers, old meannesses, old sins, rise up again in us into ugly life, and frighten us by making us in our sleep, what we were once, God forgive us! when broad awake. I am not superstitious. I know that those dreams are bred merely of our brain and of our blood. But I know that they are none the less messages from God. They tell us unmistakeably that we are the same persons that we were twenty years ago. They tell us that there is the same infection of nature, the same capability of sin, in us, that there was of old. That in our flesh dwells no good thing: that by the grace of God alone we are what we are: and that did his grace leave us, we might be once more as utter fools as we were in the wild days of youth. Yes: let us thank God for everything which reminds us of what we once were. Let us humble ourselves before him whenever those memories return to us; and let us learn from them what St. Paul learnt. To be charitable to all who have not yet learnt the wisdom which God (as we may trust) has taught to us; to feel for them, feel with them, be sure that they are our brothers, men of like passions with ourselves, who will be tried by the same standard as we; whom therefore we must not judge, lest we be judged in turn: and let us have, as St. Paul had, hope for them all; hope that God, who has forgiven us, will forgive them; that God who has raised us from the death of sin, to something of the life of righteousness, will raise them up likewise, in his own good time. Amen.

SERMON XVII.

THE BROKEN AND CONTRITE HEART.

ISAIAH, lvii. 15—21.

For thus saith the high and lofty One that inhabiteth eternity, whose name is Holy; I dwell in the high and holy place, with him also that is of a contrite and humble spirit, to revive the spirit of the humble, and to revive the heart of the contrite ones. For I will not contend for ever, neither will I be always wroth: for the spirit should fail before me, and the souls which I have made. For the iniquity of his covetousness was I wroth, and smote him: I hid me, and was wroth, and he went on frowardly in the way of his heart. I have seen his ways, and will heal him: I will lead him also, and restore comforts unto him and to his mourners. I create the fruit of the lips: Peace, peace to him that is far off, and to him that is near, saith the Lord; and I will heal him. But the wicked are like the troubled sea, when it cannot rest, whose waters cast up mire and dirt. There is no peace, saith my God, to the wicked.

THIS is part of Isaiah's prophecy. He is telling the Jews that they should come back safe at last to their own land. He tells them why God had driven them out, and why God was going to bring them back.

He had driven them out for their sins. But he was not going to bring them back for their righteousness. He was going to bring them back out of his own free grace, his own pure love and mercy, which was wider, deeper, and higher, than all their sins, or than the sins of the whole world. He had sworn to

Abraham to be the friend of those foolish rebellious Jews, and he would keep his promise for ever. Their wickedness could not conquer his goodness, or their denying him make him deny himself.

But one thing he did require of them. Not that they should turn and do right all at once. That must come afterwards. But that they should open their eyes, and see that they had done wrong. He wanted to produce in them the humble and the contrite heart.

Now, as I told you last Sunday, a contrite heart does not merely mean a broken heart; it means more. It means literally a heart crushed; a heart ground to powder. You can have no stronger word.

It was this heart which God wished to breed in these rebellious Jews. A heart like Isaiah's heart, when he said, after having seen God's glory, 'Woe is me, for I am a man of unclean lips, and dwell among a people of unclean lips.' A heart like Jeremiah's heart, when he said, 'Oh, that my head were waters, and mine eyes a fountain of tears, that I might weep day and night for the slain of the daughter of my people.' A heart like Daniel's heart, when he confessed before God that, to him and all his people belonged shame and confusion of face.

Why do I mention these three men? They were not bad men, but good men. What need had they of a contrite heart?

I mention them, because they were good men. And why were they good men? For any good works of their own? Not in the least. What made them good men was, just the having the humble and the contrite heart; just feeling that in themselves they were as bad as the sinners round them; that the only thing which kept them out of the idolatry and profligacy of their neighbours was confessing their own weakness, and clinging fast to God by faith; confessing that their own righteousness was as filthy rags, and that God must clothe them with his righteousness.

Do you suppose that Isaiah, Jeremiah, and Daniel would have been good men, if they had said to themselves, 'We are prophets; we are inspired; we know God's law: and therefore we are righteous; we are safe: but these people—these idolaters, these drunkards, these covetous, tyrannous, profligate people round, to whom we preach, and who know not the law—they are accursed.' If they had, they would have said just what the Pharisees said afterwards. And what came of their saying so? Instead of knowing the Lord Christ, when he came they crucified him, showing that they were really worse at heart than the ignorant common people, instead of better.

No, my friends, Isaiah, and Jeremiah, and Daniel, were, better men than those round them, just because they had the humble and contrite heart; because they confessed that the root of sin was in them too, as much as in their fellow-countrymen; because they took their share of the public blame, their share of the public burden.

And their work and wish was, to breed in their fellow-countrymen the same humble and contrite heart which they had; to make them confess that their only hope lay in turning back to God, and doing right. But they could not succeed. Sin was too strong for them. So as Isaiah had warned the Jews, God did the work himself. God took the matter into his own hands, and arose out of his place to punish those Jews, and to make short work with them, by famine, and pestilence, and earthquake, and foreign invasion, till they were all carried away captive to Babylon: to see if that would teach them to know that God was the Lord; to see if that would breed in them the humble and contrite heart.

But God says to these poor Jews, Do not fancy that I have taken a spite against you. Not so. I will not contend for ever. I will not be always angry; for then the spirit would fail before me, and the souls which I have made. I have made you, God says; and I love you. I wish to save you, and not to destroy you. If God really hated any man, do you suppose that he would endure that man for a moment in his universe? Do you suppose that he would not sweep that man away, as easily and as quickly as we do a buzzing gnat when it torments us? Do you fancy that God lets you, or me, or any man, or any creature live one single instant, except in the hope of saving him, and of making him better than he is; of making him of some use, somewhere, some day or other? Do you suppose, I say, that God endures sinners one moment, save because he loves sinners, and willeth not the death of a sinner, but that he should be converted and live? No. 'God our Saviour,' says St. Paul to Timothy, 'willeth that all men should be saved, and come to the knowledge of the truth;' and therefore if they are not saved it must be their own fault, and not God's; it must be they who will not be saved, though God wills that they should be, as Isaiah goes on to show. For he says—God cries to men, Peace! I create the fruit of the lips; that is, I give men cause to thank me. I create it. I make it without their help. I do not sell them my mercy. I give it them freely. I say, Peace, peace, to them all, To him who is near, and him who is afar off; peace to all mankind; peace on earth, and goodwill to men. God is everlastingly at peace with himself, and at peace with all his creatures, and with all his works; and he wills, in his boundless love, to bring them all into his peace, the peace which passeth understanding; that they may be at peace with him; and, therefore at peace with themselves, and at peace with each other.

But how can they be at peace, when there is no peace in them? If they will do wrong; if they will quarrel; if they will defraud each other; if they will give way to the lusts and passions which war within them: how can they be at peace? They are like a troubled sea, says Isaiah, when it cannot rest, which casts up mire and dirt; and there is no peace to them. It is not God who casts up the mire and dirt. It is they who cast it up. God has not made them restless: but they themselves, with their pride, selfishness, violent passions, longings after this and that. God has not made them foul and dirty, but they themselves, with their own foul words and foul deeds, which keep them from being at peace with themselves, because they are ashamed of them all the while; which keep them from being at peace with their neighbours; which make them hate and fear their neighbours, because they know that their neighbours do not respect them, or are afraid of their neighbours finding them out.

What says brave, plain-spoken St. James?—'Let no man say when he is tempted, I am tempted of God : for God cannot be tempted with evil, neither tempteth he any man.' 'From whence come wars and fightings among you? Come they not hence, even of your lusts that war in your members? Ye lust, and have not: ye kill, and desire to have, and cannot obtain: ye fight and war, yet ye have not, because ye ask not.'

But as for God, he says, from him comes nothing but good. Do not fancy anything else. 'Do not err, my beloved brethren. Every good gift and every perfect gift is from above, and cometh down from the Father of lights, with whom is no variableness, neither shadow of turning. Of His own will begat He us with the word of truth, that we should be a kind of firstfruits of His creatures.'

My friends, all these things were written for our examples. God grant that we may lay the lesson to heart. A dark night may come to any one of us, a night of darkness upon darkness, and sorrow upon sorrow, and bad luck upon bad luck; till we know not what is going to happen next; and are ready to say with David—'All thy waves and thy billows are gone over me;' and with Hezekiah—'I reckoned till morning, that, as a lion, so will he break all my bones: from day even to night wilt thou make an end of me.'

God grant, that before that day comes, we may have so learnt to know God, as to know that the billows are God's billows, and the storms his storms; and, after a while, not to be afraid, though all earthly hope and help seem swept away.

God grant that when trouble comes after trouble, we may be able to see that our Father in heaven is only dealing with us as he dealt with those poor Jews; that he is all the while saying 'Peace!' to us, whether we be near him, or far off from him; and is ready to heal us, the moment that he has worked in us the broken and contrite heart. And we may trust him that he will do it. With him one day is as a thousand years. And in one day of bitter misery he can teach us lessons, which we could not teach ourselves in a thousand years of reading and studying, or even of praying. But our prayers, we shall find, have not been in vain. He has not forgotten one of them; and there is the answer, in that very sorrow. In sorrow, he is making short work with our spirits. In one terrible and searching trial our souls may be, as the Poet says—

> Heated hot with burning fears,
> And bathed in baths of hissing tears;
> And battered by the strokes of doom,
> To shape and use.

Yes. He will make short work at times with men's spirits. He grinds hearts to powder, that they may be broken and contrite before him: but only that he may heal them; that out of the broken fragments of the hard, proud, self-deceiving heart of stone, he may create a new and harder heart of flesh, human and gentle, humble and simple. And then he will return and have mercy. He will show that he will not contend for ever. He will show that he does not wish our spirits to fail before him, but to grow and flourish before him to everlasting life. He will create the fruit of the lips, and give us cause to thank him in spirit and in truth. He will show us that he was nearest when he seemed furthest off; and that just because he is the high and lofty One that inhabiteth eternity, whose name is Holy, who dwelleth in the high and holy place, for that very reason he dwells also with the humble and the contrite heart; because that heart alone can confess his height and its own lowliness, confess its own sin and his holiness; and so can cling to his majesty by faith, and partake of his holiness by the inspiration of his Holy Spirit.

God grant that we may all so humble ourselves under his mighty hand, whenever that hand lies heavy upon us, that he may raise us up in due time, changed into his divine likeness, from glory to glory; till we come to the measure of Christ, and to the stature of perfect men, renewed into the image of the Son of Man, Jesus Christ our Lord! Amen.

SERMON XVIII.

ST. PETER.

MATT. xvi. 18.

Thou art Peter, and on this rock I will build my Church.

THIS is St. Peter's day. It will be well worth our while to think a little over St. Peter, and what kind of man he was. For St. Peter was certainly one of the most important and most famous men who ever lived in the whole world. You just heard what our Lord said to him in the text. And certainly, from those words, and from many other things which are told of St. Peter, he was the chief of the apostles—at least till St. Paul arose.

St. Paul says himself, that he had as much authority as St. Peter, and that he was not a whit behind the very chiefest of the apostles: but St. Peter, for some time after our Lord's death, seems to have been looked up to, by the rest of the apostles and the disciples, as their leader, the man of most weight and authority among them. It was to St. Peter especially that our Lord looked to strengthen the other apostles, after he had been converted himself. It was to St. Peter that our Lord first revealed that great gospel, that the Gentiles were fellow-heirs with the Jews in all God's promises. The same thing was afterwards revealed to St. Paul too, and far more fully: but it was St. Peter who had the great honour of baptizing the first heathen; and of using, as our Lord had bid him do, the keys of the kingdom of heaven, to open its doors to all the nations upon earth.

Now, what sort of a man was this on whom the Lord Jesus Christ put so great an honour? If we say that St. Peter was nothing in himself; that all the goodness and worth in him was given him by Jesus Christ, then we must ask, what sort of goodness, what sort of worth, did the Lord give St. Peter to make him fit for so great an office? And how did he use Christ's gifts? For, mind, he might have used them wrongly, as well as rightly; and the greater gifts he had, the more harm he would have done if he had used them ill. We shall see, presently, how he did use them ill, more than once; and how our Lord had to reprove him, and say very stern and terrible words to him, to bring him to his senses.

But this we may see, that St. Peter was always a frank, brave honest, high-spirited man; who, if he thought that a thing ought to be done, would do it at once.

The first thing we hear of him is, how Jesus, walking by the Lake of Galilee, saw Peter with his brother, casting a net into the sea, for they were fishers. And he said unto them, 'Follow me, and I will make you fishers of men. And they straightway left their nets, and followed him.' This was most likely not the first time that St. Peter had seen our Lord, or heard him speak. Living in the same part of the country, he must have known all his miracles: but still it was a great struggle, no doubt, for him (and doubly so because he was a married man), to throw up his employment, and go wandering after one who had not where to lay his head: yet he did it, and did it at once. And you may see that he did it for a much higher and nobler reason than if he had only gone to wonder at our Lord's miracles, as the multitude did, or even to be able to work miracles himself. Jesus did not say to him, Follow me, and I will give you the power of working miracles, and being admired, and wondered at; all he says is, I will make you fishers of men; I will make you able to get a hold on men's hearts, and teach them, and make them happier and better. And for that St. Peter followed him. It seems as if from the first his wish was to do good to his fellow-creatures.

And, gradually, he seems to have become the spokesman for the other apostles. When they wished to ask our Lord anything, we generally find St. Peter asking; and when (as in the gospel for to-day), our Lord asks them a question, St. Peter answers for them all. Whom say ye that I am? And Peter answered and said, 'Thou art the Christ, the Son of the Living God.'

This is what St. Peter had learnt; because he had kept his eyes and his ears open, and his heart ready and teachable, that he might see God's truth when it should please God to show it him; and God did show it him: and taught him something which his own eyes and ears could not teach him; which all his thinking could not have taught him; which no *man* could have taught him; flesh and blood could not reveal to him that Jesus was the Son of God; flesh and blood could not draw aside the veil of flesh and blood, and make him see in that poor man of Nazareth, who was called the carpenter's son, the only-begotten of the Father, God made man. No. God the Father only could teach him that, by the inspiration of his Holy Spirit: but do you think that God would have taught St. Peter that, or that St. Peter could have learnt it, if his mind had been merely full of thoughts about himself, and what honour he was to get for himself, or what profit he was to get for himself, out of the Lord Jesus Christ?

No: St. Peter loved the Lord Jesus; loved him with his whole heart. When afterwards our Lord asked him, 'Simon, son of Jonas, lovest thou me?' He answered, 'Lord, thou knowest that I love thee.' And because he loved him, he saw how beautiful and glorious the Lord's character was; and his eyes were opened to see that the Lord was too beautiful, too glorious, to be merely a mortal man; and, at last, to see that he was the brightness of God's glory, and the express image of his Father's person.

But, as I said just now, St. Peter's great and excellent gifts might have made him only the more dangerous man, if he used them ill. And this seems to have been his danger. He was plainly a very bold and determined man, who knew his own power, and was ready to use it fearlessly: and what would he be tempted to do ! To fancy that his power belonged to him, and not to Christ; that his wisdom belonged to himself; that his faith belonged to himself; his authority belonged to himself; and that, therefore, he could use his excellent gifts as he liked, and not merely as Christ liked. He was liable, as we say in homely English, to 'have his head turned' by his honour and his power.

For instance, immediately after our Lord had put this great honour on him, 'I will give thee the keys of the kingdom of heaven,' we find Peter mistaking his power, and, therefore, misusing it. 'From that time forth began Jesus to show unto his disciples, how that he must go unto Jerusalem, and suffer many things of the elders and chief priests and scribes, and be killed, and be raised again the third day. Then Peter took him, and began to rebuke him, saying, Be it far from Thee, Lord: this shall not be unto thee. But he turned, and said unto Peter, Get thee behind me, Satan: thou art an offence unto me: for thou savourest not the things that be of God, but those that be of men.' St. Peter's words, in the Greek tongue, really seem to mean that St. Peter fancied that *he* could protect our Lord; that he had the power of delivering him, by binding his enemies the Jews, and loosing the Lord himself. That seems to have been the way in which he took our Lord's words : but what does our Lord answer? As stern words as man could hear. 'Get thee behind me, Satan ; for thou art an offence unto me.' Or, rather, thou art my stumbling-block. So that St. Peter, while he fancied himself near to the angels, found out, to his shame, that he was behaving like a devil, and had to be called Satan to his face ;

and that while he thought he could save the Lord Jesus, he found that he was doing all he could to harm and ruin his master; trying to do the very work which the Devil tried to do, when he tempted the Lord Jesus in the wilderness. So near beside each other do heaven and hell lie. So easy is it to give place to the Devil, and fall into the worst of sin, just when we are puffed up with spiritual pride.

And more than once afterwards, St. Peter had to learn that same lesson; when, for instance, he leaped boldly overboard from the boat, and came walking towards Jesus on the sea. That was noble: worthy of St. Peter: but he fancied himself a braver man than he was. He became afraid; and the moment that he became afraid, he began to sink. Jesus saved him, and then told him why he had become afraid: because his faith had failed him. He had ceased trusting in Christ's power to keep him up; and became helpless at once.

That should have been a lesson to St. Peter, that he was not to be so very sure of his own faith and his own courage; that without his Lord he might become cowardly and helpless any moment: but he did not take that gentle lesson; so he had to learn it once and for all by a very terrible trial. We all know how he fell;—one day protesting vehemently to his Lord, 'Though I die with thee, I will not deny thee;' the next, declaring, with oaths and curses, 'I know not the man.' No wonder that when Jesus turned and looked on him, Peter went out and wept bitterly, as bitter tears of shame as ever were shed on earth. For he knew, he was sure, that he loved his Lord all along: and now he had denied him. He who was so bold and confident, to fall thus! and into the very sins most contrary to his nature! the very sins in which he would have expected least of all to fall! He, so frank and honest and brave—He to turn coward. He to tell a base lie! I dare say, that for the moment he could hardly believe himself to be himself.

But so it is, my friends. If we forget that all which is good and strong in us comes from God, and not from ourselves; if we are conceited, and confident in ourselves; then we cut ourselves off from God's grace, and give place to Satan the Devil, that he may sift us like wheat, as he did St. Peter; and then in some shameful hour, we may find ourselves saying and doing things which we would never have believed we could have done. God grant, that if ever we fall into such unexpected sin, it may happen to us as it did to St. Peter. For Satan gained little by sifting St. Peter. He sifted out the chaff: but the wheat was left behind safe for God's garner. The chaff was St. Peter's rashness and self-conceit, which came from his own sinful nature; and that went, and St. Peter was rid of it for ever. The wheat was St. Peter's courage, and faith, and honour, which came from God; and that remained, and St. Peter kept them for ever. That, we read, was St. Peter's conversion; that worked the thorough and complete change in his character, and made him a new man from that day forth. And then, after that terrible and fiery trial, St. Peter was ready to receive the gift of the Holy Spirit, which gave him courage with fervent zeal to preach the gospel of his Crucified Lord, and at last to be crucified himself for that Lord's sake; and so fulfil the Lord's words to him. 'When thou wast young, thou girdedst thyself, and walkedst whither thou wouldest: but when thou shalt be old, thou shalt stretch forth thy hands, and another shall gird thee, and carry thee whither thou wouldest not.' By that our Lord seems to have meant, 'You were strong and proud and self-willed enough in your youth. The day will come when you will be tamed down, ready and willing to suffer patiently, even agony from which your flesh and blood may shrink;' and the Lord's words came true. For, say the old stories, when St. Peter was led to be crucified, he refused to be crucified upright, as the Lord Jesus had been, saying, 'That it was too great an honour for him, who had once denied his Lord, to die the same death as his Lord died.' So he was crucified, they say, with his head downward; and ended a glorious life in a humble martyrdom.

And what may we learn from St. Peter's character? I think we may learn this. Frankness, boldness, a high spirit, a stout will, and an affectionate heart; these are all God's gifts, and they are pleasant in his eyes, and ought to be a blessing to the man who has them. Ought to be a blessing to him, because they are the stuff out of which a good, and noble, and useful Christian man may be made. But they need not be a blessing to a man; they are *excellent* gifts: but they will not of themselves make a man an *excellent* man, who *excels;* that is, surpasses others in goodness. We may see that ourselves, from experience. We see too many brave men, free-spoken men, affectionate men, who come to shame and ruin.

How then can we become excellent men, like St. Peter? By being baptised, as St. Peter was, with the Holy Ghost and with fire.

Baptized with the Holy Ghost, to put into our hearts good desires; to make us see what is good, and love what is good, long to do good: but baptized with fire also. 'He shall baptize you, John the Baptist said, with the Holy Ghost and with fire.'

Does that seem a hard saying? Do not some at least of you know what that means? Some know, I believe. All will know one day; for it is true for all. To all, sooner or later, Christ comes to baptise them with fire; with the bitter searching affliction which opens the very secrets of their hearts, and shows them what their souls are really like, and parts the good from the evil in them, the gold from the rubbish, the wheat from the chaff. 'And he shall gather the wheat into his garner, but the chaff he shall burn up with unquenchable fire.' God grant to each of you, that when that day comes to you, there may be something in you which will stand the fire; something worthy to be treasured up in God's garner, unto everlasting life.

But do not think that the baptism of fire comes only once for all to a man, in some terrible affliction, some one awful conviction of his own sinfulness and nothingness. No; with many

—and those, perhaps, the best people—it goes on month after month, year after year: by secret trials, chastenings which none but they and God can understand, the Lord is cleansing them from their secret faults, and making them to understand wisdom secretly; burning out of them the chaff of self-will and self-conceit and vanity, and leaving only the pure gold of his righteousness. How many sweet and holy souls look cheerful enough before the eyes of man, because they are too humble and too considerate to intrude their secret sorrows upon the world. And yet they have their secret sorrows. They carry their cross unseen all day long, and lie down to sleep on it at night: and they will carry it for years and years, and to their graves, and to the Throne of Christ, before they lay it down: and none but they and Christ will ever know what it was; what was the secret chastisement which he sent to make that soul better, which seemed to us to be already too good for earth. So does the Lord watch his people, and tries them with fire, as the refiner of silver sits by his furnace, watching the melted metal, till he knows that it is purged from all its dross, by seeing the image of his own face reflected in it. God grant that our afflictions may so cleanse our hearts, that at the last Christ may behold himself in us, and us in himself; that so we may be fit to be with him where he is, and behold the glory which his Father gave him before the foundation of the world.

SERMON XIX.

ELIJAH.

(*Tenth Sunday after Trinity.*)

---

1 KINGS XXI. 19, 20.

And thou shalt speak unto him, saying, Thus saith the Lord, Hast thou killed, and also taken possession? and thou shalt speak unto him, saying, Thus saith the Lord, In the place where dogs licked the blood of Naboth, shall dogs lick thy blood, even thine. And Ahab said to Elijah, Hast thou found me, O mine enemy? And he answered, I have found thee: because thou hast sold thyself to work evil in the sight of the Lord.

OF all the grand personages in the Old Testament, there are few or none, I think, grander than the prophet Elijah. Consider his strange and wild life, wandering about in forests and mountains, suddenly appearing, and suddenly disappearing again, so that no man knew where to find him; and, as Obadiah said when he met him, 'If I tell my Lord, Behold, Elijah is here; then, as soon as I am gone from thee, the Spirit of the Lord shall carry thee whither I know not.' Consider, again, his strange activity and strength, as when he goes, forty days and forty nights, far away out of Judea, over the waste wilderness, to Horeb the mount of God; or, as again, when he girds up his loins, and runs before Ahab's chariot for many miles to the entrance of Jezreel. One can fancy him from what the Bible tells us of him, clearly enough; as a man mysterious and terrible, not merely in the eyes of women and children, but of soldiers and of kings.

He seems to have been especially a countryman; a mountaineer; born and bred in Gilead, among the lofty mountains and vast forests, full of wild beasts, lions and bears, wild bulls and deer, which stretch for many miles along the further side of the river Jordan, with the waste desert of rocks and sand beyond them. A wild man, bred up in a wild country, he had learnt to fear no man, and no thing, but God alone. We do not know what his youth was like; we do not know whether he had wife, or children, or any human being who loved him. Most likely not. He seems to have lived a lonely life, in sad and bad times. He seems to have had but one thought, that his country was going to ruin, from idolatry, tyranny, false and covetous ways; and one determination; to say so; to speak the truth, whatever it cost him. He had found out that the Lord was God, and not Baal, or any of the idols; and he would follow the Lord; and tell all Israel what his own heart had told him, 'The Lord, he is God,' was the one thing which he had to say; and he said it, till it became his name; whether given him by his parents, or by the people, his name was Eli-jah, 'The Lord is God.' 'How long halt ye between two opinions?' he cries, upon the greatest day of his life. 'If the Lord be God, then follow him; but if Baal, then follow him.' How grand he is, on Carmel, throughout that noble chapter which we read last Sunday. There is no fear in him, no doubt in him. The poor wild peasant out of the savage mountains stands up before all Israel, before king, priests, nobles, and people, and speaks and acts as he, too, were a king; because the Spirit of God is in him: and he is right, and he knows that he is right. And they obey him as if he were a king. Even before the fire comes down from heaven, and shows that God is on his side, from the first they obey him. King Ahab himself obeys him, trembles before him—'And it came to pass, when Ahab saw Elijah, that Ahab said unto him, Art thou he that troubleth Israel? And he answered, I have not troubled Israel; but thou, and thy father's house, in that ye have forsaken the commandments of the Lord, and thou hast followed Baalim. Now therefore send, and gather to me all Israel unto mount Carmel, and the prophets of Baal four hundred and fifty, and the prophets of the groves four hundred, which eat at Jezebel's table. So Ahab sent unto all the children of Israel, and gathered the prophets together unto mount Carmel.' The tyrant's guilty conscience makes a coward of him; and he quails before the wild man out of the mountains, who has not where to lay his head, who stands alone against all the people, though Baal's prophets are four hundred and fifty men, and the prophets of the groves four hundred, and they eat at the queen's table; and he only is left and they seek his life:—yet no man dare touch him, not even the king himself. Such power is there, such strength is there, in being an honest and a God-fearing man.

Yes, my friends, this was the secret of Elijah's power. This is the lesson which Elijah has to teach us. Not to halt between two opinions. If a thing be true, to stand up for it; if a thing be right, to do it, whatsoever it may cost us. Make up your minds then, my friends, to be honest men like Elijah the prophet of old.

For your own sake, for your neighbour's sake, and for God's sake, be honest men.

For your own sake. If you want to be respected; if you want to be powerful—and it is good to be powerful sometimes —if God has set you to govern people, whether it be your children and household, your own farm, your own shop, your own estate, your own country or neighbourhood—Do you want to know the great secret of success?—Be honest and brave. Let your word be as good as your thought, and your deed as good as your word. Who is the man who is respected? Who is the man who has influence? The complaisant man—the cringing man—the man who cannot say No, or dare not say No? Not he. The passionate man who loses his temper when anything goes wrong, who swears and scolds, and instead of making others do right, himself does wrong, and lowers himself just when he ought to command respect? My experience is—not he: but the man who says honestly and quietly what he thinks, and does fearlessly and quietly what he knows. People who differ from him will respect him, because he acts up to his principles. When they are in difficulty or trouble, they will go and ask his advice, just because they know they will get an honest answer. They will overlook a little roughness in him; they will excuse his speaking unpleasant truths: because they can trust him, even though he is plain-spoken.

For your neighbour's sake, I say; and again, for your children's sake; for the sake of all with whom you have to do, be honest and brave. For our children—O my friends, we cannot do a crueller thing by them than to let them see that we are inconsistent. If they hear us say one thing and do another—if, while we preach to them we do not practice ourselves, they will never respect us, and never obey us from love and principle. If they do obey us, it will be only before our faces, and from fear. If they see us doing only what we like, when our backs are turned they will do what they like.

And worse will come than their not respecting us—they will learn not to respect God. If they see that we do not respect truth and honesty, they will not respect truth and honesty; and he who does not respect them, does not respect God. They will learn to look on religion as a sham. If we are inconsistent, they will be profane.

But some may say—'I have no power; and I want none. I have no people under me for whom I am responsible.'

Then, if you think that you need not be honest and brave for your own sake, or for other peoples' sake, be honest and brave for God's sake.

Do you ask what I mean? I mean this. Recollect that truth belongs to God. That if a thing is true, it is true because God made it so, and not otherwise; and therefore, if you deny truth, you fight against God. If you are honest, and stand up for truth, you stand up for God, and what God has done.

And recollect this, too. If a thing be right for you to do, God has made it right, and God wills you to do it; and, therefore, if you do not do your duty, you are fighting against God; and if you do your duty, you are a fellow-worker with God, fulfilling God's will. Therefore, I say, Be honest and brave for God's sake. And in this way, my friends, all may be brave, all may be noble. Speak the truth, and do your duty, because it is the will of God. Poor, weak women, people without scholarship, cleverness, power, may live glorious lives, and die glorious deaths, and God's strength may be made perfect in their weakness. They may live, did I say? I may say they have lived, and have died, already, by thousands. When we read the stories of the old martyrs who, in the heathen persecution, died like heroes rather than deny Christ, and scorned to save themselves by telling what they knew to be a lie, but preferred truth to all that makes life worth having:—how many of them—I may say the greater part of them—were poor creatures enough in the eyes of man, though they were rich enough, noble enough, in the eyes of God who inspired them. 'Few rich and few noble,' as the apostle says, 'were called.' It was to poor people, old people, weak women, ill-used and untaught slaves, that God gave grace to defy all the torments which the heathen could heap on them, and to defy the scourge and the rack, the wild beasts and the fire, sooner than foul their lips and their souls by denying Christ, and worshipping the idols which they knew were nothing, and worth nothing.

And so it may be with any of you here; whosoever you may be, however poor, however humble. Though your opportunities may be small, your station lowly, your knowledge little;

though you may be stupid in mind, slow of speech, weakly of body, yet if you but make up your mind to say the thing which is true, and to do the thing which is right, you may be strong with the strength of God, and glorious with the glory of Christ.

It is a grand thing, no doubt, to be like Elijah, a stern and bold prophet, standing up alone against a tyrant king and a sinful people; but it is even a greater thing to be like that famous martyr in old time, St. Blandina, who, though she was but a slave, and so weakly, and mean, and fearful in body, that her mistress and all her friends feared that she would deny Christ at the very sight of the torments prepared for her, and save herself by sacrificing to the idols, yet endured, day after day, tortures too horrible to speak of, without cry or groan, or any word, save 'I am a Christian;' and, having outlived all her fellow-martyrs, died at last victorious over pain and temptation, so that the very heathen who tortured her broke out in admiration of her courage, and confessed that no woman had ever endured so many and so grievous torments. So may God's strength be made perfect in woman's weakness.

You are not called to endure such things. No: but you, and I, and every Christian soul are called on to do what we know to be right. Not to halt between two opinions: but if God be God, to follow Him. If we make up our minds to do that, we shall be sure to have our trials: but we shall be safe, because we are on God's side, and God on ours. And if God be with us, what matter if the whole world be against us? For which is the stronger of the two, the whole world, or God who made it, and rules it, and will rule it for ever?

SERMON XX.

THE LOFTINESS OF HUMILITY.

1 Peter v. 5.

Be clothed with humility: for God resisteth the proud, and giveth grace to the humble.

THIS is St. Peter's command. Are we really inclined to obey it? For, if we are, there is nothing more easy There is no vice so easy to get rid of as pride: if one wishes. Nothing so easy as to be humble: if one wishes.

That may seem a strange saying, considering that self-conceit is the vice of all others to which man is most given; the first sin, and the last sin, and that which is said to be the most difficult to cure. But what I say is true nevertheless.

Whosoever wishes to get rid of pride may do so. Whosoever wishes to be humble need not go far to humble himself.

But how? Simply by being honest with himself, and looking at himself as he is.

Let a man recollect honestly and faithfully his past life; let him recollect his sayings and doings for the past week; even for the past twenty-four hours: and I will warrant that man that he will recollect something, or, perhaps, many things which will not raise him in his own eyes; something which he had sooner not have said or done; something which, if he is a foolish man, he will try to forget, because it makes him ashamed of himself; something which, if he is a wise man, he will not try to forget, just because it makes him ashamed of himself; and a very good thing for him that he should be so. I know that it is so for me; and therefore I suppose it is so for every man and woman in this Church.

I am not going to give any examples. I am not going to say,—'Suppose you thought this and this about yourself, and were proud of it; and then suppose that you recollected that you had done that and that: would you not feel very much taken down in your own conceit?'

I like that personal kind of preaching less and less. Those random shots are dangerous and cruel; likely to hit the wrong person, and hurt their feelings unnecessarily. It is very easy to say a hard thing: but not so easy to say it to the right person and at the right time.

No. The heart knoweth its own bitterness. Almost every one has something to be ashamed of, more or less, which no one but himself and God knows of; and which, perhaps, it is better that no one but he and God should know.

I do not mean any great sin, or great shame—God forbid; but some weak point, as we call it. Something which he had better not say or do; and yet which he is in the habit of saying and doing. I do not ask what it is. With some it may be a mere pardonable weakness; with others it may be a very serious and dangerous fault. All I ask now is, that each and every one of us should try and find it out, and feel it, and keep it in mind; that we may be of a humble spirit with the lowly, which is better than dividing the spoil with the proud.

But why better?

The world and human nature look up to the proud successful man. One is apt to say, 'Happy is the man who has plenty to be proud of. Happy is the man who can divide the spoil of this world with the successful of this world. Happy is the man who can look down on his fellow-men, and stand over them, and manage them, and make use of them, and get his profit out of them.'

But that is a mistake. That is the high-mindedness which goes before a fall, which comes not from above, but is always earthly, often sensual, and sometimes devilish. The true and safe high-mindedness, which comes from above, is none other than humility. For, if you will look at it aright, the humble man is really more high-minded than the proud man. Think. Suppose two men equal in understanding, in rank, in wealth, in what else you like, one of them proud, the other humble. The proud man thinks—'How much better, wiser, richer, more highly born, more religious, more orthodox, am I than other people round me.' Not, of course, than all round him, but than those whom he thinks beneath him. Therefore he is always comparing himself with those below himself; always watching those things in them in which he thinks them worse, meaner than himself; he is always looking down on his neighbours.

Now, which is more high-minded; which is nobler; which is more fit for a man; to look down, or to look up? At all events the humble man *looks up*. He thinks, 'How much worse, not how much better, am I than other people.' He looks at their good points, and compares them with his own bad ones. He admires them for those things in which they surpass him. He thinks of—perhaps he loves to read of— men superior to himself in goodness, wisdom, courage. He pleases himself with the example of brave and righteous deeds, even though he fears that he cannot copy them; and so he is always looking up. His mind is filled with high thoughts, though they be about others, not about himself. If he be a truly Christian man, his thoughts rise higher still. He thinks of Christ and of God, and compares his weakness, ignorance, and sinfulness with their perfect power, wisdom, goodness. Do you not see that this man's mind is full of higher, nobler thoughts than that of the proud man? Is he not more high-minded who is looking up, up to God himself, for what is good, noble, heavenly? Even though it makes him feel small, poor, weak, and sinful in comparison, still his mind is full of grace, and wisdom, and glory. The proud man, meanwhile, for the sake of feeding his own self-conceit at other men's expense, is filling his mind with low, mean, earthly thoughts about the weaknesses, sins, and follies, of the world around him. Is not he truly low-minded, thinking about low things?

Now, I tell you, my friends, that both have their reward. That the humble man, as years roll on, becomes more and more noble, and the proud man becomes more and more low-minded; and finds that pride goes before a fall in more senses than one. Yes. There is nothing more hurtful to our own minds and hearts than a domineering, contemptuous frame of mind. It may be pleasant to our own self-conceit: but it is only a sweet poison. A man lowers his own character by it. He takes the shape of what he is always looking at; and, if he looks at base and low things, he becomes base and low himself; just as slave-owners, all over the world, and in all time, sooner and later, by living among slaves, learn to copy their own slaves' vices; and, while they oppress and look down on their fellow-man, become passionate and brutal, false and greedy, like the poor wretches whom they oppress.

Better, better to be of a lowly spirit. Better to think of those who are nobler than ourselves, even though by so doing we are ashamed of ourselves all day long. What loftier thoughts can man have? What higher and purer air can a man's soul breathe? Yes, my friends; believe it, and be sure of it. The truly high-minded man is not the proud man, who tries to get a little pitiful satisfaction from finding his brother men, as he chooses to fancy, a little weaker, a little more ignorant, a little more foolish, a little more ridiculous, than his own weak, ignorant, foolish, and, perhaps, ridiculous self. Not he; but the man who is always looking upwards to goodness,

THE LOFTINESS OF HUMILITY.

to good men, and to the all-good God : filling his soul with the sight of an excellence to which he thinks he can never attain ; and saying, with David, ' All my delight is in the saints that dwell in the earth, and in those who excel in virtue.'

But I do not say that he cannot attain to that excellence. To the goodness of God, of course, no man can ; but to the goodness of man he may. For what man has done, man may do ; and the grace of God which gave power to one man to rise above sin, and weakness, and ignorance, will give power to others also. But only to those who look upward, at better men than themselves : not to those who look down, like the Pharisee, but to those who look up like the Publican ; for, as the text says, ' God resisteth the proud, but giveth grace to the humble.'

And why does God resist and set himself against the proud ? To turn him out of his evil way, of course, if by any means he may be converted (that is, turned round) and live. For the proud man has put himself into a wrong position ; where no immortal soul ought to be. He is looking away from God, and down upon men ; and so he has turned his face and thoughts away from God, the fountain of light and life ; and is trying to do without God, and to stand in his own strength, and not in God's grace, and to be somebody in himself, instead of being only in God, in whom we live and move and have our being. So he has set himself against God ; and God will, in mercy to that foolish man's soul, set himself against him. God will humble him ; God will overthrow him ; God will bring his plans to nought ; if by any means he may make that man ashamed of himself, and empty him of his self-conceit, that he may turn and repent in dust and ashes, when he finds out what those proud Laodicæan Christians of old had to find out—that all the while that they were saying, ' I am rich, and increased with goods, and have need of nothing,' they did not know that they were wretched, and miserable, and poor, and blind, and naked.

And how does God give grace to the humble? My friends, even the wise heathen knew that. Listen to a heathen;* a good and a wise man, though; and one who was not far from the kingdom of God, or he would not have written such words as these,—

'It is our duty,' he says, 'to turn our minds to the best of everything; so as not merely to enjoy what we read, but to be improved by it. And we shall do that, by reading the histories of good and great men, which will, in our minds, produce an emulation and eagerness, which may stir us up to imitation. We may be pleased with the work of a man's hands, and yet set little store by the workman. Perfumes and fine colours we may like well enough: but that will not make us wish to be perfumers, or painters: but goodness, which is the work, not of a man's hands, but of his soul, makes us not only admire what is done, but long to do the like. And therefore,' he says, he thought it good to write the lives 'of famous and good men, and to set their examples before his countrymen. And having begun to do this,' he says in another place, 'for the sake of others, he found himself going on, and liking his labour, for his own sake: for the virtues of those great men served him as a looking-glass, in which he might see how, more or less, to order and adorn his own life. Indeed, it could be compared,' he says, 'to nothing less than living with the great souls who were dead and gone, and choosing out of their actions all that was noblest and worthiest to know. What greater pleasure could there be than that,' he asks, ' or what better means to improve his soul? By filling his mind with pictures of the best and worthiest characters, he was able to free himself from any low, malicious, mean thoughts, which he might catch from bad company. If he was forced to mix at times with base men, he could wash out the stains of their bad thoughts and words, by training himself in a calm and happy temper to view those noble examples.' So says the wise heathen. Was not he happier,

* Plutarch.

wiser, better, a thousand times, thus keeping himself humble by looking upwards, than if he had been feeding his petty pride by looking down, and saying, 'God, I thank thee that I am not as other men are?'

If you wish, then, to be truly high-minded, by being truly humble, read of, and think of, better men, wiser men, braver men, more useful men than you are. Above all, if you be Christians, think of Christ himself. That good old heathen took the best patterns which he could find: but after all, they were but imperfect, sinful men: but you have an example such as he never dreamed of; a perfect man, and perfect God in one. Let the thought of Christ keep you always humble: and yet let it lift you up to the highest, noblest, purest thoughts which man can have, as it will.

For all that this old heathen says of the use of examples of good men, all that, and far more, St. Paul says, almost in the same words. By looking at Christ, he says, we rise and sit with him in heavenly places, and enjoy the sight of His perfect goodness; ashamed of ourselves, indeed, and bowed to the very dust by the feeling of our own unworthiness; and yet filled with the thought of his worthiness, till, by, looking we begin to admire, and, by admiring, we begin to love; and so are drawn and lifted up to him, till, by beholding as in a glass the glory of the Lord, and the perfect beauty of his character, we become changed into the same image, from glory to glory: and thus, instead of receiving the just punishment of pride and contempt, which is lowering our characters to the level of those on whom we look down, we shall receive the just reward of true humility, which is having our characters raised to the level of him up to whom we look.

Oh young people, think of this; and remember why God has given you the advantage of scholarship and education. Not that you may be proud of the very little you know; not that you may look down on those who are not as well instructed as you are; not that you may waste your time over silly books, which teach you only to laugh at the follies and ignorance of some of your fellow-men, to whom God has not given as much as to you; but that you may learn what great and good men have lived, and still live, in the world; what wise, and good, and useful things have been, and are being, done all around you; and to copy them: above all, that you may look up to Christ, and through Christ, to God, and learn to copy him; till you come, as St. Paul says, to be perfect men; to the measure of the stature of the fulness of Christ. To which may he bring you all of his mercy. Amen.

SERMON XXI.

THE KNOWLEDGE OF GOD.

(*Trinity Sunday.*)

JOHN v. 19.

Then answered Jesus and said unto them, Verily, verily, I say unto you, The Son can do nothing of himself, but what he seeth the Father do: for what things soever he doeth, these also doeth the Son likewise.

THIS is Trinity Sunday; and on this day we are especially to think of the mystery of the ever-blessed Trinity, and on the Athanasian Creed, which was read this morning. Now there is much in this Athanasian Creed, which simple country people, however good their natural abilities may be, cannot be expected to understand. The Creed was written by scholars, and for scholars; and for very deep scholars, too, far deeper than I pretend to be; and the reasonable way for most men to think of the Athanasian Creed, will be to take it very much upon trust, as a child takes on trust what his father tells him, even though he cannot understand it himself; or, as we all believe, that the earth moves round the sun, and not the sun round the earth, though we cannot prove it; but only believe it, because wiser men than we have proved it. So we must think of the Athanasian Creed, and say to ourselves—'Wiser men than I can ever hope to be have settled that this is the true doctrine, and the true meaning of Holy Scripture, and I will believe them.

They must know best.' Still, one is bound to understand as much as one can; one is bound to be able to give some reason for the faith which is in us; and, above all, one is bound not to hold false doctrines, which are contrary to the Athanasian Creed and to the Bible.

Some people are too apt to say now-a-days, ' But what matter if one does hold false doctrine? That is a mistake of the head and not of the heart. Provided a man lives a good life, what matter what his doctrines are?" No doubt, my friends, if a man lives a good life, all is well : but *do* people live good lives? I am not speaking of infidels. Thank God, there are none here; to God let us leave them, trusting in the Good Friday collect, and the good-will of God, which is, that all should be saved and come to the knowledge of the truth.

But, as for Christian people, this I will tell you, that unless you hold true doctrines, you will *not* lead good lives. My experience is, that people are often wrong, when they say false doctrine is a mistake of the head and not of the heart. I believe false doctrine is very often not bred in the head at all, but in the heart, in the very bottom of a man's soul; that it rises out of his heart into his head; and that if his heart was right with God, he would begin at once to have clearer and truer notions of the true Christian faith. I do not say that it is always so; God forbid! But I do say that it is often so, because I see it so; because I see every day false doctrines about God making men lead bad lives, and commit actual sins; take God's name in vain, dishonour their fathers and mothers, lie, cheat, bear false witness against their neighbours, and covet other men's goods. I say, I see it, and I must believe my own eyes and ears; and when I do see it, I begin to understand the text which says, ' This is eternal life, to know thee, the only God, and Jesus Christ, whom thou hast sent ;' and I begin to understand the Athanasian Creed, which says, that if a man does not believe rightly the name of God, and the Incarnation of our Lord Jesus Christ, he will perish everlastingly; his soul will decay more and more, become more and more weak, unhealthy and corrupt, till he perishes everlastingly. And whatsoever that may mean, it must mean something most awful and terrible, worse than all the evil which ever happened to us since we were born.

There is a very serious example of this, to my mind, in what is called the Greek Church; the Greeks and Russians. They split off from the rest of Christ's Catholic Church, many hundred years ago, because they would not hold with the rest of the Church that the Holy Spirit proceeded from the Son as well as from the Father. They said that the Holy Spirit proceeded from the Father alone. Now that may seem a slight matter of words: but I cannot help thinking that it has been a very solemn matter of practice with them. It seems to me—God forgive me if I am judging them hardly!—that because they denied that the Holy Spirit proceeded from the Son, they forgot that he was the Spirit of the Son, the Spirit of Jesus Christ, by whom he says for ever, 'Father, not my will but thine be done!' and so they forgot that the Holy Spirit is the Spirit of Sonship, the Spirit of adoption, which must proceed and come from Christ to us, that we may call God our Father, and say with Christ, 'Father, I come to do thy will;' and so, in course of time, they seem to have forgotten that Christian men were in any real practical sense, God's children; and when people forget that they are God's children, they forget soon enough to behave like God's children, and to live righteous and Godlike lives.

I give you this as an example of what I mean; how not believing rightly the Athanasian Creed may make a man lead a bad life.

Now let me give an example nearer home; one which has to do with you and me. God grant that we may all lay it to heart. You read, in the Athanasian Creed, that we are not to confound the persons of the Trinity, nor divide the substance; but to believe that such as the Father is, such is the Son. and such is the Holy Ghost, the Glory equal, the Majesty co-eternal. Now there is little fear of our confounding the persons, as some people used to do in old times; but there is great fear of our dividing God's substance, parting God's substance, that is, fancying that God is made up of different parts, and not perfectly one God.

For people are very apt to talk as if God's love and God's justice were two different things, different parts of God; as if his justice had to be satisfied in one way, and his love in another; as if his justice wished to destroy sinners, and his love wished to save sinners; and so they talk as if there was a division in God; as if different attributes of God were pulling two different ways, and that God has parts of which one desires to do one thing, and one part another. It sounds shocking, I am sure you will feel, when I put it into plain English. I wish it to sound shocking. I wish you to feel how wrong and heretical it is; that you may keep clear of such notions, and believe the orthodox faith, that God has neither parts nor passions, nor division in his substance at all, but is absolutely and substantially one; and that, therefore, his love and his justice are the very same things; his justice, however severe it may seem, is perfect love and kindness; and his love is no indulgence, but perfect justice.

But you may say—Very likely that is true; but why need we take so much care to believe it?

It is always worth while to know what is true. You are children of the Light, and of the Truth, adopted by the God of truth, that you may know the truth and do it, and no mistake or falsehood can, by any possibility, do anything for you, but harm you. Always, therefore, try to find out and believe what is true concerning everything; and, above all, concerning God, on whom all depend, in whom you live, and move, and have your being. For all things in heaven and earth depend on God; and, therefore, if you have wrong notions about God, you will sooner or later have wrong notions about everything else.

For see, now, how this false notion of God's justice and love being different things, leads people into a worse error still. A man goes on to fancy, that while God the Son is full of love towards sinners, God the Father is (or at least was once) only full of justice and wrath against sinners; but if a man thinks that God the Son loves him better than God the Father does, then, of course, he will love God the Son better than he loves God the Father. He will think of Christ the Son with pleasure and gratitude, because he says to himself, Christ loves me, cares for me; I can have pity and tenderness from him, if I do wrong. While of God the Father he thinks only with dread and secret dislike. Thus, from dividing the substance, he has been led on to confound the persons, imputing to the Son alone that which is equally true of the Father, till he comes (as I have known men do) to make for himself, as it were, a Heavenly Father of Jesus Christ the Son.

Now, my dear friends, it does seem to me, that if anything can grieve the Spirit of Christ, and the sacred heart of Jesus, this is the way to grieve him. Oh read your Bibles, and you will see this, that whatever Jesus came down on earth for, it certainly was not to make men love him better than they love the Father, and honour him more than they honour the Father, and rob the Father of his glory, to give it to Jesus. What did the Lord Jesus say himself? That he did not come to seek his own honour, or shew forth his own glory, or do his own will: but his Father's honour, his Father's glory, his Father's will. Though he was equal with the Father, as touching his Godhead, yet he disguised himself, if I may so say, and took on him the form of a servant, and was despised and rejected of men. Why! That men might honour his Father rather than him. That men might not be so dazzled by his glory, as to forget his Father's glory. Therefore he bade his apostles, while he was on earth, tell no man that he was the Christ. Therefore, when he worked his work of love and mercy, he took care to tell the Jews that they were not his works, but the works of his Father who sent him; that he was not doing his own will, but his Father's. Therefore he was always preaching of the Father in heaven, and holding him up to men as the perfection of all love and goodness and glory: and only once or twice, it seems, when he was compelled, as it were, for very truth's sake, did he say openly who he was, and claim his co-equal and co-eternal glory, saying, 'Before Abraham was, I am.'

And, after all this, if anything can grieve him now, must it not grieve him to see men fancying that he is better than his Father is, more loving and merciful than his Father is, more worthy of our trust, and faith, and adoration, and gratitude than his Father is?—His Father, for whose honour he was jealous with a divine jealousy—His Father, who, he knows well, loved the world which shrinks from him so well that he spared not his only begotten Son, but freely gave him up for it.

Oh, my friends, believe me, if any sin of man can add a fresh thorn to Christ's crown, it is to see men, under pretence of honouring him, dishonouring his Father. For just think for once of this—What nobler feeling on earth than the love of a son to his father? What greater pain to a good son than to see his father dishonoured, and put down below him? But what is the love of an earthly son to an earthly father, compared to the love of The Son to the Father? What is the jealousy of an earthly son for his father's honour, compared with the jealousy of God the Son for God the Father's honour?

All men, the Father has appointed, are to honour the Son, even as they honour the Father. Because, as the Athanasian Creed says, 'such as the Father is, such is the Son.' But, if that be true, we are to honour the Father even as we honour the Son; because such as the Son is, such is the Father. Both are true, and we must believe both; and therefore we must not give to Christ the honour which we should to a loving friend, and give to the Father the honour which we should to an awful judge. We must give them both the same honour. If we have a godly fear of the Father, we ought to have a godly fear of

Christ; and if we trust Christ, we ought to trust the Father also. We must believe that Jesus Christ, the Son, is the brightness of the Father's glory, and the express image of his person; and therefore we must believe that because Jesus is love, therefore the Father is love; because Jesus is long-suffering, therefore the Father is long-suffering; because Jesus came to save the world, therefore the Father must have sent him to save the world, or he would never have come; for he does nothing, he says, of himself. Because we can trust Jesus utterly, therefore we can trust the Father utterly. Because we believe that the Son has life in himself, to give to whomsoever he will, we must believe that the Father has life in himself likewise, and not, as some seem to fancy, only the power of death and destruction. Because nothing can separate us from the love of Jesus, nothing can separate us from the love of his Father and our Father, whose name is Light and Love.

If we believe this, we shall indeed honour the Father, and indeed honour the Son likewise. But if we do not, we shall dishonour the Son, while we fancy we are honouring him: we shall rob Christ of his true glory, to give him a false glory, which he abhors. If we fancy that he does anything for us without his Father's commands; if we fancy that he feels anything for us which his Father does not feel, and has not always felt likewise: then we dishonour him. For his glory is to be a perfectly good and obedient Son, and we fancy him—may he forgive us for it!—a self-willed Son. This is Christ's glory, that though he is equal with his Father, he obeys his Father. If he were not equal to his Father, there would be less glory in his obeying him. Take away the mystery of the ever-blessed Trinity, and you rob Christ of his highest glory, and destroy the most beautiful thing in heaven, except one. The most beautiful and noble thing of all in heaven—that (if you will receive it) out of which all other beautiful and noble things in heaven and earth come, is the Father for ever saying to the Son, 'Thou art my Son; this day have I begotten thee. And in thee I am well pleased.' The other most beautiful thing is the co-equal and co-eternal Son for ever saying to the Father, 'Father, not my will, but thine be done. I come to do thy will, O God. Thy law is written in my heart.'

Do you not see it? Oh, my dear friends, I see but a very little of it. Who am I, that I should comprehend God? And who am I, that I should be able to make you understand the glory of God, by any dull words of mine? But God can make you understand it. The Spirit of God can and will shew you the glory of God. Because he proceedeth from the Father, he will shew you what the glory of the Father is like. Because he proceedeth from the Son, he will shew you what the glory of the Son is like. Because he is consubstantial, co-equal, and co-eternal with the Father and the Son, he will shew you that the glory of the Father and the Son is not the glory of mere power; but a moral and spiritual glory, the glory of having a perfectly glorious, noble, and beautiful character. And unless he shews you that, you will never be thoroughly good men. For it is a strange thing that men are always trying, more or less, to be like God. And yet, not a strange thing; for it is a sign that we all came from God, and can get no rest till we are come back to God, because God calls us all to be his children, and be like him. A blessed thing it is, if we try to be like the true God: but a sad and fearful thing, if we try to be like some false god of our own invention. But so it is. It was so even among the old heathen. Whatsoever a man fancies God to be like, that he will try himself to be like. So if you fancy that God the Father's glory is stern and awful power, that he is extreme to mark what is done amiss, or stands severely on his own rights, then you will do the same; you will be extreme to mark what is done amiss; you will stand severely on your rights; you will grow stern and harsh, unfeeling to your children and workmen, and fond of shewing your power, just for the sake of shewing it. But if you believe that the glory of the Father, Son, and Holy Spirit is all one: and that it is a loving glory;

if you believe that such as Jesus Christ is, such is his Father, gracious and merciful, slow to anger, and of great kindness, and repenting him of the evil; if you believe that your Father in heaven is perfect, just because he sendeth his sun to rise on the evil and on the good, and sendeth rain on the just and on the unjust, and is good to the unthankful and the evil—if you believe this, I say, then you will be good to the unthankful and the evil; you will be long-suffering and tender; good fathers, good masters, good neighbours; and your characters will become patient, generous, forgiving, truly noble, truly godlike. And all because you believe the Athanasian Creed in spirit and in truth.

In like manner, if you believe that Jesus Christ is not a perfect Son; if you fancy that he has any will but his Father's will; that he has any work but what his Father gives him to do, who has committed all things into his hands; that he knows anything but what his Father sheweth him, who sheweth him all things, because he loveth him; then you will be tempted to wish for power and honour of your own; to become ambitious, self-willed, vain, and disobedient to your parents.

But if you believe that Jesus is a perfect Son, all that you would wish your son to be to you, and millions of times more; and if you believe that that very thing is Christ's glory; that his glory consists in being a perfect Son, perfectly obedient, having no will or wish but his Father's; then will you, by thus seeing Christ in spirit and in truth, see how beautiful and noble it is to be good sons; and you will long to try to be good sons: and what you long for, and try for, you will surely be, in God's good time; for he has promised,—'Blessed are they who hunger and thirst after righteousness: for they shall be filled.' And all through believing the Athanasian Creed? All? Yes, all.

But will not the Holy Spirit teach us, without the Athanasian Creed?

The Holy Spirit will teach us. Must teach us, if we are really to learn one word of all this in spirit and in truth. But whether the Holy Spirit does teach us, will depend, I fear, very much upon whether we pray for him; and whether we pray for him aright will depend on whether we know who he is, and what he is like; and that, again, the Athanasian Creed will tell us.

Now, go home with God's blessing. Remember that such as the Son is, such is the Father, and such is the Holy Ghost. Pray to be made good fathers, after the likeness of The Father, from whom every fatherhood in heaven and earth is named; good sons, after the likeness of God The Son; and good and holy spirits, after the likeness of The Holy Spirit; and you will be such at last, in God's good time, as far as man can become like God; for you will be praying for the Holy Spirit himself, and he will hear you, and come to you, and abide with you, and all will be well.

SERMON XXII.

THE TORMENT OF FEAR.

(*First Sunday after Trinity.*)

---

1 JOHN iv. 16, 18.

And we have known and believed the love that God hath to us. God is love; and he that dwelleth in love dwelleth in God, and God in him. Herein is our love made perfect, that we may have boldness in the day of judgment: because as he is, so are we in this world. There is no fear in love; but perfect love casteth out fear: because fear hath torment. He that feareth is not made perfect in love.

THE text tells us how to get one of the greatest blessings; a blessing which all long for, but all do not find; and that is a happy death. All wish to die happily; even bad men. Like Balaam when he was committing a great sin, they can say, 'Let me die the death of the righteous, and let my last end be like his.' But meanwhile, like Balaam, they find it too hard to live the life of the righteous, which is the only way to die the death of the righteous. But something within them (if false preachers will but leave them alone) tells them that they will not succeed. Reason and common sense tell them so: for how can a man expect to get to a place without travelling the road which leads to it? And the Spirit of God, the Spirit of truth and right, tells them that they will not succeed: for how can a man win happiness, save by doing right? Every one shall 'receive the things done in his body, according to that he hath done, whether it be good or bad.' So says Scripture; and so say men's own hearts, by the inspiration of God's Holy Spirit. And therefore such men's fear of death continues. And why? The text tells us the secret. As long as we do not love God, we shall be tormented with fear of death. And as long as we do not love our neighbour, we shall not love God. We may try, as thousands have tried, and as thousands try still, to love God without loving their neighbour; to be very religious, and worship God, and sing His praises, and think over all His mercy to them, and all that he has done for them, by the death of His blessed Son Jesus Christ; and so to persuade themselves and God that they love Him, while they keep in their hearts selfishness, pride, spite, uncharitableness: but they do not succeed. If they think they succeed, they are only deceiving themselves. So says St. John. 'He who loveth not his brother whom he hath seen, how can he love God whom he hath not seen?' But they cannot deceive themselves long. You will see, if you watch such people, and still more if you watch yourselves, that if you do not love your neighbours in spirit and in truth, then those tormenting fears soon come back again, worse than ever. Ay, whenever we indulge ourselves in hard words and cruel judgments, the thought of God seems darkened to us there and then; the face of God seems turned from us; and peace of mind and brightness of spirit, and lightness of soul, do not come back to us, till we have confessed our sins, and have let the kindly, the charitable, the merciful thoughts rise up in us once more, as, by the grace of Christ, they will rise up.

Yes, my friends, as far as I can see, people are filled with the peace of God just in as far as they are at peace with their fellow-men. They are bright, calm, and content, looking forward with cheerfulness to death, and with a humble and holy boldness to judgment, just in as far as their hearts are filled with love, gentleness, kindness, to all that God has made.

They dwell in God, and God in them, and perfect love has cast out fear.

But if a man does not live in love, then sooner or later he will hear a voice within him, which whispers, Thou art going wrong; and, if thou art going wrong, how canst thou end at the right place? None but the right road can end there. The wrong road must lead to the wrong place.

Then the man gets disturbed and terrified in his mind, and tormented with fears, as the text says. He knows that the day of judgment is coming, and he has no boldness to meet it. He shrinks from the thought of death, of judgment, of God. He thinks—How shall I meet my God? I do not love my neighbour. I do not love God; and God does not love me. The truth is, that the man cannot love God even if he will. He looks on God as his enemy, whom he has offended, who is coming to take vengeance on him. And, as long as we are afraid of any one, and fancy that they hate us, and are going to hurt us, we cannot love them. So the man is tormented with fear; fear of death, fear of judgment, fear of meeting God.

Then he takes to superstition; he runs from preacher to preacher; and what not?—There is no folly men have not committed, and do not commit still, to rid themselves of that tormenting fear. But they do not rid themselves of it. Sermons, church-goings, almsgivings; leaving the Church and turning Dissenters or Roman Catholics; joining this sect and that sect; nothing will rid a man of his superstitious fear: nothing but believing the blessed message of the text.

And what does the text say? It says this,—'God is love.' God does not hate thee, He loves thee. He willeth not thy death, O sinner, but rather that thou shouldest turn from thy wickedness and live. Thy sins have not made Him hate thee: but only pity thee; pity thy folly, which will lead on the road to death, when He wishes to put thee on the road to life, that thou mayest have boldness in the day of judgment, instead of shrinking from God like a guilty coward. And what is the way of life? Surely the way of Christ, who *is* the life. Live like Him, and thou wilt not need to fear to die. So says the text. We are to have boldness in the day of judgment, because as Christ is, so are we in this world. And how was, and is, and ever will be, Christ in this world? Full of love; of brotherly-kindness, charity, forgiveness, peace, and good will to men. That, says St. John, is the life which brings a joyful death; for God is love; and he that dwelleth in love dwelleth in God, and God in him.

Oh consider this, my good friends. Consider this; lest when you come to die the ghosts of all your sins should rise up at your bedside, and torment you with fear—the ghosts of every cruel word which you ever spoke against your fellow men; of every kind action which you neglected; as well as of every unjust one which you ever committed. And, if they do rise up in judgment against you, what must you do?

Cast yourself upon the love of God, and remember that God is love, and so loved us that He sent His Son to be the propitiation for our sins. Ask Him to forgive you your sins, for the sake of that precious blood which was shed on the cross: but not that you may keep your sins, and may escape the punishment of them. God forbid. What use in having your past sins forgiven, if the sinful heart still remains to run up fresh sins for the future? No. Ask Him not merely to forgive the past, but to mend the future; to create in you a new heart, which wishes no ill to any human being, and a right spirit, which desires first and utterly to do right, and is filled with the Holy Spirit of God, the Spirit of love, by which God made and redeemed the world, and all that therein is.

So will all tormenting fears cease. You will feel yourself in the right way, the way of charity, the way in which Christ walked in this world, and have boldness in· the day of judgment, facing death without conceit, indeed, but also without superstitious fear.

SERMON XXIII.

THE FLESH AND THE SPIRIT.

(*Eighth Sunday after Trinity.*)

ROMANS viii. 12.

Therefore, brethren, we are debtors, not to the flesh, to live after the flesh; for if ye live after the flesh, ye shall die.

WHAT does walking after the flesh mean? St. Paul tells us himself, in Gal. v., where he uses exactly the same form of words which he does here. 'The works of the flesh,' he says, 'are manifest.' When a man gives way to his passions and appetites—when he cares only about enjoying his own flesh, and the pleasures which he has in common with the brutes, then there is no mistake about the sort of life which he will lead—' Now the works of the flesh are manifest, which are these; adultery, fornication, uncleanness, lasciviousness, idolatry, witchcraft, hatred, variance, emulations, wrath, strife, seditions, heresies, envyings, murders, drunkenness, revellings, and such like.' An ugly list, my friends; and God have mercy on the man who gives way to them. For disgraceful as they are to him, and tormenting also to him in this life, the worst is, that if he gives way to them, he will die.

I do not mean that he will bring his mortal body to an untimely end; that he will ruin his own health; or that he will get himself hanged, though that is likely enough—common enough.

I think St. Paul means something even worse than that. The man himself will die. Not his body merely: but his soul, his character, will die. All in him that God made, all that God intended him to be, will die. All that his father and mother loved in him, all that they watched over, and hoped and prayed that it might grow up into life, in order that he might become the man God meant him to be, all that will die. His soul and character will become one mass of disease. He will think wrong, feel wrong, about everything of which he does think and feel: while, about the higher matters, of which every man ought to know something, he will not think or feel at all. Love to his country, love to his own kinsfolk even; above all, love to God, will die in him, and he will care for nothing but himself, and how to get a little more foul pleasure before he goes out of this world, he dare not think whither. All power of being useful will die in him. Honour and justice will die in him. He will be shut up in himself, in the ugly prison-house of his own lusts and passions, parted from his fellow-men, caring nothing for them, knowing that they care nothing for him. He will have no faith in man or God. He will believe no good, he will have no hope, either for himself or for the world.

This, this is death, indeed; the death of sin; the death in which human beings may go on for years, walking, eating, and drinking; worse than those who walk in their sleep, and see nothing, though their eyes are staring wide.

Oh pitiable sight! The most pitiable sight in the whole world, a human soul dead and rotten in sin! It is a pitiable sight enough, to see a human body decayed by disease, to see a poor creature dying, even quietly and without pain. Pitiable, but not half so pitiable as the death of a human soul by sin. For the death of the body is not a man's own fault. But that death in life of sin, is a man's own fault. In a Christian country, at least, it is a man's own fault, if he goes about the world, as I have seen many a one go, having a name to live, and yet dead in trespasses and sins, while his soul only serves to keep his body alive and moving. How shall we escape this death in life? St. Paul tells us, 'If ye through the Spirit do mortify the deeds of the body, ye shall live.

Through the Spirit. The Spirit of God and of Christ. Keep that in mind, for that is the only way, the right way, to mortify and kill in us these vices and passions, which, unless we kill them, will kill us. The only way. For men have tried other ways in old times, do try other ways now: but they fail. I could mention many plans which they have tried. But I will only mention the one which you and I are likely to try.

A young man runs wild for a few years, as young men are too apt to do: but at last he finds that ill-living does not *pay*. It hurts his health, his pocket, his character. He makes himself ill; he cannot get employed; he has ruin staring him in the face, from his wild living. He must mend. If he intends to keep out of the workhouse, the gaol, the grave, he must mortify the deeds of the body. He must bridle his passions, give up lying about, drinking, swearing, cheating, running after bad women: and if he has a strong will, he does it from mere selfish prudence. But is he safe? I think not, as long as he loves still the bad ways he has given up. He has given them up, not because he hates them, because he is ashamed of them, because he knows them to be hateful to God, and ruinous to his own soul: but because they do not pay. The man himself is not changed. His heart within is not converted. The outside of his life is whitewashed; but his heart may be as foul as ever; as full as ever of selfishness, greediness, meanness. And what happens to him? Too often, what happened to the man in the parable, when the unclean spirit went out of him, and came back again. The unclean spirit found his home swept and garnished: but empty. All very neat and respectable: but empty. There was no other spirit dwelling there. No good spirit, who could fight the unclean spirit and keep him out. So he took to himself seven other spirits worse than himself—hypocrisy, cant, cunning, covetousness, and all the smooth-shaven sins which beset middle-aged and elderly men; and they dwell there, and so does the unclean spirit of youth too.

Alas! How often have I seen men whom that description would fit but too well—men who have kept themselves respectable till they have got back their character in the world's eyes: and when they get into years, and have risen perhaps in life, and made money, are looked up to by their fellows: but what are they at heart? As great scoundrels as they were thirty years before—cunning, false, covetous, and hypocritical—and indulging, perhaps, the unclean spirit of youth, as much as they dare without being found out. God help them! for their last state is worse than their first. But that is the fruit of trying to mortify and kill their own vices by mere worldly prudence, and not by the Spirit of God, which alone can cleanse the heart of any man, or make him strong enough really to conquer and kill his sins.

And what is this spirit of God? We may know in this way. What says our Lord in the Gospel? 'The tree is known by its fruits.' Then if we know the fruits of the Spirit, we shall surely know something at least of what the Spirit is like. What then says St. Paul, 'The fruit of the Spirit is love, joy, peace, longsuffering, gentleness, goodness, faith, meekness, temperance.' Therefore the Spirit is a loving spirit—a peaceable, a gentle, a good, a faithful, a sober and temperate spirit. And if you follow it, you will live. If you give yourselves up honestly, frankly, and fully, to be led by that good spirit, and obey it when it prompts you with right feelings, you, your very self, will live. You will be what God intended you to be; you will grow as God intended you to grow; grow as Christ did, in grace; in all which is graceful, amiable, worthy of respect and love; and therefore in favour with God and man. Your character will improve and strengthen day by day; and rise day by day to fuller, stronger, healthier spiritual life. You will be able more and more to keep down low passions, evil tempers, and all the works of the flesh, when they tempt you; you will despise and hate them more and more ; for having seen the beauty of goodness, you will see the ugliness of sin. So the bad passions and tempers, instead of being merely put to sleep for a while to wake up all the stronger for their rest, will be really mortified and killed in you. They will die out of you ; and you, the real *you* whom God made, will live and grow continually. And, instead of having your character dragged down, diseased, and at last ruined, it will rise and progress, as you grow older, in the sure and safe road of eternal life. To which God bring us all in his mercy! Amen.

SERMON XXIV.

THE UNRIGHTEOUS MAMMON.

(*Ninth Sunday after Trinity.*)

LUKE xvi. 1—8.

And he said also unto his disciples, There was a certain rich man, which had a steward; and the same was accused unto him that he had wasted his goods. And he called him, and said unto him, How is it that I hear this of thee? give an account of thy stewardship; for thou mayest be no longer steward. Then the steward said within himself, What shall I do? for my lord taketh away from me the stewardship: I cannot dig; to beg I am ashamed. I am resolved what to do, that, when I am put out of the stewardship, they may receive me into their houses. So he called every one of his lord's debtors unto him, and said unto the first, How much owest thou unto my lord? And he said, An hundred measures of oil. And he said unto him, Take thy bill, and sit down quickly, and write fifty. Then said he to another, And how much owest thou? And he said, An hundred measures of wheat. And he said unto him, Take thy bill and write fourscore. And the lord commended the unjust steward, because he had done wisely: for the children of this world are in their generation wiser than the children of light.

THIS parable has always been considered a difficult one to understand. Fathers and Divines, in all ages, have tried to explain it in different ways; and have never, it seems to me, been satisfied with their own explanations. They have always felt it strange, that our Lord should seem to hold up, as an example to us, this steward who, having been found out in one villainy, escapes, (so it seems, from the common explanation) by committing a second. They have not been able to see either, how we are really to copy the steward. Our Lord says, that we are to copy him by making ourselves friends of the Mammon of unrighteousness: but how? By giving away a few alms, or a great many? Does any rational man seriously believe, that if his Mammon was unrighteous, that is, if his wealth were ill-gotten, he would save his soul, and be received into eternal life, for giving away part of it, or even the whole of it?

No doubt, there always have been men who will try. Men who, having cheated their neighbours all their lives, have tried to cheat the Devil at last, by some such plan as the unjust steward's, but that plan has never been looked on as either a very honourable or a very hopeful one. I think, that if I had been an usurer or a grinder of the poor all my life, I should not save my soul by founding almshouses with my money when I died, or even ten years before I died. It might be all that I was able to do: but would it justify me in the sight of God? That which saves a soul alive is repentance; and of repentance there are three parts, contrition, confession, and satisfaction— in plain English, making the wrong right, and giving each man back, as far as one can, what one has taken from him. To each man, I say; for I have no right to rob one man and then give to another. I ought to give back again to the man whom I have robbed. I have no right to cheat the rich for the sake of the poor; and after I have cheated the rich, I do not make satisfaction, either to god or man, by giving that money to the poor. Good old Zaccheus, the publican, knew better what true satisfaction was like. He had been gaining money not altogether in an unjust way, but in a way which did him no credit; he had been farming the taxes, and he was dissatisfied with his way of life. Therefore, Behold, Lord, he says, the half of my goods, of what I have a right to in the world's eyes

—what is my own, and I could keep if I liked—I give to the poor. But if I have done wrong to any man, I restore to him fourfold. Then said the Lord, 'This day is salvation come to this man's house; forsomuch as he also is a son of Abraham;' a just and faithful man, who knows what true repentance is.

But now, my friends, suppose that this was just what our Lord tells us to do in this parable. Suppose that this was just what the unjust steward did. I only say, suppose; for I know that more learned men than I explain the difficulty otherwise. Only I ask you to hear my explanation.

The steward is accused of wasting his lord's goods.

He will be put out of his stewardship.

He goes to his lord's debtors, and bids them write themselves down in debt to him at far less sums than they had thought that they owed.

Now, suppose that these debtors were the very men whom he had been cheating. Suppose that he had been overcharging these debtors; and now, in his need, had found out that honesty was the best policy, and charged them what they really owed him. They were, probably, tenants under his lord, paying their rents in kind, as was often the custom in the East. One rented an olive garden, and paid for it so many measures of oil; another rented corn-land, and paid so many measures of meal. Now suppose that the steward, as he easily might, had been setting these poor men's rents too high, and taking the surplus himself. That while he had been charging one tenant a hundred, he had been paying to his lord only fifty, and so forth.

What does he do, then, in his need? He does justice to his lord's debtors. He tells them what their debts really are. He sets their accounts right. Instead of charging the first man a hundred, he charges him fifty; instead of charging the second a hundred, he charges him eighty; and he does not, as far as we are told, conceal this conduct from his lord. He rights them as far as he can now. So he shews that he honestly repents. He has found out that honesty is the best policy; that the way to make true friends is to deal justly by them; and, if he cannot restore what he has taken from them already (for I suppose he had spent it), at least to confess his sin to them, and to set the matter right for the time to come.

This, I think, is what our Lord bids us do, if we have wronged any man, and fouled our hands with the unrighteous mammon, that is, with ill-gotten wealth. And I think so all the more from the verses which come after. For, when he has said, 'Make yourselves friends of the mammon of unrighteousness,' he goes on in the very next verse to say, 'He that is faithful in that which is least, is faithful also in that which is much. If, therefore, ye have not been faithful in the unrighteous mammon, who will commit to your trust the true riches?' Now, surely, this must have something to do with what goes before. And, if it has, what can it mean but this—that the way to make friends out of the mammon of unrighteousness, is to be faithful in it, just in it, honest in it?

But some one may say, If mammon be unrighteous, how can a man be righteous and upright in dealing with it? If money be a bad thing in itself, how can a man meddle with it with clean hands?

So some people will say, and so some will be glad to say. But why? Because they do not want to be righteous, upright, just, and honest in their money dealings; and, therefore, they are glad to make out that they could not be upright if they tried; because money being a bad thing altogether, a man must needs, if he has to do with money, do things which he knows are wrong. I say some people are glad to believe that. I do not mean any one in this congregation. God forbid! I mean in the world in general. We do see people, religious people too, do things about money which they know are mean, covetous, cruel, and then excuse themselves by saying,—Well, of course I would not do so to my own brother; but, in the way of business, one can't help doing these things. Now, I do not quite believe them. I have seldom seen the man who cheated his neighbour, who would not cheat his own brother if he had a chance: but so they say. And, if they be religious people, they will quote Scripture, and say,—Ah! it is the fault of the unrighteous mammon; and, in dealing with the unrighteous mammon, we cannot help these little failings, and so forth: till they seem to have two quite different rules of right and wrong; one for the saving of their own souls, which they keep to when they are hearing sermons, and reading good books; and the other for money, which they keep to when they have to pay their debts or transact business.

Now, my dear friends, be not deceived: God is not mocked. God tempts no man. Man tempts himself by his own lusts and passions. God does not tempt us when he gives us money, puts us in the way of earning money, or spending money. Money is not bad in itself; wealth is not bad in itself. If mammon be unrighteous, we make money into mammon, when we make an idol of it, and worship it more than God's law of right and justice. We make it unrighteous, by being unrighteous, and unjust ourselves.

Money is good; for money stands for capital; for money's worth; for houses, land, food, clothes, all that man can make; and they stand for labour, employment, wages; and they stand for human beings, for the bodily life of man. Without wealth, where should we be now? If God had not given to man the power of producing wealth, where should we be now? Not here. Four-fifths of us would not have been alive at all. Instead of eight hundred people in this parish, all more or less well off, there would be, perhaps, one hundred—perhaps far less, living miserably on game and roots. Instead of thirty millions of civilized people in Great Britain, there would be perhaps some two or three millions of savages. Money, I say, stands for the lives of human beings. Therefore money is good; an ordinance and a gift of God; as it is written, 'It is God that giveth the power to get wealth.' But, like every other good gift of God, we may use it as a blessing; or we may misuse it, and make it a snare and a curse to our own souls. If we let into our hearts selfishness and falsehood; if we lose faith in God, and fancy that God's laws are not well-made enough to prosper us, but that we must break them if we want to prosper; then we turn God's good gift into an idol and a snare; into the unrighteous Mammon.

It is not the quantity of money we have to deal with which is the snare, it is our own lusts and covetousness which are the snares. It is just as easy to sell our souls for five pounds as for five thousand. It is just as easy to be mean and tricky about paying little debts of a shilling or two, as it is about whole estates. I do not see that rich people are at all more unjust about money than poor ones; and if any say Yes, but the poor are tempted more than the rich; I answer, then look at those who are neither poor nor rich; who have enough to live on decently, and are not tempted as the poor are, to steal, or tempted as the rich are, to luxury and extravagance. Are they more honest than either rich or poor? Not a whit. All depends on the man's heart. If his heart be selfish and mean, he will be dishonest as a poor man, as a middle-class man, as a great lord. If his heart be faithful and true, he will be honest, whether he lives in a cottage or in a palace. Any man can do justly, and love mercy, if his heart be right with God. I have seen day-labourers who had a hard struggle to live at all, keep out of debt, and out of shame, and live in a noble poverty, rich in the sight of God, because their hearts were rich in goodness. I have seen tradesmen and farmers, among all the temptations of business, keep their honour as bright as any gentleman's— brighter than too many gentlemen's, because they had learnt to fear God and work righteousness. I have seen great merchants and manufacturers, because that they were their brothers' keepers, spread not only employment, but comfort, education, and religion, among the hundreds of workmen whom God had put into their charge. I have seen great landowners live truly royal lives, doing with all their might the good which their hand found to do; and, after the likeness of their heavenly Father, causing their sun to shine on the evil and on the good, and their rain to fall on the just and on the unjust. Yes; in every station of life, thy dealings will be right with men, if thy heart be right with God.

Yes. Let us bear in mind this—that whatever we cannot be, we can at least be honest men. Let us go to our graves, if possible, with the feeling that there is not a man on earth, a penny the worse for us. And if we have ever fouled our hands with the unrighteous Mammon, let us cleanse them by the only possible plan, by making restitution to those whom we have wronged; and so make friends of the Mammon of unrighteousness, who shall forgive us, and receive us as friends in heaven, instead of making enemies, and going out of the world with the fearful thought, that we shall meet at God's judgment-seat people whom we have made miserable, who will rise up to accuse us, and demand payment of us when it is too late for ever.

Let us bear in mind, even though we cannot copy, the dying words of Muhammed the Arab, who, when he found his end draw near, went forth into the market-place, and asked before all the people, 'Was there any man whom he had wronged? If so, his own back should bear the stripes. Was there any man to whom he owed money? and he should be paid.' 'Yes,' cried some one, 'those coins which you borrowed from me on such a day.' 'Pay him,' said Muhammed: 'better to be shamed now on earth, than shamed in the day of judgment.' He was a heathen. And shall we Christians be worse than he? Then let us pray for the Holy Spirit of God, the Spirit of truth, which will make us faithful and true; so that no man may be the worse for us in this life; no man may have to say of us, when he hears that we lie dying, 'He wronged me, he cheated me, he lied to me; God forgive him:' but that our friends, as they carry us to the grave, may feel that they have lost one whom they could respect and trust; and say, as the earth rattles in upon the coffin lid, 'There lies an honest man.'

SERMON XXV.

THE SIGHS OF CHRIST.

(*Twelfth Sunday after Trinity.*)

MARK vii. 34, 35.

And looking up to heaven, he sighed, and saith unto him, Ephphatha, that is, Be opened. And straightway his ears were opened, and the string of his tongue was loosed, and he spake plain.

WHY did the Lord Jesus look up to heaven? And why, too, did he sigh?

He looked up to heaven, we may believe, because he looked to God the Father; to God, of whom the glorious collect tells us, that he is more ready to hear than we to pray, and is wont to give more than either we desire or deserve. He looked up to the Father, who is the fountain of life, of order, of health, of usefulness; who hates all death, disease, infirmity; who wills that none should perish, body or soul.

My friends, think of these cheering words; and try to look up to God the Father, as Christ looked up. Look up to him, I say, if but once, as a Father. Not merely as your Father, but as the Father of the spirits of all flesh; the good God who creates, and delights to create; who orders all worlds and heavens with perfect wisdom, perfect power, perfect justice, perfect love; and peoples them with immortal souls and spirits, that they may be useful, happy, blessed, in keeping his laws, and doing the work which he has ordained for them. Oh think, if but once, of God the perfect and all-loving Father; and then you will know why Jesus looked up to him.

And you will see, too, why Jesus sighed. He sighed because he was one with the Father. He sighed because he had the mind of God. Because God, the Lord of health and order, hates disease and disorder. Because God, the Lord of bliss and happiness, hates misery and sorrow. Because God made the world at first very good; and, behold, by man's sin, it has become bad.

Why did he sigh? Surely, also, from pity for the poor man. His infirmity was no such great one; he had an impediment in his speech, and with it, as many are apt to have, deafness also: but it was an infirmity. It was a disease. It was something out of order, something gone wrong in God's world; and as such, Christ could not abide it; he grieved over it. He sighed because there was sickness in a world where there ought to be nothing but health, and sorrow where there ought to be nothing but happiness. He sighed, because man had brought this sickness and sorrow on himself by sin; for, remember, man alone is subject to disease. The wild animal in the wood, the bird upon the tree, seldom or never know what sickness is; seldom or never are stunted or deformed. They live according to their nature, healthy and happy, and die in a good old age. While man——Why should I talk of what man is, of how far man is fallen from what God the Father meant him to be, while one hundred thousand corpses of brave men are now fattening the plains of Italy for next year's crop; while even in our favoured land, we find at every turn prisons and reformatories, lunatic asylums, hospitals for numberless kinds of horrible diseases; sickness, weakness, and death all round us? Only look up yonder to Windsor Forest, and see the vast building now in progress there before your eyes, for lunatic convicts—the most miserable, perhaps, and pitiable of human beings,—and let that building be a sign to you, how far man is fallen, and what cause Jesus had to sigh, and has to sigh still, over the miseries of fallen man.

Yes, my friends, not without reason did the old heathen poet, who had no sure and certain hope of everlasting life, say, that man was the most wretched of all the beasts of the field; not without reason did St. Paul say, that if in this life only we have hope in Christ, then the Christian man, who dare not indulge his passions and appetites, dare not say, Let us eat and drink, for to-morrow we die: but must curb himself, and give up his own pleasure and his own fancy at every turn, is of all men most miserable.

If Christ's work is done; if his mercy and help ended when he died upon the cross; if all he did was to heal the sick for three short years in Judea a long while ago: then what have we to which we can look forward? What hope have we, not merely for ourselves, who are here now, but for all the millions who have died and suffered already? Yes: what reasonable hope for mankind can they have, who do not believe that Christ is Very God of Very God, the perfect likeness of the heavenly Father?

But what if that which was true of him then, is true of him now? What if he be the same yesterday, to-day, and for ever? What if he be ascended on high, that he might fill all things with his almighty power, and declare that almighty power most chiefly by shewing mercy and pity? What if he be for ever looking up to his Father and our Father, to his God and our God, interceding for ever for mankind; for ever offering up to the Father that sacrifice of himself which he perfected upon the Cross, for the sins of the whole world? What if he be for ever sighing over every sin, every sorrow, every cruelty, every injustice, over all things, great and small, which go wrong throughout the whole world; and saying for ever, 'Father, this is not according to thy will. Let thy will be done' on earth, as in heaven.' And what, if he does not look up in vain, nor sigh in vain? What if the will of God the Father be, that sin and sorrow, disease and death, being contrary to his will and law, should be at last rooted out of this world, and all worlds for ever? What if Christ have authority and commission from God to fight against all evil, sin, disease, and death, and all the ills which flesh is heir to ; and to teach men to fight them likewise, till they conquer them by his might, and by his light? What if he reigns, and will reign, till he has put all enemies under his feet, and he has delivered up the kingdom to God, even the Father, that God may be all in all? What if the day shall come, when all the nations of the earth shall thus see Christ's good works, and glorify his Father and their Father who is in heaven? and by obeying the Law of their being, and the commandment of God, which is life eternal, shall live for ever in that glory, of which it is written, that a river of water of life shall proceed out of the throne of God and of the Lamb ; and the leaves of the trees which grow thereby shall be for the healing of the nations ; and there shall be no more curse, but the throne of God and of the Lamb shall be in the city of God, and his servants shall serve him ; and the Lord God shall give them light ; and they shall reign for ever and ever.

What those words mean I know not, and hardly dare to think : but as long as those words stand in the Bible, we will have hope. For God the Father, who willeth that none should perish, and Jesus the only-begotten Son, who sighed over the poor man's infirmity in Judea, are the same yesterday, to-day, and for ever.

SERMON XXVI.

THE WOMAN OF SAMARIA.

(*Twelfth Sunday after Trinity*, 1856.)

2 KINGS xviii. 9—12.

And it came to pass in the fourth year of King Hezekiah, which was the seventh year of Hoshea son of Elah king of Israel, that Shalmaneser, king of Assyria, came up against Samaria, and besieged it. And at the end of three years they took it: even in the sixth year of Hezekiah, that is the ninth year of Hoshea king of Israel, Samaria was taken. And the king of Assyria did carry away Israel unto Assyria, and put them in Halah and in Habor by the river of Gozon, and in the cities of the Medes: because they obeyed not the voice of the Lord their God, but trangressed his covenant, and all that Moses the servant of the Lord commanded, and would not hear them, nor do them.

THESE are very simple words: but they are awful words enough. Awful enough to the poor creatures of whom they speak. You here, most of you, can hardly guess all that these words mean. You may thank God that you do not. That you do not know the horrors of war, and the misery of a conquered country, in old times.

To lose all they had ever earned; all that makes life worth having. To have their homes burnt over their heads, their crops carried off their fields. To see their women dishonoured, their old men and children murdered—to be insulted, beaten, and tortured to make them tell where their money was hidden;

and after they and theirs had suffered every unspeakable shame and misery from the hands of brutal enemies, to be stripped, bound, and marched away, for hundreds of miles across the deserts, into the cold and dreary mountains of the north of Assyria, there to live and die as slaves, and never again to see their native land. And such a land as it was, and is still: or rather might be still, if there were men in it worthy the name of men. For of all countries in the world, that land of Israel is one of the most rich and beautiful. The climate and the soil there is such, that two crops can often be grown in the year, of almost any kind which man may need; there are rich valleys well watered, where not only wheat and every grain-crop, but the olive, and the fig, and the vine, flourish in perfection; rich park-like uplands, where sheep and cattle without number may find pasture; great forests of timber, fit for every use; and all kept cool and fruitful, even beneath that burning eastern sun, by the clear streams which flow for ever down from Hermon, the great snow-mountain ten thousand feet high, which overlooks that pleasant land. There is hardly, travellers say, a lovelier or richer country upon earth, than the land of Israel, from Hebron on the south to Hermon on the north; nor a country which might have been stronger, and safer, and more prosperous, if these Jews had been but wise.

It is, so to speak, one great castle, rising most of it two thousand feet high, and walled in by God in a way as is seen hardly in any other land. On the west lies the sea; on the south and on the east vast wildernesses of sandy desert; and on the north, the mighty mountains of Hermon and Lebanon, which no invading army could have crossed, if the Jews had had courage to keep them out. And that, the noble and divine Law of Moses would have given them. It would have made them one free, brave, God-fearing people, at unity with itself; and the promise of Moses would have been fulfilled—that one of them should chase a thousand, and no man or nation be able to stand against them. In David's time, and in Solomon's time also, that promise came true; and that small people of the Jews became a very powerful nation, respected and feared by all the kingdoms round.

But when they fell into idolatry, and forsook the true God, and his law: all was changed. Idolatry brought sin, and sin brought bad passions, hatred, division, weakness, ruin.

The first beginning was, the breaking up of the nation into two;—the kingdom of Judah to the south, the kingdom of Israel to the north. And with that division came envy, spite, quarrels; wars between Israel and Judah, which were but madness. For what could come of those two brother-nations fighting against each other, but that both should grow weaker and weaker, and so fall a prey to some third nation stronger than them both? The ruin of the kingdom of Israel, of which the text tells us, arose out of some unnatural quarrel of this kind. Pekah, the king of Israel, had made friends with the heathen king of Syria, and got him to join in making war on Judah: and a fearful war it was; for the Israelites, according to one account, killed in that war a hundred and twenty thousand of the Jews, men of their own blood and language, all Abraham's descendants as well as they. On which, Ahaz, king of Judah, not to be behind-hand in folly, sent to the heathen king of Assyria to help him, just as the king of Israel had sent to the king of Damascus. He had better have been dead than to have done that. For those terrible Assyrians, who had set their hearts on conquering the whole east, were standing by, watching all the little kingdoms round tearing themselves to pieces by foolish wars, till they were utterly weak, and the time was ripe for the Assyrians to pounce upon them. The king of Assyria came. He swept away all the heathen people of Damascus, and killed their king. But he did not stop there. In a very few years, he came on into the land of Israel, besieged Samaria for three years, and took it, and carried off the whole of the inhabitants of the country; and there was an end of that miserable kingdom of Israel, which had been sinking lower and lower ever since the days of Jeroboam. This was the natural outcome of all their sin and folly, of which we have been reading for the last few Sundays.

Elijah's warnings had been in vain, and Elisha's warnings also. They liked, at heart, Ahab's and Jezebel's idolatries better than they did the worship of the true God. And why? Because, if they worshipped God, and kept his laws, they must needs have been more or less good men, upright, just, merciful, cleanly and chaste livers: while, on the other hand, they might worship their idols, and nevertheless be as bad as they chose. Indeed, the very idol-feasts and sacrifices were mixed up with all sorts of filthy sin, drunkenness and profligacy; so that it is a shame even to speak of the things which went on, especially at those sacrifices to Ashtaroth, the queen of heaven, of which they were so fond. They choose the worse part, and refused the better; and they were filled with the fruit of their own devices, as every unrepenting sinner surely will be.

But did the Jews of Judea and their king escape, who had thus brought the king of Assyria down to murder their own countrymen, and lay that fair land waste? Not they. A very few years more, the Assyrians were back again, and overran Judea itself, laying the country waste with fire and sword, till nothing was left to them, but the mere city of Jerusalem. And so they, too, were filled with the fruit of their own devices. In their madness they had destroyed their brethren, the people of Israel, who ought to have been a safeguard for them to the north; now there was nothing and no man to prevent the Assyrians, or any other invaders, from pouring right down into their land. Truly says Solomon, 'He that diggeth a pit, shall fall into it, and he who breaketh a hedge, a serpent shall bite him.' From that day, Judah became weaker and weaker, standing all alone. Good king Hezekiah, good king Josiah, could only stave off her ruin for a few years; a little while longer, and her cup was full too, and the Babylonians came and swept the Jews away into captivity, as the Assyrians had swept away Israel, and that fair land lay desolate for many a year.

The king of Assyria, we read, after he had carried away the people of Israel, brought heathens from Assyria, and settled them in the Holy Land, instead of the Israelites. But the Lord sent lions among them, we read; the land, I suppose, lying waste, the wild beasts increased, and became very dangerous: so these poor ignorant settlers sent to the king of Assyria, to beg for a Jewish priest, to teach them, as they said, the manner of the god of that land, that they might worship him, and not be terrified by the lions any more. It was a simple, confused notion of theirs: but it brought a blessing with it; for the king of Assyria sent them one of the Jewish priests who had been carried away from Samaria; and he came and lived at Beth-el, and taught them to fear the Lord. So these poor people got some confused notion of the one true God: but they mixed it up sadly with their old heathen idolatry, and made gods of their own, and some of them even burnt their children in the fire, to Adrammelech and Anammelech, the gods of Sepharvaim, from which town they had come. And so they went on for several hundred years, marrying with the remnant of the Israelites who were left behind, and worshipping idols and the true God at the same time. Now these people are the Samaritans, of whom you read so often in the New Testament. The Jews, when they came back, hated and despised the Samaritans, and would not speak to them, eat with them, trade with them, because they were only half-blooded Jews, and did not observe Moses' law rightly; and so they were left to themselves: but as time went on, they seemed to have got rid of their old idolatry, and built themselves a temple on Mount Gerizim, by Samaria, in Jacob's old haunts, by Jacob's well, and there worshipped they knew not what. But still they did their best. And their reward came at last.

Many a hundred years had passed away. The proud Pharisees of Jerusalem were still calling them dogs and infidels; when there came to that half-heathen city of Samaria such a one as never came there before or since; and yet had been very near that place, and those poor Samaritans, for a thousand years.

And being wearied with his journey, he sat down upon the edge of Jacob's well, by Joseph's tomb. The well is still there, choked with rubbish to this very day; and Joseph's tomb by it, all in ruins, among broad fields of corn. And on the edge of that well he sat. Along the very road which was before him, Jeroboam, and Ahab, and many a wicked king of Israel, had gone in old times, travelling between Shechem and Samaria: along that road the terrible Assyrians had marched back to their own land, leading strings of weeping prisoners out of their pleasant native land, to slavery and misery in the far North. He knew it all; and doubt not that he thought over it all, as never man thought on earth. Doubt not that his heart yearned over these poor ignorant Samaritans, and over the sinful woman who came to draw water at the well. After all, half-heathens as they were, Jacob's blood was in their veins; and if not, were they not still human beings? They were worshipping they knew not what: but still they were worshipping the best which they knew.

'Jesus saith unto her, Woman, believe me, the hour cometh, when ye shall neither in this mountain, nor yet at Jerusalem, worship the Father. Ye worship ye know not what: we know what we worship: for salvation is of the Jews. But the hour cometh, and now is, when the true worshippers shall worship the Father in spirit and in truth: for the Father seeketh such to worship him. God is a spirit: and they that worship him must worship him in spirit and in truth. The woman saith unto him, I know that Messias cometh, which is called Christ: when he is come, he will tell us all things. Jesus saith unto her, I that speak unto thee am he. . . . . So when the Samaritans were come unto him, they besought him that he would tarry with them: and he abode there two days. And many more believed because of his own word; and said unto the woman, Now we believe, not because of thy saying: for we have heard him ourselves, and know that this is indeed the Christ, the Saviour of the world.'

Oh, my friends, despise no man; for Christ despises none. He is no respecter of persons: but in every nation, he that feareth God and worketh righteousness is accepted with him. Despise no man; for by so doing you deny the Father, who has made of one blood all nations of men to dwell on the earth, and has appointed them their times, and the bounds of their habitation; if haply they may feel after him, and find him: though he be not far from any of us; for in him we live and move and have our being, and are the offspring of God. For hundreds of years those poor ignorant Samaritans had felt after him; in that foreign land to which the cruel Assyrian conqueror had banished them: but it was God who had appointed them their habitation there, and their time also; and, in due time, they found God: for he came to them, and found them, and spoke with them face to face.

Better to have been one of those ignorant Samaritans, than to have been King Ahab, or King Hoshea, in all their glory, with all their proud Jewish blood. Better to have been one of those ignorant Samaritans than one of those conceited Pharisees at Jerusalem, who, while they were priding themselves on being Abraham's children, and keeping Moses' law, ended by crucifying him who made Abraham, and Moses, and his law, and them themselves. Better to be the poorest negro slave, if, in the midst of his ignorance and misery and shame, he believes in Christ, and works righteousness, than the cleverest and proudest and freest Englishman, if, in the midst of his great light, he works the works of darkness, and, while he calls himself a child of God, lives the sinful life, on which God's curse lies for ever.

So you who have many advantages, take warning by the fate of those foolish Jews, who knew a great deal, and yet did not do it, and so came to shame and ruin. And you who have few advantages, take comfort by those poor Samaritans, who knew a very little, and yet made the best of it, and so at last saw a great light, after sitting in darkness for so long. Schools, books, church-going, ordinances of all kinds, they are good. If you can get them, use them, and thank God for them : but remember, God does not ask for learning, but for goodness and holiness : he does not ask for knowledge, but for a right life. And do not fancy, that because your children have a good education now, and you had none, that God does not love you as well as he loves them. His mercy is over all his works; and the promises are to you as well as to your children. There is many a poor soul who never read a book in her life, who is nearer God than many a great scholar, and fine preacher, and learned divine. All Christ asks of you is, to receive him when he comes to you; and to love, and thank, and admire him, and try to be like him, because he will make you like him : while for the rest to whom little is given, of him shall little be required; and to him who uses what he has, be it little or much, more shall be given, and he shall have abundance. For God is no respecter of persons ; but in every nation, he that feareth God, and worketh righteousness, is accepted by him.

SERMON XXVII.

THE INVASION OF THE ASSYRIANS.

(Thirteenth Sunday after Trinity, Morning.)

---

2 KINGS xix. 15-19.

And Hezekiah prayed before the Lord, and said, O Lord God of Israel, which dwellest between the cherubims, thou art the Lord, even thou alone, of all the kingdoms of the earth; thou hast made heaven and earth. Lord, bow down thine ear, and hear: open, Lord, thine eyes, and see: and hear the words of Sennacherib, which hath sent him to reproach the living God. Of a truth, Lord, the kings of Assyria have destroyed the nations and their lands, and have cast their gods into the fire: for they were no gods, but the work of men's hands, wood and stone: therefore they have destroyed them. Now, therefore, O Lord our God, I beseech thee, save thou us out of his hand, that all the kingdoms of the earth may know that thou art the Lord God, even thou only.

THIS noble story, which we read in Church every year, seems to have had a great hold on the minds of the Jews. They plainly thought it a very important story. For it is told three times over in the Bible: first in the Book of Kings, then in the Book of Chronicles, and again in that of the Prophet Isaiah. Indeed, many chapters of Isaiah's prophecies speak altogether of this invasion of the Assyrians and their destruction.

But what has this story to do with us, you may ask? There are no miracles in our day. We can expect no angels to fight for our armies. We must fight for ourselves.

THE INVASION OF THE ASSYRIANS. 371

True, my friends: but the lesson of these old stories, the moral of them stands good for ever. And I am thankful that this very story is appointed to be read publicly in church once a year, to put us in mind of many things, which all men are too apt to forget.

For instance: to learn one lesson out of many which this chapter may teach us. We are too apt to think that peace and prosperity are the only signs of God's favour. That if a nation be religious, it is certain to thrive and be happy. But it is not so. We find from history that the times in which nations have shewn most nobleness, most courage, most righteousness, most faith in God, have been times of trouble, and danger, and terror. When nations have been invaded, persecuted, trampled under foot by tyrants, then all the good which was in them has again and again shewed itself. Then to the astonishment of the world they have become greater than themselves, and done deeds which win them glory for ever. Then they are truly purged in the fire of affliction, that whatever dross and trash is in their hearts may be burnt out, and the pure gold left.

So it was with the Jews in Hezekiah's time. So again in the time of the Maccabees. So with the old Greeks, when the great Kings of Persia tried to enslave them. So with the old Romans, when the Carthaginians set upon them. So it was with us English, three hundred years ago, when for a time the whole world seemed against us, because we alone were standing up for the Gospel and the Bible against the Pope of Rome. Then the king of Spain, who was then as terrible a conqueror and devourer of nations, as the Assyrians of old, sent against us the Great Armada. Then was England in greater danger than she had ever been before, or has been since.

And what came of it? That that dreadful danger brought out more faith, more courage, than perhaps has ever been among us since. That when we seemed weakest we were strongest. That while all the nations of Europe were looking on to see us devoured up by those Spaniards, our laws and liberties taken from us, the Popish Inquisition set up in England, and England made a Spanish province, what they did see was, the people of this little island rising as one man, to fight for themselves on earth, while the tempests of God fought for them from heaven; and all that mighty fleet of the King of Spain routed and scattered, till not one man in a hundred ever saw their native country again.

And in England, after that terrible trial had passed over us, there rose up the best and noblest time which she had ever yet beheld.

Yes, my friends, three hundred years ago we went through just such a fiery trial as the Jews went through in Hezekiah's time; and God grant that we may never forget that lesson.

But what is true of whole nations, is often true also of each single person; of you and me.

To almost every man, at least once in his life, comes a time of trial—what we call a crisis. A time when God purges the man, and tries him in the fire, and burns up the dross in him, that the pure sterling gold only may be left.

To some people it comes in the shape of some terrible loss, or affliction. To others it comes in the shape of some great temptation. Nay, if we will consider, it comes to us all, perhaps often, in that shape. A man is brought to a point where he must choose between right and wrong. God puts him where the two roads part. One way turns off to the broad road, which leads to destruction: the other way turns off to the narrow road which leads to life. The man would be glad to go both ways at once, and do right and wrong too: but it so happens that he cannot. Then he would be glad to go neither way, and stay where he is: but he cannot. He must move on. He must do something. Perhaps he is asked a question which he does not wish to answer: but he must. It would be well worth his while to tell a lie. It would be very safe for him, profitable for him; while it would be very dangerous for him to tell the truth. He might ruin himself once and for all, by being an honest man. Now which shall he do? He would be glad to do both, glad to do neither: but choose he must; speak he must. He must either lie or tell the truth. Then comes the trial, whether he believes in God and in Christ, or whether he does not. If he only believes, as too many do without knowing it, in a dead God, a God far away, he will lie. If he only believes, as too many do without knowing it, in a dead Christ, a Christ who bore his sins on the cross eighteen hundred years ago, but since then has had nothing to do with him to speak of, as far as he knows—then he will lie. And that is the God and the Christ which most people believe in: and therefore when the time of trial comes, they fall away, and do and say things of which they ought to be ashamed, because their trust is not in God, but in man.

But if that man believes in the living God, and believes that he lives, and moves, and has his being in God, he cannot lie. As it is written, 'he that is born of God, sinneth not, for his seed remaineth in him, and that wicked one toucheth him not.' He will say, Whatever happens, I must obey God, and not man. The Lord is on my side, therefore I will not fear what man can do to me.

And what is the seed which remains in that man, and keeps him from playing the coward? Christ himself, the seed and Son of God. If he believes in the living Christ; if he believes that Christ is really his master, his teacher, who is watching over him, training him, from his cradle to his grave;—if he believes that Christ is dwelling in him, that whatever wish to do right he has comes from Christ, whatever sense of honour and honesty he has comes from Christ; then it will seem to him a dreadful thing to lie, to play the hypocrite, or the coward; to sin against his own better feelings. It will be sinning against Christ himself.

Remember the great Martin Luther, when he stood on one side, a poor monk standing up for the Bible and the Gospel, and against him were arrayed the Pope and the Emperor, cardinals, bishops, and almost all the princes in Europe; and his friends wanted him to hold his tongue, or to say Yes and No at once; in short, to smooth over the matter in some way. —What conceit, said many, of one poor monk standing up against all the world; and what folly, too! He would certainly be burnt alive. But Luther could not hold his tongue. He was afraid enough, no doubt. He disliked being burnt as much as other men. But he felt he must speak God's truth then or never. He must bear witness for Christ's free gospel, against Pope, Emperor, all the devils in hell, if need be, or else hereafter for ever hold his peace. He must play the honest man that day, or be a hypocrite and a rogue for ever. His friends said to him, 'If you go to the Council, Duke George will have you burnt.' He answered, 'If it snowed Duke Georges nine days together, I must go.' They said, 'If you go into that town, you will never leave it alive.' He said, 'If there were as many devils in the town as there are tiles on the houses, I must go.' And he went, Bible in hand, and said, 'Here I stand; I can do no otherwise. God help me!' He went, and he conquered.

And so it will be with you, my friends, if you will believe in the living God, and in the living Christ; then, when temptation comes, you will be able to stand in the evil day, and having done all, to stand. And you will feel yourselves better men from that day forward. You will feel that you have made one one great step upward; you will look back upon that time of temptation and perplexity as the beginning of a new life; as a sign to you that Christ is with you, and in you, training you and shaping your character, till he makes you, at last, somewhat like himself; somewhat of the stature of a true man; somewhat like what he has bidden you to be, 'perfect as your Father in heaven is perfect.'

SERMON XXVIII.

THE TEN LEPERS.

(*Fourteenth Sunday after Trinity.*)

LUKE xvii. 17, 18.

Were there not ten cleansed, but where are the nine? There are not found that returned to give glory to God, save this stranger.

NO men, one would have thought, had more reason to thank God than those nine lepers. Afflicted with a filthy and tormenting disease, hopelessly incurable, at least in those days, they were cut off from family and friends, cut off from all mankind; forced to leave their homes, and wander away; forbidden to enter the houses of men, or the churches of God; forbidden, for fear of infection, to go near any human being; keeping no company but that of wretched lepers like themselves, and forced to get their living by begging; by standing (as the Gospel says) afar off, and praying the passers-by to throw them a coin.

In this wretched state, in which they had been certain of living and dying miserably, they met the Lord: and suddenly, instantly, beyond all hope or expectation, they found themselves cured, restored to their families, their homes, their power of working, their rights as citizens; restored to all that makes life worth having, and that freely, and in a moment. If such a blessing had come to us, should we have thought any thanks too great! Would not our whole lives have been too short to bless God for his great mercy? Should we have gone away. like those nine, without a word of thanks to God, or even to the man who had healed us? What stupidity, hardheartedness, ingratitude of those nine, never to have even thanked the Lord for their restoration to health and happiness.

Ay, so we think. Yet those nine lepers were men of like passions with ourselves; and what they did, we perhaps might do in their place. It is very humbling to think so: but the Bible is a humbling book: and, therefore, a wholesome book, profitable for reproof, for correction, for instruction in righteousness. And I am very much afraid that when the Bible tells us that nine out of ten of those lepers were ungrateful to God, it tells us that nine out of ten of us are ungrateful likewise.

Ungrateful to God? I fear so; and more ungrateful, I fear, than those ten lepers. For which of the two is better off, the man who loses a good thing, and then gets it back again; or the man who never loses it at all, but enjoys it all his life? Surely the man who never loses it at all. And which of the two has more cause to thank God? Those lepers had been through a very miserable time; they had had great affliction; and that, they might feel, was a set-off against their good fortune in recovering their health. They had bad years to balance their good ones. But we—how many of us have had nothing but good years? Oh consider, consider the history of the average of us. How we grow up tolerably healthy, tolerably comfortable, in a free country, under just laws, with the power of earning our livelihood, and the certainty of keeping what we earn. Famine we know nothing of in this happy land; war, and the horrors of war, we know nothing of—God grant we never may. In health, safety and prosperity most of us grow up; forced, it is true, to work hard: but that, too, is a blessing; for what better thing for a man, soul and body, than to be forced to work hard? In health, safety and prosperity; leaving children behind us, to prosper as we have done. And how many of us give God the glory, or Christ the thanks?

But if these be our bodily blessings, what are our spiritual blessings? Has not God given us his only-begotten son Jesus Christ? Has he not baptised us into his Church? Has he not forgiven our sins? Has he not revealed to us that he is our Father, and we his children? Has he not given us the absolutely inestimable blessing of his commandments? Of knowing what the right thing to be done is, that we may do it and live for ever; that treasure of which not only Solomon, but the wise men of old held, that to know what was right was a more precious possession than rubies and fine gold, and all the wealth of Ind? Has he not given us the hope of a joyful immortality, of everlasting life after death, not only with those whom we have loved and lost, but with God himself?

And how many of us give God the glory, and Christ the thanks? Do we not copy those nine lepers, and just shew ourselves to the priest?—Come to church on the Sunday, because it is the custom; people expect it of us; and God, we understand, expects it too: but where is the gratitude? Where is the giving of glory to God for all his goodness? Which are we most like? Children of God, looking up to our Father in heaven, and saying, at every fresh blessing, Father, I thank thee. Truly thou knowest my necessities before I ask, and my ignorance in asking?—Or, like the stalled ox, which eats, and eats, and eats, and never thanks the hand which feeds him?

We are too comfortable, I think, at times. We are so much accustomed to be blest by God, that we take his blessings as matters of course, and feel them no more than we do the air we breathe.

The wise man says—

> Our torments may by length of time become
> Our elements;

and I am sure our blessings may. They say that people who endure continual pain and misery, get at length hardly to feel it. And so, on the other hand, people who have continual prosperity get at length hardly to feel that. God forgive us! My friends, when I say this to you, I say it to myself. If I blame you, I blame myself. If I warn you, I warn myself. We most of us need warning in these comfortable times; for I believe that it is this very unrighteousness of ours which brings many of our losses and troubles on us. If we are so dull that we will not know the value of a thing when we have got it, then God teaches us the value of it by taking it from us. He teaches us the value of health by making us feel sickness; he teaches us the value of wealth by making us feel poverty. I do not say it is always so. God forbid. There are those who suffer bitter afflictions, not because they have sinned, but that, like the poor blind man, the glory of God may be made manifest in them. There are those too who suffer no sorrow at all, even though they feel, in their thoughtful moments, that they deserve it. And miserable enough should we all be, if God punished us every time we were ungrateful to him. If he dealt with us after our sins, and rewarded us according to our iniquities, where should we be this day?

But still, I cannot but believe that if we do go on in prosperity, careless and unthankful, we are running into danger; we are likely to bring down on ourselves some sorrow or anxiety which will teach us, which at least is meant to teach us —from whom all good things come; and to know that the Lord has given, when the Lord has taken away.

God grant that when that lesson is sent to us we may learn it. Learn it, perhaps, at once, and in a moment, we cannot. Weak flesh and blood cannot enter into the kingdom of God, and see that he is ruling us, and all things, in love and justice; and our eyes are, as it were, dimmed with our tears, so that we cannot see God's handwriting upon the wall against us. But at length, when the first burst of sorrow is past, we may learn it; and, like righteous Job, justify God; saying,—The Lord gave, and the Lord hath taken away, blessed be the name of the Lord. If we do that, and give God the glory, it may be with us, after all, as it was with Job, when God gave him back sevenfold for all that he had taken away, wealth and prosperity, sons and daughters. For God doth not afflict willingly, nor grieve the children of men out of spite. His punishments are not revenge, but correction; and, as a father, he chastises his children, not to harm, but to bless them.

And God grant that if that day, too, comes—if after sorrow comes joy, if after storm comes sunshine—we may not forget God afresh in our prosperity, nor go our ways like those dull-hearted Jews, after they were cleansed from their leprosy: but, like the Samaritan, return, and give glory to God, who gives, and delights in giving; and only takes away, that he may lift up our souls to him, in whom we live, and move, and have our being: and so, knowing who we are, and where we are, may live in God, and by God, and for God, in this life, and for ever.

SERMON XXIX.

PARDON AND PEACE.

(Twenty-first Sunday after Trinity.)

PSALM xxxii. 1—7.

Blessed is he whose transgression is forgiven, whose sin is covered. Blessed is the man unto whom the Lord imputeth not iniquity, and in whose spirit there is no guile. When I kept silence, my bones waxed old through my roaring all the day long. For day and night thy hand was heavy upon me: my moisture is turned into the drought of summer. I acknowledge my sin unto thee, and mine iniquity have I not hid. I said, I will confess my transgressions unto the Lord; and thou forgavest the iniquity of my sin. For this shall every one that is godly pray unto thee in a time when thou mayest be found: surely in the floods of great waters they shall not come nigh unto him. Thou art my hiding place; thou shalt preserve me from trouble; thou shalt compass me about with songs of deliverance.

THE collect for to-day is a very beautiful one. There is something musical in the sound of the very words; so musical, that it is sung as an anthem in many churches. Let us think a little over it. 'Grant, we beseech thee, merciful Lord, to thy faithful people pardon and peace; that they may be cleansed from all their sins, and serve thee with a quiet mind, through Jesus Christ our Lord. Amen.' That is a noble prayer; and a prayer for each and every one of us, every day. I say for every day. It is not like the fifty-first psalm, the prayer of a man who has committed some black and dreadful crime; who fears lest God should take his Holy Spirit from him, and leave him to remorse and horror; who feels that he needs to be utterly changed, and have a new heart created within him. It is not a prayer of that kind. It is rather the prayer of a man who is weary with the burden of sinful mortality; who finds it very hard work to do his duty, even tolerably well; who is dissatisfied with himself, and ashamed of himself, not about one great fault, but about many little faults; and who wants to be cleansed from them; who is tempted to be fretful, anxious, out of heart, because things go wrong; and because he feels it partly his own fault that things go wrong; and who, therefore, wants peace, that he may serve God with a quiet mind.

Now then, dear friends, did I not speak truth, when I said, this is a prayer for every one of us, and for every day? For which of us does his duty as he ought? I take for granted, we are all trying to do our duty, better or worse: but I take for granted, too, that the more we try to do our duty, the more dissatisfied with ourselves we are; and the more we find we have sins without number to be cleansed from. For the more we try to do our duty, the higher notion we get of what our duty is; the more we do, the more we feel we ought to do; and the more we feel that we leave undone a great many things which we ought to do, and do a great many things which we ought not to do, and that there is no health in us: but a great deal of disease and weakness;—disease of soul, in the way of conceit, pride, selfishness, temper, obstinacy; weakness, in the way of laziness, fearfulness, and very often of sheer stupidity; we do not see, or rather will not take the trouble to see, what we ought to do, and how to do it. And therefore, we must be, or rather ought to be, dissatisfied with ourselves; and our consciences accuse us when we lie down at night, of a hundred petty miserable mistakes, which we ought to have avoided. We are continually knowing what is right, and doing what is wrong, till we get deservedly angry with ourselves; and think at times, that

God must be deservedly angry with us; that we are such poor paltry creatures that he can only look on us with dislike and contempt: and even worse ; that, perhaps, he does not care to see us mend ; that our struggles to do right are of no value in his eyes : but that he has sternly left us to ourselves, to struggle through life, right or wrong, as best we may ; and to be punished at last, for all that we have done amiss.

Such thoughts will cross our minds. They have crossed the minds of all mankind since the first man's conscience awoke, and he discovered that he was not a brute animal, by finding in himself that awful thought, which no brute animal can have —' I have done wrong.' And therefore the consciences of men will cry for pardon, just in proportion as they are worthy of the name of men, and not merely a superior sort of animals ; and therefore just in proportion as our souls are alive in us, alive with the feeling of duty, of justice, of purity, of love, of a just and orderly God above—just in that proportion shall we be tormented by the difference between what we are, and what we ought to be ; and the sense of sin, and the longing for pardon, will be more keen in us ; and we shall have no rest till the sins are got rid of, and the pardon sure. That is the price we pay for having immortal souls. It is a heavy price truly : but it is well worth the paying, if it be only paid aright. If that tormenting feeling of being continually wrong in this life, ends by making us continually right for ever in the world to come ; if Christ be formed in us at last ; if out of our sinful and mortal manhood a sinless and immortal manhood is born ;—then shall we, like the mother over her new-born babe, forget our anguish, for joy that a man is born into the world.

But, again, besides pardon, we want peace. Who does not know that state of mind in which, perhaps, without any great reason in reality, one has no peace ? When everything seems to go wrong with a man. When he suspects everybody to be against him. When little troubles, which he could bear easily enough at other times, seem quite intolerable to him. When he is troubled with vain regrets about the past—'Ah, if I had done this and that!' and vain fears for the future, conjuring up in his mind all sorts of bad luck which may, but most probably never will, happen; and yet from off which he cannot turn his mind. Who does not know this frame of mind?

True, a great deal of this may depend on ill-health; and will pass away as the man's bodily condition gets better. We know, in the same way, that the strange anxiety which comes over us in sleepless nights, comes from bodily causes. That is merely because, the circulation of our blood being quickened, our brain becomes more active; and because we are lying alone in the silent darkness, with nothing to listen to or look at, we cannot turn our attention away from the thoughts which get possession of us and torment us. That is only bodily; and yet it may be very useful to our souls. As we lie awake, our own past lives, our own past mistakes and sins, and God's past blessings and mercies, too, may rise up before us with clearness, and teach us more than a hundred sermons; and we may find, with David, that our reins chasten us in the night-season. 'When I am in heaviness, I will think upon God; when my heart is vexed, I will complain. Thou holdest mine eyes waking. . . . I have considered the days of old, and the years that are past. I call to remembrance my song, and in the night I commune with my own heart, and search out my spirits. Will the Lord absent himself for ever, and will he be no more intreated? Is his mercy clean gone for ever: and is his promise come utterly to an end for evermore? Hath God forgotten to be gracious: and will he shut up his loving-kindness in displeasure? And I said it is mine own infirmity. But I will remember the years of the right hand of the Most Highest.' These sleepless hours taught the Psalmist somewhat; and they may teach us likewise. And so, again, with these sad and fretful frames of mind. Even if they do partly come from our bodies, they have a real effect, which cannot be mistaken, on our souls; and they may have a good effect on us, if we choose. I believe that we shall find, that even if they do come from ill health and weak nerves, what starts them is—that we are dissatisfied with ourselves. We feel something wrong, not merely in our bodies, but in our souls, our characters; and then we try to lay the blame on the world around us, and shift it off ourselves; saying in our hearts, 'I should do very well, if other people, and things about me, would only let me:' but the more we try to shift off the blame, the less peace we have. Nothing mends matters less than throwing the blame on others. That is plain. Other people we cannot mend; they must mend themselves. Circumstances about us we cannot mend; God must mend them. So, as long as we throw the blame on them, we cannot return to a cheerful and hopeful frame of mind. But the moment we throw the blame on ourselves, that moment we can have hope, that moment we can become cheerful again; for whatsoever else we cannot mend, we can at least mend ourselves. Now a man may forget this in health. He may be put out and unhappy for a while: but when his good spirits return, he does not know why. Things have not improved; but, somehow, they do not affect him as they did before. Now this is not wrong. God forbid! In such a world as this, one is glad to see a man rid of sadness by any means which is not wrong. Better anything than that a poor soul should fret himself to death.

But it may be very good for a man now and then not to forget; to be kept low, whether by ill health or by any other cause, till he faces fairly his own state, and finds out honestly what does fret him and torment him.

And then, I believe, his experience will generally be like David's,—'As long as I kept silence, my bones waxed old through my groaning all the day long.

Think over these words, I beg you. I chose them for my text, just because they seem to me to contain all that I wish you to understand. As long as the Psalmist held his peace—as long as he did not confess his sin to God—all seemed to go wrong with him. He fretted his very heart away. The moment that he made a clean breast to God, peace and cheerfulness came back to him.

This psalm may speak of some really great sin which he had committed. But that makes all the more strongly for us. For if he got forgiveness for a great sin, by merely confessing it, how much more may we hope to be forgiven, for the comparatively little sins of which I am now speaking? Surely there is forgiveness for them. Surely we, Christians, are not worse off than the old Jews. God forbid! What does the Bible tell us? If we confess our sins, he is faithful and just to forgive us our sins, and to cleanse us from all unrighteousness. If we say that we have not sinned, we make him a liar, and his word is not in us. And again, if we walk in the light; that is, if we look honestly at our own hearts, and confess honestly to God what we see wrong there; then we have fellowship one with another; all our frettings and grudgings against our fellowmen pass away; and the blood of Jesus Christ cleanseth us from all sin. God forbid again! For what is the message of the Absolution, whether general in the church, or private by the sick-bed, but this—that there is continual forgiveness for those who really confess and repent? God forbid again! For what is the message of the Holy Communion, but that we really are forgiven, really helped by God not to do the like again; that the stains and scars of our daily misdoings are truly healed by God's grace; and power given us to lead a healthier life, the longer we persevere in the struggle after God.

Therefore, instead of proudly laying the blame of our unhappiness on our fellow-men, much less on God and his providence, let us cast ourselves, in every hour of shame or of sadness, on the boundless love of him who hateth nothing that he hath made; who so loved the world that he spared not his own Son, but delivered him up for us all. How shall he not with him freely give us all things? Let us open our weary hearts to him who watches with tender interest, as of a father watching the growth of his child, over every struggle of ours from worse to better; and so we shall have our reward. The more we trust to the love of God, the more shall we feel his love—feel that we are pardoned—feel that we are at peace. We may not grow more cheerful as we grow older; but we shall grow more peaceful. Sadder men, it may be; but wiser men also; caring less and less for pleasure; caring even less and less for mere happiness: but finding a lasting comfort in the knowledge that we are doing our life's work not altogether ill, under the smile of Almighty God; aware more and more of our own weakness, and of our own failings: but trusting that God will take the will for the deed, and forgive us what we have left undone, and accept what we have done, for the sake of Christ, in whom, and not in our own poor paltry selves, he looks upon us as his adopted children.

Only let us remember to ask for pardon and to ask for peace, that we may use them as the collect bids us;—To ask for pardon, not merely that we may escape punishment; not even to escape punishment at all, if punishment be wholesome for us, as it often is: but that we may be cleansed from our sins; that we may not be left to our own weakness and our own bad habits, to grow more and more useless, more and more unhappy, day by day, but that we may be cleansed from them; and grow purer, nobler, juster, stronger, more worthy of our place in God's kingdom, as our years roll by. Let us remember to ask for peace, not merely to get rid of unpleasant thoughts, or unpleasant people, or unpleasant circumstances; and then sit down and say, Soul, take thine ease, eat and drink, for thou hast much goods laid up for many years: but let us ask for peace, that we may serve God with a quiet mind; that we may get rid of the impatient, cowardly, discontented, hopeless heart, which will not let a man go about his business like a man; and get, instead of it, by the inspiration of God's Holy Spirit, the calm, contented, brave, hopeful heart, in the strength of which a man can work with a will wherever God may put him, even amidst vexation, confusion, disappointment, slander, and persecution; and, in his place and calling, serve the Lord, who served him when he died for him, and who serves him, and all his people, now and for ever in heaven.

So shall we have real pardon, and real peace. A pardon which will make us really better; and a peace which will make us really more useful. And to be good and to be useful were the two ends for which God sent us into the world at all.

SERMON XXX.

THE CENTRAL SUN.

(*Sunday after Ascension, Evening.*)

EPHESIANS iv. 9. 10.

Now that he ascended, what is it but that he also descended first into the lower parts of the earth? He that descended is the same also that ascended up far above all heavens, that he might fill all things.

THIS is one of those very deep texts which we are not meant to think about every day; only at such seasons as this, when we have to think of Christ ascending into heaven, that he might send down his Spirit at Whitsuntide. Of this the text speaks; and therefore, we may, I hope, think a little of it to-day, but reverently, and cautiously, like men who know a very little, and are afraid of saying more than they know. These deep mysteries about heaven we must always meddle with very humbly, lest we get out of our depth in haste and self-conceit. As it is said,

Fools rush in where angels fear to tread.

For, if we are not very careful, we shall be apt to mistake the meaning of Scripture, and make it say what we like, and twist it to suit our own fancies, and our own ignorance. Therefore we must never, with texts like this, say positively, 'It must mean this. It can mean only this.' How can we tell that?

This world, which we do see, is far too wonderful for us to understand. How much more wonderful must be the world which we do not see? How much more wonderful must heaven be? How can we tell what is there, or what is not there? We can tell of some things that are not there, and those are sin, evil, disorder, harm of any kind. Heaven is utterly good. Beyond that, we know nothing. Therefore I dare not be positive about this text, for fear I should try to explain it according to my own fancies. Wise fathers and divines have differed very much as to what it means; how far any one of them is right, I cannot tell you.

The ancient way of explaining this text was this. People believed in old times that the earth was flat. Then, they held, hell was below the earth, or inside it in some way: and the burning mountains, out of which came fire and smoke, were the mouths of hell. And when they believed that, it was easy for them to suppose that St. Paul spoke of Christ's descending into hell. He went down, says St. Paul, into the lower parts of the earth. What could those lower parts be, they asked, but the hell which lay under the earth?

Now about that we know nothing. St. Paul himself never says that hell is below the earth. Indeed (and this is a very noteworthy thing) St. Paul never, in his epistles, mentions in plain words hell at all; so what St. Paul thought about the matter, we can never know. Whether by Christ's descending into the lower parts of the earth, he meant descending into hell, or merely that our Lord came down on this earth of ours, poor, humble, and despised, laying his glory by for a while, this we cannot tell. Some wise men think one thing, some another. Two of the wisest and best of the great old fathers of the Church think that he meant only Christ's death and burial. So how dare I give a positive opinion, where wiser men than I differ?

But about the other half of the text, which says, that he ascended high above all heavens, there is no such difficulty.

All agree as to what that means : though, perhaps, in old times they would have put it in different words.

The old belief was, that as hell was below the flat earth, so heaven was above it; and that there were many heavens, seven heavens, in layers, as it were, one above the other ; and that the seventh heaven, which was the highest of all, was where God dwelt. Now, whether St. Paul believed this, we cannot tell. He speaks of being himself caught up into the third heaven, and here Christ is spoken of as ascending above all heavens.

My own belief, though I say it very humbly, is, that St. Paul spoke of these things only as a figure of speech, for the sake of the ignorance of the people to whom he was writing. They talked in that way; and he was forced now and then to talk in that way, too, to make them understand him. I think that, when he spoke of being caught up into the third heaven, he did not mean that he was lifted bodily off the earth into the skies : but that his soul was raised up and enlightened to understand high and wonderful heavenly matters, though not the highest or most wonderful. If he had meant that, he would have said, that he was caught up into the seventh heaven. We know that our Lord, in the same way, continually used parables ; because, as he said, the ignorant people could not understand the mysteries of the kingdom of heaven; and he had, therefore, to put them into parables, taken from the common country matters, and country forms of speech, if by any means he might make them understand. And so, I suppose, it was with St. Paul. He had to speak in such a way that he could be understood ; and no more.

But when he says that Christ ascended far above all heavens, we are to believe this—that he ascended to God himself. So high that he could go no higher; so far that he could go no farther.

We, now, do not believe that there are seven heavens above the earth ; and we need not. It is no doctrine of the Church, or of the Creeds. We know that the earth is round, and not flat; and that the heavens, if by that we mean the sky, is neither above it, nor below it, but round it on every side. But some may say, whither, then, did our Lord ascend? To what place did his body go up? And that is a right question; for we must always bear in mind that not merely Christ's godhead but his manhood, not merely Christ's soul but his body also, ascended into heaven. If we do not believe that, we do not hold the Catholic faith. Whither, then, did Christ ascend?

My friends, we know this. That this earth and the planets move round the sun, which is in the centre of them. We know this, too; that all the countless stars which spangle the sky are really suns likewise, perhaps, with worlds which we cannot see, moving round them, as we move round the sun. We know, too, that these fixed stars, as they seem to be, are not really fixed, but have some regular movements among themselves, which seem very slow and small to us, from their immense distance, but which really are very great and fast.

Now all these suns and stars, it is reasonable to believe, most probably have a centre. There must be order among them; and they most probably move round one thing, one place, one central sun, as it were, which is the very heart of all the worlds, and the whole universe. Where that place is, or what it is like, we know not, and cannot know. Only this we may believe, that it is glorious beyond all that eye hath seen, and ear heard, or hath entered into the heart of man to conceive. If this world be beautiful, how beautiful must that world of all worlds be. If the sun be glorious, how glorious must the sun of all suns be. If the heaven over us be grand, how grand must that heaven of heavens be. We will not talk of it; for we cannot imagine it: and if we tried to, we should only lower it to our own low fancies. But is it not reasonable to suppose, that there God the Father does, perhaps, in some unspeakable way, shew forth his glory? That there, in the heart of all the worlds, Cherubim and Seraphim continually adore him, crying day and night, 'Holy, holy, holy, Lord God of Sabaoth: Heaven and earth are full of the majesty of thy glory!' before his throne, from which goes forth light, and power, and life, to all worlds and all created things.

And is it not reasonable to believe, that there Christ is, in the bosom of the Father, and at the right hand of God? We know that those, too, are only figures. That God is a Spirit, everywhere and nowhere; and has not hands as we have. But it is only by such figures that the Bible can make us understand the truth, that Christ is the highest being in all heavens and worlds; equal with God the Father, and sharer of his kingdom, and power, and glory, God blessed for ever. Amen.

What then does St. Paul mean, when he says, 'That he may fill all things?' I do not know. And I will take care not to lessen and spoil St. Paul's words, by any ignorant words of my own. But one thing I know it will mean one day, for St. Paul says so. That Christ reigns, and will reign, triumphant over sin, and death, and hell, till he have put all enemies under his feet, and the last enemy that shall be destroyed is death. Then shall he deliver up the kingdom to God, even the Father; that God may be all in all. What that means I do not know. But this I can say, and you can say. We can pray that God will finish the number of his elect and hasten his kingdom, that we, with all that are departed in the true faith, may have our perfect consummation and bliss, both in body and soul, in his eternal kingdom. And this I can say, that it means now, for you and me; for Whitsuntide tells me:—that whatever else Christ can or cannot fill, he can at least fill our hearts, because he is in the bosom of the Father himself; and therefore from him, as from the Father, proceeds the Holy Spirit, the Lord and Giver of life. That Spirit will proceed even to us, if we will have him. He will fill our hearts with himself; with the Spirit of goodness, which proceeds out of the heaven of heavens, and out of the bosom of God himself; with love, peace, longsuffering, gentleness, goodness; with truth, honour, duty, earnestness, and all that is the likeness of Christ and of God. Oh let us pray for that Spirit; the Spirit of truth, which Christ promised us when he ascended up into the heaven of heavens, to keep us sound in our most holy faith; and the Spirit of goodness, to give us strength to live the good lives of good Christian men.

And then it will matter little what opinions we hold about deep things, which the wisest man can never put into words. And it will matter little, whether what I have been telling you to-day about the heaven of heavens be exactly true or not; for what says St. Paul of such deep matters? That we know in part, and prophesy in part; and that prophecies shall fail, and knowledge vanish away: but charity, love, and right feeling, and right doing, which is the very Holy Spirit of God, shall abide for ever. And if that Spirit be with us, he will guide us in due time into all truth: teach us all we need to know, and enable us to practise all we ought to do. Amen.

SERMON XXXI.

CHRISTMAS PEACE.

(*Sunday before Christmas.*)

Phil. iv. 4.

Rejoice in the Lord alway: and again I say, Rejoice.

THIS is a glorious text, and one fit to be the key-note of Christmas-day. If we will take it to heart, it will tell us how to keep Christmas-day. St. Paul has been speaking of two good women, who seem to have had some difference; and he beseeches them to make up their difference, and be of the same mind in the Lord. And then he goes on to tell them, and all Christian people, why they should make up their differences. And for that reason, I suppose, the Church has chosen it for the epistle before Christmas-day, on which all men are to make friends with each other, and rejoice in the Lord. Let your moderation, he says, be known to all men. The Greek word signifies forbearance, reasonable dealing, consideration for one another, readiness to give way, not standing too severely on one's own rights. Now this is just the temper in which we ought to meet our friends at Christmas—forbearance. They may not have always behaved well to us. Be it so. No more have we to them. Let us, once in the year at least, forget old grudges. Let us do as we would be done by; give and forgive;

live and let live; bury our past quarrels, and shake hands over their graves.

For the Lord is at hand. Close to all of us: watching all we do, and setting the right value on it. He cannot mistake. He sees both sides of a matter, and all sides—a thousand sides which we cannot see. He can judge better than we. Let him judge. Why do I say, Let him judge? He has judged already, weeks, months ago, as soon as each quarrel happened: and, perhaps, he found us in the wrong as well as our neighbours; and, if so, the least said the soonest mended. Let us forgive and forget, lest we be neither forgotten nor forgiven.

And, because the Lord is at hand, be anxious about nothing. The word here is the same as in the Sermon on the Mount. It means do not fret; do not terrify yourselves; for the Lord is at hand; he knows what you want: and will he not give it? Is not Christmas-day a sign that he will give it—a pledge of his love? What did he do on the first Christmas-day? What did he shew himself to be on the first Christmas-day? Now, here is the root of the whole matter, and a deep root it is; as deep as the beginning of all things which are, or ever were, or ever will be. And yet if we will believe our Bibles, it is a root which we all may find. What did the angels say the first Christmas night? Peace on earth, and goodwill to men. That is what God proclaimed. That is what he said that he had, and would give.

Now, says the apostle, if you will believe the latter half of this same Christmas message, then the first half of it will come true to you. If you will believe that God's will is a good will to you, then you will have peace on earth. For believe in Christmas-day; believe that the Lord is at hand; that he has been made man for ever and ever; and that to the Man Christ Jesus all power is given in heaven and earth: and then, if you want aught, instead of grudging or grinding your neighbours, ask him. In everything let your requests be made known unto God: and then the peace of God will keep your hearts through Christ Jesus.

You will feel at peace with God through Christ Jesus, because you have found out that God is at peace with you; that God is not against you, but for you; that God does not hate you, but love you; and if God is at peace with you, what cause have you to be at war with him? And so the message of Christmas-day will bring you peace.

You will be at peace with your neighbours, through Christ Jesus. When you see God stooping to make peace with sinful men, you will be ashamed to be quarrelling with them. When you see God full of love, you will be ashamed to keep up peevishness, grudging, and spite. When you see God's heaven full of light, you will be ashamed to be dark yourselves; your hearts will go out freely to your fellow-creatures; you will long to be friends with every one you meet; and you will find in that the highest pleasure which you ever felt in life. But mind one thing—what sort of a peace this peace of God is. It passes all understanding; the very loftiest understanding. The cleverest and most learned men that ever lived could not have found it—we know they did not find it—by their own cleverness and learning. No more will you find God's peace, if you seek for it with your understanding. Thinking will not bring you peace, think as shrewdly as you may. Reading will not bring it, read as deeply as you may. Some people think otherwise; that they can get the peace of God by understanding. If they could but understand more, their minds would be at rest. So they weary themselves with reading, and thinking, and arguing, perhaps trying to understand predestination, election, assurance; perhaps trying to understand which is the true Church. What do they get thereby? Certainly not the peace of God. They certainly do not set their minds at rest. They cannot. Books cannot give a live soul rest. Understanding cannot. Nothing can give you or me rest, save God himself. The peace is God's; and he must give it himself, with his own hand, or we shall never get it. Go then to God himself. Thou art his child, as Christmas-day declares: be not afraid to go unto thy

Father. Pray to him; tell him what thou wantest: say, Father, I am not moderate, reasonable, forbearing. I fear I cannot keep Christmas-day aright, for I have not a peaceful Christmas spirit in me; and I know that I shall never get it by thinking, and reading, and understanding; for it passes all that, and lies far away beyond it, does peace, in the very essence of thine undivided, unmoved, absolute, eternal Godhead, which no change nor decay of this created world, nor sin or folly of men or devils, can ever alter; but which abideth for ever what it is, in perfect rest, and perfect power, and perfect love. O Father, give me thy peace. Soothe this restless, greedy, fretful soul of mine, as a mother soothes a sick and feverish child. How thou wilt do it I do not know. It passes all understanding. But though the sick child cannot reach the mother, the mother is at hand, and can reach it. Though the eagle, by flying, cannot reach the sun, yet the sun is at hand, and can reach all the earth, and pour its light and warmth over all things. And thou art more than a mother: thou art the everlasting Father. Pour thy love over me, that I may love as thou lovest. Thou art more than the sun: thou art the light and the life of all things. Pour thy light and thy life over me, that I may see as thou seest, and live as thou livest, and be at peace with myself and all the world, as thou art at peace with thyself and all the world. Again, I say, I know not how; for it passes all understanding: but I hope that thou wilt do it for me. I trust that thou wilt do it for me, for I believe the good news of Christmas-day. I believe that thou art love, and that thy mercy is over all thy works. I believe the message of Christmas-day: that thou so lovest the world, that thou hast sent thy Son to save the world, and me. I know not how; for that, too, passes understanding: but I believe that thou wilt do it; for I believe that thou art love; and that thy mercy is over all thy works, even over me. I believe the message of Christmas-day, that thy will is peace on earth, even peace to me, restless and unquiet as I am; and goodwill to men, even to me, the chief of sinners.

SERMON XXXII.

THE LIFE OF THE SPIRIT.

(*First Sunday after Christmas.*)

ISAIAH xxxviii. 16.

O Lord, by these things men live, and in all these things is the life of my spirit.

THESE words are the words of Hezekiah, king of Judah: and they are true words, words from God. But, if they are true words, they are true words for every one—for you and me, for every one here in this church this day: for they do not say, By these things certain men live, one man here and another man there; but all men. Whosoever is really alive, that is, has life in his spirit, his soul, his heart, the life of a man and not a beast, the only life which is worthy to be called life, then that life is kept up in him in the same way that it was kept up in Hezekiah, and by the same means.

Let us see, then, what things they were which gave Hezekiah's spirit life. Great joy, great honour, great success, wealth, health, prosperity and pleasure? Was it by these things that Hezekiah found men lived? Not so, but by great sorrow. 'In those days was Hezekiah sick unto death. And Isaiah the prophet the son of Amos came unto him and said, Thus saith the Lord, Set thine house in order; for thou shalt die and not live. Then Hezekiah turned his face towards the wall and prayed unto the Lord; and Hezekiah wept sore.'

Trouble upon trouble came on Hezekiah; and that just when he might have expected a little rest. The Lord had just delivered Hezekiah and the Jews from a fearful danger, of which we read in the chapter before. Hezekiah had believed God's promise by the mouth of Isaiah. He held fast his faith in God when Sennacherib and his Assyrian army were camping round Jerusalem; for God had said, 'I will defend this city to save it for my own sake and for my servant David's sake.' He defended his city bravely and nobly, and showed himself a true, and valiant, and godly king. And perhaps Hezekiah expected to be rewarded for his faith, and rewarded for having done his duty: but it was not so. He had to wait, and to endure more. And now this fresh trouble was come upon him. Isaiah told him he should die and not live: and he must prepare himself to meet death.

Hezekiah, you see, was horribly afraid of death. I do not mean that he was afraid of going to hell, for he does not say so: but he felt, to use his own words, 'The grave cannot praise thee, death cannot celebrate thee: they that go down into the pit cannot hope for thy truth.' And, therefore, death looked to him an ugly and an evil thing—as it is; the Lord's enemy, and his last enemy, the one with which he will have the longest and sorest fight. He conquered death by rising from the dead: but nevertheless we die; and death is an ugly, fearful, hateful thing in itself, and rightly called the King of Terrors: for terrible it is to those who do not know that Christ has conquered it. Hezekiah lived before the Lord Jesus came into the flesh to bring life and immortality to light, by rising from the dead; and, therefore, the life after death was not brought to light to him, any more than it was to David, or any other Old Testament Jew. He dreaded it, because he knew not what would come after death. And, therefore, he prayed hard not to die. He did not pray altogether in a right way: but still he prayed. 'Remember now, O Lord, I beseech thee, how I have walked before thee in truth and with a perfect heart, and have done that which was good in thy sight.' And the Lord heard his prayer. 'Then came the word of the Lord to Isaiah, saying, Go, and say to Hezekiah, Thus saith the Lord, I have heard thy prayer, I have seen thy tears, behold I will add unto thy days fifteen years.'

Then what was the use of God's warning to him? What was the use of his sickness and his terror, if, after all, his prayer was heard, and after the Lord had told him, Thou shalt die and not live—that did not come to pass: but the very contrary happened, that he lived, and did not die?

Of what use to him was it? Of this use at least, that it taught him that the Lord God would hear the prayers of mortal men. Oh my friends, is not that worth knowing? Is not that worth going through any misery to learn—that the Lord will hear us? That he is not a cold, arbitrary tyrant, who goes his own way, never caring for our cries and tears, too proud to turn out of his way to hear us: but that he is very pitiful and of tender mercy, and repenting him of the evil? Hezekiah did not pray rightly. He thought himself a better man than he was. He said, 'Remember now, O Lord, I beseech thee, how I have walked before thee in truth and with a perfect heart, and have done that which is good in thy sight.' And Hezekiah wept sore. But he did pray. He went to God, and told his story to him, and wept sore; and the Lord God heard him, and taught him that he was not as good as he fancied; taught him that, after all, he had nothing to say for himself—no reason to shew why he should not die. 'What shall I say? He hath both spoken unto me, and himself hath done it: I shall go softly all my years in the bitterness of my soul.' And so he felt that, instead of justifying himself, he must throw himself utterly on God's love and mercy; that God must undertake for him. 'O Lord, I am oppressed, crushed—the heart is beaten out of me. I have nothing to say for myself. Undertake for me. I have nothing to say for myself, but I have plenty to say of thee. Thou art good and just. Thou wilt not leave my soul in hell. I can say no more.'

And then he found that the Lord was ready to save him. That what the Lord wished was, not to kill him, but to recover him, and make him live—live more really, and fully, and wisely, and manfully—by making him trust more utterly in God's goodness, and love, and mercy; making him more certain that, good as he thought himself, and perfect in heart, he was full of sins: and yet that the Lord had cast all these sins of his behind his back, forgotten and forgiven them, as soon as he had made him see that all that was good and strong in him came from God, and all that was evil and weak from himself. And then he says, 'O Lord, by these things men live, and in all these things is the life of my spirit.' God meant all along to receive me, and make me live. He chastened me, and brought me low, to shew me that my own faith, my own righteousness, was no reason for his saving me: but that his own love and mercy was a good reason for saving me. 'Behold,' he goes on to say, 'for peace I had great bitterness: but thou hast in love to my soul delivered it from the pit of corruption: for thou hast cast all my sins behind thy back.'

And, my dear friends, what Hezekiah saw but dimly, we ought to see clearly. The blessed news of the Gospel ought to tell us it clearly. For the blessed Gospel tells us that the same Lord who chastened and taught, and then saved, Hezekiah, was made flesh, and born a man of the substance of a mortal woman; that he might in his own person bear all our sicknesses and carry our infirmities; that he might understand all our temptations, and be touched with the feeling of our infirmities, seeing that he himself was tempted in all points likewise, yet without sin.

Oh hear this, you who have had sorrows in past times. Hear this, you who expect sorrows in the times to come.

He who made, he who lightens, every man who comes into

the world; he who gave you every right thought and wholesome feeling that you ever had in your lives: he counts your tears; he knows your sorrows; he is able and willing to save you to the uttermost. Therefore do not be afraid of your own afflictions. Face them like men. Think over them. Ask him to help you out of them: or if that is not to be, at least to tell you what he means by them. Be sure that what he must mean by them is good to you: a lesson to you, that in some way or other they are meant to make you wiser, stronger, hardier, more sure of God's love, more ready to do God's work, whithersoever it may lead you. Do not be afraid of the dark day of affliction, I say. It may teach you more than the bright prosperous one. Many a man can see clearly in the cloudy day, who would be dazzled in the sunlight. The dull weather, they say, is the best weather for battle; and sorrow is the best time for seeing through and conquering one's own self. Therefore do not be afraid, I say, of sorrow. All the clouds in the sky cannot move the sun a foot further off; and all the sorrow in the world cannot move God any further off. God is there still, where he always was; near you, and below you, and above you, and around you; for in him you live and move and have your being, and are the offspring and children of God. Nay, he is nearer you, if possible, in sorrow, than in joy. He is informing you, and guiding you with his eye, and, like a father, teaching you the right way which you should go. He is searching and purging your hearts, and cleansing you from your secret faults, and teaching you to know who you are and to know who he is—your Father, the knowledge of whom is life eternal. By these things, my friends —by being brought low and made helpless, till ashamed of ourselves, and weary of ourselves, we lift up eyes and heart to God who made us, like lost children crying after a Father—by these things, I say, we live, and in all these things is the life of our spirit.

SERMON XXXIII.

THE UNCHANGEABLE ONE.

PSALM cxix. 89—96.

For ever, O Lord, thy word is settled in heaven. Thy faithfulness is unto all generations : thou hast established the earth, and it abideth. They continue this day according to thine ordinances : for all are thy servants. Unless thy law had been my delight, I should then have perished in mine affliction. I will never forget thy precepts : for with them thou hast quickened me. I am thine, save me ; for I have sought thy precepts. The wicked have waited for me to destroy me : but I will consider thy testimonies. I have seen an end of all perfection ; but thy commandment is exceeding broad.

THE Psalmist is in great trouble. He does not know whom to trust, what to expect next, whom to look to. Everything seems failing and changing round him. His psalm was most probably written during the Babylonish captivity, at a time when all the countries and kingdoms of the east were being destroyed by the Chaldean armies.

Then, he says, Be it so. If everything else changes, God cannot. If everything else fails, God's plans cannot. He can rest on the thought of God; of his goodness, his faithfulness, order, providence. God is governing the world righteously and orderly. Whatever disorder there is on earth, there is none in heaven. God's word endures for ever there.

Then he looks on the world round him ; all is well ordered—

seasons, animals, sun, and stars abide. They continue this day according to God's ordinances. The unchangeableness of nature is a comfort to him; for it is a token of the unchangeablenes of God who made it.

Now, I do beg you to think carefully over this verse; because it is quite against the very common notion that, because the earth was cursed for Adam's sake, therefore it is cursed now; that because it was said to him, Thorns and thistles shall it bring forth to thee, therefore that holds good now. It is not so, my friends; neither is there, as far as I know, in any part whatsoever of Scripture, any mention of Adam's curse continuing to our day. St. John, in the Revelations, certainly says, 'And there shall be no more curse.' But if you will read the Revelation, you will find that what he plainly refers to is to the fearful curses, the plagues, the vials of wrath, as he calls them, which were to be poured out on the earth; and then to cease when the New Jerusalem came down from heaven.

St. Paul, again, knows nothing about any such curse upon the earth. He says that death came into the world by Adam's sin: but that must be understood only of man, and the world of man; and for this simple reason, that we know, without the possibility of doubt, that animals died in this world just as they do now, not only thousands, but hundreds of thousands of years before man appeared on earth.

What St. Paul says of the creation, in one of his most glorious passages, is this—not that it is cursed, but that it groans and travails continually in the pangs of labour, trying to bring forth; trying to bring forth something better than itself; to develop, and rise from good to better, and from that to better still; till all things become perfect in a way which we cannot conceive, but which God has ordained before the foundation of the world.

Besides, as a fact, the earth does not bring forth thorns and thistles to us, but good grain, and fruitful crops, and an abundant return for our labour, if we choose to till the ground.

And wise men, who study God's works, can find no curse at all upon the earth, nor sign of a curse, neither in plants nor beasts, no, nor in the smallest gnat in the air. The more they look into the wonders of God's world, the more they find it true that there is order everywhere, beauty everywhere, fruitfulness everywhere, usefulness everywhere—that all things continue as at the beginning; that, as the psalmist says in another place, God has made them fast for ever and ever, and given them a law which cannot be broken. And if you will look at Genesis viii. 21, 22, you will find from the plain words of Scripture itself, that Adam's curse, whatever it was, was taken off after the flood, 'And the Lord smelled a sweet savour : and the Lord said in his heart, I will not again curse the ground any more for man's sake ; for the imagination of man's heart is evil from his youth ; neither will I again smite any more everything living, as I have done. While the earth remaineth, seed-time and harvest, and cold and heat, and summer and winter, and day and night shall not cease.'

Therefore, my friends, open your eyes and your hearts freely to the message which God is sending you, in summer and winter, in seed-time and in harvest, in sunshine and in storm; that God is not a hard God, a revengeful God, a God of curses, who is extreme to mark what is done amiss, and keepeth his anger for ever. No : but that he is your Father in heaven, who hateth nothing that he has made, and whose mercy is over all his works; who made heaven and earth, the sea, and all that therein is; who keepeth truth for ever; who helpeth them to right that suffer wrong; who feedeth the hungry ; a God who feeds the birds of the air, though they sow not, neither do they reap, nor gather into barns ; and who clothes the grass of the field, which toils not, neither doth it spin ; and who will much much more clothe and feed you, to whom he has given reason, understanding, and the power of learning his laws, the rules by which this world of his is made and works, and of turning them to your own profit in rational and honest labour.

And think, my friends, if the old Psalmist, before Christ came, could believe all this, and find comfort in it, much more ought we. Shame to us if we do not. I had almost said, we deny Christ, if we do not. For who said those last words concerning the birds of the air, and the grass of the field? Who told us that we have not merely a Master or a Judge in heaven, but a Father in heaven? Who but that very Word of God, whom the Psalmist saw dimly and afar off? He knew that the Word of God abode for ever in heaven: but he knew not, as far as we can tell, that that same Word would condescend to be made flesh, and dwell among men that we might see his glory, full of grace and truth. The old Psalmist knew that God's word was full of truth, and that gave him comfort in the wild and sad times in which he lived; but he did not know —none of the Old Testament prophets knew,—how full God's word was of grace also. That he was so full of love, condescension, pity, generosity, so full of longing to seek and save all that was lost, to set right all that was wrong, in one word again, so full of grace, that he would condescend to be born of the Virgin Mary, suffer under Pontius Pilate, to be crucified, dead and buried, that he might become a faithful High Priest for us, full of understanding, fellow-feeling, pity, love, because he has been tempted in all things like as we are, yet without sin.

My friends, was not the old Psalmist a Jew, and are not we Christian men? Then, if the old Psalmist could trust God, how much more should we? If he could find comfort in the thought of God's order, how much more should we? If he could find comfort in the thought of his justice, how much more should we? If he could find comfort in the thought of his love, how much more should we? Yes; let us be full of troubles, doubts, sorrows; let times be uncertain, dark, and dangerous; let strange new truths be discovered, which we cannot, at first sight, fit into what we know to be true already: we can still say, 'I will not fear, though the earth be moved, and the hills be carried into the midst of the sea.' For the word of God abideth for ever in heaven, even Jesus Christ, who is the Light of the world and the Life of men. To him all power is given in heaven and earth. He is set on the throne, judging right, and ministering true judgment among the people. All things, as the Psalmist says, come to an end. All men's plans, men's notions, men's systems, men's doctrines, grow old, wear out, and perish.

> The old order changes, giving place to the new :
> But God fulfils himself in many ways.

For men are not ruling the world. Christ is ruling the world; and his commandment is exceeding broad. His laws are broad enough for all people, all countries, all ages; and strangely as they may seem to work, in the eyes of us short-sighted timorous human beings, still all is going well, and all will go well; for Christ reigns, and will reign, till he has put all enemies under his feet, and God be all in all.

SERMON XXXIV

EN TOYTΩ NIKA.

(*Good Friday*, 1860.)

---

1 CORINTHIANS i. 23-25.

But we preach Christ crucified, unto the Jews a stumbling-block, and unto the Greeks foolishness; but unto them which are called, both Jews and Greeks, Christ the power of God, and the wisdom of God. Because the foolishness of God is wiser than men; and the weakness of God is stronger than men.

THE foolishness of God? The weakness of God? These are strange words. But they are St. Paul's words, not mine. If he had not said them first, I should not dare to say them now.

But what do they mean? Can God be weak? Can God be foolish? No, says St. Paul. Nothing less. For so strong is God, that his very weakness, if he seems weak, is stronger than all mankind. So wise is God, that his very foolishness, if he seems foolish, is wiser than all mankind.

Why then talk of the weakness of God, of the foolishness of God, if he be neither weak nor foolish? Why use words which seem blasphemous, if they are not true?

I do not say these ugly words for myself. St. Paul did not say these ugly words for himself. But men have said them; too many men, and too often. The Jews, who sought after a sign, said them in St. Paul's time. The Corinthian Greeks, who sought after wisdom, said them also. There are men who say them now. We all are tempted at times to say them in our hearts. As often as we forget Good Friday, and what Good Friday means, and what Good Friday brought to all mankind, we do say them in our hearts; and charge God—though we should not like to confess it even to ourselves—with weakness and with folly.

Now, how is this? Let us consider, first, how it was with these Jews and Greeks.

Why did the cross of Christ, and the message of Good Friday, seem to them weakness and folly? Why did they answer St. Paul, 'Your Christ cannot be God, or he would never have allowed himself to be crucified?'

The Jews required a sign; a sign from heaven; a sign of God's power. Thunder and earthquakes, armies of angels, taking vengeance on the heathen; these were the signs of Christ which they expected. A Christ who came in such awful glory as that, they would accept, and follow, and look to him to lead them against the Romans, that they might conquer them, and all the nations upon earth. And all that St. Paul gave them, was a sign of Christ's weakness. 'He was despised and rejected of men; a man of sorrows, and acquainted with grief. . . . . He hath borne our griefs, and carried our sorrows, yet we did esteem him stricken, smitten of God, and afflicted. He was oppressed, and he was afflicted, yet he opened not his mouth: he is brought as a lamb to the slaughter, and as a sheep before her shearers is dumb, so he opened not his mouth.' Then said the Jews—This is no Christ for us, this weak, despised, crucified Christ. Then answered St. Paul—Weak? I tell you that what seems to you weakness, is the very power of God. You Jews wish to conquer all mankind: and behold, instead, you yourselves are rushing to ruin and destruction: but what you cannot do, Christ on his cross can do. Weak, shamed, despised, dying man as he seemed, he is still conqueror; and he will conquer all mankind at last, and draw all men to himself. Know that what seems to you weakness, is the very power of God; the power of doing good, and of suffering all things, that he may do good : and that *that* will conquer the world, when riches and glory, and armies, aye, the very thunder and the earthquake, have failed utterly.

The Greeks, again, sought after wisdom. If St. Paul was (as he said) the apostle of God, then they expected him to argue with them on cunning points of philosophy; about the being of God, the nature of the world and of the soul; about finite and infinite, cause and effect, being and not being, and all those dark questions with which they astonished simple people, and gained power over them, and set up for wise men and teachers to their own profit and glory, pampering their own luxury and self-conceit. And all St. Paul gave them, seemed to them mere foolishness. He could have argued with these Greeks on those deep matters; for he was a great scholar, and a true philosopher, and could speak wisdom among those who were perfect : but he would not. He determined to know nothing among them but Jesus Christ, and him crucified; and he told them, You disputers of this world, while you are deceiving simple souls with enticing words of man's wisdom and philosophy, falsely so called, you are trifling away your own souls and your hearers' into hell. What you need, and what they need, is not philosophy, but a new heart and a right spirit. Sin is your disease; and you know that it is so, in the depth of your hearts. Then know this, that God so loved you, sinners as you are, that he condescended to become mortal man, and to give himself up to death, even the shameful and horrible death of the cross, that he might save you from your sins; and he that would be saved now, let him deny himself, and take up his cross and follow him. And to that, those proud Greeks answered,—That is a tale unworthy of philosophers. The Cross? It is a death of shame—the death of slaves and wretches. Tell your tale to slaves, not to us. To give himself

up to the death of the cross is foolishness, and not the
wisdom which we want. Then answered St. Paul and said,—
True. The cross is a slave's and a wretch's death; and
therefore slaves and wretches will hear me, though you will
not. 'For you see your calling, brethren, how that not many
wise men after the flesh, not many mighty, not many noble, are
called: but God hath chosen the foolish things of the world to
confound the wise; and God hath chosen the weak things
of the world to confound the things which are mighty; and
base things of the world, and things which are despised, hath
God chosen, yea, and things which are not, to bring to nought
things that are: that no flesh should glory in his presence.'
For the foolishness of God is wiser than all the wisdom of men.
You Greeks, with all your philosophy and your wisdom, have
been trying, for hundreds of years, to find out the laws of
heaven and earth, and to set the world right by them; and you
have not done it. You have not found out the secrets of
the world. You have not set the world right. You have not
even set your own hearts and lives right. But what your
seeming wisdom cannot do, the seeming foolishness of Christ
on his cross will do. Does it seem to you foolish of him,
to believe that he could save the world, by giving himself up to
a horrible and shameful death? Does it seem to you foolishness
in me, to preach nothing but him crucified, and to say, Behold
God dying for men? Then know, that what seems to you
foolishness, is the very wisdom of God. That God knows the
secret of touching, convincing, and converting the hearts of
men, though you do not. That God knows how the world is
made, and how to set it right, though you do not. That God
knows the law which keeps all heaven and earth in order,
though you do not; and that that law is charity,—self-sacrificing
love, which shines out from the cross of Christ. Know, that
when all your arguments and philosophies have failed to teach
men what they ought to do, one earnest penitent look at Christ
upon his cross will teach them. That their hearts will leap up

in answer, and cry, If this be God, I can believe in him. If this be God, I can trust him. If this be God, I can obey him. That one look at Christ upon his cross will make them—what you could never make them—new men, filled with a new thought; the thought that God is love, and that he who dwelleth in love, dwelleth in God, and God in him; and that the poor slaves and wretches, whom you despise, will look unto the cross and be saved, and become new men, and lead new lives, and rise to be saints and martyrs to God and to his Christ, giving themselves up to torments and death, as Christ did before them; and that out of them shall spring that church of Christ, which shall reign over all the world, when you and your philosophies have crumbled into dust.

My friends, let us look, earnestly, humbly, and solemnly this day, at Christ upon his cross. Let us learn that love, the utter self-sacrificing love which Christ shewed on his cross, is stronger than all pomp and might, all armies, riches, governments; aye, that it is the very power of God, by which all things consist, which holds together heaven and earth and all that is therein.

Let us learn that love, the utter self-sacrificing love which Christ shewed on his cross, is wiser than all arguments, doctrines, philosophies, whether they be true or false; aye, that it is the very wisdom of God, by which he convinces and converts all hearts and souls; and let us look to the cross, and see there the wisdom of God, and the power of God, mighty to save to the uttermost all who come through Christ to him.

And let us remember this, that whenever we fancy ourselves to be strong and powerful, and think to aggrandize ourselves at our neighbour's expense, and to crush those who are weaker than ourselves, then we are forgetting the lesson of Good Friday; that whenever we fancy that the way to be wise is, to use our wit and our knowledge for our own glory, and by them to manage our fellow-men, and make them admire us and bow down to us, then we forget the lesson of Good Friday. For whosoever gives himself up to selfish ambition, or to selfish cunning, charges Christ upon his cross with weakness and with foolishness, and denies the Lord who bought him with his blood.

My friends, I have no more to say. Much more I might say. For Good Friday has many other meanings, and all the sermons of a lifetime would not exhaust them all.

But one thing seemed to me fit to be said, and I say it again, and entreat you to carry it home with you, and live by the light of it all the year round.

Do you wish to be powerful? Then look at Christ upon his cross; at what seems to men his weakness; and learn from him how to be strong. Do you wish to be wise? Then look at Christ upon the cross; and at what seemed to men his folly; and learn from him how to be wise. For sooner or later, I hope and trust, you will find that true, which St. Buonaventura (wise and strong himself) used to say,—That all the learning in the world had never taught him so much as the sight of Christ upon the cross.

SERMON XXXV.

THE ETERNAL MANHOOD.

(*First Sunday after Easter.*)

JOHN xx. 29.

Jesus saith unto him, Thomas, because thou hast seen me, thou hast believed; blessed are they that have not seen, and yet have believed.

ON the eighth day after the Lord Jesus rose from the dead, he appeared a second time to his disciples. On this day he strengthened St. Thomas's weak faith, by giving him proof, sensible proof, that he was indeed and really the very same person who had been crucified, wearing the very same human nature, the very same man's body.

'Blessed are they who have not seen, and yet have believed.' You have not seen. You have never beheld with your bodily eyes, or touched with your bodily hand, as St. Thomas did, the Lord Jesus Christ. And yet you may be more blessed now, this day, than St. Thomas was then. We are too apt to fancy, that, to have seen the Lord with our eyes, to have walked with him, and talked with him, as the apostles did, was the greatest honour and blessing which could happen to man. We fancy, perhaps, at times, that if the Lord Jesus were to come visibly among us now, we should want nothing more to make us good; that we could not help listening to him, obeying him, loving him.

But the Scriptures prove to us that it was not so. The

Scribes and Pharisees saw him and talked with him; yet they hated him. Judas Iscariot, yet he betrayed him. Pilate, yet he condemned him. The word preached profited them nothing, not being mixed with faith in those who heard him. Jesus Christ, the Lord of glory, came and preached himself to them; declared to them who he was, proved who he was by his mighty works of love and mercy, and by fulfilling all the prophecies of Scripture which spoke of him; and yet they did not believe him, they hated him, they crucified him; because they had no faith.

You see, therefore, that something more than seeing him with our bodily eyes is wanted to make us believe in the Lord Jesus Christ; something more than seeing him with our bodily eyes is wanted to make us blessed. St. Thomas saw him; St. Thomas was allowed, by the boundless condescension and mercy of the Lord Jesus, to put his hand into his side. And yet the Lord does not say to him,—See how blessed thou art; see how honoured thou art, by being allowed to touch me. No; our Lord rather rebukes him for requiring such a proof.

There are those who will not believe without seeing; who say, I must have proof. What I hear in church is too much for me to believe without many more reasons than are given for it all. Many people, for instance, stumble at the stumbling-block of the cross, and cannot bring themselves to believe that God would condescend to suffer and to die for men. Others cannot make up their minds about the resurrection. It seems to them a strange and impossible thing that Jesus' body should have risen from the grave and ascended to heaven, and that our bodies should rise also. That was the great puzzle to the Greeks, who thought themselves very learned and cunning, and were great arguers and disputers about all deep matters in heaven and earth. When St. Paul preached to them on Mars' Hill, they heard him patiently enough, till he spoke of Jesus rising from the dead; and then they mocked; laughed at the notion as absurd. And we find that the Corinthians, even after they were converted and baptised Christians, were puzzled about this same matter. They could not understand how the dead were raised, and with what body they would come.

With such the Lord is not angry. If they really wish to know what is true, and to do what is right; if they really are, as St. Paul says, 'feeling after the Lord, if haply they may find him;' then the Lord will give them light in due time, and shew them what they ought to believe, and give them the sort of proof which they want. All such he treats as he did Thomas, when he said, in his great condescension, 'Reach hither thy finger, and behold my hands, and reach hither thy hand, and thrust it into my side, and be not faithless but believing.'

So the Lord sent to those Corinthians the very sort of proof which they wanted, by the hand of the learned apostle, St. Paul. They were great observers of the works of nature, of the strange movement and change, birth and death, which goes on in beasts, and in plants, and in the clouds, and the rivers, and the very stones under our feet. And they said, We cannot believe in the resurrection of the dead, because we see nothing like it in the world around us. And St. Paul was sent to tell them. No: you do see something like it. If you will look deeper into the working of the world around you, you will see that the rising again of the dead, instead of being an unnatural or an absurd thing, is the most reasonable and natural thing, the perfect fulfilment, and crowning wonder of wonderful laws which are working round you in every seed which you sow; in the flesh of beasts and fishes; in bodies celestial and bodies terrestrial: and so in that glorious chapter which we read in the Burial Service, St. Paul tells the Corinthians, who went altogether by sense, and reasoning about the things which they could see and handle, that sense and reasoning were on his side, on God's side; and that the mysteries of faith, like the resurrection of the body, were not contrary to reason, but agreed with it.

So does the Lord clear up the doubts of his people, in the way which is best for them. But he does not call them as blessed as others. There is a higher faith than that. There is a better part. The same part which Mary chose. The same faith of which our Lord says,—' Blessed are they who have not seen, and yet have believed.' The faith of the heart; the childlike, undoubting, ready, willing faith, which welcomes the news of the Lord; which runs to meet it, and is not astonished at it; and, if it ever doubts for a moment, only doubts for very joy and delight; and feeling that the news of the gospel is good news, cannot help feeling now and then that it is too good news to be true; shewing its love and its faith in its very hesitation. This is the childlike heart, whereof it is written, ' Except ye be converted and become as little children, ye shall in no wise enter into the kingdom of heaven.'

The hearts of little children; the hearts which begin by faith and love toward God himself; the hearts which know God; the hearts to whom God has revealed himself, and taught them, they know not how, that he is love. They are so sure of God's goodness, so sure of his power, so sure of his love, his willingness to have mercy, and to deliver poor creatures, that they find nothing strange, nothing difficult, in the mysteries of faith. To them it is not a thing incredible, that God should have come down and died upon the cross. When they hear the good news of him who gave his own life for them, it seems a natural thing to them, a reasonable thing: not of course a thing which they could have expected; but yet not a thing to doubt of or to be astonished at. For they know that God is love.

And now some of you may say, Then are we more blessed than Thomas? We have not seen, and yet we have believed. We never doubted. We never wanted any arguments, or learned books, or special inward assurances. From the moment that we began to learn our catechisms at school we believed it, of course, every word of it. Do we not say the Creed every Sunday; I believe in—and so forth? O my friends, do you believe indeed? If you do, blessed are you. But are you sure that you speak truth?

You may believe it. But do you believe in it? Have you faith in it? Do you put your trust in it? Is your heart in it? Is it in your heart? Do you love it, rejoice in it, delight to think over it; to look forward to it, to make yourselves ready and fit for it. Do you believe in it, in short, or do you only believe it, as you believe that there is an Emperor of China, or that there is a country called America, or any other matter with which you have nothing to do, for which you care nothing, and which would make no difference at all to you, if you found out to-morrow that it was not so. That is mere dead belief; faith without works, which is dead, the belief of the brains, not the faith of the heart and spirit.

Oh, do you really believe the good news of this text, in which the Son of God himself said to mortal men like ourselves, 'Handle me and see that it is I, indeed; for a spirit hath not flesh and bones as ye see me have.' Do you believe that there is a Man evermore on the right hand of God? That now as we speak a man is offering up before the Father his perfect and all-cleansing sacrifice? That, in the midst of the throne of God, is he himself who was born of the Virgin Mary, and crucified under Pontius Pilate? Do you wish to find out whether you believe that or not? Then look at your own hearts. Look at your own prayers. Do you think of the Lord Jesus Christ, do you pray to the Lord Jesus Christ, as a man, very man, born of woman? Do you pray to him as to one who can be touched with the feeling of your infirmities, because he has been tempted in all things like as you are, yet without sin? When you are sad, perplexed, do you take all your sorrows and doubts and troubles to the Lord Jesus, and speak them all out to him honestly and frankly, however reverently, as a man speaketh to his friend? Do you really cast all your care on him, because you believe that he careth for you? If you do, then indeed you believe in the resurrection of the Lord Jesus Christ; and you will surely have your reward in a peace of mind, amid all the chances and changes of this mortal life, which passes man's understanding. That blessed knowledge that the Lord knows all, cares for all, condescends to all—That thought of a loving human face smiling upon your joys, sorrowing over your sorrows, watching you, educating you from youth to manhood, from manhood to the grave, from the grave to eternities of eternities—Whosoever has felt that, has indeed found the pearl of great price, for which, if need be, he would give up all else in earth or heaven.

Or do you say to yourselves at times, I must not think too much about the Lord Jesus's being man, lest I should forget that he is God? Do you shrink from opening your heart to him? Do you say within yourself, He is too great, too awful, to condescend to listen to my little mean troubles and anxieties? Besides, how can I expect him to feel for them; I, a mean, sinful man, and he the Almighty God? How do I know that he will not despise my meanness and paltriness? How do I know that he will not be angry with me? I must be more reverent to him, than to trouble him with very petty matters. He was a man once when he was upon earth: but now that he is ascended up on high, Very God of Very God, in the glory which he had with the Father before the worlds were made, I must have more awful and solemn thoughts about him, and keep at a more humble distance from him.

Do you ever have such thoughts as those come over you, my friends, when you are thinking of the Lord Jesus, and praying to him? If you do, shall I tell you what to say to them when they arise in your minds, 'Get thee behind me, Satan.' Get thee away, thou accusing devil, who art accusing my Lord to me, and trying to make me fancy him less loving, less condescending, less tender, less understanding, than he was when he wept over the grave of Lazarus. Get thee away, thou lying hypocritical devil, who pretendest to be so very humble and reverent to the godhead of the Lord Jesus, in order that thou mayest make me forget what his godhead is like, forget what God's likeness is, forget that it was in his manhood, in his man's words, his man's thoughts, his man's actions, that he shewed forth the glory of God, the express image of his person, and fulfilled the blessed words, 'And God said, Let us make man in our image, after our likeness.' Get thee behind me, Satan. I believe in the good news of Easter Day, and thou shalt not rob me of it. I believe that he who died upon the Cross, rose again the third day, as very and perfect man then and now, as he was when he bled and groaned on Calvary, and shuddered at the fear of death, in the garden of Gethsemane. Thou shalt not make my Lord's incarnation, his birth, his passion, his resurrection, all that he did and suffered in those thirty-three years, of none effect to me. Thou shalt not take from me the blessed message of my Bible, that there is a man in heaven in the midst of the throne of God. Thou shalt not take from me the blessed message of the Athanasian Creed, that in Christ the manhood is taken into God. Thou shalt not take from me the blessed message of Holy Communion, which declares that the very human flesh and blood of him who died on the Cross is now eternal in the heavens, and nourishes my body and soul to everlasting life. Thou shalt not, under pretence of voluntary humility and will-worship, tempt me to go and pray to angels or to saints, or to the Blessed Virgin, because I choose to fancy them more tender, more loving and condescending, more loving, more human, than the Lord himself, who gave himself to death for me. If the Lord God, the Son of the Father, is not ashamed to be man for ever and ever, I will not be ashamed to think of him as man; to pray to him as man; to believe and be sure that he can be touched with the feeling of my infirmities; to entreat him, by all that he did and suffered as a man, to deliver me from those temptations which he himself has conquered for himself; and to cry to him in the smallest, as well as in the most important matters—' By the mystery of thy holy incarnation ; by thine agony and bloody sweat ; by thy cross and passion ; by thy precious death and burial ; by thy glorious resurrection and ascension ;' by all which thou hast done, and suffered, and conquered, as a man upon this earth of ours, good Lord, deliver us !

SERMON XXXVI.

THE BATTLE WITHIN.

(*Fourteenth Sunday after Trinity*, 1858.)

GALATIANS, V. 16, 17.

This I say then, Walk in the spirit, and ye shall not fulfil the lust of the flesh. For the flesh lusteth against the spirit, and the spirit against the flesh: and these are contrary the one to the other: so that ye cannot do the things that ye would.

DOES this text seem to any of you difficult to understand? It need not be difficult to you; for it does not speak of anything which you do not know. It speaks of something which you have all felt, which goes on in you every day of your lives. It speaks of something, certainly, which is very curious, mysterious, difficult to put into words: but what is not curious and mysterious? The commonest things are usually the most curious? What is more wonderful than the beating of your heart; your pulse which beats all day long, without your thinking of it?

Just so this battle, this struggle, which St. Paul speaks of in this text, is going on in us all day long, and yet we hardly think of it. Now what is this battle? What are these things which are fighting continually in your mind and in mine? St. Paul calls them the flesh and the spirit. 'The flesh,' he says, 'lusts against the spirit, and the spirit against the flesh.' They pull opposite ways. One wants to do one thing, and the other the other. But if so, one of them must be in the right, and the other in the wrong. Now, St. Paul says, when these two fall out with each other, the spirit is in the right, and the flesh in the wrong. And therefore, the secret of life is, to walk in the spirit, and so not to fulfil the lusts of the flesh.

But if so, it must be worth our while to find out which is flesh, and which is spirit in us, that we may know the foolish part of us from the wise. What the flesh is, we may see by looking at a dumb beast, which is all flesh, and has no immortal soul. It may be very cunning, brave, curiously formed, beautiful, but one thing you will always see, that a beast does what it likes, and only what it likes. And this is the mark of the flesh, that it does what it likes. It is selfish, and self-indulgent, cares for nothing but itself, and what it can get for itself.

True, you may raise a dumb beast above that, by taming and training it. You may teach a horse or dog to do what it does *not* like, and give it a sense of duty, and as it were awaken a soul in it. That is very wonderful, that we should be able to do so. It is a sign that man is made in God's likeness. But I cannot stay to speak of that now. I say our flesh, our animal nature, is selfish and self-indulgent. I do not say, therefore, that it is bad : God forbid. God made our bodies and brains, as well as our souls ; and God makes nothing bad. It is blasphemous to say that he does. No, our bodies as bodies are good; the flesh as flesh is good, when it is in its right place ; and its right place is to be servant, not master. We are not to walk after the flesh, says St. Paul : but the flesh is to walk after the spirit—in English, our bodies are to obey our spirits, our souls. For man has something higher than body in him. He has a spirit in him ; and it is just having this spirit which makes him a man. For this spirit cares about higher things than mere gain and comfort. It can feel pity and mercy, love and generosity, justice and honour ; and when a man not only feels them, but obeys them, then he is a true man—a Christian man : but, on the other hand, if a man does not; if he be a man in whom there is no mercy or pity, no generosity, no benevolence, no justice or honour; who cares for nothing and no one but himself, and filling his own stomach and his own purse, and pleasing his own brute appetites in some way, what should you say of that man? You would say, he is like a brute beast—and you would say right—you would say just what St. Paul says. St. Paul would say, that man is fulfilling the lusts of the flesh; and you and St. Paul would mean just the same thing. Now, St. Paul says, 'The flesh in us lusts against the spirit, and the spirit against the flesh.' And what do we gain by the spirit in us lusting against the flesh, and pulling us the opposite way? We gain this, St. Paul says, 'that we cannot do the things that we would.'

Does that seem no great gain to you? Let me put it a little plainer. St. Paul means this, and just this, that you may not do whatever you like. St. Paul thought it the very best thing for a man not to be able to do whatever he liked. As long, St. Paul says, as a man does whatever he likes, he lives according to the flesh, and is no better than a dumb beast: but as soon as he begins to live according to the spirit, and does not do whatever he likes, but restrains himself, and keeps himself in order, then, and then only, he becomes a true man.

But why not do whatever we like? Because if we did do so, we should be certain to do wrong. I do not mean that you and I here like nothing but what is wrong. God forbid. I trust the Spirit of God is with our spirits. But I mean this:—That if you could let a child grow up totally without any control whatsoever, I believe that before that lad was twenty-one he would have qualified himself for the gallows seven times over. Thank God, that cannot happen in England, because people are better taught, most of them at least; and more, we dare not do what we like, for fear of the law and the policeman.

But, if you knew the lives which savages lead, who have neither law outside them to keep them straight by fear, nor the Spirit of God within them to keep them straight by duty and honour, then you would understand what I mean only too well.

Now St. Paul says,—It is a good thing for a man not to be able to do what he likes. But there are two ways of keeping him from it. One is by the law, the other is by the Spirit of God. The law works on a man from the outside by fear; but the Spirit of God works in a man by honour, by the sense of duty, by making him like and love what is right, and making him see what a beautiful and noble thing right is.

Now St. Paul wants us to restrain ourselves, not from fear of being punished, but because we like to do right. That is what he means when he says that we are to be led by the Spirit, instead of being under the law. It is better to be afraid of the law than to do wrong: but it is best of all to do right from the Spirit, and of our own free will.

Am I puzzling you? I hope not: but, lest I should be, I will give you one simple example which ought to make all clear as to the struggle between a man's flesh and his spirit, and also as to doing right from the Spirit or from law.

Suppose you were a soldier going into battle. You see your comrades falling around you, disfigured and cut up; you hear their groans and cries; and you are dreadfully afraid: and no shame to you. It is the common human instinct of self-preservation. The bravest men have told me that they are afraid at first going into action, and that they cannot get over the feeling. But what part of you is afraid? Your flesh, which is afraid of pain, just as a beast is of the whip. Then your flesh perhaps says, Run away—or at least skulk and hide —take care of yourself. But next, if you were a coward, the law would come into your mind, and you would say, But I dare not run away; for, if I do, I shall be shot as a deserter, or broke, and drummed out of the army. So you may go on, even though you are a coward : but that is not courage. You have not conquered your own fear—you have not conquered yourself—but the law has conquered you.

But, if you are a brave man, as I trust you all are, a higher spirit than your own speaks to your spirit, and makes you say to yourself, I dare not run away; but, more, I cannot run away. I should like to—but I cannot do the things that I would. It is my duty to go on; it is right; it is a point of honour with me to my country, my regiment, my Queen, my God, and I must go on.

Then you are walking in the Spirit. You have conquered yourself, and so are a really brave man. You have obeyed the Spirit, and you have your reward by feeling inspirited, as we say; you can face death with spirit, and fight with spirit.

But the struggle between the Spirit and the flesh is not ended there. When you got excited, there would probably come over you the lust of fighting; you would get angry, get mad and lose your self-possession.

There is the flesh waking up again, and saying, Be cruel; kill every one you meet. And to that the Spirit answers, No; be reasonable and merciful. Do not fulfil the lusts of the flesh, and turn yourself into a raging wild beast. Your business is not to butcher human beings, but to win a battle.

Well; and even if you have conquered the enemy, you may not have conquered your worst enemy, which is yourself. For, after having fought bravely, and done your duty, what would the flesh say to you? I am sure it would say it to me. What but —Boast : talk of your own valiant deeds and successes; get all the praise and honour you can; and shew how much finer a person you are than any of your comrades. But what would the Spirit say?—and I trust you would all listen to the Spirit. The Spirit would say, No; do not boast; do not lower yourself into the likeness of a vain peacock : but be just, and be modest. Give every man his due; try to praise and recommend every one whom you can ; and trust to God to make your doing your duty as clear as the light, and your brave actions as the noon-day.

So, you see, all through, a man's flesh might be lusting, and would be lusting, against the Spirit, and the Spirit against the flesh; and see, too, how in each case, the flesh is tempting the man to be cowardly, brutal, vain, selfish, and wrong in some way, and the Spirit is striving to make him forget himself, and think of his comrades and his duty.

Now when a man is led by the Spirit, if he is tempted to do wrong, he does not say, I will not do this wrong thing, but I cannot. I cannot do what you want me. I like to hear a man say that. It is a sign that he feels God's voice in him, which he must obey, whether he likes or not; as Joseph said when he was tempted. Not, I had rather not, or I dare not: but, How *can* I do this great wickedness against my master, who has trusted me, and put everything into my hand, and so, by being a treacherous traitor, sin against God?

Now, is this Spirit part of our spirits, or not? I think we confess ourselves that it is not. St. Paul says that it is not. For he says, there is one Spirit—that is, one good Spirit—of whom he speaks as the Spirit; and this, he says, is the Spirit of God, and the Spirit of Christ, and the Spirit which inspires the spirits of all noble, Christ-like, God-like men.

In this Spirit there is nothing proud, spiteful, cruel; nothing selfish, false, and mean; nothing violent, loose, debauched. But he is an altogether good and noble spirit, whose fruit is love, joy, peace, longsuffering, gentleness, goodness, faith, meekness, temperance. This, he says, is the Spirit of God; and this Spirit he gives to those spirits,—souls, as we call them now,—who desire it, that they may become righteous with the righteousness of Christ, and good with the goodness of God.

And is not this good news? I say, my friends, if we will look at it aright, there is no better news, no more inspiriting news for men like us, mixed up in the battle of life, and often pulled downward by our own bad passions, and ashamed of ourselves more or less, every day of our lives ;—no better news, I say, than this, that what is good and right in us is not our own, but God's; that our longings after good, our sense of duty and honour, kindliness and charity, are not merely our own likings or fancies: but the voice of God's almighty and everlasting Spirit. Good news, indeed! For if God be for us, who can be against us? If God's Spirit be with our spirits, they must surely be stronger than our selfish pleasure-loving flesh. If God himself be labouring to make us good; if he be putting into our hearts good desires; surely he can enable us to bring those desires to good effect: and all that is wanted of us, is to listen to God's voice within, and do the right like men, whatever pain it may cost us, sure that we, by God's help, shall win at last in the hardest battle of all battles, the victory over our own selves

SERMON XXXVII.

HYPOCRISY.

MATTHEW xvi. 3.

Oh ye hypocrites, ye can discern the face of the sky; but can ye not discern the signs of the times?

IT will need, I think, some careful thought thoroughly to understand this text. Our Lord in it calls the Pharisees and Sadducees hypocrites; because, though they could use their common sense and experience to judge of the weather they would not use them to judge of the signs of the times; of what was going to happen to the Jewish nation.

But how was their conduct hypocritical? Stupid we might call it, or unreasonable: but how hypocritical? That, I think, we may see better, by considering what the word hypocrite means.

We mean now, generally, by a hypocrite, a man who pretends to be one thing, while he is another; who pretends to be pious and good, while he is leading a profligate life in secret; who pretends to believe certain doctrines, while at heart he disbelieves them; a man, in short, who is a scoundrel, *and knows it;* but who does not intend others to know it: who deceives others, but does not deceive himself.

My friends, such a man is a hypocrite: but there is another kind of hypocrite, and a more common one by far; and that is, the hypocrite who not only deceives others, but deceives himself likewise; the hypocrite who (as one of the wisest living men puts it) is astonished that you should think him hypocritical.

I do not say which of these two kinds is the worse. My duty is to judge no man. I only say that there are such people, and too many of them; that we ourselves are often in danger of becoming such hypocrites; and that this was the sort of people which the Pharisees for the most part were. Hypocrites who had not only deceived others, but themselves also; who thought themselves perfectly right, honest, and pious; who were therefore astonished and indignant at Christ's calling them hypocrites.

How did they get into this strange state of mind? How may we get into it?

Consider first what a hypocrite means. It means strictly neither more nor less than a play-actor; one who personates different characters on the stage. That is the one original meaning of the word hypocrite.

Now recollect that a man may personate characters, like a play-actor, and pretend to be what he is not, for two different objects. He may do it for other people's sake, or for his own.

1. For other people's sake. As the Pharisees did, when they did all their works to be seen of men; and therefore, naturally, gave their attention as much as possible to outward forms and ceremonies, which could be seen by men.

Now, understand me, before I go a step further, I am not going to speak against forms and ceremonies. No man less: and, above all, not against the Church forms and ceremonies, which have grown up, gradually and naturally, out of the piety, and experience, and practical common sense of many generations of God's saints. Men must have forms and ceremonies to put them in mind of the spiritual truths which they cannot see or handle. Men cannot get on without them; and those who throw away the Church forms have to invent fresh ones, and less good ones, for themselves.

All, I say, have their forms and ceremonies; and all are in danger, as we churchmen are, of making those forms stand instead of true religion. In the Church or out of the Church, men are all tempted to have, like the Pharisees, their traditions of the elders, their little rules as to conduct, over and above what the Bible and the Prayer-book have commanded; and all are tempted to be more shocked if those rules are broken, than if really wrong and wicked things are done; and like the Pharisees of old, to be careful in paying tithe of mint, anise, and cummin, the commonest garden herbs, and yet forget the weighty matters of the law, justice, mercy, and judgment. I have known those who would be really more shocked at seeing a religious man dance or sing, than at hearing him tell a lie. But I will give no examples, lest I should set you on judging others. Or rather, the only example which I will give is that of these Pharisees, who have become, by our Lord's words about them, famous to all time, as hypocrites.

Now you must bear in mind that these Pharisees were not villains and profligates. Many people, feeling, perhaps, how much of what the Lord had said against the Pharisees would apply to them, have tried to escape from that ugly thought, by making out the Pharisees worse men than our Lord does. But the fact is, that they cannot be proved to be worse than too many religious people now-a-days. There were adulterers, secret loose-livers among them. Are there none now-a-days? They were covetous. Are no religious professors covetous now-a-days? They crept into widows' houses, and, for a pretence made long prayers. Does no one do so now? There would, of course, be among them, as there is among all large religious parties, as there is now, a great deal of inconsistent and bad conduct. But, on the whole, there is no reason to suppose that the greater number of them were what we should call ill-livers. In that terrible twenty-third chapter of St

Matthew, in which our Lord denounces the sins of the Scribes and Pharisees, he nowhere accuses them of profligate living; and the Pharisee of whom he tells us in his parable, who went into the Temple to pray, no doubt spoke truth when he boasted of not being as other men are, extortioners, unjust, adulterers. He trusted in himself that he was righteous. True. But whatever that means, it means that he thought that he was righteous, after a fashion, though it proved to be a wrong one. What our Lord complains of in them is, first, their hardness of heart; their pride in themselves, and their contempt for their fellowmen. Their very name Pharisee meant that. It meant separate—they were separate from mankind; a peculiar people; who alone knew the law, with whom alone God was pleased: while the rest of mankind, even of their own countrymen, knew not the law, and were accursed, and doomed to hell. Ah God, who are we to cast stones at the Pharisees of old, when this is the very thing which you may hear said in England from hundreds of pulpits every Sunday, with the mere difference, that instead of the word law, men put the word gospel.

For this our Lord denounced them; and next, for their hypocrisy, their play-acting, the outward show of religion in which they delighted; trying to dress, and look, and behave differently from other men; doing all their good works to be seen of men; sounding a trumpet before them when they gave away alms; praying standing at the corners of the streets; going in long clothing, making broad their phylacteries, the written texts of Scripture which they sewed to their garments; washing perpetually when they came from the market, or any public place, lest they should have been defiled by the touch of an unclean thing, or person; loving the chief seats in their religious meetings, and the highest places at feasts; and so forth,—full of affectation, vanity, and pride.

I could tell you other stories of their ridiculous affectations: but I shall not. They would only make you smile: and we could not judge them fairly, not being able to make full allowance for the difference of customs between the Jews and ourselves. Many of the things which our Lord blames them for, were not nearly so absurd in Judea of old, as they seem to us in England now. Indeed, no one but our Lord seems to have thought them absurd, or seen through the hollowness and emptiness of them :—as he perhaps sees through, my friends, a great deal which is thought very right in England now. Making allowance for the difference of the country, and of the times, the Pharisees were perhaps no more affected, for Jews, than many people are now, for Englishmen. And if it be answered, that though our religious fashions now-a-days are not commanded expressly by the Bible or the Prayer Book, yet they carry out their spirit:—remember, in God's name, that that was exactly what the Pharisees said, and their excuse for being righteous above what was written; and that they could, and did, quote texts of Scripture for their phylacteries, their washings, and all their other affectations.

Another reason I have for not dwelling too much on these affections; and it is this. Because a man may be a play-actor and a self-deceiver in religion, without any of these tricks at all, and without much of the vanity and pride which cause them. For recollect that a man may act for his own amusement, as well as for other people's. Children do so perpetually, and especially when no one is by to listen to them. They delight in playing at being this person and that, and in living for a while in a day-dream. Oh let us take care that we do not do the same in our religion ! It is but too easy to do so. Too easy; and too common. For is it not play-acting, like any child, to come to this church, and here to feel repentance, feel forgiveness, feel gratitude, feel reverence; and then to go out of church and awake as from a dream, and become our natural selves for the rest of the week, till Sunday comes round again; comforting ourselves meanwhile with the fancy that we had been very religious last Sunday, and intended to be very religious next Sunday likewise ?

Would there not be hypocrisy and play-acting in that, my friends?

Now, my dear friends, if we give way to this sort of hypocrisy, we shall get, as too many do, into the habit of living two lives at once, without knowing it. Outside us will be our religious life of praying, and reading, and talking of good things, and doing good work (as, thank God, many do whose hearts are not altogether right with God, or their eyes single in his sight) good work, which I trust God will not forget in the last day, in spite of all our inconsistencies. Outside us, I say, will be our religious life: and inside us our own actual life, our own natural character, too often very little changed or improved at all. So by continually playing at religion, we shall deceive ourselves. We shall make an entirely wrong estimate of the state of our souls. We shall fancy that this outward religion of ours is the state of our soul. And then, if any one tells us that we are play-acting, and hypocrites, we shall be as astonished and indignant as the Pharisees were of old. We shall make the same mistake as a man would, who because he always wore clothes, should fancy at last that his clothes were himself, part of his own body. So, I say, many deceive themselves, and are more or less hypocrites to themselves. They do not, in general, deceive others; they are not, on the whole, hypocrites to their neighbours. For their neighbours, after a time, see what they cannot see themselves, that they are play-acting; that they are two different people without knowing it: that their religion is a thing apart from their real character. A hundred signs shew that. How many there are, for instance, who are, or seem tolerably earnest about religion, and doing good, as long as they are actually in church, or actually talking about religion. But all the rest of their time, what are they doing? What are they thinking of? Mere frivolity and empty amusement. Idle butterflies, pretending to be industrious bees once in the week.

Others again, will be gentle and generous enough about

everything but religion; and as soon as they get upon that, will become fierce, and hard, and narrow at once. Others again (and this is most common) commit the very same fault as the Pharisees in the text, who could use their common sense to discern the signs of the weather, and yet could not use it to discern the signs of the time, because they were afraid of looking honestly at the true state of public feeling and conscience, and at the danger and ruin into which their religion and their party were sinking. For about all worldly matters, these men will be as sound-headed and reasonable as they need be: but as soon as they get on religious matters, they become utterly silly and unreasonable; and will talk nonsense, listen to nonsense, and be satisfied with nonsense, such as they would not endure a moment if their own worldly interest, or worldly character, were in question.

But most of all do these poor souls not deceive their neighbours when a time of temptation comes upon them. For then, alas! it comes out too often that they are of those whom our Lord spoke of, who heard the word gladly, but had no root in themselves, and in time of temptation fell away. For then, before the storm of some trying temptation, away goes all the play-acting religion; and the man's true self rises up from underneath into ugly life. Up rise, perhaps, pride, and self-will, and passion; up rise, perhaps, meanness and love of money; up rise, perhaps, cowardice and falsehood; or up rises foul and gross sin, causing some horrible scandal to religion, and to the name of Christ; while fools look on, and, laughing an evil laugh, cry,—'These are your high professors. These are your Pharisees, who were so much better than everybody else. When they are really tried, it seems they behave no better than we sinners.'

Oh, these are the things which make a clergyman's heart truly sad. These are the things which make him long that all were over; that Christ would shortly accomplish the number of his elect, and hasten his kingdom, that we, with all those who are departed in the true faith of his holy name, may rest in peace for ever from sin and sinners.

Not that I mean that some of these very people, in spite of all their inconsistency, will not be among that number. God forbid! How do we know that? How do we know that they are one whit worse than we should be in their place? How do we know, above all, that to have been found out may not be the very best thing that has happened to them since the day that they were born? How do we know that it may not be God's gracious medicine to enable them to find themselves out; to make them see themselves in their true colours; to purge them of all their play-acting; and begin all over again, crying to God, not with the lips only, but out of the depth of an honest and a noble shame, as David did of old—Behold I was shapen in wickedness, conceived in sin, and I have found it out at last. But thou requirest truth in the inward parts, in the very root and ground of the heart, and not merely truth in the head, in the lips, and in the outward behaviour. Make me a clean heart, O God, and renew a right spirit within me. Thou desirest no sacrifice, else would I give it thee: but thou delightest not in burnt-offerings. The sacrifice of God is a broken spirit, as mine is now. A broken and a contrite heart, ground down by the shame of its own sin, that, O God, thou wilt not despise.

And then—when that prayer has gone up in earnest, and has been answered by the gift of a clean heart, and of a right spirit, which desires nothing but to be made clean and made right, to learn its duty and to do it—then, I say, that man may go back safely and freely, to such forms and ceremonies, as he has been accustomed to, and have been consecrated by the piety and wisdom of his forefathers. For, says David, though forms and ceremonies, sacrifice and burnt-offering cannot make any peace with God, yet I am not going to give up forms and ceremonies, sacrifice and burnt-offerings. No. When my peace is made, when the broken and the contrite heart has put me in my true place again, and my heart is clean, and my spirit right once more; then, he says, will God be pleased with my sacrifices, with my burnt-offerings and oblations; because they will be the sacrifice of righteousness, of a righteous man desiring to shew honour to that God from whom his righteousness comes, and gratitude to that God to whom he owes his pardon.

And so with us, my friends, if ever we have fallen, and been pardoned, and risen again to a new, a truer, a more honest, a more righteous life. Our forms of devotion ought then to become not a snare and a hypocrisy, but honest outward signs of the spiritual grace which is within us; as honest and as rational as the shake of the hand to the friend whom we truly love, as the bowing of the knee before the Queen for whom we would gladly die.

O may God give us all grace to seek first the kingdom of God and his righteousness. To seek first the kingdom of God; to work earnestly, each in his place, to do God's will, and to teach and help others to do it likewise. To seek his righteousness, which is the righteousness of the heart and spirit: and then all other things will be added to us. All outward forms and ceremonies, ways of speaking, ways of behaving, which are good and right for us, will come to us as a matter of course; growing up in us naturally and honestly, without any affectation or hypocrisy, and the purity and soberness, the reverence and earnestness of our outward conversation, will be a pattern of the purity and soberness, the reverence and earnestness, which dwells in our hearts by the inspiration of the Holy Spirit of God.

SERMON XXXVIII.

A PEOPLE PREPARED FOR THE LORD.

EPHESIANS iii. 3—6.

How that by revelation he made known unto me the mystery (as I wrote afore in few words, whereby, when ye read, ye may understand my knowledge in the mystery of Christ), which in other ages was not made known unto the sons of men, as it is now revealed unto the holy apostles and prophets by the Spirit; that the Gentiles should be fellow-heirs, and of the same body, and partakers of his promise in Christ by the Gospel.

THIS day is the feast of the Epiphany. Epiphany, as many of you know, means 'shewing,' because on this day the Lord Jesus Christ was first shewn to the Gentiles; to the Gentile wise men who, as you heard in the Gospel, saw his star in the east, and came to worship him. And the part of Scripture from which I have taken my text, is used for the Epistle this day, because in it St. Paul explains to us the meaning of the Epiphany. The meaning of those wise men being shewn our Lord, and worshipping him, though they were not Jews as he was, but Gentiles. He says that it means this, that the Gentiles were fellow-heirs with the Jews, and of the same body as them, and partakers of God's promise in Christ by the Gospel.

This does not seem so very wonderful to us; and why? Because we, though we are Gentiles like those wise men, have lived so long, we and our forefathers before us, in the light of the Gospel, that we are inclined to take it as a matter of course; forgetting what a wonderful, unspeakable, condescension it was of God, not to spare his only begotten Son, but freely to give him for us. God forgive us! We are so heaped with blessings that we neglect them, forget them, take them as our right, instead of remembering our sins and ungratefulness, and saying, Thy mercies are new every morning; it is only of thy mercies that we are not consumed.

But to St. Paul it was very wonderful news. A mystery, as he said; quite a new and astonishing thought, that heathens had any share in God's love and Christ's salvation.

And so it was to St. Peter. God had to teach it him by that wonderful vision, in which he saw coming down from heaven all sorts of animals, and God bade him kill and eat; and when he refused, because they were common and unclean, God forbade him to call anything common or unclean, now that God had cleansed all things by the precious blood of his dear Son. Then Peter was bidden to go to the Gentile Roman soldier Cornelius. And he went, though, he said, he had been used to think it unlawful for a Jew even to eat with a Gentile. And when he went, he found, to his astonishment, that God's love was over that Gentile soldier and his family, because they were good men, as far as they had light and knowledge, just as much as if they had been good Jews. And God gave St. Peter a sign which there was no mistaking, that he really did care for those Gentile Romans, just as much as if they had been Jews; for, as he was preaching Christ to them, the Holy Ghost fell on them, not after, but before they were baptised. So that St. Peter, astonished as he was, was forced by his own consience and reason to say, 'Can any man forbid water, that these should not be baptised, who have received the Holy Ghost as well as we' (Jews)? Then he commanded them to be baptised in the name of the Lord.

And what was the lesson which God taught St. Peter by this?

St. Peter himself tells us; for he opened his mouth and said, 'Of a truth I see that God is no respecter of persons; but in every nation, he that feareth God, and worketh righteousness, is accepted by him.'

Now, my dear friends, this is (as the Lord Jesus Christ tells us) God's everlasting law, 'That he that hath, to him shall be given, and he shall have more abundantly; but from him that hath not, shall be taken away even that which he seems to have.'

So it was, as I have just shewn you, with Cornelius; and so it was with those wise men. They were worshippers (as is supposed) of the one true God, though in a dim confused way: but they had learnt enough of what true faith was, and of what true greatness was, too, not to be staggered and fall into unbelief, when they saw the King of the Jews, whom they had come so many hundred miles to see, laid, not in a palace, but in a manger; and attended not by princesses and noblewomen, but by a poor maiden, espoused to a carpenter. Therefore God bestowed on them that great honour, that they, first of all the Gentiles, should see the glory and the love of God in the face of Jesus Christ, his Son.

And so it was with our forefathers, my friends. And I think that on this Epiphany, we ought to thank God, among all his other blessings, for having given us such forefathers, and letting us be born of that noble stock, to whom he gave the kingdom of God, after he took it away from the faithless and rebellious Jews, and afterwards from the false and profligate Greeks and Romans, to whom the epistles of the apostles were written. I will tell you what I mean.

When the Lord Jesus came on earth; our forefathers did not live here in England, but in countries across the sea, in Germany, Denmark, and Sweden, which did not belong to the Roman Empire; for the Romans, who had conquered all the world beside, could never conquer our forefathers. It was God's will, that whenever they tried they were beaten back with shame and slaughter; and our forefathers, almost alone of all, remained free men, even as we are at this day. But for that very reason, the apostles could never come among us to preach the Gospel to us; for they could not pass the bounds of the Roman empire; and that was so large, that they had enough to do to preach the Gospel in it; so that it was not till at least 400 years after the apostles' death, that their successors, zealous missionaries, priests and bishops, came and preached to our forefathers; and when they came, they found us a people prepared for the Lord, who heard the word gladly, and turned, thousands sometimes in one day, from vain idols to serve the living God, and were baptised into that holy church in which we now stand. And it has been among us, and the nations who are our kinsmen, that the light of the gospel has shone ever since, while all through the East, where the apostles preached most and earliest, it has died out. So that our Lord's words have been fulfilled, that many that are last shall be first, and those that are first shall be last. God grant that it may not always be so. God grant that his kingdom may return to its ancient seat at Jerusalem, and that all nations may go up to the mountain of the Lord's house, in the day of which St. Paul prophesies, when the times of the Gentiles are fulfilled, and all Israel shall be saved, when the earth shall be full of the knowledge of the Lord, as the waters cover the sea. But it is not so now; and cannot be so, as far as we can see, for many a year to come.

But in the meanwhile, why were our forefathers—heathens though they were, and sinners in many things, being truly children of wrath, fierce, bloodthirsty, revengeful, without the grace of Christ, which is Love and Charity—nevertheless a people prepared for the Lord? How was it true of them that to him that hath shall be given?

I will tell you. There is an old book, written in Latin by a heathen gentleman of Rome, who lived in St. Paul's time, and wrote this book about twenty years after St. Paul's death. It is a little book; but it is a very precious one : and I think it is a great mercy of God that, while so many famous old books have been lost, this little book should have been preserved: for this Roman gentleman had travelled among our forefathers; and when he returned he wrote this book to shame his countrymen at Rome. In it he calls us 'Germans;' but that was the Roman fashion. By Germans they meant not only the people who now live in Germany, but the English and the Danes, and the Swedes, and the Franks, who afterwards conquered France. In fact he meant our own forefathers. And he said to the Romans,—

'Look at these wild Germans. You despise them because they go half-naked, and cannot read or write, and live in mud cottages; while you go in silk and gold, and have all sorts of learning, and live in great cities, palaces, and temples, in worldly pomp and glory. But I tell you,' he said, 'that these wild Germans are better men than you; for, while you are living in sin, in cheating and falsehood, in covetousness, adultery, murder, and every horrible iniquity, they are honest, chaste, truthful; they honour their fathers and mothers; they are obedient and loyal to their kings and their laws; they shew hospitality to strangers; they do not commit adultery, steal, bear false witness, covet their neighbours' goods. And therefore,' this Roman felt (and really it seems as if a spirit of prophecy from God had come on him), 'something great and glorious will come out of these wild Germans, while the Romans will rot away and perish in their sins.' That was true enough. We see it true at this day.

For what happened? That great Roman empire, Babylon the great, as St. John calls it in the Revelations, perished miserably and horribly by its own sins; while our forefathers rose and conquered it all, and live and thrive till this day. But it is curious that they never throve really, though they made great conquests, and did many wonderful deeds, till they became Christians : but as soon as they became Christians, they began to thrive at once, and settled down, and became that great family of nations, and kingdom of God, which we call Christendom; England, France, Spain, Italy, Germany, Sweden, and the other countries of Christian Europe; which God has so prospered for his Son Jesus Christ's sake, in spite of many sins and shortcomings, with wealth and numbers, skill, and learning, and strength, that now the empire of the whole world depends upon these few small Christian nations, which in our Lord's time were only tribes of heathen savages: so that here again our Lord's great parable was fulfilled.

The gospel seed which the apostle sowed in those rich, luxurious, clever, learned, Romans, was like the seed which fell on thorny ground; and the cares and pleasures of this life, and the deceitfulness or riches, sprang up, and choked the word, and it remained unfruitful. But the gospel seed which was sown among our poor, wild, simple, ignorant forefathers, was the seed which fell on an honest and good heart, and took root, and brought forth fruit, some thirty, some fifty, and some one hundred fold. Epiphany came late to us—not for three hundred years after our Lord's birth: but, when it came, the light which it brought remained with us, and lights us even now from our cradle to our grave: and so again was fulfilled the Scripture, which says, that God chooses the weak things of this world to confound the strong; the foolish to confound the wise; yea, and things which are not, to bring to nought the things which are, that no flesh should glory in his presence.

That no flesh should glory in his presence. For mind, my friends, our business is not to be high-minded but to fear. And we English are too apt to be high-minded now. We pride ourselves on our English character, English cleverness, English courage, English wealth. My friends, be not high-minded but fear. We have no right to pride ourselves on being Englishmen, if we do the very things which our forefathers were ashamed to do even when they were heathens. They honoured their fathers and mothers. Do we? They were loyal and obedient to law. Are we? They were chaste and clean livers: adultery was seldom heard of among them; and, when it was, they punished it in the most fearful way : while what astonished that old Roman gentleman, of whom I spoke, most of all, was the pure and respectable lives of the young men and women. Is it so now-a-days among us, my friends? They were honest, too, and just in all their dealings. Are we? They were true to their word; no men on earth more true. Are we? They hated covetousness and overreaching. Do we? They were generous, open-handed, hospitable. Are we? My friends, this was the old English spirit, which God accepted in our forefathers. Is it in us now? We must not pride ourselves on it, unless we have it. Nay, more, what is it but a shame to us, if, while our forefathers were good heathens, we are bad Christians? They had but a small spark, a dim ray, as it were, of the light which lighteth every man who comes into the world : but they were more faithful to that little than many are now, who live in the full sunshine of God's gospel, in the free dispensation of God's spirit, with Christ's sacraments, Christ's Churches, means of grace and hopes of glory, of which they never dreamed. May they not rise up against some of us in the day of judgment, and condemn us, and say,—'Are you our children? Do you boast of knowing God better than we did, while you did things which we dared not do? We knew that God hated such sins, and therefore we kept from them. You should know that better than we ; for you had seen God's horror of sin in the death of his own Son Jesus Christ ; and yet you went on committing the very sins which crucified the Lord of Glory.'

My friends, I speak sober earnest. God grant that our old heathen forefathers may not rise up against us in the day of judgment, and condemn us. Let us turn to the Lord this day with all our hearts, and come to this holy table, confessing all our sins and unfaithfulness, and backslidings, that we may get there cleansing from his most precious blood, strength from his most precious body, life from his life, and spirit from his spirit; that so we may go away to lead new lives, following the commandments of God, and living up to our great light and knowledge, at least as well as our forefathers lived up to their little light. And so we shall really keep the feast of Epiphany in spirit and in truth : for Epiphany means the shewing of Jesus Christ to us Gentiles; and the way to prove that Jesus Christ has been shewn to us, and that we have seen his glory, the glory as of the only-begotten of the Father, full of grace and truth, is to keep his commandments, and live lives like his.

SERMON XXXIX.

THE WRATH OF LOVE.

PSALM cvii. 6.

Then they cried unto the Lord in their trouble, and he delivered them out of their distresses.

IF I were asked to give a reason why I believed the Old Testament to be an inspired and divine book, as well as the New, I could not do better, I think, than to lay my hand on this 107th psalm, and say,—This is my reason for believing the Old Testament to be inspired. I have hundreds of others: but this one is enough—this one psalm. It contains an account of God's dealings with men, such as the world never heard before, and very seldom since, save from a very few men, who really saw what the Bible meant, and honestly followed its teaching. It gives a notion of the justice of God, and an explanation of the chances and changes of this mortal life, such as you will find nowhere else save in the Bible, and in the books of Christian men who have been taught by the Bible. The man who wrote that psalm knew so much more than other men, that he must have been indeed inspired by the Spirit of Truth, and the Holy Ghost of God.

And, I should say, I have come to this opinion mainly by comparing this psalm with the writings of heathens, even the wisest and the best of them. For the heathens, like all men,

THE WRATH OF LOVE. 447

used to have their troubles, and to ask themselves, Who has sent this trouble? And why has he sent it? And their answers remain to us in their writings, some worse, some better, some very foolish, some tolerably wise. But when one compares the heathen writings with this psalm, or with any psalms or passages of the Old Testament which talk of God's dealings with man, then we shall be altogether astonished at the superiority of the Bible. The Bible will seem to us quite infinitely wiser than heathen books, on this matter, as on others—so much more simple, and yet so much more deep; so much more rational also, and so much more true: agreeing so much more with the facts which we see happen round us: agreeing so much more with our own reason, experience, inward conscience, about what is just and unjust:—that we shall begin to see as much difference between heathen books and the Old Testament, as there is between the dim dawn of morning, and the full blaze of noonday light.

One of the earliest heathen notions why troubles came was, it seems, that the gods were offended with men, because they had not shown them due honour, flattered them enough, or offered sacrifices enough to them: or else they fancied that the gods envied men: grudged their prosperity, did not like to see them too happy.

That dark and base notion gradually faded away, as men got higher notions of right and wrong, and of the gods, as the judges and avengers of wrong. Then they began to think these troubles were punishments for doing wrong. The Gods, or God, punished sin; inflicting so much pain for so much sin, very much as the heathens are apt to punish their criminals still, and as Christian nations used to punish theirs, namely, with shameful and horrible tortures; before they began to find out that the end of punishment is not to torment, but to reform, the criminal, wherever it is possible.

But then the thought would come—Why, after all, should God, if he be just and merciful, punish my sin by pain and misery? How can it profit God, how can it please God, to give me pain? Because it satisfies his justice? How can it do that? It would not satisfy mine. Suppose my child, or even my dog, disobeyed me, would it satisfy my sense of justice to beat him? It might satisfy my passion: but God has no passions. It would be base, blasphemous to fancy that he takes pleasure in hurting me, as I take pleasure in beating my dog when I lose my temper with it. God forbid! The old prophets saw that, and cried—'Have I any pleasure in the death of him, saith the Lord, and not rather that he should turn from his wickedness, and live?'

Then, naturally, the thought would come into the mind of a wise and serious man—I punish my child, or my dog, and God punishes me. May he not punish me for the same reason that I punish them? I punish them to correct them and make them better. Surely God punishes me, to correct me, and make me better. I punish my child, because I love him, and wish him good. God punishes me because he loves me and desires that I may be a partaker of his holiness.

And as soon as that blessed thought had risen up in any man's mind, by the inspiration of God's Holy Spirit, all the world would begin to look bright and clear and full of hope. This earth, with all its sorrows and sufferings, would look no longer to him as God's prison house, where poor sinners sat tortured and wailing, fast bound in misery and iron, till they should pay the uttermost farthing, which they never could pay. No. It would look to him as God's school-house, God's reformatory, in which he is training and chastening and correcting the souls of men, that he may deliver them from the ruin and misery which sin brings on them, both the original sin which is born in them and the actual sin which they commit. Then God appears to him a gracious and merciful father. He can see a blessed meaning and a wholesome use in all human suffering; and he can break out, as the Psalmist does in this glorious psalm, into praise and thanksgiving, and call on mankind to give thanks to the Lord; for he is gracious, and his mercy endureth for ever.

In every kind of human suffering, I say, he sees now a meaning and a use.

First, he takes, it seems, his own countrymen, the Jews, coming back from Babylon into their own country after the seventy years' captivity. They had been punished for their sins. But for what purpose? That they might know (as Ezekiel said), that God was the Lord. And when they cried unto him in their trouble, he delivered them out of their distress.

Then he goes on to those who have brought themselves into poverty and shame, and sit fast bound in misery and iron. It is their own fault. They have brought it on themselves by rebelling against the word of the Lord, and lightly regarding the counsel of the Most Highest. But God does not hate them. God is not going to leave them to the net which they have spread for their own feet. When they cry unto the Lord in their troubles, he delivers them out of their distress. God himself, by strange and unexpected ways, will deliver them from their darkness of ignorance and sin, and from the danger and misery which they have brought upon themselves.

Then he goes on to those who have injured their health by their own folly, till their soul abhors all manner of food, and they are even hard at death's door. Neither does God hate them, They, too, are in God's school-house. And when they cry to the Lord in their trouble, he will deliver them, too, out of their distress, and send his word, and heal them, and save them from destruction.

Then he goes on to men who are exposed to danger, and terror, and death in their lawful calling; and his instance is the seamen—those who go on to the sea in ships, and occupy their business in great waters.

The storms come up, they know not when or how : but they are not the sport of a blind chance ; they are not the victims of the wrath of God. The wild sea, too, is his school-house, where they are to see the works of the Lord, and his wonders in the deep; and so, by strange dangers and strange deliverances, learn, as I have seen many a seaman learn, a courage and endurance, a faith, a resignation, which puts us comfortable landsmen to shame.

Then he goes on to even a deeper matter—to those terrible changes in nature, so common in the East, in which whole districts, by earthquake or drought, are rendered worthless and barren. They too, he says, are God's lessons, though sharp ones enough. 'He turneth the rivers into a wilderness, and the water-springs into dry ground; a fruitful land into barrenness, for the wickedness of them that dwell therein. Again, he turneth the wilderness into a standing water, and dry ground into water-springs. And there he maketh the hungry to dwell, that they may prepare a city for habitation; and sow the fields, and plant vineyards, which may yield fruits of increase.'

Lastly, he goes on to political changes, which bring a whole nation low, into oppression and misery. 'They are minished and brought low through oppression, affliction and sorrow. He poureth contempt upon princes, and causeth them to wander in the wilderness, where there is no way. Yet setteth he the poor on high from affliction, and maketh him families like a flock. The righteous shall see it, and rejoice: and all iniquity shall stop her mouth. Whoso is wise, and will observe these things, even they shall understand the loving-kindness of the Lord.'

And so, in all the changes of this mortal life, he sees no real chance, no real change, but the orderly education of a just and loving Father, whose mercy endureth for ever; who chastens men as a father chastens his children, for their profit, that they may be partakers of his holiness, in which alone is life and joy, health and wealth.

Surely, here is a Gospel, and good news;—news so good, that it turns what seems to the superstitious the worst of news, into the very best. For it seems at first sight the worst of news, that which the ninth Article tells us, that our original sin, in every person born into this world, deserves God's wrath and damnation. And so it would be the worst of news, if God were merely a judge, inflicting so much pain and misery for so much sin, without any wish to mend us and save us. But if we remember only the blessed message of this psalm; if we will remember that God is our Father; that God is educating us; that God hath neither parts nor passions; and that, therefore, God's wrath is not different or contrary to his love, but that God's wrath is his love in another shape, punishing men just because he loves men;—then the ninth Article will bring us the very best of news. We shall see that it is the best thing that can possibly befall us, that our sin deserves God's wrath and damnation; and that it would have been the worst thing which could possibly have befallen us, if our sin had not deserved God's wrath and damnation. For if our sin had not deserved God's anger, then he would not have been angry with it; and then he would have left it alone, instead of condemning it, and dooming it to everlasting destruction as he has done; and then, if our sin had been left alone, we should have been left alone to sin and sin on, growing continually more wicked, till our sin became our ruin. But now God hates our sin, and loves us; and therefore he desires above all things to deliver us from sin, and burn our sin up in his unquenchable fire, that we ourselves may not be burned up therein. For if our sins live, we shall surely die: but if our sins die, then, and then only, shall we live.

Do these words seem strange to some of you? I doubt not that they will: but if they do, that will be only a fresh proof to me, that the Bible is inspired by the Holy Ghost. Yes, nothing shews me how wide, how deep, how wise, how heavenly the Bible is, as to see how far average Christians are behind the Bible in their way of thinking; how the salvation which it offers is too free for them, the love which it proclaims too wide for them, the God whom it reveals too good for them: so that they shrink from taking the Bible and trusting the Bible, in its fulness; and are perpetually falling back on heathen notions—the very old heathen notions from which this psalm delivers us—concerning what God's anger means, and what God's punishment means; because they are afraid of taking the words of Scripture literally and fully, and believing honestly the blessed news, that God is Love.

They try to make God's ways as their ways, and God's thoughts as their thoughts. But do not you do so. Receive the Bible in its fulness. Believe that it tells you infinitely more of God's character and dealings, than you can ever tell yourselves; that God's ways are not as your ways, nor God's thoughts as your thoughts, even at their best: but that God's ways are always wider and deeper than yours, were you the most learned of men; God's thoughts are always more loving and just than yours, were you the most holy of men, and that when you have learned all that you can learn, or that any man can learn, out of the Bible, there will be still left behind treasures beside, which you have not yet found out. For the riches of Christ are unsearchable; like the depth of the riches of the wisdom and knowledge of God, whose only-begotten son, and perfect likeness, he is; and the man who reads the Scripture with a single eye, and an humble heart, will see that the more he finds in the Bible, the more he has yet to find; and that if he studied it to all eternity, he would have fresh and fresh cause for ever to cry with the Psalmist, 'Oh give thanks to the Lord; for he is gracious, and his mercy endureth for ever!'

THE END.

www.ingramcontent.com/pod-product-compliance
Lightning Source LLC
Chambersburg PA
CBHW022116300426
44117CB00007B/732